YALE
HISTORICAL PUBLICATIONS

MISCELLANY

XXI

PUBLISHED UNDER THE DIRECTION OF
THE DEPARTMENT OF HISTORY
FROM THE INCOME OF
THE FREDERICK JOHN KINGSBURY
MEMORIAL FUND

WILLIAM BLATHWAYT

BY SIR G. KNELLER

WILLIAM BLATHWAYT

A LATE SEVENTEENTH CENTURY
ENGLISH ADMINISTRATOR

BY

GERTRUDE ANN JACOBSEN, Ph.D.

*Assistant Professor of History and the Social Sciences
in Hunter College*

NEW HAVEN: YALE UNIVERSITY PRESS
LONDON: HUMPHREY MILFORD
OXFORD UNIVERSITY PRESS
MDCCCCXXXII

1448

PREFACE

INCREASING attention has been paid in recent years to administrative history, and more credit has been given to a nation's permanent governors, those civil servants who give direction to public policies and who keep the wheels of government well oiled and working smoothly. William Blathwayt, who was, in a sense, the forerunner of the modern undersecretary, was a late Stuart administrator whose activities represent one stage in the evolution of England's civil service and fit into a critical period in constitutional development. He has been selected as a prototype of administrators of his day, not because he possessed intrinsic genius or unusual originality—he was, as a matter of fact, lacking in both—but because he was an uncommonly energetic and enduring pluralist. He was so successful and intelligent in the various administrative offices which he held simultaneously that his activities serve as a cross section of administrative organization and development at the time. It is the rare individual, either in Blathwayt's day or now, who has sufficient physical endurance or orderly mental capacity to be active at one and the same time in four offices—plantations, war, secretary of state, Privy Council. Modern constitutional limitations alone would forbid it. Blathwayt suffered from no constitutional handicaps—either in the governmental or in the physical sense of the word—and he achieved his unusual feat with considerable success. As a medium, therefore, for an administrative study, he is a convenient and easily justified choice; though as a subject for a biography, either in the heroic or in the modern style, he is distinctly a bad one. Heroic biographers, therefore, would never bother their heads about him, and the modern, or psychological one, would stop in passing, only long enough to rescue him from the New Englanders—a group of colonial leaders and historians to whom Blathwayt was anathema because he took an active part in the movement for the revocation of the charters.

Efforts to find Blathwayt the person, as well as Blathwayt the administrator, have been difficult, but the attempt has been made; even administrators become more convincing when attached to a personality. But Blathwayt has proved elusive. In all his offices, he hides behind, and often completely loses his identity in, an array of official documents. Many of his private papers—and with them, possibly, whatever was colorful in his record—have been permanently or temporarily lost to view through a series of sales and may therefore never be reassembled. The mass of public papers, even with careful study, have produced a fainter image of the true Blathwayt than might be desired. This, however, is a common complaint when the activities of civil servants are undergoing investigation. To preserve the spirit of the time, current spelling and methods of dating have been retained, though not with unfailing accuracy.

This study has not been a lone task. I wish to express my indebtedness to a number of persons. First and foremost, to Professor Charles McLean Andrews, without whose invaluable counsel and constant aid and encouragement, it could never have been brought to completion; to Professor Wallace Notestein, who first introduced me to the problems and fascinations of Stuart England; to the late Professor Cephas D. Allin, whose brilliant lectures on English government are not easily forgotten; to the late Professor Thomas F. Tout, under whose kindly and able direction it was my pleasure to begin the work; and to Mr. and Mrs. C. S. S. Higham, who first presented William Blathwayt to me and outlined some of the problems surrounding his public career. I also wish to express my gratitude to the librarians and attendants of the Public Record Office, the British Museum, the John Rylands Library, the Library of Congress, and the Huntington Library; especially to Mr. Stamp, of the Public Record Office, who put at my disposal proofs of certain manuscripts in the Historical Manuscripts Commission, which were in the process of being printed and were not at the time in accessible form; to Mr. Haselden, of the Huntington Library, who carefully piloted me to then uncatalogued manuscripts; to Dr. Guppy, of the John Rylands Library, whose unfailing courtesy and willing aid made work in the library a rare pleasure; and to the Prince Society of Boston, from whose photogravure of the Kneller portrait of Blathwayt the reproduction in this volume has been made. To William Blathwayt's descendant, Mr. George Wynter Blathwayt, of West Porlock House, Somerset, I owe a special debt for permitting me to examine certain family papers and for extending to me innumerable courtesies. In the arrangement and preparation of the manuscript, Miss Amy Clare Giffin has been a useful editorial assistant.

G. A. J.

New York City,
February, 1932.

CONTENTS

CHRONOLOGY OF BLATHWAYT'S LIFE

1649 [?]	Birth, London.
1665, February	Entrance into the Middle Temple.
1668, Fall	Entrance into the office of Sir William Temple, the ambassador to The Hague.
1672, January	Return to England.
May	Departure with the Duke of Richmond on a special diplomatic mission to Denmark.
August	On a temporary diplomatic mission to Sweden.
1672–1673	Grand Tour of Germany and Italy.
1675, September	Entrance into the plantation office.
1676, May	Permission to attend the meetings of the Lords of Trade.
1678, July	Flying mission to Paris with Dr. Tabor.
	Clerk in extraordinary of the council.
November	Permission to attend the meetings of the Privy Council.
1679, December	Virtual secretary of the Lords of Trade.
1680, May	Surveyor and auditor general of plantation revenues.
1681, February	Clerk to Lord Conway, secretary of state.
1683, March	Dismissal of Lord Conway.
August	Purchase of the secretaryship at war.
1685	Election to the house of commons for Newton, Isle of Wight.
1686, October	Clerk in ordinary of the council.
December	Marriage to Mary Wynter of Dyrham Park.
1688, June	Principal witness at the Trial of the Seven Bishops.
November	Attendant to James II on the march to Salisbury.

1689	Renewal of various offices under William III.
1691, November	Death of Mary Wynter Blathwayt.
1692	First summer of attendance on William III in Flanders.
1693	Election to the House of Commons for Bath.
1696, May	Member of the Board of Trade.
1700	Rumor that he might be created Earl of Bristol.
1701	Last summer of attendance on William III in Flanders.
1702	Renewal of various offices under Anne.
1704, April	Loss of the secretaryship at war.
1707, April	Dismissal from the Board of Trade.
1710	Loss of his seat in the house of commons.
1717, August	Death at Dyrham Park.

ILLUSTRATIONS

CHAPTER I

WHITEHALL IN WILLIAM BLATHWAYT'S DAY

THE civil servant of any period finds few champions, but
none, with the exception of his eighteenth century successors, has suffered more from harsh and unwarranted
stricture than the civil servant of the Restoration and the
late seventeenth century. He has been condemned for his
venality, his want of veneration for the best interests of
the state, his gross ignorance, general inefficiency, and
lack of application to duty. The low moral standards generally attributed to the court of the last two Stuarts have
been fastened upon him, and we have been led to believe
that England's administrative good was sacrificed to the
personal advantage of a motley group of self-seekers.
Fortunately, owing to the researches of some very notable scholars within the past few years, the general conception with regard to England's administrative agents
at this time has been altered. Two points have been revealed; first, that conditions were not as vicious as they
seemed; and second, that the civil servants were the victims of circumstances over which they had no control.
Moreover, biographical investigations and a study of the
administrative records have made it clear that England
bred a very fine group of able administrators in this period, despite all the obstacles which war, a ravaged treasury and public impecuniosity, loose moral standards,
obstreperous parliaments, and obstinate kings, could
impose. An age has nothing to be ashamed of which can

produce administrators such as those in the group to which William Blathwayt belonged; Sir George Downing, who served first as secretary to the Treasury Board, and then as a commissioner of the customs; Samuel Pepys, secretary to the Admiralty Board; Sir Joseph Williamson, who was for many years first clerk in the secretarial office, then secretary of state himself; and Sir Robert Southwell, the first secretary to the Lords of Trade and Plantations.

It would be idle to deny that the administrative system had many features which marred, although they did not vitiate, its efficiency. These were principally the widespread practice of buying and selling offices, the system of patent offices to which reversions could be secured, pluralism, the use of deputies, nepotism, and the scandalous resort to gratuities. To the modern reader, a man who buys his way into office is wholly contemptible. We must remember that in Stuart England it was a common practice, in which even the great officers of state engaged. True, it was a statutory offense by act of 5 and 6 Edward VI, c. 16, but the law had long since been a dead letter.[1] Offices were highly marketable, and few men, even the most high-minded, had any scruples in the matter. Obtaining an office was usually a question of driving a hard bargain with the incumbent, unless a man were so fortunate as to secure it as a mark of royal favor; in which case the incumbent felt that he had been cheated since he thus lost his original purchase money. So purely commercial was the transaction, men felt they had liens on offices, ranging in price according to the remuneration to be derived from them. A clerkship of the Privy Council could command only £1250, while a secretaryship of state often went as high as £6000.

Even in this period, however, public sentiment was not

[1] *Statutes of the Realm*, IV, 151–152.

wholly deadened to the vicious character of the practice, and in 1703 we find the house of lords moving that a day be set aside for considering heads for a bill to prevent the buying and selling of offices.[2] It was an abortive measure, though the practice decreased to a certain extent. One reason for the decrease was the fact that many of the offices passed into the category of party spoils. Another was the stand adopted by the Treasury in the employment of men engaged by them or by the various commissions under them. In 1689, they had reprimanded the commissioners of the customs for failure "to advance those who have well deserved in an inferior station." Thereupon that board responded Jesuitically: "The constant opinion and practice of this Board has been by all meanes to discountenance and discourage any private agreement for the surrendering or obteyning any of the places upon the establishment, that the filling up of the same may be without any other consideration besides the fitnesse of the person presented."[3] In 1714, the Treasury rather summarily set aside the claims of a member of the excise board who was about to be removed from his office for which he had paid £3500 and for which he wanted reimbursement. The secretary to the Treasury informed him, "The place is already disposed of, and my Lordships do not think fit there should be any money given for employments in the revenue."[4]

The system of patent offices was expensive and stultifying, particularly when the grant was made for life, as many of them were. The issuance of the patents called for an enormous outlay at the Treasury in exchequer fees, which the grantee naturally expected to make up in gra-

[2] *Hist. MSS. Com., House of Lords MSS.*, n.s., VI, 36; Dec. 6, 1703.

[3] *Cal. Treas. Papers*, 1557–1696, pp. xliv–xlvii, especially xlvi and xlvii; also Vol. XX, No. 9.

[4] *Ibid.*, 1714–1719, p. xviii.

tuities mulcted from his clients. By no means all of the important administrative offices were patent offices, and the lesser were rarely so, yet even commissions under Treasury warrant or under the sign manual or the signet required the payment of large initial fees. It was an exceedingly expensive and burdensome matter, against which frequent but unavailing protests were made.

Nothing, moreover, could be more vicious than the system of reversions to which patent offices as well as others were subject, and nothing more truly indicative of the commercial light in which officeholding was regarded. Needless to say, no man ever sought the reversion to an office which was not financially remunerative. Men were willing to wait for years for a reversion to fall due. The frequent application to the king for a life grant to a reversion, even though there were already entered five, six, or even more claims, shows that an applicant was not easily deterred.

There is a case in point early in the seventeenth century, when Blathwayt's maternal grandfather, Justinian Povey, in requesting the reversion to the office of auditor of the exchequer, was told that his chances of ever succeeding were slight, since there were six claims ahead of his. He persisted, nevertheless, won his claim, and, curiously enough, actually did succeed to the office within a few years.[5] Death, the relinquishment of claims, and various other circumstances often served an applicant better than he dared hope. There were often bewildering counterclaims, but it was frequently possible to buy out a previous claimant. Pepys, for instance, was embarrassed and annoyed to learn that the office of clerk of the acts in the navy office, to which he succeeded in 1660, had a prior claimant. Thomas Barlow appeared and gave proof that

[5] *Cal. S. P. Dom.*, Add., 1580–1625, pp. 476–477; May 7, 1606; 1603–1610, p. 316; May 6, 1606; 1625–1626, p. 536.

he, jointly with Dennis Fleming, had secured the grant in 1638, and it cost Pepys £100 a year to buy them off.[6]

A wholesale practice of pluralism in office holding prevailed, for there was no provision, statutory or otherwise, which prevented a man from holding more than one office of trust or profit under the government. On the contrary, a man could hold as many offices as he could safely lay his hands on. Blathwayt is a good example of an active pluralist, since he regarded not one of his offices as a sinecure; but there were plenty of passive pluralists, whose claims to office cluttered up the whole British system. The desire for emoluments led all types of men to reach out for one petty office after another. Poets and philosophers were grateful for official appointments. Milton, Dryden, Marvell, Locke, George Stepney, and Matthew Prior were all holders of one, and in most cases more than one, office, though be it said to their credit that most of them worked very assiduously and even displayed real administrative skill. No particular protest was made against pluralism, though occasionally the complaint was voiced that a man was monopolizing posts to the public disadvantage. Blathwayt was criticized, but not unduly, and the attacks upon him were usually bitterly partisan.

Although little progress was made in governmental quarters against the practice of holding office by deputy, public opinion was becoming less tolerant. On February 10, 1699, an order in council was issued which directed that all holders of patent offices "be obliged to actual residence upon the place and to execute their offices in their own persons."[7] The tone of the order was peremptory, but its enforcement almost nil. Too many of the great officers of state were themselves affected by it to permit its being carried out with any degree of thoroughness. In

[6] Pepys, *Diary;* entries for June 29, 1660 and February 9, 1665.
[7] C. O. 391: 20, 235; also Basye, *The Board of Trade,* p. 25.

theory, every man was willing to concede that the practice was vicious, except where he himself was concerned. To save their faces, many of them, no doubt, reasoned as did the commissioners of the customs, that it was better to have good deputies than indifferent original patentees. In answering a sharp rebuke from the Treasury that they had been encouraging the sale of offices within the customs service, the commissioners blandly replied, "But for patent offices, the Commissioners have always look't upon them as bountyes, in the hands of the Crowne or your Lordships, being generally bestowed upon persons, with power to execute by deputy; and therefore the Commissioners have always been passive and easy in the transaction of those grants, when their Lordships have been pleased to referr them to this Board; not thinking it became them to enter into the consideration of the meritts or services for which they were bestowed, nor to concerne themselves soe much about the qualifications of the person as to make provision for good deputyes, who are to execute those offices."[8]

One of the serious menaces was the dynastic tendency of secretaries and clerks. It was an age of nepotism generally, which reveals itself everywhere in the ranks of political underlings. Investigation discloses the recurrence in the departmental records of the same family name for generation after generation. Families regarded offices at Whitehall in the light of family perquisites and guarded them against the invasion of an outsider with all the zeal of a close corporation. If a man in office had no relative whose claims he wanted advanced, he almost always had a favorite clerk whom he desired to promote. There was a Whitehall tradition in the Blathwayt family; two generations of Poveys, his mother's people, had

---

[8] *Cal. Treas. Papers*, 1557–1696, p. xlvii; Vol. XXVIII, No. 78; July 23, 1694.

served before him, although not in the same offices which he filled. Blathwayt did not train his own sons for the public service, but he brought up his cousin, John Povey, as senior clerk in the plantation office, hoping that he would in turn fall heir to the secretaryship. He had similar designs for Adam Cardonnel, his clerk in the war office, but in both cases political opposition frustrated his carefully laid plans. The spoils system was necessarily to have a disrupting effect on these dynastic arrangements. Nevertheless family ramifications in the bureaucracy of England were a characteristic feature of the governmental system in the seventeenth and eighteenth centuries.

The desire for perquisites and emoluments explains the mad trafficking in offices that went on in Blathwayt's day. It would be absurd to assert that men were not in Whitehall for what they could get out of it. Men grew rich in official positions even of a minor nature. Since salaries were small, the methods men used to enrich themselves are self-evident. Critics, of which there were many, especially as party acerbities increased, attributed the growth in most officeholders' fortunes to bribery. Naval disasters, in particular, aroused men to wrath, and they blamed them on the vicious practices which permeated the whole system of naval administration. They complained bitterly that commissioners of the navy could advance themselves from salaries of £30 per annum to great estates.[9] No one who has read Pepys's *Diary* can deny that that administrator's fortune was out of all proportion to the salary he received.[10] It was a sort of refined bribery in which he indulged. In the modern sense there was no such

[9] Robert Crosfield, *Corrupt Ministers, the Cause of Publick Calamities*, a pamphlet published in London in 1701.

[10] See Albion, *Forests and Sea Power*, pp. 49–52, for some vivid comments on Pepys's peculations.

thing as an honest man in office, for not one of them was above accepting gratuities. A man had to go very far indeed, before his malpractice won him public disesteem. Conditions were worse in departments where there were contracts to be let, as may easily be assumed, but even the regular business of any office brought large fees.[11]

There was an economic as well as a moral explanation for the conditions which prevailed. Relaxed moral standards account for some of the official rapacity, but the real reason is to be found in the disordered state of public finance. As long as England failed to work out a satisfactory budget system, but was content to live from hand to mouth, depending on the shiftless method of farming out the revenue to men who had their own interests at heart, and resorting to the sale of lottery tickets and the use of tallies of various sorts when ready money failed, the situation was hopeless. The Treasury could not begin to meet the ordinary demands which were made on it at this time. Official salaries were not only inadequate; they were hopelessly in arrears. Money was never paid in advance, and officials were grateful when their salaries were received within a reasonable length of time. Payments were never made automatically. Often a man had to petition the Treasury, not once, but repeatedly. An extreme case is the petition of John Phelps, one of the seven auditors of the revenue, to the Treasury Lords in 1695, complaining that he had received no part of his salary of £200 a year for fifteen and a half years, and that a fee of £20 was in arrears for nearly seventeen years.[12] We may agree that it was his own carelessness, but the fact remains that petitions and visits to the Treasury were expensive processes, and a man was likely to use up a large amount of what

---

[11] Albion, *Forests and Sea Power*, the chapter entitled, ''Contracts, Conservatism, and Corruption,'' pp. 39–95.

[12] *Cal. Treas. Papers*, 1557–1696, pp. xxxv and 415.

was owing him in dispensing fees to Treasury attendants. Payment in tallies or lottery tickets was a mockery, for they were not infrequently at a forty per cent. discount.[13] We have the pathetic case of Thomas Rymer, who had been commissioned to compile the *Fœdera,* petitioning for his salary in 1697 and receiving of the arrears due him since 1693, £200 in malt tickets which he disposed of for £160. High and low were affected by this system of payment, and some very pitiful instances of deferred payment are to be found among the menials working in offices, the charwomen and errand boys, whose credit at best could have been none too good.[14] Conditions were at their worst during the period of recoinage, after the Coinage Act of 1696, but the embarrassment of the Treasury was constant. There were times when ready money was so scarce that the Treasury officials did not know where they were to get their own salaries, proof that the crisis was indeed acute.[15] Little wonder then that men in office were driven to take refuge in the practice of pluralism or fell back on the device of extracting gratuities from their clients. Somehow money must be obtained and the government winked at and even encouraged openly the system of fees. The resort to more scientific methods of tax collection and the creation of a sound system of national credit were to do more in the end to free officeholders from the charge of venality than partisan diatribes against official corruption.

Practices such as we have outlined prevented English administration from reaching the highest level of effici-

[13] Discount rates of course varied. See a comment in *The Memoirs of Thomas, Earl of Ailesbury,* I, 241.

[14] *Cal. Treas. Papers,* 1557–1696, pp. xxxii–xxxvi; Basye, *The Board of Trade,* pp. 11–12; Andrews, *Guide to the Materials . . . in the Public Record Office,* I, 92 and footnote.

[15] Vernon, *Letters Illustrative of the Reign of William III* (ed. by G. P. R. James), I, 184.

ency. There is another explanation which is equally valid. No one can deny that there was a widespread lack of inter-departmental coördination, and this at first glance might be attributed to the low standards of public administrators. There was a more basic reason, however, growing out of the fact that England was in a state of transition. A modern spirit was creeping into English governmental practices. This made the organization of political offices more akin to present-day administration than was that of the Tudors or the early Stuarts. Some of the liberating forces which impelled England during the Civil Wars and the Commonwealth remained unchecked by the Restoration, and though an effort was made by such devotees of the earlier system as the Earl of Clarendon to restore English administration to the *status quo ante,* the attempt was unavailing. It is more than a matter of orthography that the modern student has a sense of familiarity with the records of the late seventeenth century which he never has for those of the late sixteenth or early seventeenth centuries.

England entered on a great period of transition, rather than of restoration, in 1660. Gone was the tradition of romanticism and high religious purpose in the field of colonization; instead, England faced a series of matter-of-fact problems in colonial administration. In trade also a new spirit had been awakened, which brought about great commercial expansion. Where England had once depended on buccaneers to bring in the spoils of commerce and the ships captured from her trade rivals, she now placed her trust in naval and customs officials, instructed to effect a rigid enforcement of the Acts of Trade and Navigation. An avowed interest in, and eagerness for, trade rapidly superseded the old interest in religious conflict, although it was to be years before the earlier issues were entirely laid aside. The constitutional struggle reflected the new scene, for the absorption which English merchants manifested in the problem of parliamentary supremacy was admittedly based on the desire to further their own material concerns and was very remotely, if at all, connected with constitutional theory.

The expansion in England's resources after 1660, called for a corresponding expansion in English administration. The real problem of the period, then, was not parliamentary but executive and administrative; the creation of a smooth-working, well-oiled, and financially solvent governmental machine.

From the days of the early Tudors to the eve of the Civil Wars, the heart of English administration was the Privy Council. With the Restoration, Clarendon as well as others assumed that the council would resume its former position. "For by the constitution of the kingdom, and the very laws and customs of the nation, as the privy council and every member of it is of the king's sole choice and election of him to that trust, . . . so the body of it is the most sacred, and hath the greatest authority in the government next the person of the king himself, to whom all other powers are equally subject: and no king of England can so well secure his own prerogative, or preserve it from violation, as by a strict defending and supporting the dignity of his privy-council."[16]

Though in theory the Privy Council still held such an exalted position after 1660, in practice it was otherwise, and all the vain subscriptions of the Earl of Clarendon to this tenet were pathetic attempts to arrest new, unwelcome forces. The council was being devoured by its own

---

[16] *Continuation of the Life of Edward, Earl of Clarendon* (Oxford, 1857), § 912. See the article by E. I. Carlyle, "Clarendon and the Privy Council, 1660–1667," *Eng. Hist. Rev.* (1912), XXVII, 251–273.

committees, one of which, the committee of trade, set up in 1675, as the Lords of Trade and Plantations, was soon to assume the size and importance of a colonial department, although it lacked every vestige of constitutional authority and independence. Other offices were in practice asserting their independence of the Privy Council. Thus the secretary of state, once little better than a clerk of the council in importance and dignity, was passing out from under the ægis of the council, as earlier he had moved out of the household of the king, and was setting up a great and independent department of state. The same evolution was going on in the Treasury and the Admiralty, where the resort to commissions instead of Lord High Admirals and Lord High Treasurers, at first as a temporary expedient but ultimately as a permanent device, permitted a degree of independence of the Privy Council hitherto unknown. The growth of the army after 1660, in particular after the accession of James II, meant a rapid development in the machinery of administrative control, and a war office came into being, subservient in its character to be sure, but dependent in civil matters on the secretary of state, not the Privy Council. New specialized boards—the Board of Trade, the customs commission, the excise commission, the transport board, the victualling board, the commission for sick and wounded—sprang into existence. Some were mere war-time expedients, others were permanent parts of the administration. Only one, the Board of Trade, was dependent by its commission on the Privy Council. In many cases the line of responsibility was not clear; often, as in the case of the transport board, it was joint. As a result, important matters were sometimes delayed when the commissioners were at a loss to know which of their superiors to consult.

The rapid expansion in governmental agencies after

1660, was confusing to all concerned. The old unifying force, the Privy Council, was losing its power, despite all efforts to strengthen it; the new centralizing body, the cabinet, was in process of development but had not yet overcome the onus of its extra-legal character. The king's leadership was passing, but the new leader, the prime minister, had not yet appeared. Hence it was not only a period of transition, but one of conflict. Sovereigns were struggling to regain a lost preëminence. Parliament was laboring to enhance and increase its newly acquired powers. King's ministers were busy evolving new theories of responsibility which would enable them to be loyal to crown and parliament at one and the same time. Administrative agents were struggling to make smooth a system in which the lines of responsibility were often so confusing as to be lost to view. Methods in administration were hence unavoidably, rather than wilfully, cumbersome and circuitous. A new energizing, unifying force was the desideratum and, consciously or unconsciously, was awaited. The evolution of political parties, and their recognition as the keynote to the whole parliamentary system, were in the end to form the real solution. "Until the party system had been evolved, and the functions of criticism and protest had passed to his Majesty's Opposition, it was impossible for Parliament to enter into the domain of the executive. For it would thereby have deserted its own nature. The whole cruel problem of Charles's reign lies in this one fact. The distance between the executive and legislature was lessening, the embryonic elements of the eighteenth century, cabinet government and the party system, were beginning chaotically to evidence themselves, but neither side could force the development or anticipate the result. The gulf between them was not bridged, and as a result the executive on the one hand was starved and weakened and the Parliament on the other became the deluded tool of Louis XIV.''[17]

The emergence of new departments and branches of the government added to the number on the civil list and brought into being a new group of professional administrators, who are the forerunners of the modern permanent undersecretaries. These were the secretaries of the secretaries of state, of the Treasury Board, of the Admiralty Board, of the Lords of Trade, and presently of the Board of Trade, also the secretary at war, and to an extent, the entire membership of the lesser boards. They now gained ground at the expense of the clerks of the more ancient departments (Chancery, the Exchequer, the Privy Seal), whose duties had long since become formal and stereotyped. Many of these new agents were also clerks of the council, or had originally been so.

Some of the secretaryships which were rising to prominence were not new, but their character was changing. Thus the secretary to the secretary of state had originally been nothing more than the private secretary of that official, a member of his household and in every way dependent upon him. The personal nexus between the secretary of state and his "writing clerks" continues to an extent throughout the entire seventeenth century, but the increasing use of the appellation, "undersecretary of state," gives proof of the growing public character of the office. It is likewise significant that, during these years, the system of payment out of the public coffers rather than out of the secretary of state's private means made a partial beginning.[18]

[17] *Cal. Treas. Bks.*, 1676–1679, VI, p. xlii. Mr. Shaw confines his statement to the reign of Charles II, but, save for the reference to Charles's foreign policy, it can be applied with equal truth to the reigns of his three successors.

[18] Evans, *The Principal Secretary of State*, pp. 164–165; see also Clarke, *Life of James II*, II, 641.

The secretaries to the Treasury and Admiralty Boards had also been originally nothing more than personal attendants of the Lord High Treasurer and the Lord High Admiral. They now became the public secretaries of composite boards and were paid out of the exchequer. Even the temporary revival of the offices of Lord High Treasurer and Lord High Admiral could not rob these secretaries of their recently acquired public dignity. The secretary at war, who differed from his colleagues on the boards just mentioned in that he had no superior board over him but was in immediate attendance on the king, also threw off the yoke of close dependence on the commander-in-chief, whose office was frequently in abeyance during this period.

Further evidence that these new officials were taking on a public character is to be seen in the notice which they attracted. Chamberlayne, the public annalist, began to list them by name in his *Angliae Notitia*. *The London Gazette* and the news-letters also referred to them in a way that indicated their public capacity. Luttrell, the author of the political diary usually known as *A Brief Relation,* frequently gave information with regard to changes in office among them.

These administrative agents were now left to organize and operate their departments or branches of the government in the face of the difficulties which we have mentioned. The tendency of ministers of state to allow the administration of their offices to rest in the hands of their secretaries is not peculiar to any age. Ministers of strong political susceptibilities are not content to be glorified clerks. Admiralty and Treasury Boards must necessarily relegate much of the actual work of their departments to their secretaries. The late seventeenth century was no exception to the rule. The general moral relaxation of the period, and the all engrossing political situation, made many ministers wilfully negligent of their duties. The tremendous expansion of administrative business prevented the most assiduous minister from acting independently of his secretaries and clerks. There were, of course, ministers of state who labored at their posts. Sir Joseph Williamson, who served as secretary of state from 1674 to 1679, was the outstanding example of a ministerial drudge, but since he had graduated from a mere clerkship, this is not to be wondered at. So great a political dignitary as the Earl of Nottingham, secretary of state under William III, was a hardworking official. Lord Ailesbury relates of him in his *Memoirs,* "In comparison to Secretaries before and after him, he played the clerk as well as the chief, and he often told me that he never ate until he had finished in the office in parliament time, and that he was obliged to go to Kensington . . . for to have the King to sign, and although fasting, he stayed often one or two hours before the King came out, who was in council with his Dutch favorites."[19]

Nottingham's colleague in office, the Earl of Shrewsbury, who went to the opposite extreme, was, Ailesbury informs us, far more typical of his age. Ailesbury arrived one day at Shrewsbury's office to accompany him on an excursion into the country. "Before we went out of his house, the door-keeper of the office brought in a velvet bag with great quantities of letters, the foreign mails, and several coming in at one time. The man took them out of the bag and laid them on a table in that lord's chamber, on which I told him I supposed that he could not go along with us. He, with a smiling countenance, asked me what should hinder him. I pointing to the heap of letters, he replied, 'What is that to me? I never read or write a letter.' I asking him who did, he told me that Mr. William Bridgeman, the first secretary in his office, read all the

19 *Memoirs of Thomas, Earl of Ailesbury,* I, 247–248.

letters and reported to him the material contents, on which he drew what answers were requisite, and then he set his name to them, and, in ending, 'that is all I do.' "[20]

Most of the seventeenth-century administrators were qualified as a result of their training to accept the responsibilities which were placed upon them. The prerequisites laid down for the upper ranks in the civil service were of a high standard and did not differ intrinsically from the standards set today. Training was general, rather than specific, and there was a more or less definite course to be run before an office could be obtained. Clarendon, in speaking of the disposition made for younger sons in an earlier age, described very nearly the training for public servants in his own day and since. "As for Exsample in Queen Elizabeth's dayes a gentleman would put his younger son, to the universety, then to the Ins of Courts, to have a smakering in the Lawe, afterwardes to wayte of an Embassador, afterwards, to bee his secretary, Then to bee lefte as Agente or resedent, behind him, then sent of many forrayne Imployments,—and after some 30 yeares breeding, to bee made a Clarke of the signett, or a Clarke of the Counsell,—itt may bee afterwardes secretary of state,—this was not onely breeding, but a breed of statesmen, fitt to serve the greatest monarke in the world."[21]

Although Clarendon wrote regretfully, as if he spoke of a past practice, the training for the administrators of the Restoration was substantially the same, although no one of the qualifications which he outlined was an absolute prerequisite. Native wit, favoritism, political wirepulling, allowed some men to rise from the ranks. The majority of appointees were sons of gentlemen commoners, but a fairly democratic spirit pervaded Whitehall. Blathwayt

[20] *Ibid.*, 246–247.

[21] Clarendon MSS. 109, f. 67; quoted in Turner, *The Privy Council*, II, 445–446.

was an exception to the rule that a man had to be university trained, for we find no record of his matriculation at either Oxford or Cambridge. However, he had the necessary "smakering in the Lawe" and had made the Grand Tour although he did so in a semiofficial diplomatic capacity.

Nor were these administrators without cultural pursuits. They were not the proverbial dry-as-dust bureaucrats of the popular conception of their class. Many were prominent members of the Royal Society, Pepys, as well as Sir Joseph Williamson and Sir Robert Southwell, Blathwayt's political patrons, serving as presidents. All were widely read and some, like Pepys, Thomas Povey (Blathwayt's uncle), and Blathwayt himself, were true bibliophiles. Williamson was an antiquarian of distinction, and Povey had a critical sense in art that marked him as a connoisseur. Some were even fairly skilful musicians. Blathwayt loved his violin as much as Pepys his flageolet. Each one had some cultural diversion to which his mind often turned.

As a rule they were not unduly solemn. They were men of the world, fond of good living and given to gay, convivial pursuits—the theatre, fair ladies, fine horses, and hard drinking. None of them was a rake or sank to any low level of dissipation. Apparently they were conscientious, law-abiding public servants, constantly seeking to advance themselves in the royal favor, and careful to conceal those little weaknesses which sometimes led them into irregular paths. Few of them bothered their heads much about matters of religious dogma, although, like Pepys, some found themselves embroiled in the endless investigations of alleged Papists. Blathwayt appears to have been ever a light-hearted Conformist.

As a coterie of public servants, they developed an *esprit de corps,* despite the decentralized state of affairs

at Whitehall. Petty jealousies and hatreds appear, but
the strong bonds of friendship in matters apart from official duties indicate that among most of them relations
were harmonious. They were all aware of their superior
knowledge. Ignorant though they might be of their duties
when they entered upon them, they worked very hard to
overcome initial deficiencies. Pepys took up his work as
clerk to Sir George Downing, then one of the tellers of the
exchequer, with a very hazy knowledge of public finance,
but once he had mastered the multiplication tables and
some of the rudimentary principles of arithmetic, he became a very satisfactory accountant. As clerk of the acts,
his conception of naval matters was at first so negligible
that, according to modern tradition, he would have qualified for the first lordship of the Admiralty Board. Blathwayt, as we shall see, was an exception, in that he prided
himself on his understanding of trade and the colonies
even before he entered the plantation office.

Pride, the advantage of good general training, and a
wholesome fear of parliamentary commissioners of accounts, drove all of them forward, and most of them soon
displayed a bellicose omniscience in matters relating to
their special departments. Blathwayt regarded himself as
an oracle in colonial affairs, though, quite rightly, he
never displayed so intrepid an attitude in military concerns. Pepys's assurance—for it was more than mere
bluster—was typical when he stated, "Among the many
thousands under whose observation my employment must
have placed me, I challenge any man to assign one day
from my first admission to this service in July 1660, to
the determination of the war, August 1667 . . . of which
I am not this day able upon oath to give an account of the
particular manner of my employing the same."[22] They

[22] Pepysian MSS., No. 2554; Pepys's testimony before the commissioners

had a clerk's contempt for the deficiencies of their superiors, as when Pepys recorded, "Mr. Burgby, one of the
writing clerks belonging to the Council, a knowing man,
. . . complains how most of the Lords of the Council do
look after themselves and their own ends, and none the
publique, unless Sir Edward Nicholas."[23]

Permanency of tenure was no more guaranteed these
administrators than it is today. Almost none of their
offices were patent offices, and those that were so classed
were usually not life grants, but renewable at the beginning of every reign. Everything supposedly rested on the
rule of good behavior. A young man entering almost any
of the offices had good reason, provided he gave satisfaction to his superiors, to look forward to ten, twenty, or
even thirty years of service.

William Bridgeman, the secretary on whom Shrewsbury depended so completely in 1690, had been in the
secretarial office for over a decade, although as Sunderland's clerk, in 1681, he had to share in the latter's disgrace over the Exclusion Bill. The confidential secretaries
of the secretaries of state, who were often bound to them
by ties of family relationship, were frequently required
to leave office with their superiors, but the other secretaries and clerks usually continued in office. John Cooke
and Robert Yard were prominent in one or other of the
secretarial offices from the early years of the Restoration
until the Revolution, and in Yard's case for another decade. Blathwayt's services at the Privy Council board
totaled thirty-eight years, from 1678 to 1716, although
during the last six years he was more or less inactive. He
served at the plantation office from 1675 to 1696, and at
the war office from 1683 to 1704. Pepys was connected

of public accounts in 1669. Quoted by J. R. Tanner in *Mr. Pepys, an Introduction to the Diary*, p. xii.

    [23] Pepys, *Diary;* entry for March 2, 1664.

with the navy board and the Admiralty from 1660 to 1689, with the exception of the years from 1679 to 1684, when, as a result of the Popish Plot and the Duke of York's disgrace, he was in enforced retirement. William Lowndes served the Treasury in one capacity or another, but preeminently as secretary, for almost fifty years, from 1679 to 1724.[24]

Crises from time to time might threaten to cut short a secretary's or a clerk's services. Thus the Popish Plot landed Pepys temporarily in the Tower, and the Trial of the Seven Bishops came near to unseating Blathwayt. The Roman Catholic predilections of James II turned many ministers of state, as well as officers of the army, out of office, but did not seriously affect the rank and file. The Revolution of 1688 probably took the heaviest toll. It counted Pepys among its victims, but not the indomitable Blathwayt, even though he was suspected of having Jacobite leanings. The government continued with a surprisingly large number of its former secretaries and clerks on the Treasury lists. Considering the nature of the Revolution, it was natural that this should be so, and from the point of view of stability in government, it was exceedingly fortunate.

The dangers attendant on permanency of tenure, atrophy, and inbreeding, did not manifest themselves in

[24] For interesting articles on Lowndes and his predecessor, Henry Guy, see *Dict. Natl. Biog.*, XXXIV, 210–212, XXIII, 388–389. Lowndes succeeded Guy, whose chief clerk he had been, in 1695 when the latter was forced to resign and was committed to the Tower for having accepted a bribe of 200 guineas. As a Tory Guy may have been the victim of the Whig return to power in 1695. Mercenary he undoubtedly was, however, for the story goes that when Henry St. John first came to court, Guy especially warned him "to be very moderate and modest in applications for friends, and very greedy and importunate when he asked for himself." He seems to have acted on the same principle himself. Apparently Lowndes did also, for according to reports, Lowndes's share of fees for his first year of office approached £2400.

any alarming proportions. There was, on the whole, a sustained virility in administration, and the neglect of duty characteristic of some of the ministers of state did not extend to their clerical staffs. The spoils system made very little headway before the opening years of the eighteenth century. This was a fortunate state of affairs, and the degree of success achieved by the administrative system during this period was due not only to the character and the preliminary training of these undersecretaries but also, to the fact that neither they nor their clerks were easily turned out of office.

Few comprehensive sets of rules were laid down for the administration of these offices, but standing rules existed, either written or unwritten, which were closely adhered to. Within an office a business-like atmosphere prevailed. Duties were carefully assigned to the clerks, and, if efficiency sometimes suffered, this was often due to the tedium of copying hour after hour duplicates and triplicates of papers that even at first reading were not very absorbing. Work came in waves also, for mails were irregular, especially in plantation business, and often weary clerks locked up their desks and crawled up to their lodgings, which were frequently on the floor above their offices, at the hours of two and three in the morning.[25] For a clerk to be at his desk at seven or even earlier was not uncommon, although he found relief in the long dinner hour in the middle of the day. No psychological theories with regard to fatigue were being tested out; instead, as best they could, secretaries followed for themselves and their clerks the sounder principles of common sense.

The secretaries in charge of public offices were severe taskmasters in their dealings with their clerks, for none of them ever forgot the hard apprenticeships they had themselves served. These secretaries had a certain

25 Andrews, *Guide to Materials . . . in the Public Record Office*, II, 45.

amount of independence when it came to the engaging of their clerks, although ministers of state and superior boards, no doubt, were often guilty of arbitrary interference. Blathwayt seems to have been fortunate in exercising a considerable amount of independence. Few definite standards were set down in writing to guide secretaries, but they looked around for young men who had gone through much the same training as themselves. Personal interrogation of the candidate after the necessary letters of recommendation had come in, and the request that he produce a fair copy of some stipulated exercise to test penmanship and spelling, constituted a usual test of ability. Such men as Pepys and Blathwayt were looking for clerks who were, in the words of the diarist, "business, active men" and prided themselves "upon having things do well" under their hands—and their search was rarely unavailing, since they never, if possible, went outside the bounds of their own immediate families or acquaintanceships! A very good clerk could be engaged for fifty pounds a year, and Blathwayt considered a youthful Oxford graduate as none too good for a clerkship of that sort in the plantation office, although the young man's family chose to take an opposite view.[26]

As far as is known, the commissioners of the customs were the only ones to insist on a system of competitive examinations, and they did so by order from the Treasury. It was a method applied, not to the clerks under the immediate surveillance of the commissioners, but to the

[26] Add. MSS. 11759, ff. 76–77. The young man in question, Thomas Lane, wrote to Sir Robert Southwell, Blathwayt's patron, for advice. He said his family was threatening to disinherit him if he accepted the clerkship, saying, "If you have anything of rising pride in your temper, methinke it should secure you from debasing your degree, your standing and your gentile [sic] education." His place at Oxford—that of tutor—was worth nearly one hundred pounds they argued. If he went into the plantation office he could not travel or do anything to improve himself.

various collectors. The determination to weed out the in-
effectuals in the customs service dates back to 1689, when
an examination for applicants to the office of landwaiter
was set.[27] The candidate was first examined by the commissioners of the customs and then sent for a second examination to the surveyor of the port. Some of the papers
given them in mathematics are still extant.[28] The system
was carried out with difficulty, however, the commissioners of the customs lending it only a half-hearted support, as the frequent complaints of the Treasury indicate.

In all the offices there was a definite tendency to promote the clerk next in line, although this could be set aside
whenever ministers of state chose to do so. We have a
definite resolution on this practice in the case of the commissioners of the customs. In 1706, they received notice
from the Lord Treasurer that "henceforth no person
shall be made a Collector of the Customes unless he hath
been bred a Clerke in the businesse of the Customes and
that the Collector for the lesser ports be preferred according to their merits to the greater, and that no person
be received as Collector without giving sufficient security.
This to be a standing Rule to be signified to the Commissioners of Customes.''[29]

All the administrative agents of the government had
impressed upon them the importance of departmental
records, and, although an unfortunate amount of laxity in
the care of the archives is to be discerned, it is clear that
all of the offices were following definite standards. There
were standing orders with regard to the keeping of rough
and perfected journals, minute books, and entry books of
in-letters and out-letters, and for the classification and
cataloguing of papers. The order which the newly created

27 *Cal. Treas. Papers*, 1557–1696, pp. xliii–xlvi.
28 *Ibid.*, 1697–1702, pp. xliii, 560–561.
29 *Treas. Min. Bk.*, XV, 185.

Treasury Board issued to its secretary, Sir George Downing, on May 27, 1667, is typical. He was instructed to "keepe a book singly for registring the breife notes he should take for framing any orders upon, or pursuing other their Lordships directions, which notes at their next meeting, and before they entered upon any new buisnes, he should acquaint them with, and what was done thereupon, and so from time to time what progress was made, upon any directions then unperfected, that he should enter the names of the Commissioners present at every meeting and constantly observe this method."[30] In 1689 a rather belated regulation was made by the Treasury to the effect "that when petitions are brought in, the day on which they are exhibited be entered on the back thereof," a rule which was commonly followed in all of the departments.[31]

Most of the departmental records reflect the painstaking efforts of the secretaries and clerks to fulfil requirements with regard to the records, and occasional references reveal the pride which they took in the imposing rows of office books and well-kept files. Only the secretarial office persistently lagged behind. There, the administrative method employed, since there was no superior board to enforce regularity, depended on the will or whim of the secretary of state. Even in the Treasury office, however, which was subject to strict discipline and apparently prided itself on its system, there must have been an appalling amount of carelessness, or a suitor would not have written, "I pray, good Sirs, endeavour to find these two petitions, for we shall be undone if they are lost; else lett Esquire Lowndes [the secretary] make me keeper of his petitions, and I will be bound in ten thousand pounds not one shall be lost while I live; now I have waited above

3 quarters of a year, and now my petition is mislaid."[32]
And in 1726 conditions became so bad that it was necessary to appoint such a paper keeper, for clerks not only
lost documents but fell into the habit of lighting the fires
with them.[33]

The lack of space and of proper facilities for hous-
ing the archives caused the government a certain amount
of concern. The need of a Public Record Office was already felt, for in lieu of one great central repository, any
vacant rooms which could be found either in Whitehall
or in the Tower were used for documents as they over-
flowed their departmental bounds.[34] The matter became
the subject of a parliamentary inquiry early in the eighteenth century. Shocking conditions were disclosed in the
state-paper office, where the papers of the secretary of
state were supposed to be deposited. Sir Joseph Williamson had purchased the office of keeper of these records in
1661 and held it until his death in 1702. His negligence,
which arose partly out of the unwillingness of secretaries
of state to relinquish their papers, was then disclosed by
his successor, John Tucker, one of the clerks in the office of
the secretary of state. Tucker reported that Williamson
had "left the office very much out of repair, without so
much as one whole window or door." No papers had been
turned into the office since 1684. Such important state
documents as the treaties of Breda and Ryswick were
missing. Williamson had kept no catalogue, "not even of
those papers that he bequeathed by his will to be placed
in the office (which appear most of them have been

[32] *Cal. Treas. Papers*, 1557–1696, Vol. XLI, No. 53; also Vol. XLII, No. 42.

[33] *Notes of Materials for the History of Public Departments* (compiled by Francis S. Thomas, 1846), p. 6.

[34] Only Chancery records were kept in the Tower and there was an official keeper. On the question of archives see a statement by James II in Clarke, *Life of James II*, II, 641.

formerly taken out of it by himself)." "It will be a work of time," Tucker declared, "to inspect such a multitude of papers, and to digest them and put them in order, with proper references for finding each particular paper."[35] Investigation of certain other office records, however, those of chancery in particular, revealed "these papers or records to be carefully and regularly kept."[36]

The government was aware of the grave and constant danger from fire, the frequent recurrence of which in Whitehall was enough to put men on their guard. There was practically nothing which could be done to prevent documents from being burned up, except to provide iron chests in which to store them (and this the Privy Council did for some of its documents in 1678)[37] or to furnish facilities which would enable records to be easily removed in case a fire broke out. In 1699 warned by the fire in Whitehall the preceding year, the Board of Trade decided to take precautionary measures, although their records had not been affected by the conflagration. "Upon occasion of a chimney in the Cockpit being on fire, their Lordships resolved to consider of a means for getting all the books in this office transcribed, to be kept in some other place, in case of fire should happen here. In the meantime ordered that a competent number of sacks be provided for carrying away the books upon any such accident."[38]

The greatest sin committed by secretaries and clerks in

[35] *Hist. MSS. Com., House of Lords MSS.*, n.s., VI, 42; also pp. 36–49.

[36] *Ibid.*, p. 47. See, however, *Cal. Treas. Papers*, 1714–1719, CCXIV, No. 69; CCXX, No. 9. On July 29, 1718, the Board of Works reported, "The magazine of gunpowder belonging to the Tower is at present under the rooms where the most valuable records of the kingdom are kept." On June 10, 1719, the Ordnance responded curiously that the situation was not so bad as it might have been since only 60 or 70 barrels of gunpowder were in the storeroom.

[37] *Privy Council Register*, LXVI; October 11, 1678. Quoted in Turner, *The Privy Council*, II, 446.

[38] *Cal. S. P. Col.*, 1699, p. 580.

connection with the archives was the tendency, to which all were prone, of carrying off papers to their lodgings or houses, frequently forgetting to bring them back again, if indeed they had any serious intention of doing so. This was a cardinal sin of ministers of state as well, despite the standing rule that they hand over all public papers to their successors in office. There was no clear-cut line of distinction drawn between public and private papers and since ministers were jealous of their rights, they too often overstepped legitimate bounds in removing documents from their offices, as the labors of the Historical Manuscripts Commission testify. In this respect Blathwayt was a notorious offender.[39]

Although in the duties assigned them and in the responsibilities which they assumed, these first secretaries in governmental offices were clearly the seventeenth-century forerunners of the modern permanent undersecretaries, there was one essential difference in their official character. Whitehall was, as yet, no citadel of bureaucracy. There was an easy channel of communication between Westminster and Whitehall, but it was not the counterpart of the modern parliamentary undersecretary who kept it open. Such administrators as Blathwayt and his colleagues were themselves members of parliament, where they represented their departments as effectively as the modern parliamentary undersecretary. Had the provision of the Act of Settlement which prevented ministers of the crown from sitting in the house of commons been enforced, the cleavage which now exists between the permanent undersecretary and the legislature would have been created at this time; but actually its enforcement

[39] Subsequent sales of private libraries have resulted in the further dissemination of official papers and made the problem of the modern researcher almost insurmountable, except in the fairly rare cases where the manuscripts have been bought by government archivists.

was as much a dead letter in the case of these lesser administrative officers as it was among the great ministers of state.

As a matter of fact, the bureaucracy of the late seventeenth century enjoyed neither political nor social isolation, for it was as closely bound up with the court of the king as it was with the legislature. Whitehall was still the royal palace, and while William III might prefer Kensington, and all the sovereigns might withdraw from time to time to Windsor and Hampton Court, Whitehall was never entirely deserted by those courtiers and their ladies who had apartments there. Whitehall was, like Versailles, the social, as well as the political, heart of the kingdom. Crowded in between Charing Cross on the north and the "city" of Westminster on the south, the Thames on the east and St. James's Park on the west, it lay cluttered like a rabbit warren with buildings some of which were the palaces of the sovereign and his queen, others the London houses of grandees, the apartments of the royal mistresses, or the public offices of England's administration. This grouping of England's social and administrative activities presented a scene that defies description except to facile pens like that of Pepys, who, living as he did in the midst of it, let no colorful detail escape him. It was a medieval life in a modern setting and was already passing, although to men of Blathwayt's day the change was not discernible.

Amid scenes of courtly wantonness and gayety, Blathwayt drudged over his office books. Not even at night did he escape them, for as early as 1675, he secured lodgings from the king in Scotland Yard. After the Revolution, William III granted him a lease of Little Wallingford House, which lay on the Great Street, running from Charing Cross to Westminster. From the war office, facing the main thoroughfare, the plantation office in Scotland Yard, or the council chamber in the Cockpit, Blathwayt could look out on idling courtiers or fashionably gowned ladies. He heard their gay voices and merry laughter as these floated up from the privy gardens or St. James's Park, and their cries to the boatmen as they descended the privy stairs to the river, to take boat for Windsor or Hampton Court. As he passed along King Street he brushed elbows with nobles and leading officers of state, to many of whom, in that small world which then constituted England's officialdom, he was personally known. He was often an onlooker at royal balls and banquets, for as secretary at war he had access to the royal chambers. He was *au courant* with the life of the royal palace as no modern official at Whitehall could ever be. The conditions among which he and his colleagues worked would have maddened a modern efficiency expert and must have distracted even the officials of that day, though never lastingly did they regret the circumstances which placed them so near the heart of the court. This close proximity to the social side of court life was so much a matter of course that officials never dreamed an administrative system could be conducted otherwise. They rather pitied their brethren in the ordnance or the navy or the customs service whose offices perforce lay in the City, along the wharves, or in the Tower. To have introduced the cold impersonalism of the modern Whitehall would have been to rob them of life's greatest pleasure, their endless fund of court gossip, leaving them nothing in its place save peace and quiet, two conditions on which, in contrast, they set little store.

Engraving by J. Kip

WHITEHALL IN 1724

Showing the Banqueting Hall, the Holbein Gateway, the old Guards House, and
Great Wallingford House

CHAPTER II

WILLIAM BLATHWAYT—A MORE INTIMATE PICTURE

"Now for myself, I never pretended to any estate. My father died as soon as I was born, leaving his estate which had been more considerable extremely embroiled and impaired. Other things happened since and particularly the Fire of London that reach't me with others. I have had three sisters provided for and two married since that time, so that I am under no obligation to them other than that of brotherly kindness.'" This very modest recital, the most intimate utterance of Blathwayt's on record, might well have been the opening passage of his memoirs. It was written, however, in his thirty-seventh year and in no specially reminiscent mood. It was to serve merely as a credential to establish the eligibility of Blathwayt in the eyes of the man he had selected as his father-in-law. The tone, that usually adopted by the self-made man in explaining his rise to fortune, has an unmistakable quality. At the time he wrote Blathwayt's fortunes had been administrative rather than financial, but he was definitely on a solid footing, in modern parlance a "career man," and, best of all, considering the occasion, free from family encumbrances.

A diary does not necessarily make a man, nor do his memoirs necessarily damn him. Both help to reconstruct

---

[1] Porlock MSS.; a letter written to Sir Robert Southwell, September 28, 1686.

him more or less as he really was. A private correspondence can be of great assistance in the matter of motives.
Blathwayt's private papers are a bleak array, startling
in their paucity as compared with the mass of his public
papers. Only a few scattered letters remain and although
they occasionally contain descriptive phrases, vignette-
like in their clarity, they are often only tantalizing—
valuable for what they imply rather than for what they
prove. Contemporary gossip about Blathwayt was rare.
As we know, few newsmongers bothered their heads
about anything save the indiscretions of Whitehall's
servants and, since Blathwayt was a most cautious man,
what he said or did was rarely "news." Fate infrequently
played tricks on him by thrusting him nearer the centre
of the political stage, but Blathwayt never courted pub-
licity and having temporarily achieved it, hastily sought
refuge in self-ordained anonymity.

We know that Blathwayt was essentially a man of action rather than words, too busy, apparently, in building
a public memorial for himself in the form of orderly rows
of office books to prepare a private legacy in the shape of
a diary. If he did keep one, it could not have been very in-
trospective. Blathwayt never felt any great need of a confidant, animate or otherwise, not because his nature was
so complex but because it was so simple. In his case it was
his motives, not his heart, that he wore pinned to his coat
sleeve. He craved material success both for himself and
his country, and in his own case he hoped to achieve it as
the result of very careful planning and prodigious industry, combined with whatever flukes a kindly providence
chose to bestow.

On first glance we might assume that Blathwayt's work
was his life, engrossing so much of his time that he had no
opportunity to live apart from it. This, however, was far
from the case. Seventeenth-century man of affairs that he

was, Blathwayt had cultural tastes and interests far too highly developed ever to permit himself to be lost in the minutiæ of business. He probably was not as deeply interested as most of his friends and contemporaries in scientific discovery, since he never joined the Royal Society. His bent apparently was literary and musical, if we are to judge from his fondness for Shakespeare and Purcell; from his zest for the acquisition of lexicons he must have had ability as a philologist as well as a linguist. He craved elegant surroundings in private life and the effect on him of a newly acquired arras was like that of a very stirring wine.

The most pronounced of Blathwayt's attributes, perhaps, was this emphasis which he put on things external rather than things spiritual. Possessions, or the desire for them, occupied a much larger place in his mind than introspection on abstract subjects. They meant far more to him than people or popular favor and, while we find that he was a loyal friend and a doting father, it is not unjust to say that it was the possessive spirit that prompted many of his actions. Never meanly calculating nor basely covetous, he longed for this world's goods with a passion that did not desert him to his dying day. It was not a desire to compensate himself for earlier privations that impelled him, for despite the implication in the letter we have quoted, he had never known want nor been deprived of the ordinary comforts of life; he merely had the zeal of a collector, a connoisseur's love of beauty, which meant that he never begrudged the money he spent on pictures and books or the time involved in arranging them, whereas he must often have found irksome the half hours spent with friends and acquaintances.

A process of indirection has brought out certain other definite impressions about Blathwayt. He was unmistakably the product of early family influences, the traces of which he could never have eradicated, if indeed he had desired to do so. Although politically he chose to pursue a middle course, mild Toryism, at heart he had strong convictions which won him a few warm friends and a fairly large number of adversaries whose cruel thrusts he could not easily parry, for while his pen flowed smoothly, his tongue faltered and stumbled. He had a calm, genial disposition, and was inclined to be jocose. Indeed, he sometimes embarrassed his well-wishers, particularly as he grew older, by his heavy wit, which more often than not took the form of a pun. William III set a royal stamp upon him by pronouncing him dull; it was a strange judgment for William to have made since his own company was not the most enlivening, but with his usual acuteness he struck very near the truth.

In the records, Blathwayt's early years are an utter blank. Perhaps that is why we conclude that he was never really young. He was such a solemn young man in his early twenties, when he first comes to our attention, that we cannot picture him ever as a rollicking boy, freely exercising the prerogatives which go with youth, teasing his sisters, badgering his playmates, playing truant. He probably never caused his family a moment's alarm as to his ultimate welfare. Never wayward, always diligent, the sort of youth more often to be found in the library than disporting himself on the street or in the garden—to other youth, no doubt, a sore trial, to his elders, however, a model of good sense and decorum.

He was born in London, presumably in the year 1649, although no parish record has so far disclosed the precise date. He was destined to spend most of his life within the narrow confines of the City or Whitehall, although through his marriage he became a country gentleman with a large estate in Gloucestershire and manors in Somersetshire. The rôle of country squire was becoming to him and the traces of his London upbringing not so deep but what he could fit into the habits of the gentry with great ease and satisfaction to himself. The family strains which came together in him were at the time of his birth virtually indigenous to the capital, but had originally come from the north country. His mother, Anne Povey, belonged to a family which had its seat in Cheshire.[2] The Blathwayts hailed from either Cumberland or Yorkshire, and the name belongs rather to the valleys and lakes of the north than to the narrow streets of London.[3] The exodus of both families antedated William Blath-

[2] The Povey family had several distinguished members though not in the direct line. Sir John Povey who died in 1679 and served, first as baron of the exchequer in Ireland, then as chief justice of king's bench, was related to Blathwayt, but there seems never to have been any intimate connection. Charles Povey, that curious projector of, and writer on, fire and marine insurance, was a distant cousin. See the *Dict. of Natl. Biog.*, XLVI, 233–235; for the Povey pedigree, County Cheshire, see Add. MSS. 5529, f. 53.

[3] The name, Blathwayt, is variously spelled Blathwait, Blathwaite, Blathwayte, but the first is the form William Blathwayt preferred and is the one used by the family today. There were Blathwayts to be found in the two northern counties in the days of Elizabeth, and in the seventeenth century a Blathwayt from Cumberland lost his life for adherence to the parliamentary cause during the Civil Wars. On May 11, 1654, Mary Blathwayt, his widow, residing at Seckmurther, Cumberland, petitioned Cromwell, saying that she and her husband had suffered for their loyalty to parliament and that as a result her husband had lost his memory and subsequently died. (*Cal. S. P. Dom.*, 1654, p. 167.) For much of the material on the Blathwayts of Cumberland and Yorkshire I am indebted to Mr. George Wynter Blathwayt of West Porlock, Somersetshire. He tells me that he has attempted to trace the family lineage, but has found it impossible to find any clear line of descent. The registries at Carlisle furnished him with some scattered bits of information with regard to the Blathwayts of the sixteenth century.

Blathwayt has been erroneously referred to as a Welshman, the error arising out of William Penn's reference to the Welsh ''Mr. Secretary'' when making his suggestion that his grant of land be called New Wales. He was referring to the secretary of state, Sir Leoline Jenkins, not to the secretary of the Lords of Trade, William Blathwayt. The fact that Blathwayt drafted Penn's charter led to the assumption that Penn had him in mind. (C. M. Andrews, *Colonial Self-Government*, p. 175. Professor Andrews quotes from one of Penn's letters to be found in *Penn. Hist. Soc. Memoirs*, I, 208–209.)

wayt's birth by more than half a century. We know that the Blathwayts were comfortably established in London at the time of his grandfather, Thomas Blathwayt, while on the Povey side we may definitely go back a generation earlier to his great-grandfather, John Povey.

Both families originally belonged to the merchant class and apparently had never had any great landed interests. They were, however, aristocratic guildsmen. John Povey, the great-grandfather, was a member of the Embroiderers' Company of London. Thomas Blathwayt, the grandfather, was a cutler and a prominent member of that liveried order, the London Cutlers' Company. Singularly little can be learned about these early family antecedents of William Blathwayt, the administrator, but the records of the Cutlers' Company yield a colorful account of Thomas Blathwayt and show us that his grandson came honestly by some of his conservative tendencies. Thomas Blathwayt was a man of fortune and for many years one of the members of the company's governing body, the court of assistants. The beginning of James I's reign found him engaged in a mighty battle with the more radical wing of the company over the question of a new charter. Blathwayt was aligned with the hated "non-workers" against the "workers" who were led by a so-called pirate, or interloper, Oliver Plucket. The latter, alleging that the old charter was defective and endangered the company's title to its lands, had applied successfully to James for a new charter, the cost of which the aristocratic members of the guild refused to pay. Their chief grievance lay in the fact that the new charter specifically dispossessed them of their offices and exalted position in the company. In this contest, which represented the struggle of new economic forces with old, Blathwayt stood firmly by his contention that the position of all the guilds would be imperiled if Plucket and his henchmen were triumphant. He and others were dismissed from the company by Plucket who had won a temporary ascendency, and, only after the matter had been referred to the Lord Mayor and the Board of Aldermen, did they succeed in getting reinstated. The lively combat extended over a period of years, but in the end conservatism triumphed and Blathwayt again took his place among the governors of the company. As late as 1616 he was serving as a junior warden. He apparently forgot his ill will, although at his death he left the company only three pounds for "a drinking."[4]

From the Povey branch of the family came the Whitehall tradition which was to govern the life of William Blathwayt. Both families had, in fact, forsaken their mercantile pursuits before Blathwayt's birth, but the Blathwayts had deserted the City for the almost cloistered shelter of the Inns of Court. His mother's father, Justinian Povey, however, made his fortune in the service of the government. For many years he acted as accountant general to Queen Anne of Denmark and as early as 1606 received the reversion to the office of auditor of the exchequer.[5] From 1606 to 1642, his name often appears in the official records and it is apparent that he went through a course of training not unlike that which his grandson was to receive, except that it was in a small way and never netted him the same measure of success. We hear of him in various minor connections. He secured the remunerative, though scarcely arduous, post of justice of the peace for Middlesex.[6] He was appointed receiver for life of the counties of Suffolk and Huntingdon.[7] There were

---

[4] For this material on Thomas Blathwayt, see Charles Welch, *A History of the Cutlers' Company*, II, 198–208, 274, 290–298, 314–318.

[5] *Cal. S. P. Dom.*, 1603–1610, pp. 316, 574.

[6] *Ibid.*, 1635, pp. 284, 483. [7] *Ibid.*, 1611–1618, p. 277.

few official opportunities of adding to his fortune which he neglected.

Conformity to established religious and political precepts seems to have characterized the actions of both of Blathwayt's grandfathers. Thomas Blathwayt's life, apart from his profession, is more or less a complete blank to us, but we know that he served as churchwarden of Trinity the Less.[8] We have proof of Justinian Povey's religious conformity, although surely in no creditable connection. His record, if true, makes a blot on the family escutcheon, for a case was brought in the court of Star Chamber by the attorney-general against him and ten others, all lay vestrymen of St. Botolph's without Aldersgate, for imposing illegal and excessive fees upon the parishioners.[9] It might have furnished a precedent, so William Blathwayt's enemies would have said, for some of the latter's official extortions.

The Civil Wars and the hideous political imbroglios of the 1640's took their toll from both families. Thomas Blathwayt was long dead, but the disasters fell heavily on his son, William Blathwayt's father, while Justinian Povey saw swept away from him the accumulation of years of labor. A fatal tendency toward conservatism and a respect for the established order, were largely responsible. Perhaps there had never been any great wealth in either family, but they had certainly been in more than comfortable circumstances. References to houses and gardens owned by Thomas Blathwayt, and the provisions of his will, mentioning rings set with rubies and diamonds to be bestowed on his daughters, show him, in fact, to

[8] Porlock MSS. Trinity the Less was situated at the corner of great Trinity Lane and Little Trinity Lane, Breadward, and was destroyed in the Fire. Wilberforce Jenkinson, *London Churches before the Great Fire* (S. P. C. K.), pp. 200–201.

[9] *Cal. S. P. Dom.*, 1633–1634, p. 353.

have been a man of substance.[10] As Justinian Povey's fortunes increased, we find that he decided to remove from London and purchase a fine house at Hounslow, called the Priory, where he and his family lived in comparative affluence.

William Blathwayt, the father of the administrator, was brought up in a manner which befitted the son of a gentleman commoner. He was one of a large family (for Thomas Blathwayt had been thrice married), in which the feminine element predominated. His only brother to survive was the child of the third marriage, while he was his father's first-born.[11] In December, 1609, at the age of fifteen, he was matriculated at Brasenose College, Oxford.[12] When he was eighteen, his father transferred him to the Middle Temple, evidence that Thomas Blathwayt had no desire to have his son follow in his own footsteps by entering the Cutlers' Company. To the end of his days, William's interests were centered in the Inns of Court.[13] In time, after years of faithful apprenticeship, he became one of the worthies of the Middle Temple and was ap-

[10] Thomas Blathwayt, we know, had two houses, one which lay outside of Cripplegate in Whitecross Street and another called Throgmorton House. The latter may have taken its name from the fact that it lay on the street of that name, or it may have been in Stepney parish which then lay far from the heart of the City, for we know that Blathwayt possessed land there since he remembered the poor of the parish in his will. (Feet of Fines, co. Middlesex, Trinity, 17 James I; Porlock MSS.; Thomas Blathwayt's will, 80 Byrde, Somerset House Wills.)

[11] For information on the subject of Thomas Blathwayt's marriages I am indebted to Mr. George Wynter Blathwayt. See also Burke's *Landed Gentry*. Thomas Blathwayt died in 1624 and by his father's will William was made guardian of his brother Henry, then about fourteen years of age. Henry disappears utterly from view, although he probated his mother's will in 1648.

[12] *Oxford Hist. Soc., Brasenose College Register*, p. 110. He was admitted on February 22, 1609, matriculated December 1, 1609, and left on May 16, 1612.

[13] *Middle Temple Records, Minutes of the Parliament* (1603–1649), II, 551, 568, 591, 629, 631–632, 653, 713, 717. He was admitted on June 11, 1612.

pointed a master of the utter bar, but he never achieved the rank of bencher and hence was prevented from becoming a serjeant at law. He became a junior, then a senior, reader and was thus called upon to provide the magnificent reader's feast, a banquet so splendid that royalty was asked to attend and a reader often spent as much as £1000 to provide it.[14] His activities rarely carried him beyond the bounds of London's legal world, although he was successful in securing one of the royal stewardships, that of Colebrooke near Windsor. Occasional orders were issued by the Privy Council instructing him in his duties, and he, no doubt, derived a fair share of all the rents and royal perquisites he collected.[15]

A confirmed bachelor in his ways, he postponed the question of matrimony until he was almost fifty and then entered on it at a most inauspicious moment. In 1642, when the parliamentary leaders were absorbed in the great constitutional conflict which was soon to become a contest at arms, Blathwayt sought the hand of Anne Povey. The lady in question was only half her suitor's age. Being a Povey, she was doubtless intelligent but with expensive tastes and inclined to be erratic in her interests. Sentiment could have had very little to do with the match. Loneliness prompted Blathwayt's action; expediency, Anne Povey's, for she had a natural fear of spinsterhood. The marriage was probably arranged by her brother, Thomas Povey, a rare personality, like Blathwayt a member of the Inns of Court, though he belonged to Gray's Inn. The financial inducements for the marriage were slight. At the time Anne's father's, Justinian Povey's, fortunes were very definitely on the down grade.

14 For an account of the organization of the Middle Temple, see W. Herbert, *Antiquities of the Inns of Court and Chancery*, pp. 165–181, 211–272.

15 *Cal. S. P. Dom.*, 1636–1637, p. 138.

What was worse, he was in difficulties over the Queen Dowager's accounts, though he protested his innocence of the charges of defalcation brought against him.[16] Disaster, however, had not actually overtaken him when Blathwayt came to plead for his daughter's hand. The marriage was solemnized with due rejoicing in the chapel at Hounslow on October 19, 1642. Dowered or not, Anne Povey found herself a bride; while her husband cheerfully paid the fine of ten pounds with which he was taxed at the time for failing to read at the Middle Temple. On that score he was in good company, for Sir Simonds D'Ewes was fined with him for staying away for reasons equally personal.[17]

Very little is known of Anne and William Blathwayt after their marriage. They settled in London, probably in the parish of St. Mary Savoy, and four children were born, three daughters and a son, William Blathwayt, the administrator. He was the youngest child and, as we have stated, was probably born in 1649. Over the birth of this son, whose arrival would ordinarily have been a source of great joy, a shadow was cast. The parliamentary conflict, little calculated to improve a lawyer's estate, had ruined the elder Blathwayt. Filled with dark forebodings but too old to find recourse elsewhere, he remained in his chambers at the Middle Temple and in 1646 was referred to— although he was only fifty-two—as one of the "most ancient masters of the utter bar."[18] His practice virtually gone, debts began to accumulate and the family to feel the pinch of poverty. Death mercifully overtook him shortly

[16] *Ibid.*, 1641–1643, pp. 118–119. The charges were apparently dropped. Even so, Povey's day was over and he blamed the parliamentary crisis for his misfortunes.

[17] Porlock MSS.; *Middle Temple Records, Minutes of the Parliament* (1603–1649), II, 928.

[18] *Middle Temple Records, Minutes of the Parliament* (1603–1649), II, 943; November 24, 1646. Also pp. 947–948; March 27, 1647.

after 1650, and Anne Povey Blathwayt, a young woman of thirty-two, was left to face life as a widow with four children and no very visible means of support.[19] Her husband's will, which was proved in 1654, left her his goods and chattels—and his debts.[20]

Dire as the situation was, it had its mitigating aspects, for her brother, Thomas Povey, came to the rescue and with some of the skill in orderly execution which Cromwell was beginning to find useful in government business, began to straighten out the family's affairs. His remedies were simple. For the time being, his sister and her children were taken under his wing, a step which his finances at the time made possible. Unlike his brother-in-law, he had decided after some initial hardships to desert the law for trade and politics and thus improve his fortunes. He now proceeded to collect as many of his sister's debts as possible and, since he was convinced that her loss was not inconsolable, to find her a second husband. Business and political interests frequently took him to Cornwall, where he met and probably had business relations with the Vivians, a local family of very good standing.[21] One of its members, Thomas Vivian, had betaken himself to London, where he was apparently in business for himself. Once Povey had brought her to his attention, Vivian saw in Anne Povey Blathwayt a lady after his own heart.

[19] The date of his death is unknown, but it was either 1649 or 1650; Blathwayt himself said that his father died about the time of his birth. Porlock MSS.

[20] Porlock MSS.; an excerpt from the will. See also Royalist Composition Papers, S. P. 23: 212, p. 441, for a reference to a suit in the court of chancery brought by Blathwayt against Sir Edward Fisher of Mickleton, Gloucester, in 1647. The amount involved was only £100. (Index Library, *Index Nominum to the Royalist Composition Papers*, I, A-F; also Chancery Proceedings, C 5: 401, 48.)

[21] For a genealogical table of the Vivian family, see MacLean, *Deanery of Trigg Manor*, II, 251 *et seq.*

Some time after 1655 Anne found herself for a second time a bride.

Thomas Povey relinquished his sister and her daughters very willingly to Vivian's care. Not so his young nephew, William. Povey, who was childless, regarded his nephew with the affection of a father for a son and with the fervor of a priest for a promising neophyte. To his uncle, Blathwayt probably owed all that he subsequently became. From him directly came the Whitehall tradition and the drift toward pluralistic practices. Without him and under his father's tutelage, had the latter lived, he would doubtless have gone into the law and thus been forever lost to English administration. Instead he was not merely prepared for a very commendable public career, but came under the constant supervision of a man who, if Pepys's and Evelyn's comments are to be taken at their face value, was, in spite of all of his idiosyncrasies, one of the most ingenious and cultivated men of his day. In taking Blathwayt in tow, Povey wisely made no attempt to separate him from his family. Blathwayt's affections for his mother and his stepfather were ever of the warmest and his feeling for his stepsisters, Jane and Mary, as deep as that for his real sisters. Neither the Poveys nor the Blathwayts ever ignored or neglected family ties and responsibilities.[22]

To students of English colonial policy, Thomas Povey's name is familiar, for he and his associate, the merchant, Sir Martin Noel, were pioneer figures in colonial administration.[23] To those who know the court of Charles II from

[22] The tie between the Blathwayts and the Vivians was drawn even closer, for on April 26, 1665, Blathwayt's sister, Frances, married another Thomas Vivian, a physician and a cousin or nephew of her stepfather. They were married apparently at St. Mary Savoy, Middlesex. (*Harleian Soc. Publications*, XXIV, 87; Marriage Licenses issued from the Faculty Office of the Archbishop of Canterbury.)

[23] Andrews, *British Committees . . . of Trade and Plantations, 1622–*

the pages of Pepys, Povey is also well known, for while no courtier himself, he vied with the greatest noble in setting up a London establishment to startle and command the admiration of the most critical connoisseur of art and letters. Had Blathwayt like his uncle had as clever a pen as Pepys's to describe him, the personal side of his life would not have suffered from historical anaemia. If it is not a picture of *Thomas Povey Painted to the Life* which Pepys offers us, it is at least a vivid, far from jejune, interpretation. While Evelyn was satisfied with the dignified entry ''I din'd with Mr. Povey, one of the Masters of Requests, a nice contriver of all elegances, and exceedingly formall,''[24] Pepys gives us an array of his usual succulent details.

Temperamentally we know that Blathwayt and Povey had a great deal in common. Blathwayt in his early days was his uncle's willing satellite, so that while there might have been striking initial differences in their natures, many of these were lost as the adolescent Blathwayt strove to make his tastes and manners conform to his uncle's pattern. The differences temperamentally were sufficiently real, however, so that Blathwayt could never quite recast himself in his uncle's mold. In Povey there was a trace of the jackanapes and mountebank which was utterly lacking in Blathwayt. A dull stability in the latter stands out in sharp contrast to the irritable caprices of the former and may explain why the one ended his days in comfortable security, the other in ''umbrage and inaction.''

When Pepys first met Povey, the latter was in the heyday of his success. After a checkered career during the parliamentary struggle, when for a while it seemed that

1675, pp. 51–53, and all of chapters III and IV. Egerton MSS. 2395 and Add. MSS. 11411 contain many of Povey's colonial letters and papers.

24 Evelyn, *Diary;* entry for February 29, 1676.

his moderate views might cost him very dear, Povey had turned opportunist. He secured himself in the good graces both of the Cromwellians and the leaders of the Restoration.[25] From 1660 to 1668 his fortunes ran high. Officially he was a person of some importance. He became a member of both the councils set up to administer England's commercial and colonial interests and served as secretary of the one governing the plantations. Having struck the fancy of the Duke of York, he was appointed his treasurer. He was also made one of the masters of requests, and treasurer of the commission set up to govern Tangier, as well as surveyor-general of the victualling department there. He was meanwhile a member of parliament, standing for some of the worst of Cornwall's rotten boroughs.[26] His private affairs were in equally good order. Business apparently went smoothly and he had interests in some of the stock companies set up for colonial development. Being an epicure, he knew how to turn his leisure to account. Finally he decided that the married state was preferable to bachelorhood and found himself a very rich widow. His regret was that she was inclined to be censorious.

Povey and Pepys came together over the treasurership of the commission for Tangier which Povey had decided

[25] *Dict. Natl. Biog.*, XLVI, 235–236; in 1643 Povey published a pamphlet entitled, *The Moderator, expecting sudden Peace or sure Ruine,* a plea for moderation which drew forth three acrimonious replies. He fell under a cloud, but presently decided to throw in his fortunes with the parliamentary party. In March, 1647, he was elected to parliament by the borough of Liskeard, Cornwall, but as a Presbyterian was deprived of his seat a year later. He was suspected of disloyalty to the Council of State in 1650 and a warrant issued for his arrest. His interest in the colonies subsequently won him Cromwell's attention.

[26] In 1659 when the Presbyterians were restored to parliament, he was elected for Bossiney, Trevena, and Tintagel. Some powerful patron perhaps was guiding his fortunes. His religious views he must subsequently have adjusted to suit the times.

to sell, for good trader though he was in private life, he seemed to have grave difficulty in making his official accounts balance. He would never have had the patience for his nephew's post of auditor general of plantation revenues. Pepys's initial impressions of him were most adverse. "The simple Povey, of all the most ridiculous fools that ever I knew to attend to business." But as Pepys's chances of striking a close bargain improved, so did his opinion of Povey. He forgave Povey, "the coxcomb," for being a bad mathematician and bookkeeper and decided that as a friend he could prove useful. He never quite reconciled himself to Povey's eccentricities and pedantries and frequently referred to him as a man who passed his comprehension. "Lord! to see still what a puppy that Povey is with all his show is very strange." "A cunning fellow in his way, though a strange one, and that, that I meete not in any other man, nor can describe in him."[27]

From Pepys we get an idea of the splendor in which Povey was living, a splendor to which Blathwayt's youthful eyes early grew accustomed. We learn how Povey had deserted his simple apartments in Whitehall and, although over fifty, had married a great fortune and was making havoc of it. He had set himself up in a magnificent house in Lincoln's Inn Fields and was fond of playing the host. "Thence by coach to Mr. Povey's, being invited thither . . . where really he made a most excellent and large dinner . . . he bidding us, in a frolic, to call for what we had a mind and he would undertake to give it us: and we did for prawns, swan, venison, after I had thought the dinner was quite done, and he did immediately produce it, which I thought great plenty and he seems to set up his rest in this plenty, and the neatness of his house, which he after dinner showed us, from room to room, so beset

[27] Pepys, *Diary;* entries for April 14, 1664 and December 7, 1664.

with delicate pictures, and above all, a piece of perspective in his closett in the low parlor; his stable, where was some most delicate horses, and the very racks painted and mangers, with a neat leaden painted cistern, and the walls done with Dutch tiles, like my chimnies. But still, above all things, he bid me go down into his wine-cellar, where, upon several shelves, there stood bottles of all sorts of wine, new and old, with labels pasted upon each bottle, and in the order and plenty as I never saw books in a bookseller's shop; and herein, I observe, he puts his highest content, and will accordingly commend all that he hath, but still they deserve to be so.''[28]

Povey became the avid Pepys's social mentor and secured him entrance to royal levies. Together they walked in St. James's Park or in Pepys's own garden, while Povey recounted the scandals of Whitehall. ''In the evening comes Mr. Povey about business; and he and I to walk in the garden an hour or two, and to talk of State matters. He tells me his opinion that it is out of possibility for us to escape being undone, there being nothing in our power to do that is necessary for the saving us; a lazy Prince, no Council, no money, no reputation at home or abroad. He says that to this day the King do follow the women as much as ever he did; that the Duke of York hath not got Mrs. Middleton, as I was told the other day; but says that he wants not her, for he hath others and hath always had.''[29]

Through Povey, Pepys became a member of the Royal Society and his name was brought up for a seat in the house of commons.[30] ''Comes Mr. Povey by appointment

---

[28] *Ibid.;* entry for January 19, 1663. See also Evelyn, *Diary;* entry for January 10, 1668, for a reference to Povey's ''well-contrived cellar and other elegancies.''

[29] Pepys, *Diary;* entry for June 23, 1667; also the entry for December 31, 1662.

[30] *Ibid.;* entries for February 15, 1665 and November 27, 1668. The

to dine with me; and much pleasant discourse with him, and some serious; and he tells me that he would by all meanes have me get to be a Parliament-man the next Parliament.'' Povey it was who warned Pepys that the gold-laced sleeves which he had seen him wearing in the park were too lavish for a mere clerk of the acts, and that Pepys must mind his step. Through him the diarist met some of the leaders in England's world of art and letters, for Povey prided himself on being not only a man about town but a patron of the arts. ''This afternoon, before the plan, I called with my wife at Dancre's, the great land-scape-painter, by Mr. Povey's advice and have bespoke him to come to take measure of my dining room panels.''[31] And again, ''Meeting Mr. Povey, he and I away to Dancre's to speak something touching the pictures I am getting him to make for me. And thence he carried me to Mr. Streeter's, the famous history-painter, over the way, whom I have often heard of, but did never see before; and there I found him, and Dr. Wren, and several Virtuosos, looking upon the paintings which he is making for the new theatre at Oxford . . . and I am mightily pleased to have the fortune to see this man and his work, which is very famous.''[32]

To Pepys we owe our knowledge of the decline in Povey's political fortunes, how his treasurership to the Duke of York was tottering. Already, ''the Duchess is a devil against him, and do now come like Queen Elizabeth, and sits with the Duke of York's Council, and sees what they do, and she crosses out this man's wages and prices,

death of Mrs. Pepys and Pepys's own illness prevented all thought of standing then.

[31] Pepys, *Diary;* entry for January 20, 1669. On December 21, 1662, Evelyn reported, ''I dined at Mr. Povey's, where I talk'd with Cromer, a greate musician.''

[32] *Ibid.;* entry for February 1, 1669.

as she sees fit for saving money.''[33] Povey fell victim to
gloomy fears and sought out Pepys as confidant. ''I had
some discourse with Povey, who is mightily discontented,
I find, about his disappointments at Court; and says, of
all places, if there be hell, it is here. No faith, no truth, no
love, nor any agreement between man and wife, nor
friends. He would have spoke broader, but I put it off to
another time.''[34] Pepys's comment leads us to wonder
whether Povey's misfortunes were not domestic as well
as political, and whether Mrs. Povey, whom Pepys called
''a handsome old woman that brought him money that
makes him do as he does,'' may not have interposed objections to her husband's role of Maecenas and town host.
Nevertheless, the palatial establishment at Lincoln's Inn
Fields was kept up and as late as 1676 was still arousing
the admiring comment of London.[35]

If Povey was Pepys's casual mentor and counsellor, he
daily gave young Blathwayt the benefit of his social and
political experience. Blathwayt, his eyes big with wonder,
was his uncle's willing pupil and consented to the scheme
drawn up for his education. The diplomatic service was
the first goal to be reached in his career, and accordingly
he was well grounded in modern languages.[36] In 1665 he
was enrolled at the Middle Temple, probably out of respect to his father's memory, but there was never any
serious intention that he should follow the law.[37] In the

[33] *Ibid.;* entry for January 27, 1668.

[34] *Ibid.;* entry for July 31, 1666.

[35] There was also a country house at Brentford to which Evelyn referred
on August 6, 1666; he described the house as ordinary, but commented on the
graceful avenue of trees leading to it.

[36] Sir Robert Atkyns in his volume, *Ancient and Present State of Gloucestershire,* published first in 1712, spoke of Blathwayt's great proficiency as a
linguist, p. 216 (London, 2nd ed., 1768).

[37] Blathwayt may have had his preliminary training at the Inns of Chancery. We have found only one brief reference to his schooldays; in a letter
to Dursley, one of the members of the diplomatic service in the 1690's, he

fall of 1668, a youth of less than twenty years, he turned his back on the law forever and was launched on his public career. His uncle had found a post for him in Sir William Temple's embassy at The Hague, one of the most desirable appointments to be had, especially for a young dilettante. Blathwayt was to prove more successful as an habitué of the bookshops and a worshipper of the Elzevirs than as a budding diplomat, although even in the latter capacity he was far from a failure. He set out from his uncle's house in Lincoln's Inns Fields loaded down with instructions on what to do and what not to do, more elaborate and positive than those presented to a newly appointed colonial executive.

From his days at The Hague, which came to an end in 1672, until the end of Charles II's reign, Blathwayt's personal activities elude us. On his return to England he took up his abode at Whitehall, in chambers granted him in 1675 by the king, but Povey's house was always open to him. Occasional allusions to his mother indicate that she was still alive, although she died not many years later. Kindly Thomas Vivian stood graciously at his stepson's side, ready to help in the performance of the countless trivial tasks which make a political acolyte so indispensable to his superiors. Both politically and socially, Povey did what he could for his nephew, but his political day was over and he was struggling vainly to reëstablish his footing.[38] Ultimately he settled down to live over his own career in his nephew's.

referred to him as a schoolfellow. (Add. MSS. 38700, f. 127.) There is no record of Blathwayt's matriculation at either Oxford or Cambridge. (See *Middle Temple Records*, III; February 20, 1665.)

[38] *Letters to Sir Joseph Williamson*, . . . *1673–1674* (Camden Society, n.s., II), pp. 5–6; a letter in which Povey begged Williamson to turn over his clerkship of the council to him, September 1, 1673. Povey continued as one of the masters of requests until James II's accession. He was given a pension of £100 for life in addition to the £400 he had received when he

Blathwayt in the meantime was building some substantial friendships, most of them from among his uncle's coterie. As a youth he seems to have gravitated inevitably toward older men; later on, himself an older man, his eyes turned toward youth and he was as eager to instruct as he had earlier been to learn. He rarely found it necessary to go beyond the bounds of Whitehall in making his friendships, and many of his friends displayed qualities not unlike his own. With few exceptions they were a highly cultured group; some even pedantic, like Sir Joseph Williamson. The latter's antiquarian interests aroused as much response in Blathwayt as his administrative ideas. The two could hobnob as congenially over the secretary of state's collection of rare editions as over the "shop" of Whitehall.

Pepys and Evelyn were friendly although they were never as intimate with Blathwayt as with his uncle. Blathwayt was among the list of "friends indefinite" asked to attend Pepys's funeral, but he was not presented with a mourning ring.[39]

The closest of all Blathwayt's friends was Sir Robert Southwell, whom he met through Povey and Williamson. From the start Southwell was attracted by Blathwayt and soon came to regard him with fatherly affection. Southwell's town house at Spring Gardens near Charing Cross and his country place, King's Weston in Gloucestershire, were always open to Blathwayt, and, no doubt, the latter occasionally forgot his dignity long enough to indulge in a romp with Southwell's children.[40]

resigned his office of treasurer to the Duke. See *Hist. MSS. Com., Laing Papers*, pp. 457–458.

[39] Tanner, *Private Correspondence and Miscellaneous Papers of Samuel Pepys*, 1679–1703, II, 318.

[40] Southwell's children were many years Blathwayt's junior. Edward Southwell who was to become Blathwayt's son-in-law was the only one to achieve any distinction.

Few of Blathwayt's later or early friendships were with men of rank or family. The Southwell lineage was a fine one, but the name carried more weight socially in the sixteenth than in the seventeenth century.[41] Sir William Temple's relations with Blathwayt probably never went beyond the kind concern of a man for a youth who had started out in public life under his direction. Lord Nottingham, the Tory secretary of state, 1689–1693, who was Southwell's kinsman,[42] was very friendly toward Blathwayt, but the social gulf between them was too great for Blathwayt to span and Nottingham perhaps never encouraged a personal intimacy. Charles Montagu, whose meteor-like rise in public finance in the decade from 1690 to 1700 astounded England, looked with warm approval on Blathwayt, but his attitude had in it something of the patron, a rôle Montagu enjoyed. Among colonials, the Byrds, father and son, were Blathwayt's friends, but the relationship rested on a community of economic interests. Blathwayt lacked his uncle's flair for society, and his attempts at assuming the grand manner and playing the rôle of lordly host were usually failures.

A curious attribute of Blathwayt was his penchant for singling out as his friends men who were either definitely or mildly unpopular, or who indulged in a defeatist philosophy. Williamson, Randolph, and Nottingham are three cases in point of the former class; while Sir Robert Southwell and Sir William Temple belonged in the latter, as their retreat to their country estates in the critical years from 1680 to 1688 proves. Such high-mindedness— or such show of weakness, call it what we may—was foreign to Blathwayt's own nature, for like a true opportunist he deemed official success worth a little temporizing

---

[41] Burke, *Landed Gentry; Dict. Natl. Biog.,* LIII, 292–299.

[42] Southwell's will, a portion of which is among Porlock MSS. Lady Cecilia Finch, Nottingham's daughter, was Southwell's goddaughter.

and changed his masters, although not his views, with an ease that suggests the Vicar of Bray.

Blathwayt was willing to temporize on one subject which some men consider too sacred, namely marriage. Nothing proves more definitely than his marriage how absolutely he permitted himself to be governed by his head and not his heart. Clearly his admiration of French practices extended to the marriage of convenience, and his own marriage settlement was a perfect blend of social aspirations satisfied and financial security achieved. He took a leaf out of his father's and his uncle's book by postponing matrimony until not only he but the lady in question had reached years of discretion. He improved on his father by choosing a woman of indubitable fortune. Never for a moment did he swerve from his course. Mild flirtations he occasionally indulged in, and he must have raised the hopes of many feminine hearts by that handsome appearance which even the critical Sir John Evelyn conceded. But women never greatly interested Blathwayt, unless we are to assume that he has been more successful than Pepys, for instance, in concealing his amatory weaknesses.

Youth, beauty, all such minor considerations, were thus swept aside in Blathwayt's mind. He wanted two things, a woman of fortune and a woman of family. He found both in Mary Wynter of Dyrham Park. A touch of fever on Blathwayt's part early in 1686, and a cordial invitation from Sir Robert Southwell to come down to the country to regain his health, furnished the occasion. The friendly concern of Southwell for Blathwayt's future and the geographic proximity of King's Weston to Dyrham Park did the rest.[43]

In 1686, Mary Wynter was thirty-six years old and the

[43] King's Weston lies about seven miles away from Bristol on the Channel side, Dyrham Park about seven miles to the east in the direction of Bath.

last surviving child of John Wynter.[44] Her forbears had been adventurous spirits in the piratical exploits that secured a colonial empire for the Virgin Queen, but at the end of the seventeenth century the family was again content to place a solid dependence on the land, and John Wynter's interests seem to have been wholly centered in his estate.[45] The courtship was probably more ardent on Blathwayt's side than on Mary Wynter's. In any event it was not long drawn out. The details of the settlement occupied some time, owing to Blathwayt's extreme circumspection, but at Christmas, 1686, the marriage took place in the church at Dyrham Park. Southwell was naturally an honored guest, and he wrote to Pepys a few days after the ceremony to report the pride and elation of the bridegroom. "I was at Mr. Blathwayt's wedding when your letter came to hand, and I shewed him your kind thoughts of his case, which I assure you added not a little to his comfortable importance."[46] For a month Blathwayt was away from his London offices and, when he returned, he wrote to a correspondent, Sir John Reresby, the governor

[44] For a genealogical table of the Wynter family, see Chadwyck Healey, *History of the Part of West Somerset, comprising the parishes of . . . Porlock, etc.*, facing p. 292. There had been at least five children, but all, save Mary, had died, the last John Wynter, Junior, in February, 1685.

[45] *Ibid.*, pp. 294–296. George Wynter, the first of that name at Dyrham, was a younger brother of Sir William Wynter, of Lydney, vice-admiral in command of the *Vanguard* during the attack on the Spanish Armada. George Wynter's eldest son, John, was Sir Francis Drake's second in command on the expedition to the Pacific and embarrassed his family by some of his freebooting exploits. George Wynter himself "was not without a personal and pecuniary interest" in the alleged "piracies" of his son and stated that he "adventured with Mr. Frauncis Drake the somme of £400 of money," for which Drake gave his note of hand.

[46] *Pepys's Memoirs* (Braybrooke ed.), II, 76–77; January 15, 1687. A copy of the marriage settlement was discovered by a bookseller of Colchester, Essex, in 1883, and offered to the Blathwayt family, which unfortunately did not secure possession of it. It was very long and involved.

of the garrison at York, that it was no "slight occasion" which had kept him away.

There was talk at the time of a knighthood for Blathwayt, but nothing came of it.[47] He and his wife removed to London and took a house about two miles from Hampton. They divided their time between London and Dyrham Park, where the elder Wynters still lived. Five children were born, four sons and a daughter. Two of the sons, Wynter and John, died as mere infants. William, born in 1688, and a second John, born in March, 1690, lived to survive their father by many years. The daughter, Anne, presumably the youngest child, grew up to marry Edward Southwell, the son of Sir Robert.

Almost nothing is known of Blathwayt's married life, which was of tragically short duration, for Mary Wynter died in November, 1691. Death was too frequent a visitor in those years. John Wynter, Mary's father, died in November, 1688, and was buried a few days before Blathwayt started out on the march to Salisbury with James II. Mrs. Wynter died less than a week before her daughter, in November, 1691, while that same year saw the death of Blathwayt's stepfather.[48] The times were troublous in any event, but Blathwayt's heart must have been very heavy.

His married life, however, was mildly happy, and there were many bright spots in it. Only rarely do we hear of Mrs. Blathwayt. Greetings were often enclosed in letters addressed to Blathwayt, "to his lady and fine children." Shortly after the marriage, Kneller was engaged to paint the portraits of both Mrs. Blathwayt and her husband. Hers shows her to have been a rather plain, but altogether

---

[47] Porlock MSS.

[48] Registry of Wills, Somerset House, Vere, 180; Thomas Vivian's will, drawn October 1, 1688 and proved October 7, 1691. Vivian left his estate, which was somewhat encumbered, to his daughter, Mary.

elegant and graceful lady, handsomely gowned. Blathwayt's is that of a genial and handsome figure, with long flowing curls and a face which reveals much strength of character. His dark eyes were particularly fine and luminous.[49]

Guests came to visit the Blathwayts both at Dyrham Park and the house near Hampton. One was the second Mrs. Edward Randolph, whom her husband had dispatched to England and entrusted to the care of his two good friends, Blathwayt and Southwell, after the scurrilous attacks made on her character in New England by Captain George and Captain Billop.[50] Sir John Evelyn dined with the Blathwayts at their town house in 1687 and recorded the experience, "I din'd at Mr. Blathwayt's. . . . This gentleman is Secretary of [sic] War, Clerk of the Counsel, etc., having raised himselfe by his industrie from very moderate circumstances. He is a very proper, handsome person, and very dextrous in businesse, and besides all this, has married a greate fortune."[51]

The most dramatic event during Blathwayt's brief married life was one which had not even the remotest bearing on his domestic affairs—the Trial of the Seven Bishops. In his capacity of clerk of the council, he was required to testify as principal witness for the crown. The position was awkward for a man who professed strict loyalty to his king, while his sympathies were wholly on

[49] The portraits still hang at Dyrham Park. The Prince Society has copies and that of Blathwayt has been reproduced in Goodrick, *Edward Randolph* (Prince Society), VI, frontispiece. Both have been reproduced in Chadwyck Healey, *History of the Part of West Somerset, etc.*, pp. 292, 296. There was at one time a portrait of Blathwayt at Westover, the Byrd estate in Virginia. . . . Blathwayt must have presented it to the younger Byrd who had been sent over to England to be educated by Sir Robert Southwell. *Virginia Magazine of History*, VI, 351; will of Mrs. Mary Willing Byrd, 1813.

[50] Goodrick, *Edward Randolph*, VI, 25–26, 191–193.

[51] Evelyn, *Diary;* entry for June 18, 1687.

the side of the prelates, and Blathwayt came dangerously near to being caught between the upper millstone of perjury and the nether of traitorous desertion of a monarch who had never been other than kind to him. The account of his conduct may be read in the pages of *State Trials*[52] and Macaulay.[53] It happened that he had been present in the council chamber on June 8, 1688, when the bishops had presented their petition to the king, and he had been required to read it to James. Subsequently he was called upon to testify on two main points of fact; whether the bishops had at their entrance to the council chamber admitted their signatures; and in case of such an admission, whether the king had promised them his protection.

Blathwayt, schooled by the crown officers, who had protested against his appearance as long as they dared, proved an adroit witness. He realized even before he had received his subpœna that he had evidence which was damning to the crown, and once on the stand he "shuffled, equivocated, pretended to misunderstand the questions, implored the protection of the Crown. But he was in hands not easy to escape." His conduct was masterly, if not becoming, for he avoided direct commitment on either of the two points put to him, until the court room shook with laughter, so exasperating were his evasions to the questions of Pemberton and Pollexfen, the counsel for the bishops. He declared that so much discussion had intervened between the questions put to him that he could not remember the points at issue. Pollexfen rejoined that Blathwayt understood very well the questions asked but did not care to answer, whereupon Blathwayt protested his willingness to answer any interrogations except those where his answers could be used against him. He grew irritable when Finch asked him if he had taken notes at

[52] Cobbett, *State Trials*, XII, 307–315; 344–350.
[53] Macaulay, *A History of England* (Boston, 1901), II, 369–370.

the meeting between the king and bishops, and replied
that Finch knew the procedure of the council as well as he
did, how could he take notes when he was standing at the
side of the king? All that could be gained from him was
the statement that, while the king had given no definite
promise to the bishops if they admitted the petition as
their own, there was reason for them to think that such
protection was implied. Cross-examined and re-examined,
he stood his ground firmly. He finally declared that other
clerks had been in the council chamber that day, if they
knew more about it than he did, he hoped they would be
called as witnesses! Bridgeman and Musgrave were accordingly sworn a few minutes later. Pepys, who had been
in the council chamber on the eventful occasion, was also
called upon to testify, but no one of these witnesses
proved any more satisfactory than Blathwayt, who had
made a sufficient admission. It was on the strength of his
testimony that the bishops were acquitted.

Never again was Blathwayt trapped into so critical a
position, nor were his religious views, always of the mild-
est, ever again put to so sharp a test.[54] Official life, however, became more rather than less complex after the
Revolution, and Blathwayt may have sought to forget his
domestic sorrows by spending more and more time at his
work. He did not, however, neglect his duties as a father
nor forget the fact that he was lord of a manor and had a
social position to keep up. He lavished affection on his
children, who were brought up in a manner which bespoke
their father's position as a country gentleman, and he
was never too preoccupied to satisfy their little whims

---

[54] Blathwayt always kept his religious views discreetly in the background.
He was, of course, as one of his acquaintances put it "a good Christian
gentleman." At Dyrham Park he had a living to prefer, for a very fine old
church stands on the estate. Curiously he does not seem to have been a member of the Society for Propagating the Gospel in Foreign Parts. The society
was not incorporated until 1701.

and fancies. He was willing to go to great lengths in order to find them precisely the sort of pony they wanted from Ireland. Perforce he was separated from them for months at a time from 1692 to 1701, while he was abroad, but in 1700, his son, William accompanied him to Holland. "Young Mr. Blathwayt ran his match against Mr. Rich, the page, with a great deal of applause, for he run it perfectly well, though it is true he had more odds than could be reasonably be given, half a mile in two." The thought of a second marriage apparently did not enter Blathwayt's mind.[55] Instead he arranged to have his sister Elizabeth, who was a spinster, come to Dyrham to take charge of his household, and she was still there at the time of Blathwayt's death.

William and John made the Grand Tour in 1705, accompanied by their tutor. While at Augsburg they paid their respects to the Duke of Shrewsbury, with whom their father had earlier been associated, and who was then living in retirement on the Continent.[56] In Frankfort they called on D'Avenant, the English resident, to whom their father had written announcing their arrival in Germany.[57] John was in Rome in 1707, making merry with some artists, friends of Sir John Percival, later the Duke of Egmont, and cousin to Edward Southwell. John shared his father's musical interests, and it may be that he had been sent to Italy to complete his musical education. One of Percival's letters states, "Every Friday night a

[55] Le Neve in his *Pedigree of the Knights* (p. 419) makes Blathwayt marry a daughter of Sir William Rawlinson, serjeant-at-law and one of the commissioners of the great seal. Colonel Chester wrote the present Blathwayt family that he thought Le Neve was in error since no mention of the fact or of Blathwayt appears in Sir William's or Lady Rawlinson's wills (1703 and 1712). Porlock MSS.

[56] *Hist. MSS. Com., Buccleuch MSS.*, Vol. II, Pt. II, 791; Shrewsbury secured them and their tutor, who was a relative, a pass to travel.

[57] Add. MSS. 4743, f. 158.

concert very fine at Mr. Brown's. The performers are Pauluci, Nicolini, Pipo, that famous bas violist, and two other violins; Mr. Blathwayt and Mr. Cope likewise, one with the harpsichord, the other with the violin, make no small figure in this concert.'"[58] John later joined the army as a cadet, and in 1710, after the campaign in Flanders was over for the summer, went to pay his respects to the Elector of Hanover, who in a very cordial though formal letter to Blathwayt acknowledged the visit.[59] In 1712 Blathwayt purchased him a commission as major.[60] Very obviously he had no intention of having his sons go into the civil service of the government, and, indeed, his own position in 1712 would have rendered this impossible.

William Blathwayt, III, settled down to the life of country squire, marrying Thomasina Ambrose, the daughter of a Londoner of the parish of St. Giles in the Fields, in 1718.[61] Anne Blathwayt became the second wife of Edward Southwell and was married at Dyrham Park on August 30, 1716, by the Archbishop of Dublin.[62] The Duke and Duchess of Marlborough were among the guests present at the ceremony.[63] A year later Anne died in giving birth to a son, William.

[58] *Hist. MSS. Com., Egmont MSS.*, II, 217; E. Gouge to Percival, Rome, June 18, 1707.

[59] Stowe MSS. 223, ff. 421, 457.

[60] John Blathwayt ultimately became a colonel; he settled in Amersham, Bucks. Porlock MSS.

[61] Register of Marriages in Gray's Inn Chapel, f. xviii; the marriage took place on August 17, 1718. Since it took place in Gray's Inn Chapel, it is likely that Blathwayt had been a student there.

[62] Porlock MSS.; portion of Edward Southwell's diary. See also *Allegations of Marriage Licenses of the Vicar-General, Archbishop of Canterbury,* p. 279. The marriage settlement made was almost as involved and took as much time as Blathwayt's own. It involved a dowry of £10,000 and also, apparently, the transfer of Blathwayt's clerkship of the council to his son-in-law. The archbishop was a close family friend of the Southwells.

[63] Porlock MSS.; Edward Southwell's diary.

Blathwayt took vast pride in Dyrham Park and after he had been in Holland for a summer, decided to have it rebuilt completely. The stately Tudor mansion gave way to one built on more elegant, classical Dutch lines. As much as possible of the interior of the old mansion was saved, but the exterior was completely changed. The re-building took a great many years, for it was begun in 1693 and was not completed in 1698. Talmen, the popular Dutch architect and comptroller of the works under William III, was in charge of the undertaking and the results he achieved were among his best.[64] Expense was no consideration. Year after year reports were made to Blathwayt in Flanders of the progress that was being made. Nearly all of his official correspondents knew of the project, for he had given many of them commissions to fill. He ordered deal wood from Robinson, the minister to Sweden, and marble and stone from the consuls in Italy. Randolph stopped hunting pirates and evaders of the Acts of Trade long enough to fill orders for ten tons of red cedar from the Carolinas and Bermuda and to dispatch huge quantities of black walnut wood and pine planks from Virginia and Maryland. While Blathwayt chafed over what seemed to him interminable and unwarranted delays, Randolph resentfully recounted his difficulties in finding shippers who went directly to Bristol.[65] John Povey, Blathwayt's clerk and brother-in-law,[66] was in charge of the work, and Robert Henley, Blathwayt's friend on the transport board, assisted him. The fine

[64] For accounts of Dyrham Park see Sir Robert Atkyns, *Ancient and Present State of Gloucestershire* (London, 1768), p. 216; Ralph Bigland, *Historical Collections relative to Gloucester* (London, 1791), pp. 532–536; Campbell, *Vitruvius Britannicus*, I, 94; *Country Life*, September 26, 1903, pp. 434–441, and November 4, 1916, pp. 546–552. The latter contain exquisite views.

[65] Goodrick, *Edward Randolph*, VII, 352, 382, 390, 426, 452, 465.

[66] John Povey had married Blathwayt's stepsister, Mary, in November, 1693; Porlock MSS.

cedar staircase caused Povey some trouble, because he could not find a trustworthy London joiner to come down to build it. "The London Joyner is gone some days since for London, which I reckon no great losse, if it bee true, what was hinted to me, when I was at Dirham, that he takes his pleasure 3 or 4 dayes together, for one that hee workes."[67] Henley was busy comparing specimens of Bristol glass so that the very finest quality might be had for at least the front of the house and the best rooms.[68]

The gardens were laid out by Le Nôtre, one of the court gardeners. As Tudor gable and court gave way to the balustrades and terraces of the classical period, so the informal gardens were replaced by the elaborate and dignified Dutch gardens of the day. The grounds were so sumptuously laid out "as to defy both expense and imitation." Tulip trees, spinning yuccas, Virginia pine, sassafras, and flowering oaks from Virginia gave evidence of Blathwayt's interest in the colonies.[69] There was a lovely deer park and a warren adjoining the garden, with its pleasant walks and distant view of Bristol and the forest of Kingswood. A most startling mechanical contrivance was to be found in a curious system of waterworks.

Year after year Blathwayt brought back from Holland his spoil for the interior of the house. There were silks and velvets, damasks and tapestries, some of the latter very fine arras. One of the upper rooms was completely hung in Dutch tapestries, two others had walls covered with stamped Cordova leather. There was exquisite Delft ware and fine china, which Blathwayt had had the annoyance of seeing seized by the customs officers as he was landing in England for his refusal to pay duty on them.[70]

67 Add. MSS. 9734, ff. 21–22.   68 Add. MSS. 9729, f. 27.

69 Sloane MSS. 3328, f. 88. Randolph sent many trees and seeds and had colonial gardeners interested in the matter. (Goodrick, *Edward Randolph*, VII, 425–426.)

70 The matter was apparently referred to the Treasury and ultimately the

MODERN VIEWS OF DYRHAM PARK

THE EXTERIOR IS PRACTICALLY AS IT WAS IN
WILLIAM BLATHWAYT'S DAY

Choice Dutch and Flemish paintings adorned the walls, one a Van Hoogstraten perspective, no doubt, the "Streeter" which had aroused both Pepys's and Evelyn's admiration when they saw it hanging in Povey's home, for many of Povey's treasures had found their way into Blathwayt's possession. There were also the portraits of Blathwayt and his wife by Kneller, of Charles II and James II by Lely, and of William and Mary by Wissing. Over two of the entrances were the carved inscriptions, *His mecum utere* and *Virtute et Veritate,* the one an evidence of Blathwayt's hospitality, the other of the standard which he applied to his public as well as his private life.

To Dyrham Blathwayt withdrew more and more frequently as the years went by. After 1711, when he had virtually retired from official life, he was almost constantly there, although he still kept up his London establishment, Little Wallingford House, which William III had granted him in 1689 in his capacity of secretary at war.[71] He followed the pursuits of a country gentleman,

duty was waived. The list of imports is given and has a feminine charm. It included the following: ''6 P[iece]s of Sussacs [?]; 10 Ps. of Silk flowered Cuttances; 6 flowered Pelongs; 10 Ps. printed pelongs; 3 Ps. Crimson wrought silk; 4 Ps. broad and 2 Ps. narrow Damask; 2 rich fflowered Cuttances; 1 Ps. Broad etc. [*sic*]; 1 narrow crimson velvet; 2½ lb. of Tea; 2 Doz. China Cupps; 2 Doz. D[itt]o Saucers.'' Treas. Ref. Bk., 1693–1702, Index 4621, f. 116.

71 See *Cal. Treas. Papers,* 1720–1728, p. 57 (CCXXXIV, No. 18) for a reference to the disposal of the property after Blathwayt's death. St. John, Blathwayt's successor at the war office, was exceedingly piqued because he was not showed a similar favor. He wrote to Harley in 1705, ''I hear you remove this week to the Cockpit, I hope they will think it as reasonable that I should at least have some place to be in while I am in this employment, as that Mr. Blathwayt should still enjoy a very good house for having been in it.'' *Hist. MSS. Com., Portland Papers,* IV, 257; see also *Hist. MSS. Com., Downshire MSS., Trumbull Correspondence,* Vol. I, Pt. II, 829, for an allusion by William Penn to the fine new house Anne meant to build for St. John. Blathwayt may also have had a house at Bath, or Luttrell may have

although rheumatism daily rendered him more and more
incapable. He rode over his wide estate, watched over his
fairs, instructed his tenants. He was proud of his position
and drove about in state in a fine coach drawn by yellow
horses with black manes and dappled coats, the search for
which cost him almost as much anxiety as Pepys's coach
cost the diarist.[72] He tried to forget his political disappointments and succeeded very well, although he continued to court the favor of the Duke of Beaufort, the
political patron of Gloucestershire, and once presented
him with a pair of hawks. For these he set his foreign
correspondents to work on a wide search, because he knew
the Duke was fond of falconry. Life at Dyrham Park took
on a very serene aspect!

Death came in August, 1717, after what Horatio Walpole, his successor in the auditor general's office, called a
"desperate illness." He had been ill for more than a year
and the end was probably hastened by the death of his
daughter, Anne, a few weeks earlier. He was buried on
August 30th, beside Mrs. Blathwayt, in the church at
Dyrham. His will, a matter-of-fact document, lacking the
rich, colorful fullness of his grandfather's, Thomas
Blathwayt's, as well as the pathos of his father's, stipulated briefly that the estate at Dyrham was to go to William, together with the manors in Somersetshire which
Blathwayt had held in trust for him since his mother's
death.[73] To John went Blathwayt's interest in the manor
of Egham, which he had once accepted in part payment of

referred to Dyrham Park, when he said in 1702 that Blathwayt's house was
"fitting up at Bath for [the] reception of her Majestie, who designs to goe
thither next month to drink the waters." (Luttrell, *Brief Relation*, V, 197.)
The visit according to the family was probably never made, for there is no
local tradition to the effect.

[72] Add. MSS. 21552, ff. 58–60.

[73] The manors in Somersetshire had been bequeathed to Mrs. Blathwayt by
an uncle. (Porlock MSS.) One of them was Porlock Manor.

salary owing him as secretary of state. John also received the sum of one thousand pounds, some of the family plate, and all of his father's musical instruments. Edward Southwell received the remaining portion of Anne's dowry of ten thousand pounds. Blathwayt's sister, the faithful Elizabeth, was to have a small annuity of thirty pounds, to which twenty pounds were to be added if she continued to live with her nephew, William. To Blathwayt's nephews, the two sons of his stepsister and his cousin, John Povey, went annuities of ten pounds each. The will, drawn when, as it stated, Blathwayt was of sound mind but infirm body, bore not a single trace of munificence, for not even the poor were remembered. It seemed pitifully brief by comparison with the elaborate marriage settlement which had made it possible, and it gave not a suggestion of the useful public life which the man who made it had lived.[74]

[74] Registry of Wills, Somerset House, 5 Whitefield, 560, Vol. 214, pp. 203–204. It was drawn on September 10, 1716, with a codicil dated April 20, 1717. Blathwayt may have been very generous in subscribing to public projects, but the only record of it, is his "free gift" of thirty pounds *per annum* to Chelsea Hospital, for four years and three months (£127:10:0), reference to which is to be found in Ranelagh's accounts for 1688 to 1692. (*Hist. MSS. Com., House of Lords MSS.*, n.s., 1702–1704, V, 379.)

CHAPTER III

APPRENTICESHIP FOR PUBLIC OFFICE—
CLERK IN SIR WILLIAM TEMPLE'S EMBASSY
AT THE HAGUE, 1668–1672

BLATHWAYT made his entrance into public life as clerk in
the embassy of Sir William Temple at The Hague. For
nearly three years he was under the direction of that
kindly and cultured diplomat, sent to minister to the in-
jured feelings of the Dutch in the few years of truce that
marked the relations of England and Holland from 1668
to 1672. A foil to the machinations of Louis XIV and
Charles II, Temple returned to Holland when he had
completed the arrangements for the precarious Triple Al-
liance. Although he was much loved by the Dutch, he was
summarily recalled in the fall of 1670 and was finally replaced by the adroit and irritating Sir George Downing,
whose appointment to the embassy at The Hague was little better than an open declaration of war. With the complex foreign situation of the period, we need not concern
ourselves, for Blathwayt as a minor clerk in the embassy
had no part in it. The period was crucial, but the events
were not momentous, for England was simply marking
time. On the whole, Temple and his clerks spent their days
in the performance of relatively petty tasks. The scene
did not become dramatic until the year of Temple's recall.
Then, for several months, Blathwayt was allowed to show
his mettle and level-headedness. Youth that he was, he
was left in sole charge of the embassy from June, 1671,

until January, 1672, when Downing put in a belated appearance. The fact that England was so careless of the feelings of the Dutch as to leave Blathwayt alone at The Hague as *secrétaire du roi* for a half year was more indicative of her desire to provoke Dutch wrath than of confidence in Blathwayt's ability.

The circumstances under which Blathwayt secured the notice of Temple are not important. Thomas Povey probably manoeuvred the appointment, since Temple was in his coterie of friends. Sir Joseph Williamson, Arlington's secretary, was immediately responsible for his selection.[1]

In 1668 Blathwayt was a serious youth of twenty, naïve, studious, and inclined to be priggish. He was enthusiastic over his appointment and duly impressed with the opportunity of watching at first hand England's great trade rival, for he was full of tales of the Dutch menace which he had heard related by merchants over his Uncle Povey's dinner table. Impressionable, already highly sensitive to the æsthetic side of life, he was delighted with the thought of living in close proximity to Dutch culture, then much admired. From the start he planned to spend his idle hours browsing in the famous bookmarts of Amsterdam and The Hague, poring over a host of books and manuscripts in order to fill the obscure literary commissions with which his uncle and Sir Joseph Williamson were to ply him. It may have been in anticipation of just such an appointment that he had studied Dutch, a comparatively rare accomplishment, for he was the only member of Temple's official household who had any such knowledge. Since he was also skilful in French and German and apt in his use of Latin phrases, it is plain that

---

[1] S. P. For., Holland, 184: 254; Temple to Williamson, The Hague, April 9, 1669, s.n. Temple subsequently developed a decided antipathy for Williamson, but in 1669 was apparently friendly.

his education had been thorough and in accordance with classical traditions.

An exceedingly proper young man with an exaggerated sense of decorum, Blathwayt aroused the admiration of some of his elders and the quiet amusement of others. Temple laughed gently at some of his staid habits. Povey, who observed his nephew's progress at a distance, was somewhat dismayed by his Puritanical ways and flew into a rage when he discovered that Blathwayt was ignoring his social and diplomatic opportunities by retiring to his room for study after dinner, instead of engaging in polite discourse in the Temple drawing-room. But honest and plain John Cooke, first clerk in the office of the northern secretary of state, thought Mr. Blathwayt a very fine gentleman, one to whom he could safely entrust his young son, whom he was sending over to Holland to be educated.[2] Very solemnly Blathwayt and he corresponded on the question of the selection of a tutor, and it was at Blathwayt's suggestion that the youth was entrusted to Professor Coccius at Leyden.[3]

In the office which was set up within the Temple household, there was an intimate, personal atmosphere which was very pleasant as long as the various clerks remained on terms of amity. Squalls, commensurable in spirit if not in intensity to major diplomatic conflicts, arose from time to time to try the temper of Sir William. Blathwayt fell out with the chief clerk, Temple's private secretary, a hot-headed, contemptuous young Irishman, Thomas Downton by name. He claimed that Downton was trying to make him ridiculous in the eyes of all other members of the family, and great was his joy when Downton was called to Ireland on private business in 1669 and forced to remain away for a year.[4] During his absence, Blathwayt

2 Porlock MSS.　　　　3 *Ibid.*
4 S. P. For., Holland, 186: 127; Downton to Williamson, August 1, 1670, s.n.

reigned supreme over the half-dozen clerks in the office and absorbed so large a portion of the work and responsibility that one of his subordinates broke out in protest: "My condition here with his Excellency . . . is none of the best for that I have nothing to write in French, nor English, nor High Dutch, all of which I forget for want of practice. Mr. Blathwayt, a very ingenious gentleman, being the factotum. I hear of Mr. Werden going into Sweden which is as good an opportunity as I can wish."[5]

But Downton's return in 1670 brought a reversal of the situation, and so little did Blathwayt enjoy his demotion that he fell into a morbid state and as soon as possible escaped on a three weeks' jaunt into Flanders. Meanwhile, in a fit of pique, he scribbled a childish protest which he probably intended to lay before Temple. "I thought fit to acquaint your lordship that he [Downton] takes a letter directed to me with an impertinent superscription, shows it to all the house in a ridiculous way, and endeavors to make me so upon all occasions; says that your lordship would not trust me any longer with the receiving the letters, or with any correspondency nor business but what is a mere matter of compliment, for that reason diverted my correspondence with Mr. Cooke, treats me as a cipher, says that I bid the man use that supers [sic]."[6]

Matters settled down, however, and an adjustment was made whereby Blathwayt shared the work with Downton. Life in the Temple household even took on an engaging aspect. There were young ladies, relatives of Lady Temple, who graced it, and the clerks vied with each other in

[5] S. P. For., Holland, 185: 189–190; Monsieur Jollyuet to Williamson, Dec. 6, 1669, s.n.

[6] Porlock MSS.; letter draft on the back of a letter from Cooke, dated August 30, 1670. The letter was probably addressed formally to Blathwayt as Temple's chief secretary. As a matter of fact Blathwayt's correspondence, even with Cooke, does show a gap from August 30, 1670 to June 6, 1671.

their attentions to them. Gay parties and mild flirtations broke into the dull routine of diplomatic correspondence. Blathwayt came to endure the raillery of his colleagues, and his letters to those who departed with Sir William or Lady Temple in 1670 or 1671 reveal that he was on easy terms with the other clerks and show his ability to share in light-hearted jests and pleasantries.

Work was simply organized within Temple's office. The chief correspondence was naturally with the secretarial office in England. A source of confusion was the question in whose province Holland lay, the northern or the southern secretary's. By an order of 1668, the Low Countries had very definitely been placed in the northern province, but the order was not immediately enforced, for Temple and his clerks continued to address their letters exclusively to Arlington, in the southern department, until December, 1669.[7] Blathwayt then wrote Sir Joseph Williamson that he had received orders to transfer his correspondence to the northern department, over which Sir John Trevor and his clerk, John Cooke, presided.[8] Even then, the order was laxly obeyed. Blathwayt still transmitted letters to Williamson with the utmost regularity, and while they were more or less intimate and unofficial, they contained a detailed account of the embassy. In the fall of 1671, he found himself in difficulties with the northern office because the Dutch news agent at The Hague, who was under his control, had failed to send the intelligence to Trevor with the same unfailing punctuality that he sent it to Arlington.[9] Such grievances on the part of

[7] Evans, *The Principal Secretary of State*, p. 132. The division of Europe into northern and southern provinces dates back to the Restoration, but was only beginning to be stabilized in 1668 and 1669. The reason for the transfer of the Low Countries is not clear.

[8] S. P. For., Holland, 185: 194; December 10, 1669, s.n.; also Porlock MSS., a letter from Blathwayt to Cooke of the same date.

[9] Porlock MSS.; Cooke to Blathwayt, September 19 and October 10,

one or other of the secretaries of state were common; they frequently complained of slights and would continue to do so as long as their respective provinces and duties were so loosely distributed and defined. That Trevor had some ground for complaint, since Holland lay technically within his province, is readily seen.

Temple himself assumed the official correspondence with the secretary of state, refusing an amanuensis.[10] In the event of Temple's illness or temporary absence from The Hague, the correspondence devolved on Downton, as first clerk. Very few of the letters which Temple addressed to the secretaries of state were in Blathwayt's hand, with the exception of some dispatched during Downton's stay in Ireland.

Downton was in general charge of the office, and to him fell the task of receiving and opening the mails. Blathwayt served as clerk of the intelligence and translator of the foreign news-letters which poured into the office from various parts of Holland and the Continent as a whole. Temple had great difficulty in finding competent Dutch news agents and complained repeatedly. Blathwayt spent most of his time translating the formal news-sheets, Dutch and otherwise, digesting them, and preparing them for transmission to Whitehall. He was simply another cog in that enormous news-gathering machine which had become so important a part of the English administration. His dispatches to England went out, on the average, once a week. He did not have to translate all the letters that came in from diplomatic centres. "I have not translated

1671: also S. P. For., Holland, 187: 74, 184. Blathwayt was entirely relieved of the task of sending the intelligence after Temple's departure and was allowed the necessary sums to secure news agents.

[10] An examination of State Papers Foreign for Holland during this period easily reveals this. Temple always apologized profusely when he found it necessary to employ a secretary.

the Italian news, because I believe you do not desire it,"
he wrote to Williamson in 1669.[11] His knowledge of Dutch
was at a high premium, and in his absence the office was at
a loss when it came to the Dutch letters. Downton once
wrote: "The enclosed is all the trouble I shall give you at
present from my Lord who is sorry he is forced to send
you it in Dutch as his Excellency receives it, which he
must continue till Mr. Blathwayt return from Amsterdam, having none else about him capable of translating
Dutch."[12] At first Blathwayt wrote most of the news-letters or digests in French, but this was apparently op-
tional, and he did it either as a means of keeping in practice or as proof of his proficiency. As time went on, he
lapsed into English with greater and greater frequency,
until at last French was entirely abandoned.

Neither Downton nor Blathwayt had anything to do
with entering the in-letters or the out-letters, a task at
which some of the subordinate clerks of the office must
have been employed. The archives of the embassy for this
period under Temple have been scattered. Sir William,
no doubt, carried off some of his letters to his estate at
Sheen. Blathwayt took with him on his departure from
office one or two of the entry books, all of the news-letters
he had received from London, and his personal correspondence with Cooke.[13]

Blathwayt's youthful eagerness and ambition came in
for more than one sharp blow during his first months of
apprenticeship. A few months after his arrival at The
Hague, Temple, in response to suggestions from White-

---

[11] S. P. For., Holland, 185: 97; August 8, 1669, s.n.

[12] *Ibid.*, f. 11; Downton to Williamson, April 26, 1669, s.n. See also f. 3.

[13] The Cooke letters are now at Porlock House. For references to the
others see the Sotheby Sales Catalogue of Dyrham Park MSS., sold on April
25, 1910. The news-letters mentioned there, item 118, are now in the John
Rylands Library in Manchester.

hall, decided to test out the young man's competence and discretion by dispatching him on a special mission to Amsterdam, in a case in Admiralty over a prize ship, the *Abraham's Sacrifice,* owned by a Genoese and captured by the English in the late war with the Dutch.[14] Witnesses had to be cross-examined and the advocates at The Hague, "constituted to do business for England," had refused to go to Amsterdam themselves to conduct the inquiry. Temple, therefore, sent Blathwayt, armed with instructions from the advocates and reënforced with additional powers from Sir Peter Pett of the Admiralty Board in England. Blathwayt was elated and full of self-importance. "It is his first adventure and I hope he will acquit himself well," Temple wrote to Williamson, "which I know you will be glad of."[15]

The trip, alas, proved to be only a source of deep humiliation. Blathwayt's youth was against him. The commissioners in the registry office at Amsterdam interposed obstacles, refusing to open up their records to him that he might learn the names of the assurers whom he had been sent to cross-examine. When he pleaded his instructions, they laughed and said instructions meant nothing to them. Not three weeks earlier, they had refused a similar plea on the part of the Spanish. Blathwayt was obliged to return to The Hague for further assistance. Finally he came with a letter from Williamson to the Burgomaster, requesting the latter to issue a mandamus to the registry office. The ship's assurers were equally heedless and ignored Blathwayt's summons to testify. "I send you en-

---

[14] *Cal. S. P. Dom.,* 1668–1669, p. 90. On December 4, 1668, there was a reference to the Admiralty judges of the petition of Antonio Basso, late commander of the *Abraham's Sacrifice* of Genoa. Basso claimed that his ship had been captured as a prize and the goods sold at a fifth of their value, On appeal from the Republic of Genoa, the king consented to have the case re-heard and attestations taken from merchants and factors abroad.

[15] S. P. For., Holland, 184: 234; The Hague, April 9, 1669, s.n.

closed the last I had from Mr. Blathwayt," wrote Temple, "who I doubt is a little too credulous of people's information who may have interest or be engaged to deceive him in the matter. The two points which are gained by his being there, seem to be that all search into the Assurance Office has been denied him, though at first it was promised him, and secondly that the witnesses refused to appear during the time allotted, and while he was there to have pursued their examination upon the cross interrogatories, both which circumstances may be of some consideration to the Court of Admiralty before whom the cause depends."[16] As far as Blathwayt was concerned, the whole matter was ultimately set aside, the Court of Admiralty realizing that the task was not of the kind to be entrusted to a youth.

Despite such initial defeats, Blathwayt progressed steadily in the office at The Hague, but the period was a restless, uncertain one for all concerned. In the autumn of 1670, very shortly after Downton's return, Temple was suddenly summoned to England. "Last Saturday," Blathwayt wrote Williamson, "my Lord received orders from his Majesty to hasten into England. . . . His journey is very differently interpreted here, but the most part apprehend what you find in the enclosed intelligence. . . . The hopes I had of coming into England this year are almost vanished, at least there is no appearance of it in his Lordship's absence, but if his return be suddenly I may yet have the honor of seeing you before the winter be ended."[17] Temple's summons to return ultimately proved to be a recall, but weeks lengthened into months before there was any certainty. Downton and Blathwayt were left in charge of the office and of Lady Temple, and in

16 S. P. For., Holland, 185: 146–147; Temple to Williamson, The Hague, October 10, 1669, s.n.

17 Ibid., 186: 144; September 27, 1670, s.n.

the face of the altered situation Blathwayt smothered his
wrathful feeling toward the young Irishman. In the spring
the tension lightened somewhat, and Blathwayt took advantage of the change and went into the country with his
Uncle Povey, who had come over on a visit.[18] He had
asked Downton to send the news to Williamson in his absence, but the latter failed to do so, confining his dispatches to Temple alone. With some ire, Blathwayt subsequently reported this failure to Williamson.

In June, 1671, came the definite news that Temple was
not to return to Holland. Downton was therefore ordered
to escort Lady Temple to England, and Blathwayt was
left in sole charge of the embassy.[19] His responsibilities
were only temporary, as none realized better than he did,
but meanwhile he had to endure the growing hostility and
annoying rebuffs of the Dutch. To strengthen his position, Trevor succeeded in securing official orders for him
to deliver a message to the States General. "The next
post will bring a letter from his Majesty to the States
General to be delivered by your hands: which is a favor
Mr. Secretary Trevor hath done you, to invest you in the
transaction of business there; whereas it was first intended that his Majesty's letter should have been given to
their ambassador here. It relates to the matter of Suri-
nam, where the Estates General their orders were not
well observed by their Governor Leichtenbergh in the
point of transporting our people from thence."[20] At
Whitehall, some importance was attached to Blathwayt's

18 *Ibid.*, 187: 67. Povey came over several times and it was once announced
that he was to come over in the official entourage sent to bring back Orange
to England, where he was to receive the Garter.

19 *Ibid.*, f. 84. Cooke's letter shows this to have been of Povey's contriv-
ing. Povey was then very close to Arlington, and he made good use of his
proximity. (Porlock MSS., Cooke letters.)

20 Porlock MSS.; August 15, 1671.

letters, for they were occasionally read to Charles II at the committee of foreign affairs.[21]

Late in the fall of 1671, Blathwayt, with unwarranted optimism, reported that he thought the Dutch were a little more placable.[22] This feeling was soon to vanish when the Dutch learned who their new ambassador was to be. Numerous rumors had been afloat, both at The Hague and in Whitehall, over the question of Temple's successor. Cooke had written Blathwayt: "[I] am truly sorry those people are no more inclinable to reasonable compliance with his Majesty at all times, but especially in this juncture. They would have an ambassador as once the people of Israel would have a king; and God sent them one (as our English proverbial expression is) with a vengeance. But I hope the ambassador they shall have, will come with healing in his wings."[23] There was little that was healing about Sir George Downing. His selection was a deliberate insult to Dutch sensibilities.

Blathwayt was apprised of Downing's appointment in October and was told to make his arrangements to return to England. He was to remain at The Hague, however, for about ten days after Downing's arrival. Various matters contributed toward the new ambassador's delay in putting in an appearance, and when finally all was ready, in December, 1671, a calm settled down over the Channel, and he had to wait several days for "a favorable puff of wind." Shortly after Christmas he arrived. Blathwayt lingered long enough to induct him into the business pending and made a very favorable impression on Downing, who sent back a recommendation to Williamson. "I have found him very exceeding ready and serviceable on

21 Porlock MSS.; September 5, 1671. Cooke reported that they were read with great interest.

22 *Ibid.;* December 5, 1671. Cooke to Blathwayt.

23 *Ibid.;* October 10, 1671.

all things conducing to his Majesty's service and he deserves your best kindness."[24] Glad to escape so irksome a task as his had been, Blathwayt returned posthaste to England, arriving there on January 15, 1672.[25]

The need of finding himself some other appointment was urgent, and Blathwayt felt that Downing's delay had imperiled his chances of being included in the special diplomatic mission which was then in preparation for Denmark and was to be headed by the Duke of Richmond. It developed that it, too, had been delayed. Not until April did Richmond set out, and Blathwayt was then of the party.[26] He served Richmond in some minor capacity, not as secretary, for that position was held by Dr. Thomas Henshaw.[27] Just before he left England, Blathwayt heard of the precipitate return of Sir George Downing from The Hague, "in a fright and without orders or leave," as Temple contemptuously reported.[28] Blathwayt tarried for only a few weeks in Copenhagen and was then dispatched to Sweden, apparently to take charge of the embassy in Stockholm in the interim between the departure of the English minister, Sir John Werden, who was returning to England to become the secretary of the Duke of York, and the arrival of Sir Edward Wood, Werden's successor. Werden stayed in Stockholm long enough to welcome Blathwayt and give him the necessary introductions. There was nothing of importance attached to Blathwayt's stay in the Swedish capital, and our only trace of it is in the few letters he wrote to Richmond and Williamson

24 S. P. For., Holland, 188: 12; January 12, 1672.
25 *Bulstrode Papers*, p. 215.   26 *Ibid.*, p. 233.
27 S. P. For., Denmark (1671–1674), 19: 141.
28 Add. MSS. 21948, f. 234; Blathwayt writing from Copenhagen and apologizing to Downing for not calling on him before he left London, July 17, 1672, s.v.; Temple's *Works*, II, 184; Sheen, May 23, 1672, letter to his brother.

about Swedish court life and the celebrated Swedish military manoeuvres.[29]

From Sweden, Blathwayt was dispatched to Germany, apparently in the guise of agent for Richmond, who was using him in this more or less official capacity in order to facilitate the young man's Grand Tour of Europe. Williamson, too, had a hand in the arrangement. "I intend with the first ship for Dantzick, where I expect to find your Grace's orders," Blathwayt wrote to Richmond from Stockholm, in August, 1672.[30] In October he was at Leipzig, where he was in search of a "Turkish" horse for Richmond.[31] From thence he intended to go to Dresden, "where the Elector of Saxony keeps his court and so forward toward Italy." To Hamburg he refused to venture, much as he longed to, for he felt that no one should go there in "these troublous times."[32] Richmond's sudden death in December, 1672, did not interrupt Blathwayt's peregrinations nor did the outbreak of the war with Holland affect them. He wrote to Williamson from Venice, just before Christmas, "I have been hitherto too much on the wing to write. In Germany I found everybody strongly concerned for the interest of Holland and exasperated against England because of the war, and maliciously misinformed of the reasons, progress, and success thereof, which they turn altogether to our disadvantage.

[29] S. P. For., Denmark (1671–1674), 19: 110; Add. MSS. 21948, ff. 249, 284; letters from Blathwayt to Williamson and Richmond, August, 1672. For ministerial changes in Sweden at this time, see *Bulstrode Papers*, pp. 240, 249. Werden had been in Sweden only a few months, replacing Coventry who went back to England to become secretary of state in the spring of 1672. (See Coventry's letter to Arlington, S. P. For., Sweden, 8: 83; May 22, 1672.)

[30] Add. MSS. 21948, f. 284; August 21, 1672.

[31] *Ibid.*, f. 349; Leipzig, October 3, 1672.

[32] Blathwayt was referring to the outbreak of the Dutch War of 1672, and to Hamburg's sympathy for the Dutch cause.

Here I find all merry-making and preparing for their famous carnival. I will send you the best advice I can.''[33]

Sometime in 1673 Blathwayt's diplomatic travels and his Grand Tour came to an end. Never again was he to travel on the Continent in so leisurely a fashion. As a matter of fact, he was rarely ever to cross the Channel; a hurried trip to Paris in the summer of 1678, another in the spring of 1681, and the strenuous summers spent in Flanders with William III, from 1692 to 1701, were the only occasions on which he subsequently visited the mainland.

[33] *Cal. S. P. Dom.*, 1672–1673, pp. 217–218.

CHAPTER IV

ENTRANCE INTO WHITEHALL—CLERK IN THE PLANTATION OFFICE, 1675–1679

For two years after his return from the Continent in 1673, Blathwayt dropped below the public horizon. He reappeared in the fall of 1675, as clerk in the plantation office. Only one clue has been found to his activities during this lapse of time. Sometime in 1674 he petitioned for the reversion to the office of secretary of Jamaica, our first evidence of his interest in the colonies.[1] What he intended by his petition is a question. There was a family claim to the office, which he pressed. His uncle, Richard Povey, had secured the secretaryship in 1661, when Thomas Povey stood high in colonial administrative circles, and had combined with it the office of commissary or steward general of the island.[2] A ne'er-do-well, Richard Povey proved a most unsatisfactory officeholder and ultimately returned to England,[3] but he continued to hold both of his posts by deputy, after the fashion of so many West Indian officials. In 1674 he was reported recently dead, and various claimants to his offices appeared immediately. His nephew's petition was set aside. Thomas Martyn declared himself a prior claimant, stating that he had purchased both offices from Povey, and succeeded in making good his claims.[4]

[1] *Cal. S. P. Col.*, 1669–1674, p. 550; also C. O. 1: 31, No. 6.
[2] *Ibid.*, 1675–1676, p. 518.
[3] *Ibid.*, 1669–1674, pp. 60–61, 77, 250, 306.
[4] *Ibid.*, p. 550. Martyn had had the reversion to both offices. His patent

What interests us in this connection, is not the vast amount of trafficking in minor West Indian posts which the incident reveals, but Blathwayt's intention in filing his petition. Did he really entertain the idea of emigrating to Jamaica to seek a fortune which seemed to escape him in England, or was he merely applying for the reversion to a sinecure more or less lucrative even when filled by deputy? It may be that he simply wanted to draw attention to his knowledge of colonial affairs, with a view to a clerkship in the plantation office, for his gravely worded petition stated, "But your petitioner having by his said uncle's help qualified himself in the knowledge of the affairs of the island, hopes that his industry therein may be hereafter useful to himself as well as to your Majesty's service. And having also had the honor to serve your Majesty abroad with some approbation which he humbly presumes may the better embolden him in this request."[5] If a clerkship was the real goal, the hours spent in gathering information on Jamaica and other islands in the West Indies were not to prove wasted, for fate, in the guise of his uncle, Thomas Povey, and Sir Joseph Williamson, was leading his steps to the plantation office.

In September, 1674, Sir Joseph Williamson became sec-

granted at this time was dated January 13, 1674. Something must have happened to prevent him from entering on his duties, for although he went out to Jamaica, we next hear of him as receiver of the royal revenues there, while in November, 1675, a patent for life was granted to George Harris of the offices recently given Martyn. (*Ibid.*, 1675–1676, p. 302.) Harris was still incumbent in 1691. (*Cal. S. P. Dom.*, 1690–1691, p. 462.) John Baber secured a grant in June, 1697. (*Ibid.*, 1697, pp. 202–203.) For various references to the reversion to the office of secretary and to deputy secretaryships, see *Cal. S. P. Col.*, 1669–1674, p. 528; 1675–1676, p. 192; 1677–1680, pp. 273, 583.

[5] *Cal. S. P. Col.*, 1669–1674, p. 550; C. O. 1: 31, No. 6. In his petition Blathwayt stated that he was aware of the fact that Martyn had the reversion to the office, but in view of his own superior knowledge trusted that his candidacy might be preferred.

retary of state for the northern office. That he did not
then find some employment within the secretarial office
for Blathwayt, seems strange in view of his open admiration for the youth, an admiration which went back to
Blathwayt's days at The Hague. Williamson, the biblio-
phile and antiquarian, had not been able to resist so good
an opportunity to acquire rare editions and elusive curi-
osities, so while Blathwayt was in Holland he had plied
him with one request after another for oddities that required hours of search on Blathwayt's part. Blathwayt
had complied in every instance with the best of grace; he
had hunted down rare maps of Candia, which for some
reason or other Williamson coveted; he had spent days in
pursuit of the medals struck at the end of the various
Dutch wars; he had sent over book catalogue after book
catalogue for Williamson's perusal, and Mr. Vivian,
Blathwayt's stepfather, had been kept busy delivering
the boxes of books which constantly arrived from The
Hague. Some of the commissions were so obscure that
even Blathwayt's willing spirit flagged, but Williamson
was an indomitable taskmaster and would not listen to
admissions of defeat. It had been an arduous business, but
it had one advantage, Williamson discovered that Blathwayt possessed all the qualities which go to making a
meticulous clerk.

An unwillingness to upset the regimen in the secretarial office of his successor, Lord Arlington, may have been
the reason why the timorous Williamson failed to offer
Blathwayt a permanent post. Better prospects than a
clerkship there soon presented themselves. At the time
Williamson entered the northern office, a reorganization
of colonial administration at Whitehall was impending.
The years since the Restoration had revealed a surprising
unanimity in England on the trade policies to be pursued
and the ultimate purpose of colonial possessions. The

transitory character of the boards set up to administer trade and plantations, however, indicated that colonial administration was still in an experimental stage. In 1674, alleged dissatisfaction with the work of the Shaftesbury council of trade and plantations—Danby's desire for economy was probably the underlying motive—led to the abolition of that body and the resort to a committee of the Privy Council, under the name of the Lords of Trade and Plantations.[6] England soon saw that she had sacrificed nothing in efficiency to the cause of economy; the new guardians of England's colonial and commercial interests applied themselves to their tasks with a zest and concentration that silenced any possible misgivings.

Without question the moving spirit of the committee was the secretary of state for the northern office, member *ex officio*. Although the division of duties between the northern and southern offices, as has been stated, was not absolutely fixed at this date, colonial affairs normally fell within the province of the latter, and it was with the senior secretary that colonial officials maintained their correspondence. Despite this, a large share of colonial business was engrossed by Williamson in the years of his secretaryship, from 1674 to 1678. Sir Henry Coventry, his colleague, seems to have had only a slight inclination for colonial matters, and, although he attended the meetings of the committee with fair regularity he made no protest against Williamson's monopoly of business. The bulk of colonial correspondence and a large share of the patronage fell into the latter's hands, and his notebooks on the colonies, his offers to colonial officials of his assistance and good will, his very regular attendance at the meetings of the Lords of Trade, all point to his absorbed interest.

[6] The Shaftesbury council went out of existence in December, 1674; the Lords of Trade and Plantations were appointed on February 9, 1675.

The bureaucrat in him was aroused, and he was determined to establish in the comparatively virgin field of colonial administration a system of vigilant supervision that was to make him and administrators like him—Blathwayt, Andros, and Randolph—cordially disliked in the more independent plantations. Williamson's efforts largely determined the subsequent tone of the committee and fortunately found a quickening response in Sir Robert Southwell, the committee's secretary.[7]

Economy had governed the committee in its choice of secretary. Selection was made from among the clerks in ordinary of the Privy Council. Sir Robert Southwell, who had been a clerk since 1664, was ordered "to gather together the threads of business in colonial and trade affairs left loose and at large" since December. Southwell knew Williamson intimately, from years of close association at the council board, for the latter had served as clerk of the council until his elevation to the secretariat. It was soon apparent that Southwell shared Williamson's zeal for the colonies. For several months prior to the dismissal of the Shaftesbury council, he had been manifesting concern over problems affecting trade and the plantations, arising out of the war with Holland.[8] Like Williamson, he counted many merchants among his friends, and the quondam trader, Thomas Povey, was one of them. In the early months of his work as secretary to the commit-

[7] *Cal. S. P. Col.*, 1675–1676, 1677–1680, gives ample evidence of Williamson's interest. For a very fine estimate of his activities and his importance in this matter, see Evans, *The Principal Secretary of State*, pp. 317–320. His notebooks of colonial memoranda are of special interest. For a *résumé* of them, see *Cal. S. P. Col.*, 1675–1676, pp. 154–163. There is the interesting letter that Southwell wrote Blathwayt on January 15, 1680, in which he spoke of Williamson's interest in 1675 and 1676. (*Ibid.*, 1677–1680, pp. 469–470.) A negative has been carelessly inserted in the printing, thus changing the entire context and attributing a disinterest to Williamson which was far from true.

[8] *Cal. S. P. Col.*, 1669–1674, 1675–1676; numerous references.

tee, he had been thrown into close association with Povey.
In December, 1674, the Privy Council ordered a search
made into the claims of Gorges and Mason to New Hampshire and Maine, and Povey, as secretary to one of the
earlier councils of trade and plantations, was called upon
to render his assistance.[9] On March 14, 1675, the Lords of
Trade ordered the books and papers of the Shaftesbury
council perused, so that a scheme for the government of
New England might be prepared. Povey was ordered to
help the clerks to whom the task had been assigned, and
presently Southwell also joined them.[10] Since the investigation extended over several weeks, Povey and Southwell
were thrown into almost daily contact.

Povey, who was never backward, no doubt soon gave
out the information that his very capable young nephew
was looking for a comfortable berth at Whitehall. Williamson, in passing through the council chamber, probably frequently indicated to Southwell the advisability of
getting some such enterprising youth as Blathwayt to
work at plantation business. Southwell was unfortunately
in no position to offer immediate encouragement to either
of Blathwayt's well-wishers. The work of the Lords of
Trade had been planned on the simplest and most eco-
nomical basis. No establishment had been drawn up, and
although Southwell knew that he would be reimbursed
sooner or later, it was at his own risk and expense that he
organized his office. It was impossible to work without
some assistance, so he had engaged two clerks, who were,

[9] *Cal. S. P. Col.*, 1669–1674, pp. 627–628. Although by 1675 Povey had
lost his hold in Whitehall, his name still carried weight in colonial minds.
Thus the Virginian, Giles Bland, wrote him on July 8, 1676, telling him that
he had been appointed agent for several of the Virginia counties and solicit-
ing his good offices in the distress the province was then suffering from over-
taxation, over-tobacco culture, and criminal unrest. (*Ibid.*, 1675–1676, p.
426.)

[10] *Ibid.*, 1675–1676, p. 211.

as a matter of fact, minor clerks in the Privy Council office.[11] Their work was carried on either in the Privy Council chambers or in Southwell's own house in Spring Gardens, near Charing Cross.

Southwell, with this meagre assistance, began the ambitious program which the Lords of Trade had resolved upon. The committee had determined that it would have complete information with regard to each of the colonies at its fingers' tips, and hence had an exceedingly elaborate scheme for permanent archives.[12] Southwell was to prepare general and special entry books, covering the entire commercial and colonial range. At first the work was largely of an investigatory nature and required a tremendous amount of research into official archives and an elaborate correspondence with the colonies.

As the summer of 1675 progressed, Southwell grew dismayed at the rate at which work was piling up for him. On September 24, 1675, therefore, he "acquainted the Lords that it was impossible for him to make searches up and down in offices and put together the Patents and Charters of all the Plantations, etc., as was directed on the 24th May last past without some help, he having otherwise his hands full."[13] The committee was not unreasonable and acceded to Southwell's plea for an additional clerk, thus affording Southwell an opportunity of making good his tentative promise to Povey.[14]

---

[11] C. O. 391: 1, 162-163. The two clerks were Bert Sergeant and Philip Madox. The former came in with Southwell, the latter was taken on shortly after. Madox continued to serve in the plantation office until the Revolution of 1688.

[12] *Cal. S. P. Col.*, 1675–1676, pp. 235, 269; orders of May 24 and August 11, 1675.

[13] C. O. 391: 1, 39.

[14] No mention was made at the time of the name of the clerk engaged, but the first establishment of the plantation office, which Southwell drew up and presented in April, 1676, indicated that Blathwayt entered the office in Sep-

After several months of enforced idleness, Blathwayt naturally threw himself into his work with more than his usual zeal and proved an invaluable assistant to Southwell. Early in the spring of 1676, Southwell suffered a severe nervous shock, as the result of a carriage accident in which his coachman was killed.[15] He was already worn-out from his steady application at the plantation office, so he resolved on a temporary respite from his services there. He talked the matter over with his colleague at the council board, Sir Philip Lloyd. The latter expressed his willingness to relieve Southwell, in all probability because Southwell assured him that the bulk of the work could safely be entrusted to Blathwayt, who was already regarded as first clerk in the office. Lloyd's only duty would be that of general supervision.

Accordingly the matter was laid before the Lords of Trade, who assented to Southwell's plea for release and then proposed an ingenious scheme which proved how thoroughly convinced they were of Blathwayt's capabilities. Either because they desired to leave the way open for Southwell's return, or because they were afraid that Lloyd would soon come with the same sort of complaint Southwell had, they recommended to the king, ''We think it convenient that the rest of the clerks of the Council may have liberty to declare whether they desire to take their turns in that service. And we propose that each Clerk, who will serve therein, do attend for the space of six moneths [sic] and not less.''[16]

tember, 1675, for his salary began with September 25th. (*Acts of the Privy Council, Colonial*, 1613–1680, pp. 664–665; C. O. 391: 1, 111.)

[15] *Essex Correspondence (Camden Society*, 3rd series, Vol. XXIV), p. 62; Southwell writing to his friend, the Earl of Essex, July 4, 1676.

[16] *Acts of the Privy Council, Colonial*, 1613–1680, p. 664; the report of the Lords of Trade, April 24, 1676. See also C. O. 391: 1, 111, 113. Southwell also made application to have the arrears paid him; no money had been forthcoming since the committee had been set up and he had been put

The result of this arrangement was inevitable and in all likelihood was exactly what Southwell had hoped for. The clerks of the council soon discovered that Blathwayt knew far more about the plantation office and what was going on in the colonies than they did, and they were quite willing to let him do all the work. Southwell, who recovered his health and resumed his attendance at the expiration of Lloyd's first term, was the one real exception. Although Lloyd, during his initial six months, manifested an active interest in what was going on, the other clerks gave only a nominal sort of attendance. Their interest was chiefly in the fee of £100 per annum which was attached to attendance,[17] and in the small patronage which the plantation office had to offer.[18]

to great expense. A privy seal was accordingly issued whereby he received his back payments and an establishment was set up permanently for the plantation office; £400 was to be allotted each year as salary for the clerks of the council in attendance, £150 to Blathwayt, and £50 to each of the two clerks. An office was also provided, two rooms in Scotland Yard being engaged for the purpose.

[17] Since the clerks of the council were to serve terms of six months, it would have seemed logical that the two clerks serving annually should each secure £200, but according to the bills of establishment which are to be found in the account books of the office (Add. MSS. 9767, 9768), £100 was given to each of the four clerks of the council. At least this was true after 1679, with the reorganization of the Privy Council. Of the four clerks serving in 1676, only one, the aged Sir John Nicholas, refused to attend the committee. Even after Blathwayt himself became a clerk in ordinary in 1686, the three other clerks, who certainly gave not even the semblance of attendance, continued to demand their fee. The account books give the names of the clerks in attendance up to 1685; after that time the fees are allotted simply to the ''clerk of the council in attendance.''

[18] There was very little patronage to dispense, however, for after Blathwayt's admission to the office, only one other permanent clerk was added. This occurred in March, 1677, after a petty clash between Southwell, whose six months of attendance were up, and Lloyd, who was again succeeding him. Southwell petitioned to be allowed to retain one of the two clerks in order to finish some of the entry books he had started but not brought up to date. Lloyd objected to this very strongly, saying he needed the clerk himself. The matter was finally settled by allowing Lloyd to engage a clerk in extraor-

Southwell's temporary withdrawal in April, 1676, made another change necessary. Within a month, "their Lordships order[ed] that in consideration Mr. Blathwayt is by his Majesty approved to be assistant to the clerks of the council in the business of trade and plantations, he be called in to be present and give his attendance, which was done accordingly."[19] This arrangement gave decisive proof of the dependence which the Lords of Trade and the clerks of the council intended to place upon Blathwayt. In the eighteen months of his service at the plantation office he had exhibited an intelligence and an ability superior to that of either Sergeant or Madox, the two clerks whom Southwell had originally engaged, and this preferment of 1676 made him easily the most important member of the staff.

Blathwayt had no intention of letting his efforts go unrewarded, and in September, 1677, at Williamson's or Southwell's instigation, no doubt, he petitioned for an increase in salary stating that at the time £150 was settled upon him it was "with a favorable declaration from the said lords (who had taken notice of his industry) that in convenient time his said salary should have an augmentation, as his diligence and usefulness in this service did increase."[20] He therefore trusted his majesty "would vouchsafe to order him such a salary as may be proportionable to his care and labours herein." The committee was amenable and ordered an increase of £100, stating that, even then, the establishment of the office was £200 less per annum than that of its predecessor. Even the cautious Danby concurred in the increase, and the committee as a whole expressed its appreciation of Blath-

dinary whose appointment was ultimately made permanent. C. O. 391: 2, 8-11, 139.

19 C. O. 391: 1, 118; May 18, 1676.
20 Add. MSS. 9767, f. 35; September 23, 1677.

wayt's work. "We must needs testify unto your Majesty that his diligence is very great, and hath produced good effect and benefit unto your service, and therefore we judge him worthy of encouragement."[21]

The year 1678 brought further official recognition. Williamson and Southwell were priming Blathwayt for a clerkship in extraordinary of the council. Their opportunity came in 1678, as a special mark of favor from Charles II, and had not even the remotest connection with the duties of the plantation office. At some time or other, possibly in the spring of 1678, Blathwayt had had a touch of the ague and had been cured by Dr. Tabor, whose experiments on remedies for malarial fevers, which he shrouded with deep mystery, were just beginning to attract the attention of the scientific world.[22] Early in the summer of 1678, the reports of the remarkable cure Tabor had effected reached the ears of Charles II, who was immediately interested, for his French niece lay dangerously ill with the same malady. The outcome of his interest can be learned from Southwell's letter to his friend and patron, the Duke of Ormonde. "There was a time as your Grace remembers that I named Mr. Blathwayt, and I only name him now to tell your Grace that he succeeds very well in the plantation business, and being taken notice of by his Majesty as one that was suddenly cured by Dr. Tabor (whom the king admires and very justly, for his certain cure of an ague) he lately sent Mr. Blathwayt over to

[21] Add. MSS. 9767, ff. 36-38; *Acts of the Privy Council, Colonial,* 1613–1680, p. 743. Danby came into the meeting of the Lords of Trade at the very moment Blathwayt's petition was coming up for a vote. C. O. 391: 2, 149; November 10, 1677.

[22] For a very interesting article on Dr. Tabor, or Talbor (1642–1681), see *Dict. Natl. Biog.,* LV, 288. The grave secret of Tabor's success in the treatment of ague seems to have been his discreet use of quinine, which he administered more frequently but in smaller quantities than was then customary. He conducted many of his experiments in the malarial marshes of Essex.

Paris with letters of compliment to his niece who had lain ten months without remedy and this doctor also in his company, who immediately cured her to the amazement of the court; and Mr. Blathwayt, on his return, stood so fair with his Majesty, who seems to have kindness for him, that he presently admitted him to be sworn clerk of the council extraordinary, which was the point your Grace knows we have been long aiming at and is now thus accomplished.''[23] Blathwayt was sworn on July 12, 1678, almost within a week after his return from the Continent.[24] Fortune had smiled on him again, and a touch of the ague was a small price to pay for such a mark of royal favor and a journey in state to the French capital.

The office which his ill health had won him was anomalous, and little that is definite is known about it. There was considerable demand for it at this time, since the practice that the clerks in extraordinary were to succeed by rule of seniority to the clerkships in ordinary was just beginning to be observed, and the idea that clerkships in ordinary could be sold to the highest bidder was rapidly falling into disrepute.[25] The particular duties assigned to the clerks in extraordinary who were in a sense supernumeraries, are not clear, at least prior to 1678. The tendency of the Privy Council to do more and more of its work through committees gradually strengthened and dignified the position of the clerks in extraordinary, al-

[23] *Hist. MSS. Com., Ormonde MSS.*, n.s., IV, 449; August 27, 1678.

[24] *Ibid.*, p. 444; Southwell to Ormonde, July 13, 1678. See, however, Add. MSS. 38861, ff. 7–8, where Edward Southwell in his notes on clerkships of the council erroneously gives the date as April 6, 1677. Blathwayt's passport was dated in July, 1678. (Add. MSS. 38694) Dr. Tabor was knighted almost immediately after his return, according to Southwell.

[25] For a vigorous protest against the sale of the clerkships in ordinary, see the petition of two of the clerks in extraordinary, Dolman and Bridgeman, March 22, 1676. (Add. MSS. 38861, f. 22.) They won their point for themselves, but subsequently clerks in ordinary, Sir Robert Southwell for instance, were permitted to sell their offices.

though the rebuff which the committee system met with in 1679 temporarily interrupted this practice. Within a few weeks after the reorganization of the Privy Council, however, the committee system was restored, and it was ordered, "that it was his Majesty's pleasure that Mr. Bridgeman should assist constantly at the Committee of Intelligence in like manner as Mr. Blathwayt does for the business of Trade and Plantations and as Mr. Coling is to do for the business of Tangier."[26] In a very real sense, Blathwayt's elevation to a clerkship in extraordinary in 1678 had a beneficial and clarifying effect on the office itself.

His advancement, however, did not carry with it the right to be present at the meetings of the Privy Council. That privilege was soon won. This time it was the Popish Plot that furnished the occasion. Thus out of that religious hysteria which gripped England in the fall and winter of 1678 and made even moderate men go mad with apprehension, Blathwayt reaped official advancement. His thorough knowledge of French in this case served him in good stead, for the attorney-general, who had been set to translate the Coleman letters, many of which were in French cipher, was "unskilful in the French language" and desperately in need of a competent assistant. Blathwayt was ordered to translate the letters and to "assist Mr. Attorney in justifying the translations." Lengthy discussions of the material contents of the letters were held before the Privy Council, so that on November 15, 1678, rather than depend on elaborate digests of the letters which he might draw up, the council ordered "that William Blathwayt, Esquire, clerk of the council in extraordinary be admitted to be present at the debates in

26 Add. MSS. 38861, f. 11; the Earl of Sunderland to Sir Robert Southwell. Apparently the committee for Ireland was served by one of the clerks in ordinary. (See Evans, *The Principal Secretary of State,* pp. 165, 236.)

council, for his better instruction and fitting for his Majesty's service."[27] Blathwayt came to bring his findings on the Popish Plot; and, as matters gradually resumed their usual course, he stayed to answer questions on trade and plantations.

Edward Southwell, Sir Robert's son, in his notes on the clerkships of the council, drawn up in 1697, declared that Blathwayt was the second of the clerks in extraordinary to be admitted to the sessions of the Privy Council, and that it was regarded as an unusual practice. "That noe Extraordinaries were ever admitted to the Debates of the Councill till in April 1677. That Mr. Bridgeman, then Secretary to the Lord Arlington, was after a yeares being sworne, allowed that Priviledge, in order to observe what past at the Board, that had Reference to his Lordships office of Secretary of State but he never read any of the Papers, or intermedled with the Businesse, This wholly resting uppon the Clerks in wayting. After this, in November 1678, Mr. Blathwayt, who had been alsoe for sometime in Extraordinary, had admittance to the Board on account of the Plantation Businesse, which was put into his hands by Sir Robert Southwell. And these two Examples are all that can be found in any time preceding that Extraordinaryes were admitted to the Board."[28]

Three years had seen a very definite rise in Blathwayt's position, and his fortunes were clearly in the ascendant. He had proved his own worth, so that after 1678 he was no longer much in need of sponsors like William-

[27] Add. MSS. 38861, f. 10; also *Hist. MSS. Com.*, XI. Report, App. 2, pp. 10–11, 126 (House of Lords MSS.; hearings before the committee of the house of lords, November 16, 18, 23; December 5, 6, 1678; March 27, 1679. There are scattered references to Blathwayt.)

[28] Add. MSS. 38861, ff. 72–73. Southwell drew up these notes in 1697 in order to prove his right as clerk in extraordinary to be advanced to clerk in ordinary, even though Blathwayt's clerk, John Povey, was senior claimant. He was in a combative mood.

son or Southwell, both of whom were soon to withdraw from the scene of action. He had become a familiar figure in Whitehall and must often have been seen—carrying his green bag stuffed with papers that were to come up for consideration at the committee meeting to which he was hastening—as he traversed the quadrangles that separated Scotland Yard from the council chamber. After 1678, letters began to come from some of the colonial officials addressed directly to him, evidence that his correspondents were aware of his growing power in the plantation office. Some of the Whitehall officials also began to address their missives to him, although this was not common until 1680. Among Williamson's notes for January, 1679, is to be found this slightly cryptic notation, apropos of England's state of preparedness for the threatened war with France, "Query any scheme of Mr. Blathwayt of French seamen etc. [sic]."[29]

Toward the close of 1679, Sir Robert Southwell resigned his clerkship of the council in order to accept an appointment as envoy extraordinary to Brandenburg. He had been considering the question of resignation for many months, probably because his sensitive nature longed to escape the excessive excitement of the Popish Plot, but he hesitated until he could find some satisfactory person to whom to dispose of his office. Unless he found a suitable successor, he was "unwilling to be thought a deserter in this cloudy time."[30] He finally resolved upon Francis Gwyn, a young Irishman, kinsman of the Earl of Conway and Edward Seymour, to whom he sold his clerkship for £2500.[31] In writing to the Duke of Ormonde about

29 *Cal. S. P. Dom.*, 1679–1680, p. 18.

30 *Hist. MSS. Com., Ormonde MSS.*, n.s., IV, 564–565; December 6, 1679.

31 *Ibid.;* Southwell had absolutely no intention of permitting the clerk in extraordinary next in line to have his office. Nor did he apparently consider disposing of it to Blathwayt. He did, however, state in this same letter, that he thought he would let Blathwayt have his post as one of the commissioners

the transaction, he said, "Besides, I hope, even in the post I was, my successor will acquit himself with candor and respect. And what he wants in experience shall be supplied by Mr. Blathwayt."[32]

Southwell's removal from the scene left Blathwayt virtually in sole charge of the plantation office. The clerks in ordinary continued to put in a nominal attendance at committee meetings, but Blathwayt was in control. From December, 1679, onward, therefore, it was undoubtedly proper to speak of Blathwayt as secretary to the Lords of Trade and Plantations, even though the clerks in ordinary were still the titular claimants to the office.

of the excise, since the king was willing, but the plan fell through. Apparently Southwell felt he was asking a high price for the clerkship, for he wrote, "Mr. Gwyn gives me £2500, but the place is much better than when I bought it."

[32] *Ibid.*, p. 570; letter to Ormonde, January 3, 1680. It was soon apparent that Gwyn was a chronic seeker after pleasure and that Blathwayt could supply not only information but time and effort as well.

CHAPTER V

SECRETARY TO THE LORDS OF TRADE
1679–1696

As secretary to the Lords of Trade, Blathwayt was a strict disciple of seventeenth-century mercantilism as expressed in the Acts of Trade and Navigation. No one could have been more thoroughly orthodox than he in his views on national wealth and prosperity. He was dominated by the intense nationalism which characterizes the mercantilist. He interpreted not only politics but also life in general in terms of trade and national expansion. The zeal which in some men takes the form of religious fervor and ardent out-pourings of the spirit, in Blathwayt found expression in jealous regard for England's trade interests and an unfailing determination to make the colonies subservient to them. During the course of his many years at the plantation office, he gave voice to few utterances on colonial and economic theory, for he was no expositor of ideas and apparently was so convinced of the merits of England's policy that he felt that there was rarely occasion either for explanation or argument. In one of his reports on the colonies he summed up his creed, however: "All of the plantations . . . [are] worthy of his Majesty's care as they enlarge the Empire and increase the revenues very considerably. . . . Those plantations which heretofore were looked upon as desperate ventures of little importance are now become necessary and important members of the main body and deserve as good governors as is proposed, which is the more requisite as He [the governor] is the Representative of his Majesty at so great [a] distance and has nothing else to support him but his Commission and Authority.'"[1] His Bible of trade was the Acts of Trade and Navigation; its exegesis, the works of the pamphleteers, who more than any others formulated England's economic tenets during this period.

With the theories current on the balance of trade, money and coinage, population and schemes for migration, Blathwayt was in complete accord. He visualized England as a self-contained commercial unit, and he therefore emphasized the importance of the tropical and semi-tropical colonies as against the northern, or bread, colonies, although he realized the importance of the latter as sources of naval stores. He lamented the dependence of England on the Baltic states for such supplies and constantly stimulated interest in their production in both the northern and the southern plantations. He deplored the fact that certain colonies were single-staple colonies and hoped that in time they could be brought to produce a diversity of commodities. For this reason, he set a high value on Jamaica and argued that "if any other useful product besides sugar were encouraged, it would be very beneficial and especially those of the East Indies," both for Barbados and the Leeward Islands. He was a strong believer—though not for himself—in rum, as opposed to French brandy, and maintained that "if the spirit of rum could be improved . . ., it would be of very great profit to the king and the plantations." Ireland and Scotland were both outside the pale in his scheme of trade. Spain's good will and trade were to be cultivated. France and Holland

---

[1] Huntington MSS., Blathwayt Papers relating to America, 1681–1741; draft of an undated report, "Reflections on a Paper concerning America," written about 1697. The governor's chief care was to provide places for the king's ships and stores, he said.

were England's great rivals, to be crushed through a policy of exclusion or, if necessary, war. His ideas were the usual stock in trade of the seventeenth century, but they were as full of vigor as they were lacking in originality.

He realized that the problem which lay before him, as secretary to the Lords of Trade, was one of law enforcement. A less intrepid heart than his might have been daunted. Happily he was not subject to fits of mental depression. His was a naturally buoyant disposition, and, moreover, the reigns of both Charles and James were characterized by general optimism with regard to the colonies and their ultimate compliance with the program England had before her. Certain recalcitrant colonies, Massachusetts Bay in particular, annoyed him, but years were to elapse before he was convinced of England's inability to deal with them. Like any earnest believer in a strongly centralized bureaucracy, he chose to ignore as much as possible the fact that the colonies were political entities with strong local attachments, and that the colonists did not always see eye to eye with the British government. The difficulties which England encountered in her attempts to enforce the Acts of Trade could be solved, he felt, in large part by the appointment of governors of unshaken loyalty. He did not close his eyes to the tremendous temptations which assailed the governors when once they had arrived in their provinces, and to the hapless discouragement to which they fell victims because of their great isolation. For this reason, we might suppose that he would have desired to invest the governor with very broad powers of appointment, so that the latter might at least select his own immediate group of coworkers. But his faith in the royal prerogative was too strong for him to argue in behalf of a powerful colonial executive, and this conviction prevented him—as well as

most of his contemporaries—from attacking the problem
of minor colonial appointments, and the whole question of
colonial patronage, with even a fair degree of intelligence.

He opposed the appointment of governors who intended to hold office *in absentia.* "The constituting such a
Governor or Vice Roy as is proposed to reside in England
will afford a title and some profit to a person of that eminent quality, but how it can advance His Majesty's interest in this [Jamaica] or any other Plantation does not appear since the Deputy will hold himself only accomptable
to his immediate Superior and be at a further distance
from His Majesty's directions."[2] That he was equally opposed, in practice, to the holding of minor offices in the
colonies by deputy is not so evident.

For governors who courted favor with their colonial assemblies, he had little respect, though he realized that as
long as governors were dependent on colonial largesse
for their maintenance, they could not follow an independent course. On this account he bent his efforts, both as
secretary to the Lords of Trade and auditor general of
plantation revenues, to the program in hand for improving the royal revenue in the colonies and for obtaining the
passage of permanent revenue acts. He would have preferred a system of payment out of the English exchequer,
but he knew that the costliness of such a method was pro-
hibitive. Like his contemporary, Sir Charles D'Avenant,
he was convinced of the superiority of French methods in
this matter, "In all appearance, hardly anything would
more conduce to the good government of these places than
to follow one course which the King of France observes
strictly in his Plantations, and it is to give very large appointments to the governors out of his own coffers, not

2 Huntington MSS., Blathwayt Papers relating to America, 1681–1741;
undated draft.

allowing them any perquisites, or to draw any advantages or profits from the inhabitants.'"[3]

Blathwayt, however, admired more than one feature of the French system. As a thoroughgoing bureaucrat, he was fascinated by autocratic French methods of colonial administration and would gladly have helped introduce them into the English colonies. All the changes made in England's colonial system during these years were obviously in imitation of French colonial policy. It is one of the anomalies of history that England should have advocated an absolutely autocratic system for her colonies at the very time when she was contesting most hotly a similar system for herself. Peradventure the efficiency, rather than the autocracy, of the French government appealed to England and caused D'Avenant, a far better spokesman of current theories than Blathwayt, to declare: "The present greatness of the French is chiefly derived from a succession of four very active and able men, in matter of state, viz., Richelieu, Mazarin, Colbert, and Louvoy. But Richelieu was eminent above the rest; he neglected no part of government; raising money was not his only care; for we may plainly see, he inspected into the lives and manners of the church, the discipline of the army and the corruption of the law. He fortified the frontier places of his country; he provided military stores; he put France into the way of having a naval strength; and at the same time encouraged manufactures and prompted trade, as if his thoughts had been taken up with no other business.'"[4]

It is sometimes said that the officials who governed the colonies from the safe distance of Whitehall would have been more understanding and more sympathetic with the

[3] *Works of Sir Charles D'Avenant* (London, 1771), II, 32; an essay on "Plantation Trade."

[4] *Ibid.*, I, 419–420; an essay "On the Protection and Care of Trade."

plantations had they known them at first hand; that Blathwayt, for instance, would have been a better secretary to the Lords of Trade had he made a tour of inspection in the colonies, a notion neither he nor any of his colleagues ever entertained for a moment. In the light of travellers' comments in all countries and at all times, it is exceedingly doubtful whether such a tour would have altered by one jot or tittle his point of view, for he could never have rid himself of his preconceptions. Sir George Downing, a native of New England, was, if anything, even less sympathetic in his attitude toward his native province than Blathwayt. Edward Randolph, who crossed the Atlantic fifteen times, more frequently than any man of his day, with the exception of skippers whose business it was to sail the high seas, had no more understanding of the colonial point of view at the end of his last trip than he had at the beginning. Moreover, curious though it may seem, Blathwayt was not regarded as lacking in understanding by the majority of colonies, with the exception of Massachusetts Bay and, after 1688, Maryland and New York. No one, as yet, foresaw how fundamental were the divergencies between England and her plantations, and most of the colonies, the West Indian and southern in particular, accepted very complacently their position as subservient members of the British world.

For his day, Blathwayt was exceedingly well informed on plantation affairs. He left no stone unturned in his efforts to accumulate information about them. He had a horror of ignorance. "Intelligence," he once said, "is the life of trade and the greatest merchants endeavor to be the best informed." His knowledge of colonial geography and of the printed sources for colonial discoveries and explorations was profound. A few years ago a part of his library was put on sale, and the list of early works on the colonies is impressive.[5] There is a paucity of English titles; but the outstanding authorities are there, such as, Gorges's *America Painted to the Life,* Richard Eden's *The History of Travayle in the West and East Indies and Other Countries,* John Ogilby's *America,* Morton's *New England Memorial,* and George Bishop's *New England Judged.* There are numerous treatises by French and Spanish explorers and a great many Dutch works. Champlain's *Voyages* was included and likewise the *Jesuit Relations.* It is very likely that many of these volumes had originally formed a part of the library of Thomas Povey, but we know from Blathwayt's correspondence that he was constantly on the watch for new books. We also know that his correspondents regarded his library as very extensive and complete, often stating, when he gave them a general rather than a specific commission, that they doubted whether there was any work of substance which he did not already possess.

His knowledge of the colonies was constantly being supplemented by his correspondence with colonial officials, and by copies of the proceedings of provincial councils and assemblies, and of the statutes which were remitted to him. The archives of the plantation office were at his disposal, and his work frequently required him to make extensive searches through them. He was in constant touch with the merchants, planters, and colonial agents, many of whom he first met socially at Thomas Povey's. Many of the English writers on economic questions were known to him personally. It is more than likely that he met Sir Josiah Child, who dined occasionally with Povey, and that he knew and talked with John Cary, a merchant of Bristol, less than a dozen miles distant from Dyrham; for their ideas on trade, and on the colonies in

[5] Collection of books at Dyrham Park, sold at auction at Sotheby's, November 12, 1912.

general, were very often identical.[6] It is inconceivable
that Blathwayt shared the Londoner's distrust of the out-
ports, for he used Bristol constantly for shipping goods
to Dyrham.

With one highly theoretical political economist, Sir
William Petty, cousin to Sir Robert Southwell, Blathwayt
was in intimate communication. Blathwayt was in sympathy with Petty's intricate theories on population and
money, for he offered Petty the facilities of the plantation
office for copying some essays and more than once served
as Petty's medium of communication with the king.
Either he or one of his clerks transcribed the *Quantulumcumque.* "I this day delivered the 3 sheets conteyning the
whole Doctrine of Mony to Mr. Blathwight [*sic*] who
wanted illumination in this matter. I wish it bee truely
written and well painted," Petty wrote to Southwell in
1682.[7] Again, "I am just now going to Winsor, to see what
will be done upon the Festival of our Lady's Asumption
[*sic*], and to get an Essay read to the King, that London
hath more people and Howses than Paris and Rouen put
together and for ought appears the most considerable of
the whole World; and Mr. Blathwight is to read it."[8]
Shortly before his death Petty wrote: "I send you herewith the Coppy of what Mr. Blathwight read last Thurs-

6 Porlock MSS.; Kendall to Blathwayt, July 15, 1692. Curiously enough,
however, Blathwayt does not seem to have had a correspondent at Bristol, if
the comments of Kendall, governor of Barbados, are to be believed. In 1692
Kendall wrote complaining that a letter written in December had not reached
him until the middle of July. "It is a very long time to be without any
news from you or any of my friends in England which may be prevented for
the future if you would get a correspondent at Bristol, and always have letters in his hands. For there hardly passes a month but we have one or two
ships from that city, by which means most of our merchants have intelligence from their friends in London so that there is few or none so much
neglected as myself. But I hope you will make use of this expedient." (*Ibid.*)

7 *Petty-Southwell Correspondence*, p. 104; also pp. 105–106.

8 *Ibid.*, p. 231; August 14, 1686.

day to the King at his Levy, but have a world more, part whereof you'l see in the next transactions of the Royall Society.''[9] According to Edward Southwell, Sir Robert's son, Blathwayt was a poor reader, either on account of his poor eyesight or his stumbling speech, so the picture of him at a royal "levy," faltering through the difficult phrases of Petty's essays, has a faintly comic touch.

The suggestion that Blathwayt's zeal for the colonies was inspired by ulterior motives and his own monetary necessities, need not be seriously entertained. The somewhat scandalous manner in which he drained plantation office clients of fees is dealt with elsewhere in this study, but that he himself had any great interests at stake in the colonies seems very unlikely. He was interested in the great corporate companies, and it may well be that as time went on he invested some of his fortune in stock. There is no evidence to the contrary, and certainly he had a jealous regard for the interests of the Hudson's Bay Company, the Royal Fishery Company, and the East India Company. The tales of the high-handed practices of the Royal African Company he accepted with a due amount of reserve, although in the quarrel which took place between Sir Richard Dutton, governor of Barbados and a facile tool of the company, and Sir John Witham, Dutton's deputy governor in the latter's absence, Blathwayt sympathized with Witham.[10] His stand was prompted not by hostility to Dutton as the agent for the Royal African Company but by dislike for him as a dishonest and ineffective governor.

Blathwayt's secretaryship falls logically into two pe-

[9] *Petty-Southwell Correspondence*, p. 252; January 18, 1687. The editor's note says that those must have been the *Five Essays*, which was licensed to be printed February 18, 1687.

[10] *Acts of the Privy Council, Colonial*, 1680–1720, pp. 80–81. The altercation led to a legal battle, and Blathwayt, in his capacity as clerk of the council, appeared as a witness for Witham.

riods: from 1680 to 1688; and from 1689 to the creation of the Board of Trade, in 1696. The first was the happier and more fruitful. Three main causes made the second period less satisfactory: the outbreak of the war; the appointment to the committee of members less interested in, and less informed on, colonial matters; and Blathwayt's own absorption in the campaigns on which he was required to attend William III, as secretary of state *pro tem*. Blathwayt himself felt the effect of the change no less than the colonies and the English merchants.

During the first period, Blathwayt was working with men among the Lords of Trade whose opinions in plantation affairs he respected, men who were impressed by his ability and application. Since they were predominantly Tory, they were willing to trust his judgment and to give him more or less of a free hand. Of only one, Lord Halifax, who succeeded Lord Anglesey as Lord Privy Seal in 1680, did Blathwayt manifest any profound suspicion. Halifax, according to Edward Randolph, was too great a friend of Massachusetts Bay and unable "to withstand their weighty arguments."[11]

During these years, a powerful secretary of state with ideas of his own on matters of trade and plantations would have been Blathwayt's most dangerous opponent. On this score he had nothing to fear. After Williamson and Cov-

11 Toppan, *Edward Randolph* (Prince Society), III, 146; Randolph to the Bishop of London, May 29, 1682. For references to Halifax's defence of Massachusetts Bay in 1684 at the time of the vacation of the charter, see a letter from Barillon to Louis XIV, quoted in Fox, *History of the Reign of James II*, App. ix–xi; Burnet, *History of His Own Times* (London, 1857), p. 544; Foxcroft, *The Life and Letters of. . . Halifax*, I, 428; Macaulay, *History of England* (Boston, 1901), I, 268. Time, however, was to prove Halifax a milder Whig than either Randolph or Massachusetts supposed, and in 1690 the agents of Massachusetts were as eager to have the Whig Halifax removed from the Privy Council as the Tory Earl of Danby. See Goodrick, *Edward Randolph* (Prince Society), VI, 327–328; Randolph to Blathwayt December 30, 1689, and 329–330; Randolph to Blathwayt, January 10, 1690.

entry left office in 1679 and 1680, there was no secretary in whose mind the colonies held an absorbing place. Most of the secretaries, as a matter of fact, were entirely inconsequential, the foils of Sunderland, who soon came to stand highest in the royal counsels. Sir Leoline Jenkins, who had been a judge of the High Court of Admiralty, had a thorough understanding of maritime law, which Blathwayt found very helpful in his interpretation of the Acts of Trade, but Jenkins made no attempt to interfere in matters relating to the colonies. Blathwayt admired Jenkins' great learning and culture and spent many hours in pleasant discourse with him, but he never looked to him for advice, as he had to Williamson. Sunderland might have proved dangerous, but he had greater interests at stake. Blathwayt was his placeman, completely over-awed by his high position at court and ready always to do his bidding. Fortunately there was no difference of opinion between them on matters of colonial policy, and only rarely did Sunderland direct his great but sinister ability into colonial channels. Colonial officials corresponded, as they had been directed, with the secretaries of state, but they frequently stated in their letters that they would be brief, since they had "writ at large" to Mr. Blathwayt.

Blathwayt's world was now beginning to be impressed by his official success and argued that there must be something to a man who could rise so rapidly and secure so many official appointments. Men began to court his favor and to speak of "the many kindnesses of Mr. Blathwayt." He was indeed "a man of great repute and honor," as one person wrote as early as 1684. Colonial officials importuned him with requests of all sorts, while colonial agents stormed his office and, when his help failed, begged him to secure them audiences with higher officials. This Blathwayt often did, as long as the desired gratuity was forthcoming. A change meanwhile came over Blathwayt's professional manner. The earlier diffidence vanished and in its place came a pleasant urbanity, well calculated to wear down the most importunate client who appeared at the plantation office. This new official deportment was tempered to the person he addressed, for Blathwayt never lost his awe of the "great ones" at court. An innate servility perhaps lingered, but he nevertheless had learned the importance of the grand manner and met colonial agents, particularly those of less repute, and home-coming colonial officials whose standing was not of the best, with a baffling suavity, that was designed to discourage while it did not openly offend. He was not annoyed, however, if his correspondents classed him with the officials of lesser importance, for he had no exaggerated opinion of his own position. Thus he took no offence when a colonial governor wrote, at the end of a long letter in which he begged for some financial aid: "I know ministers and statesmen so hate impertinence and tedious letters, that I durst not address this to our Lords or Mr. Secretary. You can best garble it (as the merchant says) and lay the needful before them.'"[12] He knew he was an important, though humble, medium of communication, and, true to the age, was not dissatisfied with his lack of prominence as long as his monetary rewards were secure.

The extent of his influence over colonial patronage in this early period is hard to determine, but probably it was not very conspicuous. Within the plantation office he was very much his own master, selecting his clerks as he chose. He brought in his cousin, John Povey, about 1680, intending doubtless, even at that early date, to start a Blathwayt-Povey dynasty.[13] Probably at Edward Ran-

---

[12] *Cal. S. P. Col.*, 1681–1685, pp. 395–396; Sir Thomas Lynch to Blathwayt, February 22, 1683.

[13] John Povey was a nephew, not a son of Thomas Povey, who never had any children. Where John Povey appeared from, whether he was a son of

dolph's request, he found a place in the office for Bernard Randolph in 1684, but it was an arrangement which proved temporary, since Edward Randolph found that he could make better use of his brother in the New World.[14] Blathwayt also offered a clerkship to a young Thomas Lane, a protégé of Sir Robert Southwell.[15] Outside the plantation office, he probably wielded little influence. Edward Cranfield owned Blathwayt as his patron in becoming governor of New Hampshire, but it was really Mason, Edward Randolph's kinsman, who obtained the appointment for him. Blathwayt simply lent what assistance he could, by keeping Cranfield's name before the secretary of state.[16] When it came to a selection of a secretary for the province of New Hampshire, Blathwayt wrote to the attorney general: "The Lords of Trade and Plantations request you to recommend some industrious person, well versed in the law, to be Secretary of the Colony of New Hampshire." According to Cranfield's letter to Blathwayt, the secretary appointed, Richard Chamberlain, was actually Blathwayt's nominee.[17]

As far as the governors appointed during these years are concerned, most of them were men of too great an influence to need Blathwayt's assistance. Thus, neither Sir Edmund Andros, Lord Howard of Effingham, nor the Duke of Albemarle needed to call upon him, or to ask him

Richard Povey, or whether he belonged to the Irish branch of the Povey family, we do not know.

[14] Toppan, *Edward Randolph*, I, 229. Bernard Randolph had served as his brother's deputy collector of customs in Massachusetts Bay, but returned to England while Gyles Randolph took his place. The death of Gyles, in 1683, made necessary Bernard's return to the province in 1684.

[15] Add. MSS. 11759, ff. 76–77. Lane seems to have been the son of the tutor of Edward Southwell. *Supra*, p. 23.

[16] *Cal. S. P. Col.*, 1677–1680, p. 587; see also Goodrick, *Edward Randolph*, VI, 9, 115, 120, 125, 127, 130.

[17] Goodrick, *Edward Randolph*, VI, p. 122; Cranfield to Blathwayt, December 1, 1682.

to secure them royal audiences. Blathwayt "wondered to hear that the D[uke] of Albemarle is so desirous of the government of Jamaica,"[18] and said so to the Earl of Clarendon. The latter replied: "I was indeed a little surprised to hear the Duke of Albemarle's being designed for the West Indies. I doubt he will recover neither health nor fortune by the employment; and I believe, without disparagement to his Grace, men of another sort would make better governors."[19] Competition for the governorship of the Leeward Islands, after Sir William Stapleton's death in 1686, was spirited, but there is nothing to show that Blathwayt had anything to do with the selection of Sir Nathaniel Johnson.[20]

In the eyes of the Lords of Trade, Blathwayt was probably still a subordinate figure, no matter how much they respected his intelligence. It is possible that to some extent he determined the order of business for them, though the peremptory orders which appear in the Journal to the effect that on a given day Blathwayt was to be ready with a report on a specified subject, do not point in that direction. The correspondence of Christopher Jeaffreson, the agent from St. Kitts, throws some light on the way in which Blathwayt managed the affairs of the plantation office and the business which came up before the Lords of Trade and the Privy Council. Jeaffreson implied that Blathwayt could hold back petitions to either body with comparative ease, which is not at all unlikely, though scarcely commendable. The best that can be said is that he did not wilfully hold up any important or delicate business, to a colony's or an applicant's irreparable loss. Jeaffreson, who was interested

[18] Ward, *Christopher Monck*, p. 234; Blathwayt to Southwell, April 17, 1686. Albemarle was one of the Lords of Trade.

[19] *Clarendon Correspondence*, I, 393; Dublin Castle, May 15, 1686.

[20] Jeaffreson, *A Young Squire of the Seventeenth Century*, II, 106–107.

in seeing the population of his colony increased, was much distressed because Blathwayt was not present at the time his petition, for malefactors to be sent to St. Kitts, was read at the Privy Council. "But it troubles me that Mr. Blathwait will not be in town then," he wrote. "However, I shall do my best." Later he reported that matters had not gone too well. "Mr. Blathwait not being there was much to our prejudice."[21]

Blathwayt's days were largely taken up with a round of routine duties. There was his correspondence to read, letters to dispatch, reports to draft, calls to receive and pay, and meetings of the Lords of Trade and the Privy Council to attend. Presumably he kept definite office hours. He was often called upon to make visits to the various governmental offices, for the amount of inter-departmental business was tremendous. Much of it was accomplished through correspondence; sometimes the representatives of other departments appeared at the meetings of the Lords of Trade, and sometimes Blathwayt had to pay a personal call before the desired result was achieved. The Lords of Trade very frequently asked the commissioners of the customs for information, and Blathwayt was required to transmit these requests through the medium of the secretary of the Treasury. We find him writing to Henry Guy: "My Lords desire the report of the Commissioners of Customs on two acts of Virginia: an act prohibiting the exportation of iron, wood, etc., and an act to encourage the manufacture of linen and woolen cloth."[22] There are instances where he personally interviewed the customs board, but the more common practice was to deal with the board through the Treasury. Thus when it came to the governors' instructions, Blathwayt would an-

21 Jeaffreson, *A Young Squire of the 17th Century*, II, 43–44, 44–48; March, 1683.

22 *Cal. S. P. Col.*, 1681–1685, pp. 513–514; October 6, 1683.

nounce to the Treasury that the task of preparing them was under way, whereupon the secretary to the Treasury would write to the commissioners of the customs; for example: "The King has appointed Colonel Kirke as Governor of Massachusetts Bay and other adjacent provinces in New England. The Treasury Lords desire you to draft instructions, as from his Majesty to said Governor, relating to trade and navigation. Also return the Treasury Lords your opinion on the following clause concerning trade and engrossing of commodities. Discourse with Mr. Blathwayte herein."[23]

Blathwayt's relations with the commissioners of the customs seem to have been entirely cordial, although there is one minor instance when the latter expressed their disapproval, not so much of Blathwayt as of Randolph. In 1687 the latter found it necessary to write to John Povey, asking that he might for the future forward his papers directly to the customs house in London, since the commissioners had censured him for sending them first to the plantation office.[24] Randolph, like so many other officials in the colonies, had fallen into the habit of enclosing his letters to various officials in London in the packets he addressed to Blathwayt, who then took charge of their distribution. It was a minor, though annoying, point of relative authority, not infrequently raised in inter-departmental relations, and Blathwayt himself was a victim when, years later, as secretary to William III, he had occasion to reprove Lord Lexington, minister to Austria, for enclosing letters addressed to him among those he sent to Secretary of State Trumbull.[25]

[23] *Cal. Treas. Bks.*, 1681–1685, Vol. VII, Pt. II, 1409; November 24, 1686. This was the famous appointment of Colonel Kirke which Randolph succeeded in having rescinded.

[24] Toppan, *Edward Randolph*, II, 28; May 21, 1687.

[25] *Lexington Papers*, pp. 240, 245; January, 1697.

Blathwayt always saw eye to eye with the commissioners of the customs on points connected with trade. After the Revolution, Sir Robert Southwell was on the customs board, and so was Robert Henley, a protégé and agent of both Southwell and Blathwayt.[26] But even without these personal friends to assist him, Blathwayt got on very well with the commissioners, most prominent of whom in the early period were Sir George Downing and Sir Dudley North. Downing and he were agreed "on the necessity of maintaining the present method of trade for the increase and welfare of 'old England,' " and on one occasion Downing was instructed by the secretary of the Treasury, "to go to Mr. Blathwaite at the Plantation Office in Scotland Yard on Monday morning next at 7 o'clock, when the Committee for Trade and Plantations sit upon the Newfoundland business."[27]

There is some interesting evidence of an attempt on the part of one of the Lords of Trade to induce Blathwayt to use his influence against the commissioners of the customs. Generally Blathwayt was ready to do their bidding, but only when there was no essential difference of opinion. This time, the point involved was the plantation trade with Ireland. The Earl of Clarendon had been one of the Lords of Trade, but after his appointment to the lord lieutenancy of Ireland, he had rapidly weakened in his faith on the exclusion of Ireland from the benefits of colonial commerce. His apostasy was not welcomed by anyone in England, neither by the committee of trade nor the commission of the customs—least of all by Blathwayt. Ordinarily Clarendon and Blathwayt were in agreement on commercial questions. They both stressed the im-

---

[26] Add. MSS. 9729, ff. 140–141. Henley had been a member of the board of transport, an appointment which he owed largely to Blathwayt's influence.

[27] *Cal. Treas. Bks.*, 1679–1680, VI, 448–449.

portance to England of the Levantine trade, although it is
not clear that Blathwayt agreed with Clarendon in thinking it "the most beneficial trade in England."[28] Likewise
they felt that what the colonies needed most were good
governors, and that Colonel Cony, of Bermuda, and the
Duke of Albemarle, in Jamaica, for instance, were "no fit
men for such employment." Clarendon wrote Blathwayt
in 1686, "I am very sorry for the death of Sir William
Stapleton: he was one of the best Governors the King had
in any of his Plantations: and I doubt [fear] his successor will come short of him. I am very glad Mr. Stede gives
so good satisfaction. I hope nobody is appointed to super-
sede him. I have not heard anything of late of the Duke of
Albemarle's speedy voyage into the West Indies; and so
long, I take it for granted, Colonel Molesworth is safe in
the government of Jamaica, which, I am sure, will be for
the good of the island, and for the king's interest there."[29]

The tone of Clarendon's letters indicates that he found
in Blathwayt a correspondent after his own heart. He approved, as did Blathwayt, of the appointment of Sir Edmund Andros to New England in 1686. His comment, "He
understands the people and knows how to manage them,"
shows how little either he or Blathwayt understood the
New England temperament.[30]

The point at issue between Clarendon and the English
officials, in 1686, was the result of the administrative mud-
dle in which England found herself because of parliament's failure to renew, on its expiration in 1680, the act
of 1671, which forbade the carrying of enumerated commodities to Ireland. This act had modified the act of 1660,
which required shipowners to give bond that they would

---

[28] *Clarendon Correspondence,* I, 513; Clarendon to Blathwayt, Dublin
Castle, July 29, 1686.

[29] *Ibid.,* I, 575–576; September 4, 1686.

[30] *Ibid.,* I, 393; May 15, 1686.

take the enumerated commodities directly to England and Ireland. Its expiration, therefore, automatically revived the earlier act and opened up anew the trade with Ireland. Meanwhile, the act of 1673 had been passed, which imposed the plantation duty on enumerated commodities if shipped without bond being taken out in England. In 1681, within a few months after the expiration of the act of 1671, the situation had been rectified, in part, by an order in council, which stipulated that the plantation duty of 1673 was to be paid on all enumerated commodities shipped to Ireland. With the convening of parliament in 1685, a new act was passed, again prohibiting their importation into Ireland. The arguments of Clarendon and the commissioners of the revenue in Ireland were to the effect that England would profit by the direct importation of the enumerated commodities into Ireland, because she could then collect the plantation duty. To this the English commissioners of the customs replied that the wholesale evasion of the duty proved quite clearly that it offered no real advantage. The Irish commissioners, however, had succeeded in persuading Clarendon that England did actually profit, and that in the last six months of 1685, from the duty, half of which, by an arrangement made in 1685, was paid in Ireland and not in the colony from which the goods were shipped, had amounted to £5170. Consequently, Clarendon took it upon himself to dissuade the English administration from its new course, and he plied his brother, the Earl of Rochester, then Lord Treasurer, and Blathwayt with letters in which he advanced his arguments, one by one.[31]

Blathwayt, regarding the situation from a commercial and not a fiscal point of view, looked upon the matter in the same light as did the commissioners of the customs.

[31] For a complete discussion of this matter, see Beer, *The Old Colonial System*, Pt. I, Vol. I, 91–104.

What were a few thousand pounds a year more in the English exchequer, if England lost her hold upon her trade as a result? He made his opinion clear to Clarendon, who already knew that Sir Dudley North of the customs would be "stiff in the matter" but was not quite so sure of Blathwayt's position. "I think," Clarendon wrote, "the Commissioners here have the advantage of the Commissioners of the Customs in England, in point of reason: and I am sure their assertions in matter of fact are true and plain, without any specious glosses; which I cannot say of those from the Custom-house in London."[32] Long after he saw no hope of favorable action on the part of the king in council, Clarendon continued to write Blathwayt: "I would be very glad the King were come to a resolution concerning the Plantation trade with reference to this kingdom. Since my last here are come in three ships from the West Indies; one to Coleraine, and two to Cork: they have certificates of having paid the duty in the Plantations, and think they are not within the law, not having entered into bond there to go for England. One of the ships cannot go to sea, there being two leaks in her: and neither master nor mariner will venture in her. The owners do resolve to quit that trade absolutely, and to turn their industry some other way. They are contented to go hence into England, and to enter outward from thence; but to return thither again from the plantations, and to unload in England does not, they say, quit cost, and they cannot live by it: any common tradesman, they say, may fetch tobacco from England. Upon my word, there want no discouragements to the trading men of this kingdom."[33] He finally gave up the matter in despair, though not until he had fired what he regarded as a very

[32] *Clarendon Correspondence*, I, 364; Clarendon to Rochester, April 27, 1687; also p. 330; Clarendon to Blathwayt, April 3, 1686.
[33] *Ibid.*, I, 418–419; May 30, 1686.

telling shot at Blathwayt: ''I say no more to the business of the Plantation trades, but only this, that of the ships that went from the several ports in this kingdom, (not being allowed to unlade here) when they had touched in England, and left there the ½ d. per lb. on tobacco, three of them are gone directly into Holland, thinking to find the better market there; by which means the King has lost 2 ½ d. per lb., which ought to have been paid here: and probably the rest of the ships will do the same.''[34]

Blathwayt's attitude in the controversy over this same issue which arose in 1682 between Lord Baltimore and Nicholas Badcock, surveyor and comptroller of the customs in Maryland, can easily be anticipated. Consistency was usually one of his strong points. As far as we can discover, he did not allow his friendliness toward Baltimore to alter in any particular his belief that the latter was guilty of a gross breach of England's trade laws and was justly liable for the payment of £2500, which represented the loss to England from Baltimore's failure to collect the plantation duty on enumerated goods shipped directly to Ireland from Maryland.[35] That Blathwayt was guided by principle and not by personal consideration, is to be seen from the fact, that in the endless boundary disputes which went on between Penn and Baltimore, he took the side of the latter because he believed quite impersonally that Baltimore's claims were the stronger.[36]

[34] *Clarendon Correspondence*, I, 471; June 26, 1686. Clarendon did not allow this matter to interfere with his relations with Blathwayt, which continued cordial. He appreciated Blathwayt's kindness in sending him news of plantation affairs. The two men were often in communication on military matters. In his letter of June 26, the half penny duty which Clarendon referred to was the residual duty payable in England after the drawback allowed on a re-exportation of the commodity had been calculated. The original duty was 2d., the drawback 1½d. The plantation duty, against which Clarendon was weighing this, was 3d.

[35] Beer, *The Old Colonial System*, Pt. I, Vol. I, 98–100.

[36] Blathwayt had met Baltimore through Southwell who was on very

Blathwayt and the commissioners of the customs stood together on the one act of legislation dealing with trade that was passed during this time. The only parliament called by James II, which met in the spring of 1685, agreed, in response to the king's wishes, to levy an additional duty on sugar and tobacco exported from the colonies. Unlike the plantation duty of 1673, which was supposed to prevent colonial trade with Europe, and consequently was not primarily a revenue measure, the act of 1685 was intended to provide the king with the funds he needed to meet the expenses of an increased army and navy. Even though Blathwayt, as secretary at war, was in duty bound to favor it, he was by conviction favorable to the measure. As a new member of the house of commons, without any previous parliamentary experience, he had nothing to do with the passage of the act. He was not even a member of the committee to which the bill was referred. Credit for the measure belongs to Sir Dudley North, the customs commissioner, who held out staunchly for it, even after the Lord Treasurer, the Earl of Rochester, had yielded to the wishes of the merchants and planters.[37] When the news of the act reached those colonies that were most affected by it, their distress was acute. Molesworth, the deputy-governor of Jamaica, whom Blathwayt admired for his great devotion to the crown, immediately wrote to him to say that the additional levy would have a killing effect upon trade, but when the royal letter of June 26, 1685, presumably drafted by Blathwayt, arrived in Jamaica with its explanation of the additional duty and

friendly terms with the proprietor, probably as a result of their Irish connections. For a very friendly letter from Baltimore to Blathwayt, see *Cal. S. P. Col.*, 1677–1680, p. 393. Copley, later governor of Maryland, declared that during the Penn-Baltimore case, Blathwayt had entered false minutes. Goodrick, *Edward Randolph*, VII, 354; Randolph to Povey, May 12, 1692.

[37] Stock, *Proceedings and Debates of the British Parliaments respecting North America*, I, 426–428.

of the counteracting provision for drawbacks, the situation was naturally altered in the eyes of Molesworth and the Jamaicans. Then according to the governor, "the Council was transported into a rapture of gratitude."[38] The Barbadians, also, implored Blathwayt to use his good offices to secure a revocation of the act (a curious tribute to his influence in official circles), but whether he did anything more than explain the exact nature of the imposition to the islanders, showing them that it was not so onerous as they assumed, we cannot say.[39]

Blathwayt stands out most clearly in this decade as the bulwark of English mercantile and royalist policy against the undermining attacks of corporate and proprietary colonies. He is identified at every step with the efforts made to overthrow the charters of the Massachusetts Bay and Bermuda companies. True, he had a hand in that curiously inconsistent grant of Pennsylvania to William Penn, in 1680, but in this he was only the docile tool of agents more powerful than himself. His heart was not in it, nor did he ever ask, or secure, any mark of gratitude from the distinguished Quaker. Before the century was over, Penn, in fact, became venomous in his attitude toward Blathwayt. For securing the grant, Penn paid special tribute to the Welshman, Sir Leoline Jenkins, secretary of state, and out of gratitude to him desired to name the province New Wales.[40] When asked to report on Penn's petition and its merits, Blathwayt anticipated the future difficulties over boundaries. "I have examined Mr. Penn's petition for the grant of a tract of land in America and the patent of New York granted to his Royal Highness [the Duke of York], and find that the latter is sufficiently distinguished from the grant desired by Mr. Penn.

---

[38] Cal. S. P. Col., 1685–1688, pp. 59–60, 84, 96–97, 98.
[39] Ibid., pp. 93–94.
[40] Penn. Hist. Soc. Memoirs, I, 208–209.

But I am further to offer to your lordships that there are several Dutch and Swedish plantations which have been long under the English government, that lie scattered on the westward of the Delaware river, some of them perhaps within the bounds of Mr. Penn's petition, and have for a long time either acknowledged the protection of the Duke of York or of Lord Baltimore, near whose borders they are settled.''[41] He was required to draft the charter, which appears among the Colonial Papers in his own hand.[42] When the boundary disputes between Baltimore and Penn came to a head, as they did in 1684–1685, we find that Blathwayt was always willing to slight or postpone their consideration in order to hasten, for instance, the execution of Randolph's commissions for the subjugation of New England.[43]

Randolph and Blathwayt were willing co-workers. Temperamentally, they had many traits in common, although Blathwayt's suavity stands out in sharp contrast to Randolph's brusque disregard for men's feelings. No one could have said of Blathwayt as Governor Copley said of Randolph: ''He hath indeed effected here what he hath done in all other parts of the world (wherever he sett foote), made the whole country weary of him, boastingly vaunting that he thanks God he has lived these five and twenty years upon the curses of the people, which truly I am apt to believe.''[44] Blathwayt believed that ''a soft answer turneth away wrath.'' Even in recommending

41 *Cal. S. P. Col.*, 1677–1680, p. 623; October (?), 1680.

42 C. O. 1: 46, No. 104, f. 204; February 24, 1681. For the charter, see ff. 205–223.

43 Toppan, *Edward Randolph*, I, 264; also *Cal. S. P. Col.*, 1685–1688, p. 87. Randolph to the Lords of Trade, September 2, 1685: ''[I beg] that the commission prepared by Mr. Blathwayt may be read before the Lords enter upon the matters in difference betwixt the Lord Baltimore and Mr. Penn.''

44 *Maryland Archives*, VIII, 337; Copley to the Lords of Trade, July 29, 1692. Quoted in Toppan, *Edward Randolph*, II, 140.

Randolph to the people of Massachusetts Bay, he was guided by this view, "As I cease not to persecute you at all times with business [he wrote to Randolph] you will easily take upon you the trouble of this letter to the [*sic*] Massachusetts, since it is chiefly intended to recommend you to that people, with what success I cannot tell. It is exceeding soft and gentle and meddles with nothing but the sending Agents, but I have reason to hope that things will goe never the less well for this mild way of Proceeding, there being but one thing wanting to sett all right." Irony and a grim sense of humor, however, caused him to add, "I heartily wish you and your family may have a prosperous voyage and a kind welcome at Boston where you have but one rock to avoid which you ought to be aware of. I meane your letting them come within you after which they will easily give you the Cornish Hugg."[45]

Randolph's idiosyncrasies did not annoy Blathwayt, who stood loyally behind him as did the rest of the British administration. A strong bond united the two men, their devotion to Sir Robert Southwell.[46] Socially they moved in the same circles; politically they shared the same patrons, in particular the Duke of Beaufort and the Duke of Ormonde.[47] They shared a less desirable attribute, a love of official perquisites, for they were both essentially mercenary. To find two men more bent on securing offices for themselves would be difficult. Blathwayt sponsored all of

[45] Toppan, *Edward Randolph*, III, 113–114; October 22, 1681 (quoted from *Mass. Hist. Archives*, CVI, 246). Blathwayt's stepfather, Mr. Vivian, was Cornish, hence Blathwayt's aptness for Cornish expressions such as "the Cornish Hugg," a death grapple, familiar to that part of the country.

[46] Randolph kept up an intimate correspondence with Southwell during these years. The correspondence was preserved in Sir Thomas Phillipps' collection at Cheltenham, and a large portion of it has been printed in Toppan's *Edward Randolph*.

[47] Toppan, *Edward Randolph*, I, 259, 265. Beaufort was the great patron of Gloucestershire.

Randolph's efforts to gain new posts, and we often find him hurrying the passage of one or other commission for Randolph through official channels. He appointed Randolph his deputy auditor in Massachusetts in 1681, and later in all of New England with the exception of New Hampshire, where, for good reason it may be, he felt he had no right to disturb the existing incumbent. After Maryland became a royal province, he also appointed Randolph deputy auditor there. He supported him in his efforts to secure the secretaryship of the Dominion of New England in 1688, regretting that it could not be made to include New York; "Care is already taken for the passing your patent for all New-England, and if Mr. Spragg were not in the way, it might have been for the whole new dominion."[48] He apparently did not approve of Randolph's desire that the appointment be for life, however, for we find Povey writing to Randolph: "[I] do not understand your meaning about a patent for life, not having heard of it before, it being not granted now in any case."[49]

Blathwayt showed his desire to promote Randolph's financial interests, by securing official consent to Randolph's numerous petitions for payment. He was called upon by the Treasury to audit Randolph's expense accounts for the years from 1675 to 1680, and in 1684, after the matter had been brought before the Lords of Trade, he announced to the Treasury that Randolph's petition for expenses incurred while bringing the *quo warranto* writs against the New England colonies was valid.[50] He was sympathetic with Randolph's hope that perchance

48 *Hutchinson Papers*, II, 302; Blathwayt to Randolph, March 10, 1688.

49 Toppan, *Edward Randolph*, II, 71; April 25, 1688 (quoted from *Mass. Hist. Archives*, CXXVIII, 167).

50 *Cal. Treas. Bks.*, 1681–1685, Vol. VII, Pt. I, 221; Toppan, *Edward Randolph*, III, 292–295.

the new world could be made to yield him a sudden and unexpected fortune. "I send you the gazettes [he wrote to him in March, 1688] touching the pirates and Sir R. Holmes. The King has granted him all pirates goods for 3 years and the power of pardoning for one year. He offers fair to discoverers and such as surrender themselves, and will certainly make good his promise. An accident on that account may make your fortune, as you are most in the way of that sort of people. . . . Time and patience will stand you in great stead, amidst your disappointments and afflictions."[51]

Randolph admitted his debt to Blathwayt for a variety of official favors and once said, "Sir, I owe to you the bread I eat."[52] He was constantly thinking of "handsome presents" for Mr. Blathwayt and Mr. Povey, and many were the gifts which found their way from him to the plantation office. Blathwayt's letters to him frequently contained such statements as "I am obliged to you for your kind present of cranberries, acorns, chestnuts, etc., which came very well. . . . The little box of locust trees was broken open and they are lost, which was a pity, since they are so shady as you mention. I told the king of the black fox, who taking not much notice of it, I keep it myself, unless you think otherwise to dispose of it."[53] Had Blathwayt's avarice been aroused by the glossy pelt or had the king actually been indifferent?

Randolph trusted Blathwayt's judgment, notably with regard to patronage. His disgust with West, his deputy secretary, who, as Randolph saw it, was Andros's creature led him to write to Povey as follows: "I see no reason why I should recede in my desires of getting an understanding gentleman to come from home to engage in

---

[51] *Hutchinson Papers*, II, 302–303.
[52] Goodrick, *Edward Randolph*, VI, 236; Boston, November 23, 1687.
[53] *Hutchinson Papers*, II, 302.

discharge of the secretary's and register's office, which is very beneficial to West. . . . I have wrote you of the want we have of two or three honest atturneys (if any such thing in nature); we have but two, one is Mr. West's creature, came with him from New York, and drives all before him; he also takes extravagant fees, and for want of more the country cannot avoid coming to him, so that we had better be quite without them than not to have more. I have wrote Mr. Blathwait the great necessity of judges from England. I know there are some loyal gentlemen and able lawyers, who have not practice; the judges with us, being now 3, have £390 betwixt them all, besides their fees, which they make very considerable to them: Now, two will serve our occasions. They ought to be of the councill, and their salaryes made up 400£ a yeare, apeece, they will deserve it. . . . I formerly wrote you about a fitt person to assist in my office . . . and whom Mr. Blathwayt or you should recommend will be acceptable. Capt. Nicholson tells me Mr. Martin who was to come over with Col. Kerke, is out of business and believes he would accept of the office: I would have an honest gentleman, who will not be drawn to ill company, but will mind his business. There are many about court, but now out of my mind.''[54]

Randolph's faith in Blathwayt did not lead him to take Blathwayt's word for the committee's, or to think an object had been won because it had Blathwayt's approval and support.[55] His letters to Lord Clarendon and the Bishop of London indicate this. Thus, in one of his letters urging that his petition for payment be acted upon quickly, he said: ''My Lord, I am at a great disadvantage, by reason of my distance from court, and in no condition

---

[54] *Ibid.*, pp. 299–300; Boston, January 24, 1688.

[55] Randolph declared in one instance that he sent all of his letters to the Lords of Trade open, so that nothing might reach them until Blathwayt had already seen it. Goodrick, *Edward Randolph*, VI, 304; October 15, 1689.

to sollicite his Majesties concernes and the good and well-fare of this colony, as formerly, I well remember, business with your Lordship, as with the other Lords of the Councill, sometimes intervenes, which hath occasioned not only delays, but quite alters the face of things, especially when a committee of Lords meete, who are not acquainted with the whole series of this affaire; It is therefore my humble request to your Lordships, to move that 2 or 3 Committyes may be appointed for this matter, when your Lordship, my Lord Hide, and Mr. Chancellor of the Exchequer, may be present, and the whole matter of fact examined and stated.''[56]

Randolph was careful to keep the name of Blathwayt before the New Englanders and never failed, when occasion offered, to impress them with the importance of the latter's position at Whitehall. Before the expectant eyes of the Plymouth townsmen, for instance, Randolph and Blathwayt dangled the prospect of a new charter, though their sincerity in the matter must be doubted, in view of their plans for a united New England. Randolph, made a freeman of Plymouth in 1680, intimated then that he would use his influence to secure a charter. His return to England shortly after, filled the hearts of the Plymouth men with hope, which presently faded as no news came from either Randolph or Blathwayt. On Randolph's return without the charter, Governor Hinckley wrote to Blathwayt, expressing in terms of mild reproach their keen disappointment. ''We were not out of hope but that we might receive some account of that affair from yourself, especially when Governor Cranfield should arrive; but were informed per Mr. Randolph that there was no news by him from you of our affaires.''[57]

[56] Toppan, *Edward Randolph*, III, 156; Boston, June 14, 1682.
[57] *Ibid.*, I, f.n., p. 185; Hinckley to Blathwayt, November 18, 1682; also *Mass. Hist. Soc. Coll.*, 4th ser., V, 74.

Both Randolph and Blathwayt had what they regarded as plausible reasons for their delay. Randolph said, more or less equivocally and pettishly: "I have brought you no letters because you would not trust me with any to Mr. Blathwayt; neither I believe has your agent, Jacob Jeffon. I have not, however, failed to do your colony all the service you made me capable of: which I referr till meeting, and I hope you will not fayle to send me positive word when you will be in Boston. By the enclosed papers you will see what transactions have been in England, and how far his Majesty is resolved to deal with this Colony. It therefore stands you in hand to be very careful to improve the present opportunity; for be confident, what regulation is made here will passe through all New England. I was in no way wanting with Mr. Blathwayt in your behalfe. He is very full of great business, and cannot but with great difficulty be spoaken with. He was putting me upon your business: but by some accident, either the copy of your Grant sent over by Governor Winslow is mislaid, or quite lost: for after a long search, it could not be found; so that I could not make one step about it."[58]

While Randolph preached to the Plymouth men, warning them against their misdeeds and attempting to impress them with the magnitude of Mr. Blathwayt, the latter wrote simply and directly to Hinckley. He said nothing of the charter having been lost, the report being likely a fabrication of Randolph's, but he did say, Randolph to the contrary notwithstanding, that he had intended to send a letter over by Randolph: "I intended to put this letter into your hands by the conveyance of Mr. Randolph who went lately to New England with his Majesty's writ of quo warranto against the colony of Massachusetts Bay. I have taken particular notice of your de-

[58] Toppan, *Edward Randolph*, III, 265–267; Randolph to Hinckley, Boston, October 29, 1683.

sires for the passing of a new patent for the colony of New Plymouth. But I must deal plainly with you, that it is not probable anything will be determined in that behalfe until his Majesty do see an issue of proceedings in relation to the Massachusetts Colony: and that upon regulating their charter, that Colony be brought under such an actual dependence upon the Crown as becomes his Majesty's good subjects. It will be convenient that you fully instruct Mr. Randolph with all particulars of your business, that upon his return to England, which will be in a few weeks after his arrival in your parts, we may join our endeavors in behalf of your colony.''[59] Before the arrival of Blathwayt's letter, Hinckley, thinking he had discovered where the hitch in the matter lay, transmitted a gratuity to him with the words: ''We shall not show ourselves ungrateful to either of you for your labour of love[!] therein.''[60] And since he seriously believed that the copy of the charter had been lost, he hastened to send another. We wonder whether Blathwayt was impressed by the Plymouth men's lack of guile.

Blathwayt was absolutely convinced of the utter perversity of Massachusetts Bay. He played an important part in the steps leading to the issuance of the writs against the colony, and the willingness of the Lords of Trade to leave to him the general conduct of affairs can be seen in the rough notes taken at the committee meetings. Time and again the words appear: ''Mr. Blath-[wayt] takes care.''[61] On July 17, 1683, they resolved that Randolph should carry the writ of quo warranto to Bos-

59 Toppan, *Edward Randolph*, I, f.n., p. 209; Whitehall, September 27, 1683; also *Mass. Hist. Soc. Coll.*, 4th ser., V, 91.

60 Toppan, *Edward Randolph*, I, f.n., p. 218; November 22, 1683; also *Mass. Hist. Soc. Coll.*, 4th ser., I, 94. See also *Ibid.*, I, f.n., 225.

61 ''Journal of All that Passes in the Office of Trade''; entries for July 17 and July 20, 1683.

ton. Blathwayt allowed no grass to grow under his feet. On that very day he wrote to the attorney-general, telling him to prepare the necessary papers.[62] He also wrote to Brisbane, the secretary to the Admiralty, to ask whether the frigate *Mermaid* could be secured to take Randolph speedily to New England.[63] He shared in Randolph's impatience over the delays which ensued as a result of the Admiralty's failure to provide a convenient and speedy means of conveyance.

The result of Randolph's journey with the writ of quo warranto needs no relating. On the latter's return, Blathwayt found himself engaged in an unpleasant wrangle with the attorney-general over the proceedings for the writ of scire facias. Randolph, fretting under the delays, recorded the matter in his letters to Southwell. The decision to proceed by writ of scire facias was reached on April 16, 1684, and the attorney-general was ordered to see that the writ was properly drawn. Two weeks went by with nothing done, and Randolph wrote: "I have been full of distracting business and attendance about the prosecuting the Quo Warranto and now at last we have discovered a fundamental mistake in the first step, the Clerk having directed his Writt against the particular persons in the Government whereas it ought to be against the Governor and Company, etc. This night I am to give Mr. Blathwait an account at Winsor and I believe I must be engaged to make the other voyage to New England to make a compleat service."[64] The muddled situation continued for nearly another fortnight. "Such hath been the variety and truely inconsultedness in our late method re-

---

[62] *Cal. S. P. Col.*, 1681–1685, p. 454. The order in council on the matter was not issued until July 20, 1683. (*Ibid.*, p. 456.)

[63] *Ibid.*, p. 455.

[64] Toppan, *Edward Randolph*, III, 300; Whitehall, May 3, 1684.

lating to the proceedings against the Bostoners Charter that till Thirsday last I expected his Majesty's Commands to make another trip to New England, but then with some difficulty Mr. Blathwayt convinced Mr. Atturney (who all along covered the oversight or rather neglect of his clerk), of the former errour, and now by his report we are setled in another way and I hope by the end of next term to gett Judgment entered against their Charter, unless prevented by some extraordinary providence (as the Bostoners hope for) for I find every one concerned that there hath been so great delayes in a business of such concern to his Majesty.''[65]

On October 23, 1684, the charter of Massachusetts Bay was declared forfeited. Blathwayt was directed to write to Governor Bradstreet what had happened, but the latter subsequently declared that he had no news of the cancellation until Blathwayt's letter announcing the death of Charles II reached him early in the spring of 1685. Nor had anyone else, apparently, bothered to send official notice. ''We received the letter reporting the accession of James II on 17 April, but deferred the proclamation till the 20th, to make suitable provision for the ceremony. Your intimation of the vacation of our charter by legal process was the first notice that we ever received from any correspondent in England. We did not even hear of the issue of scire facias in time to answer, so we hope that our not appearing will not be imputed to us as disloyalty, much less as contempt.''[66] So Governor Bradstreet wrote to Blathwayt, while Sewall reported in his diary for April 16, 1685, ''Mr. Blathwayt writes to Simon Bradstreet, Esq. superscribed for his Majesty's service, advising that 'twould be best for us early to do it; and our charter be-

[65] Toppan, *Edward Randolph*, III, 302–303; May 17, 1684; also I, 227–230. The attorney-general had been convinced of his error on May 13, 1684.
[66] *Cal. S. P. Col.*, 1685–1688, p. 31; April 21, 1685.

ing vacated in law and no government settled here, was the reason we were not writ to."[67]

Evidence of Blathwayt's zeal for the establishment of a united government of New England appears at every turn, and Randolph frequently mentioned him in his dispatches to Southwell. "Mr. Blathwayt is hastening my dispatches for New England," we find him writing on one occasion.[68] In January, 1685, Randolph reported, "Mr. Blathwayt is of opinion that the Road Islanders will surrender their charter upon his Majesty's letter to them."[69] On July 28, 1686, Randolph wrote to Blathwayt, saying: "Inclosed is a letter sent some time since from the government of Road Island, they call it a surrender of their charter. I have since the receipt of it called on them in my way to Hartford in Connecticut, the governor tells me they will pass a surrender in fuller termes under the seal of their colony, but are willing to have this sent. I was with the governor of Connecticut, and delivered to him the quowaranto. I suppose they intend not to stand it out."[70] In bringing the writ to Connecticut, Randolph said the colony had nothing to fear in surrendering, since "Mr. Blathwayt is much your friend."[71]

In March, 1688, Blathwayt reported to Randolph the decision to include New York and the Jerseys in the union of New England, and stated: "If the union of all New England under one governor be acceptable on your side the water, what will the joining and annexing to the same government be of all the English territories in America, from Delaware Bay to Nova Scotia? This is already determined by his Majesty, and a commission constituting

67 *Diary of Samuel Sewall*, I, 69.
68 Toppan, *Edward Randolph*, I, 263; September 1, 1685.
69 *Ibid.*, p. 250; January 29, 1685. In this, Blathwayt was correct.
70 *Hutchinson Papers*, II, 288.
71 *Cal. S. P. Col.*, 1685–1688, pp. 198–199; May 27, 1686.

Sir Edmund Andros governor also of New York, as united to and parcel of his Majesty's dominion of New England. And for the two Jersies, scire facias's are expediting towards their union. This, besides other advantages, will be terrible to the French, and make them proceed with more caution than they have lately done.''[72]

Blathwayt's comments on the project, and his belief that the French would be over-awed by these widespread plans of union, seem curious in the light of what actually happened. He was to learn to his sorrow that paper plans fell far short of the desired result and brought no real union. Inter-colonial coöperation, or the lack of it, was a new idea in 1688, and Blathwayt had yet to discover that it was one thing to declare the governments of New York and New England united, but another thing to effect the union.

Whether Blathwayt stood back of Randolph in his opposition to the proposed appointment of Colonel Kirke as governor does not appear. It seems incredible that, with his concern for the selection of good governors, he should have upheld so wretched a choice. He had undoubtedly a weakness for military men as governors, which grew naturally out of his work as secretary at war; moreover, the return of the Tangier regiment had caused him some concern in disposing of the men and officers, and it is likely that Kirke approached him on the question of a colonial appointment. On the whole, however, Blathwayt's share in the matter may be doubted, since with all his dislike for Massachusetts and her stubborn ways, he had no desire to see her scourged.[73]

[72] *Hutchinson Papers*, II, 301–302; March 10, 1688.

[73] Even Randolph, for all his subsequent opposition, had written of Kirke when first he heard of his appointment ''His Majesty has chosen Coll. Kerke, late governor of Tangier, to be your governor. He is a gentleman of very good resolution and, I believe, will not faile in any part of his duty to his

It was soon plain that merely cancelling the charter had not changed the hearts of the Massachusetts men. The struggle went on as before. Randolph reported his fears to Blathwayt: "Andros discharges the duty of an excellent governor. But this people are rivetted in their way and I fear nothing but necessity or force will otherwise dispose them."[74] Blathwayt was approached from time to time by the agents from New England. As early as June, 1686, the council of the colony drew up a memorial, which they sent to England by their agent, Stephen Mason, who was to present it to Blathwayt, to be laid before the king in council. In it they asked that the right to have an assembly and a mint be restored. They also begged, in case Rhode Island and Connecticut were annexed to Massachusetts should they resign their charters, "at least that the free commerce that hath always been between the said Colonies may be continued, without which neither can subsist."[75] Only on the last of these requests did Blathwayt take action.

In June, 1688, Increase Mather arrived on his unofficial mission in behalf of the restoration of the charter. Blathwayt reported his coming to Southwell. "Increase Mather, Sea Born Cotton, etc., are come hither from Massachusetts with addresses and have audiences of the great ones now. And there are joint endeavors to supplant Sir Edmund and discredit the Caveleros, but I hope Sir Ed[mund] Andros has taken such root in his Maj-

Majesty nor be wanting to doe all good offices for your distracted colony, if, at last, they will hear what is reason and be governed." This, however, was written before Monmouth's Rebellion and its dire aftermath. (*Hutchinson Papers*, II, 283; letter to Joseph Dudley, November 9, 1684.)

[74] Toppan, *Edward Randolph*, II, 28–29; Randolph to Blathwayt, May 21, 1687.

[75] *Mass. Hist. Soc. Proc.*, 1899–1900, 2nd ser., XIII, 238, 244; council record for June 1 and 2, 1686.

esty's good opinion as to withstand some shock.'"[76] The course upon which the great New England divine had already embarked would have proved a considerable shock to Blathwayt, had he known it. Not only had Mather determined to conciliate the "great ones," but high on his list stood the secretary of the plantation office. Within a fortnight after his arrival in London, Mather attempted, in a way curiously indirect for a Puritan, to disarm Blathwayt's hostility. In the course of his pastoral experience he had learned that feminine susceptibilities could be turned to account. In consequence, poor Mary Wynter Blathwayt emerges from anonymity to play her small part in the great conflict, and John Povey, Blathwayt's trusted clerk, apparently whole-souled in his opposition to New England, lent his hand to the petty conspiracy. On June 11th, a week before Blathwayt dispatched to Southwell the letter already quoted, Stephen Mason, the agent from Massachusetts, wrote to Mather: "Just as you went from the booksellers, I with Madame Bl—— were there [to] wait on you, & I suppose you took coach, or must have overtaken you i[n] Cheapside; but missing you, and fearing a letter by the penny post might faile, I came hither to let you know that this day Mr. P[ovey] was at her lodgings, & that he assures her that you need not doubt all things [shall be] done to your content, and that he will labour in it, but not above board, [&] so as Mr. Blathwaite shall know nothing of it, but saith it wilbe about 10 daies first, because of the present rejoycing,[77] which hinders all buissinesse; & tels her that N. E. people have been represented as such who have wronged his Majesty in his customes, & an odd humored people, which occasioned what hath been transacted in N. E., but that he will undeceiue his Majesty. He aduised

---

[76] Ward, *Christopher Monck*, f.n., p. 301; June 19, 1688.

[77] The birth of the prince.

her to goe to my Lord Bellasise, as a person much in favor, which she resolves to doe on Thursday next.'"[78]

What a tribute, this, to Blathwayt's power in plantation affairs, and what an insight into the mind of Mary Wynter Blathwayt, whose religious fervor had been aroused by this godly man even to the point of domestic disloyalty! Unfortunately the curtain falls upon the highly diverting scene with the same suddenness with which it rose. Did the interview with Lord Bellasis[79] ever take place? Did Blathwayt ever suspect Mather's strategy? If he did, Mary Blathwayt's heart must have trembled. It is likely that timidity cut short Povey's conniving, for he continued to write Randolph earnest letters full of loyalty to the policy for which Randolph stood.

Nor was there meanwhile any weakening in Blathwayt's attitude. He fell even further in New England's eyes, committing what they regarded as a dastardly piece of treachery. "Increase Mather, with two New England Gentlemen, presented a Petition and humble Proposals to the King, wherein they prayed, that the Right which they had in their Estates before the Government was changed, might be confirmed; and that no Laws might be made or money raised, without an Assembly, with sundry other particulars; which the King referred to a Committee for Foreign Plantations, who ordered them into the hands of the Attorney General to make his report. The Clerk, William Blathwait sent to the Attourney General a Copy, wherein the Essential Proposal of an Assembly was wholly left out: and being spoke to about it, he said the Earl of Sunderland blotted out that with his own hand. Likewise a Solicitor in this Cause related that the said

---

[78] *Mass. Hist. Soc. Coll.*, 4th ser., VIII, 699. See also Murdock, *Increase Mather*, pp. 200–201. Dr. Murdock thinks that *Mr. P.* must be Mr. Penn, but it is unquestionably John Povey.

[79] Lord Bellasis was a member of the Lords of Trade.

Earl of Sunderland affirmed to him, that it was by his Advice that the King had given a Commission to Sir Edmond Andros to raise moneys without an Assembly, and that he knew the King would never consent to an Alteration, nor would he propose it to his Majesty.''[80]

It probably cost Blathwayt no real effort to do Sunderland's bidding in this matter. It may even be that he hid behind Sunderland's name, and that the erasure was really his own, though he was ordinarily fearless in admitting his stand on matters in general, to say nothing of New England. His hostility to the trend of events after the Revolution can be easily understood. He was infuriated by the treatment which Andros and Randolph met at the hands of Massachusetts, long and doleful reports of which were transmittted to him by the hand of Randolph.[81] He neither liked nor furthered William III's friendly policy toward the New Englanders. As early as February 26, 1689, the decision was reached that a new charter be granted. On May 14, 1689, an item appears in Samuel Sewall's *Diary:* ''Monday, May 6th, at Westminster pleading against Mr. Blathwayt, in behalf of N[ew] E[ngland].''[82] Blathwayt and his faction were beaten, though they had fought step by step the movement for a complete restoration to Massachusetts of its former rights.[83] Much against his will, he was forced to take an

---

[80] *Andros Tracts*, II, 9–10; quoted from Increase Mather, ''A Narrative of the Miseries of New-England.'' (See also Murdock, *Increase Mather*, p. 207.)

[81] One of Blathwayt's cousins was imprisoned with Andros and Randolph, Thomas Trefry, who in 1685, when Lord Bath had raised a regiment in Cornwall, was made ensign, and was afterwards sent as lieutenant in command of a detachment of the regiment to New England. He was related to Blathwayt on the Vivian side. (*Hutchinson Papers*, II, 302; also Goodrick, *Edward Randolph*, VI, f.n., p. 208; *Cal. S. P. Col.*, 1689–1692, p. 100.)

[82] *Diary of Samuel Sewall*, I, 255; also quoted in Toppan, *Edward Randolph*, II, f.n., p. 84.

[83] Goodrick, *Edward Randolph*, VI, 328; Randolph said that Mather was reporting to the people of Massachusetts that, as a result of their stand on

active part in the drafting of the new charter in October, 1691, the account of which appears at a later point in this study.[84] Suffice it to say, that when this somewhat mangled document finally appeared, New England showed its hatred for Blathwayt by holding him responsible for all omissions. In this they were largely in error, for Cotton Mather, writing in Boston, far away from the original scene, became so confused in his account that he identified the incident of 1688 with that of 1691. His mistake is indicative of the deep grudge which he cherished against Blathwayt. "This notwithstanding, the Clerk of the Council made a false entry of the King's Order, as if wee were to be settled like Barbados, etc., at which our Tories there grew mighty brisk. But before the month was out, they grew down in the mouth. The clerk's [Blathwayt's] forgery was discovered, and by Order, our Charter was finished (though not yet sealed) by which our Colony, unto which the Eastern parts were added, have power to choose D[eputy]-Governor and Assistants, and all General Officers, on the last Wednesday of every May."[85]

Blathwayt himself was in no tender mood toward New England. He was outraged to hear of Phips's ill-starred expedition against the French, and he poured forth his feelings in a long letter to Nottingham, the Tory secretary of state, then abroad with William III. "This misfortune is not to be slighted; for besides the expense of £50,000 to a poor country and a visible damage of perhaps as much more, the king's credit and dominions have been exposed by an ignorant and perverse generation of people, declared enemies of royal authority. Under what

New England, Halifax, Danby, Southwell, and Blathwayt were to be removed from their offices. (Randolph to Blathwayt, December 30, 1689.)

[84] *Infra*, pp. 421–423.

[85] *Diary of Cotton Mather*, I, 140–141; letter to John Cotton, Boston, 14d, 7m., 1691. Mr. Ford in his footnote states that Cotton Mather "unaccountably" confuses the two incidents.

commission and by whose allowance did they undertake this unfortunate expedition, and who made this poor knight a general the same year he was publicly christened at Boston? They have not so much as thought fit formally to impart this design to his Majesty, or to have received his advice or directions which the greatest of his allies, not to say his subjects, would have done in a matter of much less importance. But the damage will not be theirs alone, and if the French take their further revenge upon New England this summer—as they, in conjunction with the Indians, have destroyed a considerable part of it already—the blow will reach all the other plantations which are under his Majesty's Government, and have an immediate effect upon the revenue of the customs and manufactures of England. This I foretold very early, as I foresee greater and irreparable mischief if not prevented by a higher hand, for how can it be otherwise while a mean and mechanical sort of people shall pretend to and abuse the highest acts of royal government under the color of an imaginary charter they have justly forfeited?''[86]

With this scorching invective, we can dismiss the problems of New England and return to some of the less controversial aspects of Blathwayt's colonial activities. He had now entered upon the second period of his secretaryship, a period of continuous conflict. During the anxious months of 1688–1689, no serious question had been raised as to whether Blathwayt was, or was not, to continue as secretary to the Lords of Trade. He was, it was true, in temporary disfavor in military circles and for a brief period was actually displaced as secretary at war, but except for his stand on New England, he had done nothing, as far as the colonies were concerned, to invite criticism either at home or in the plantations.[87] He had been a most

[86] *Cal. S. P. Dom.*, 1690–1691, pp. 297–298; March 6, 1691.

[87] Goodrick, *Edward Randolph*, VI, 34, 328, 330. Randolph congratulating

efficient secretary. A careful study of the documents reveals no instance of laxity on his part in carrying out
orders. At the same time, he had not been too officious.
While the Admiralty and the crown law officers had
shown themselves amazingly dilatory, especially in the
case of Edward Randolph and his various missions to
New England, Blathwayt had dispatched the orders of the
Lords of Trade with commendable promptness, often
sending them out on the same day they had been issued.
He did not allow the work of the plantation office to suffer
because he had more than one office to fill, and except for
occasional lapses, coöperated very effectively with the
other departments.

Believing that the governor was the keystone of sound
colonial administration, Blathwayt had been careful to
throw in his influence on the side of such able colonial executives as Stapleton, Andros, Stede, and Molesworth. He
condemned Albemarle as an improper choice. He made a
mistake, it is true, in supporting Cranfield, but he admitted this when it came to the controversy between the
latter and the so-called rebel, Gove.[88] Blathwayt condemned Governor Cony of Bermuda and tried to effect a
change there, but to no avail. It seems that he advised
Randolph to secure the post for himself, and we know that
the latter entertained the idea for a short time, in 1685.[89]

Blathwayt on having retained his secretaryship, which, he said, the New
Englanders would gladly have seen him forfeit.

[88] Toppan, *Edward Randolph*, I, 264; also Sanborn, *Edward Gove and
Walter Barefoot, 1653–1691*, p. 26. Both Randolph and Blathwayt had been
won over to the justice of Gove's complaints against Cranfield and were instrumental in securing Gove's exoneration. Randolph wrote Southwell in
September, 1685, "Mr. Blathwait has got [Gove] set at liberty upon some
slight obligation to his majesty for his good behavior, by which means his
majesty will be freed from the charge of maintaining him in the Tower at £3
a week." Gove was acquitted on September 14, 1685.

[89] Toppan, *Edward Randolph*, I, 259; IV, 28; Randolph to Southwell,
August 1, 1685.

When Randolph finally decided against it, Blathwayt brought up the name of Mason, the New Hampshire claimant, ''Last weeke Mr. Blathwayt was proposing that Mr. Mason should quitt his pretensions in New England and lay all at his Majestie's feet upon his Majestie making him Governor of Bermodos and allowing to him and his heires 2 or 300£ yearely forever to be paid out of the quitt rents which will in a short tyme arise to his Majestie upon this settlement, for the people will rather pay to his Majestie 6d. an acre than one farthing to Mr. Mason, and now since Charters are at so low an ebb I feare his Grants will hardly hold out upon a tyrall at the Councill Board, but I know not what his conceptions may bee of such proposals. I believe this day at Winsor I may have a further discourse with Mr. Blathwayt of this matter.''[90] This somewhat businesslike proposal fell through, showing that there were stronger influences at work in colonial matters than Blathwayt. With the appointment of Governor Robinson, and the subsequent re-instatement of Governor Cony, Blathwayt had nothing to do; he considered Robinson an indifferent choice, and he must have marveled at Cony's audacity in reviving his case before the king and the Lords of Trade.

Up to 1690, Blathwayt had encountered many difficulties; but now as he looked back over his work, he must have thought the path smooth and simple by comparison with what he saw before him. War, he knew, meant a paralysis of trade and a curtailment in the revenues. It also meant added expense and an interruption in intelligence from the colonies. The whole system which Blathwayt and the Lords of Trade had been building up over a period of fifteen years was threatened with disaster. Of course, since he had not been living in a fool's paradise,

[90] Toppan, *Edward Randolph*, I, 267; IV, 59; Randolph to Southwell, October 3, 1685.

he had anticipated the French conflict. His distrust of the good faith of France had come out clearly in connection with the French treaty of neutrality, into which England had entered in 1686. Stapleton and the merchants and planters of the Leeward Islands had been eager to have the treaty effected and had petitioned the king for it. Jeaffreson, the agent for St. Kitts, reported: "And having gotten this petition thus signed, I took occasion the first day that their Lordships met to present it. . . . But it was not read that day. When I brought it to Mr. Blathwait, he said he wondered the merchants would trouble themselves now that Sir William Stapleton was here; and, for the Treaty of Neutrality, he sayd it was like a ball, that must be kept up to no purpose. But that men had gotten a notion of it, and would never lay it down, and that the French did but laugh at us for it, and would never do it, and that they had long since refused it. I sayd the Count of Blanarque and the French governor in the island are and have been all along most desirous of it (as our Petition imports); but he replyed, it was no matter what the French do there, since the French here do but make sport at it. This was as neere as I can remember the words of Esquire Blathwait, who promised nevertheless it should be read; but he added that if it were done, we should but deceive ourselves in expecting the French would keep it."[91] Blathwayt's opinion showed considerable insight into French policy, for by 1690 the treaty had come to an end.

Blathwayt now (1690) foresaw that war manoeuvres would be added to his regular duties in colonial and trade administration, and that his work as secretary to the Lords of Trade would have to be more or less submerged in that as secretary at war. Up to this time, his military

[91] Jeaffreson, *A Young Squire of the Seventeenth Century*, II, 255–256; Jeaffreson to the deputy-governor of St. Kitts, January 20, 1686.

duties in connection with the colonies had been trifling. Only the independent companies stationed in Barbados, the Leeward Islands, and New York, and (after 1686) the regiment in New England, had had to be cared for, and while the task had been a trying one on account of the scarcity of money, it had been slight as compared with that involved in the military expeditions planned after the outbreak of hostilities. After 1692, indeed, Blathwayt's presence was required by William III at the war front in the Low Countries, so that for months at a time he was absent from the plantation office. John Povey, to whom the care of the office was given, proved a hard working and an able deputy, but he did not have the influence, either at Whitehall or among the colonial officials, which Blathwayt possessed. Inevitably the more important work had to be postponed until Blathwayt's return in the fall, when for weeks the latter slaved feverishly at his desk in order to clear up an overloaded calendar.

Various features of the domestic situation complicated matters still further. William III, his mind intent upon European affairs, was a much less satisfactory master to work for than either Charles or James, and could not be trusted to refrain from entering into doubtful compromises in colonial matters in order to leave the stage clear for what were to him greater issues. The character of the Lords of Trade also changed. Matters of trade and plantations were now entrusted to a committee of the whole instead of to a small standing committee. Most of the great men in colonial administration of a decade earlier were dead. Of the original group, only two remained, Danby, now the Marquis of Caermarthen; and Halifax, soon to be Duke of Leeds. The latter resigned his privy seal in 1690, so his assistance could not be counted upon. Blathwayt probably did not regret this loss, for he could never forget that Halifax had been the supporter of

Massachusetts Bay in 1684. But no men of outstanding ability in colonial affairs came to replace those who had passed away. Sir Henry Goodricke, lieutenant-general of the ordnance, was a regular attendant at the meetings of the Lords of Trade, as likewise was Boscawen, one of the commissioners of the Admiralty, but neither was notable for his interest or capabilities. The third Earl of Bridgewater was perhaps the leading member, and he fortunately proved a loyal friend to Blathwayt, setting a high value on his work as secretary to the committee. The Tory Earl of Nottingham, Southwell's kinsman, also was frequently present, but he was not very conversant with the colonial situation, though he displayed a willing dependence on Blathwayt's superior knowledge.

A strong party feeling, which as the time went on became more rancorous, was now infused into the colonial situation. The equable party arrangement of 1689 soon came to an end. The resignation of the Whig leader, Lord Shrewsbury, from the southern department, in the spring of 1690, left the Tories in control of the secretariat until 1694, when Shrewsbury returned to office. The appointment, late in 1690, of Sydney, soon to be created the Earl of Romney, while politically important, had little effect on the secretarial work of the office, for Sydney was lazy. Nottingham and Blathwayt thus came to be regarded by the Whigs as in control of the plantations, if we are to judge from the attacks made upon them in 1696 and 1697.[92] Blathwayt fell under suspicion of Jacobite leanings, the Earl of Monmouth bringing this charge against him to Queen Mary. It became more and more apparent that he was *persona non grata* in Whig circles, although

[92] Nottingham was dismissed from the secretarial office late in 1693 as a result of the naval disasters of that summer, and was succeeded by the Whiggish Trenchard.

it was not until 1696–1697 that he was to feel the full force of their enmity.

Despite Whig opposition, Blathwayt still held an important position in colonial circles, during these years, although the issuance of the Massachusetts Bay charter in 1691, in the face of his disapproval, shows that his word was no longer as weighty as it had been. How much influence he had over the post-revolutionary appointments to colonial offices is a matter of conjecture. Probably, after Shrewsbury's resignation, he and Nottingham had matters very much their own way. They were responsible for the appointment of Andros in Virginia, after Lord Howard of Effingham had refused to resume his post there, and of Colonel Fletcher in New York, who was suggested to them by Sir Robert Southwell. They also arranged for Nicholson's transfer from deputy governor of New York to a similar, but more important, post in Virginia. The first of the lists of proposed governors drawn up in 1689 is in Blathwayt's hand. Whether that indicates anything more than that he jotted down the names which came up for consideration at the meeting of the Lords of Trade, we cannot say, since he disapproved of many of the men finally selected.[93] Both he and the Lords of Trade were in favor of retaining able governors in office, Lord Howard, for instance. Blathwayt was enthusiastic over the reappointment in Jamaica of Molesworth, of whose ability he had a very high opinion, but Molesworth's death almost immediately raised the problem of a successor. Lord Inchiquin, who succeeded him, took care to solicit Blathwayt's favor.[94] As a rule, when a local man

93 *Cal. S. P. Col.*, 1689–1692, pp. 35, 39–40, 77, 99; three lists appear, one for May 4th, another for May 16th, a third for July 3rd; the final list is dated July 19, 1689.

94 Add. MSS. 9735, f. 66; August 5, 1689. Inchiquin was appointed in September.

offered himself and showed outstanding qualifications, Blathwayt supported him for governor. Beeston, a Jamaican planter of prominence, who succeeded to the governorship of the island on Inchiquin's death, was a case in point. Blathwayt wrote that he was "the most knowing and honestest man I have been acquainted with belonging to the plantations," a generally accepted opinion.[95]

Of the able governors in office during these years, the elder Codrington, alone, seems to have met with Blathwayt's disapproval. Yet it is hard to see how anyone of Blathwayt's temper could have spoken ill of Codrington's military endeavors in the West Indies. Probably he disliked the democratic and Whiggish leanings of both the Codringtons, and was piqued because the younger Codrington recognized the Earl of Peterborough, son of his own enemy, the Earl of Monmouth, as his patron, just as his father had earlier looked to Monmouth for support.[96] Of the elder Codrington he wrote: "No man is better known in the West Indies than Colonel Codrington having distinguished himself by affecting popularity in assemblies, but it is conceived His Majesty has very many subjects in those parts as well as in England more capable of serving his Majesty than he is presumed to be."[97] If any rule guided Blathwayt in recommending men for colonial governorships at this time, it was that they possess military qualifications. This was a logical stand for him to take and was based on honest conviction, not on a desire to advance the army officers whom he served as secretary at war. Thus, it was largely because he deemed Sir William Phips, "poor knight," such a bad general,

[95] Add. MSS. 34351, ff. 1–2; Blathwayt to Caermarthen, July 14, 1692. Beeston was at first merely a deputy governor.

[96] *Cal. S. P. Col.*, 1708–1709, p. 521; Parke to the Board of Trade, November 14, 1709.

[97] Huntington MSS., Blathwayt Papers relating to America, 1681–1741; undated draft of a report entitled "Reflections on the Colonies."

that he condemned him. He placed a high value on the office of governor and had no desire to see it demeaned by interlopers.

In the matter of appointments, Blathwayt had only the power of recommendation; to the men who were ever ready to thank him for his good offices in securing them their posts, he had no authority to issue commissions. We have the word of his clerk, Adam Cardonnel, that even when he was acting secretary of state in Flanders, Blathwayt was always diffident in taking the lead in the matter of recommendations. In connection with a post for Matthew Prior, the poet, then in England's diplomatic service, Cardonnel wrote in 1695; "I wish we could do something for poor Prior. Mr. Blathwayt I know here is well inclined, and would gladly serve him, but you know how slow he is in those matters and then he very seldom cares for moving the king in such concerns without a handle or staff to go by, so that if my Lord Duke [Shrewsbury] would say something of it to Mr. Blathwayt and propose the care to be taken of him, I fancy Mr. Blathwayt would make use of it."[98]

It may well be, that it was only in recommendations growing out of his work as temporary secretary of state that Blathwayt showed such reluctance to act until he had the support of his Whig colleague, the "Lord Duke." Men continued to approach him as though his influence were fairly important. When the Earl of Inchiquin died, Colonel Beckford, the president of the Jamaican council, wrote to him, "as a friend and patron of the distressed island . . . to procure a just and honest gentleman as a new governor," recommending Blathwayt's friend, Colonel Sweet. This recommendation Blathwayt ignored in

[98] S. P. For., Military Expeditions, I, 21; Cardonnel to Vernon, the duke's secretary, June 6, 1695.

favor of Beeston.[99] Even Philip Ford, Penn's agent, wrote
to Blathwayt in 1694, to urge that William Markham,
deputy governor of Pennsylvania and the proprietor's
cousin, might be freed from his dependence on Fletcher,
governor of New York, an arrangement which the war
had made advisable. In a letter, extremely illiterate and
hard to follow, he wrote: "If Secretary Blathwayt give
W[illiam] P[enn's] respects to the Duck [Duke] of
Leeds and ask it as a kindness, if cannot otherwise do it, to
be sure you two can."[100]

After the war had begun (1690), Blathwayt was naturally beset by new administrative difficulties. Prior to
1689, his inter-departmental connections had been primarily with the Treasury, the commissioners of the customs, and the secretary of state. His relations with the
Admiralty had been more or less casual, growing out of
the need for securing ship passes, frigates to patrol colonial waters, and occasional convoys. The war threw him
into daily communication with every branch of the government dealing with the army and navy. There were
four expeditions to the West Indies between 1689 and
1694. In view of the lack of official coördination, it is not
to be wondered at that preparations for these were hard
to make, and that all of them started out late and ended in
failure. The Admiralty and the commissioners of the
navy were the chief procrastinators and offenders, and
their attitude rendered the victualling board and the commissioners of transport virtually helpless. Preparations
for the expedition to Jamaica, in 1694, were begun in August, while Blathwayt was still abroad, so that John
Povey had to manage the task of whipping plans into
shape. When the latter wrote to the navy board with regard to ships to be secured, they replied that they were

[99] Porlock MS.; Jamaica, January 29, 1692.
[100] *Cal. S. P. Col.*, 1693–1696, p. 418; December 14, 1694.

too busy with the Mediterranean expedition; a stand in
which they were upheld by the Admiralty.[101] Povey, therefore, turned to the commissioners of the transport, to find
out what ships were available.[102] He was supported in his
efforts by George Clarke, Blathwayt's deputy secretary
at war. Estimates were drawn up and the Treasury gave
its promise that the necessary funds would be provided.[103]
Weeks passed, and nothing was done. On October 9th, the
victualling board announced that they could furnish no
food, since they had to equip Admiral Russell's fleet.[104]
The transport board was then ordered to accept the task.
When Blathwayt returned home, on November 18th, matters were still at a standstill. He attacked the problem immediately, insisted that the Treasury produce the money
they had promised, ordered the transport board to hurry,
and demanded that medical supplies be gathered together
at once.[105] For all his energy, the situation did not visibly
improve. In December the transport board came with a
tale of woe, that having provided for 1841 men, they now
discovered that only 1400 were actually to be sent. Who
was responsible for the error, and who was to bear the
needless expense that had been incurred? Then rose the
question of who was to be the superior authority in command, the naval or the military commander-in-chief?[106] It
was a disgraceful scene and little calculated to inspire
respect for any of the departments concerned; one, moreover, in which personal politics and party ambitions were
as much to blame as departmental disorganization.

101 *Cal. S. P. Col.*, 1693–1696, p. 334; August 20, 1694.
102 *Ibid.*, p. 335; August 21, 1694.   103 *Ibid.*, pp. 338, 339, 345, 353.
104 *Ibid.*, pp. 371, 387.   105 *Ibid.*, pp. 404, 405.
106 The expedition did not finally get under way until January. See the
entries in the *Calendar* for December 5th and 16th, 1694. The transport
board was more willing to coöperate than the victualling board even though
Blathwayt's cousin, Francis Povey, was the secretary of the latter. His
friend, Robert Henley, was then on the transport board.

On the civil side, the paralysis was almost as great. Blathwayt could not make unwilling lords attend meetings of the Lords of Trade, nor could he make them take definite action when they did come, unless they were willing to do so. There was no time for constructive work. Colonial officials began to complain that letters from Whitehall were too long in transit or did not arrive at all. Colonial agents and planters in London reported that they could not make the Lords of Trade come to any decision. Blathwayt was away from the office, engaged either in his war duties in England or abroad with William III. Disgraceful cases of negligence in colonial administration resulted. Kendall, the governor of Barbados, a man singularly unfortunate in his dealings with the island, though his motives seem to have been of the best, reported that an elections act had actually been disallowed by the king without his (Kendall's) knowing it, though the matter was familiar enough to his enemies in the colony. He did not believe that the Lords of Trade had even so much as seen his letter to Blathwayt, in which he explained the need for the act, nor heard his agent, Mr. Bridges.[107]

The situation was intolerable, and men began to talk of the need of some administrative change. As early as 1692, the first summer Blathwayt was in attendance on the king, the Earl of Mulgrave made his famous complaint against the way things were going. Highly disgruntled, he suggested that the king ''order a certain number of privy councillors to be a standing committee for the plantations, and of such as are likely to attend to it, and that it

---

[107] *Cal. S. P. Col.*, 1693–1696, pp. 162–163; Kendall to the Lords of Trade, September 18, 1693. Kendall was a military officer whose appointment Blathwayt had sponsored. He was very eager to do his best as a governor. (See *ibid.*, 1689–1692, pp. 496–499; Kendall to the Lords of Trade, July 4, 1691.)

should meet two evenings in a week, on fixed days, and not according to the leisure or the humor of a president of the council. . . . You will be pleased to observe that I propose a select number for all committees instead of all the council, as it is now; because now everybody's business is nobody's whereas the other way, such will be charged with it, who are most capable of attending and understanding it.'' He declared that much of the disorder which had crept into the council and committee meetings was unknown to the king; he called attention to the miserable way in which the clerks read petitions some of which were too ridiculous to merit attention; to the ''indecencies'' and ''irregularities'' of the clerks and the doorkeepers; and to the absurd hours of meetings. Povey may have been doing his best to fill Blathwayt's place in the latter's absence, but his best did not satisfy Mulgrave, for he said: ''If Mr. Povey give a constant weekly account to Mr. Blathwayt of all that passes at the committee of plantations in your [William's] absence, it may be seen by you. But, however, it will be some kind of obligation on that committee, to look after their business.''[108]

That the dissatisfaction which Mulgrave voiced was widespread, may be seen from an item in a news-letter of December 12, 1693: ''A commission is drawing to constitute a Committee of Trade, which is to be composed of merchants, who are to sit in the City and to transmit matters to the Lords of the Admiralty, and it is said that citizens will be added to the Lords of the Admiralty.''[109] It was clear that the influential men in trade circles had done with the Lords of Trade. Though that body had

[108] Cal. S. P. Dom., 1691–1692, pp. 543–544; undated, but the date has been fixed at 1692. Blathwayt had apparently been satisfied with Povey's work, and the latter had been communicating with him regularly. In a few instances we learn that Povey postponed a matter until Blathwayt's return. (Cal. S. P. Col., 1695–1696, p. 428.)

[109] Cal. S. P. Dom., 1693, p. 426.

served effectively for fifteen years of peace, two years of war were enough to prove its uselessness in meeting new conditions. What Blathwayt could have done, to stem the increasing popular dissatisfaction, can now only be surmised. He certainly could not have been blind to the situation, but apparently he offered no remedy. Clearly he did not take the growing demand for a change as a personal affront. He threw in his support whole-heartedly for the enactment of a more stringent act of trade in 1696, and he made no opposition to the establishment of the Board of Trade in the same year.

CHAPTER VI

SURVEYOR AND AUDITOR GENERAL OF PLANTATION REVENUES. THE FIRST PHASE, 1680–1688

IN May, 1680, Blathwayt entered upon a new relationship with the colonies. He was appointed surveyor and auditor general of the royal revenues, in the colonies under the direct control of the crown—Virginia, Jamaica, Barbados, and the Leeward Islands. Within a few months New Hampshire and Massachusetts Bay were added to the list, for the latter was drawn into the system even before the loss of its charter. As other colonies were converted into royal colonies, they too were included within the system, so that ultimately Blathwayt had supervision over ten of the plantations—the six already mentioned, and, in addition, Bermuda, New York, Maryland, and the Jerseys. North and South Carolina were later included, but not until many years after Blathwayt's day. It was a far-reaching project, and to modern eyes a Utopian one, but Blathwayt set himself to his task very gravely and in the face of serious handicaps achieved fair success. He held the post until his death, thirty-seven years later.

The office was newly created in 1680, and Blathwayt was its first incumbent. It was an expression of a colonial policy, to which the Treasury, the commissioners of the customs, and the Lords of Trade, to say nothing of the Privy Council and parliament, had committed themselves: the determination to hold the colonies to a strict accountability, financial and political, and thus to reduce them to that state of dependence which a well-ordered mercantilist state required. The Lords of Trade showed their authority in new instructions to the governors, as well as in repeated demands that they be prompt and regular in their correspondence and that colonial secretaries be punctual in their transmission of colonial acts and the proceedings of the councils and assemblies. The Treasury and the commissioners of the customs adopted an equally rigorous policy in their efforts to compel a strict enforcement of the Acts of Trade and Navigation, by means of royal collectors appointed in the colonies and through watchful surveillance by such men as Edward Randolph—collector, surveyor, and searcher of New England customs (1678). Their primary concern was to introduce a stringent fiscal policy and to relieve England of any financial burden for the ordinary civil and military needs of the royal colonies. To this end, they aimed at the passage of a perpetual revenue act in each royal colony, in order to provide an adequate civil list, and so relieve the governor from the fear of starvation if he opposed the local legislatures. In order to keep proper account of the revenues thus granted, it was necessary to introduce a system of periodic audit before an agent of the English Exchequer.

In order to develop the history of the growth of the office of auditor general of plantation revenues, certain preliminary comments on the revenues of the royal colonies are necessary, even at the risk of repetition. As students familiar with the fiscal history of the colonies know, a careful line of distinction was drawn in the royal colonies between royal and local revenues. Certain revenues were peculiarly the king's: the quit-rents and such casual revenues as fines, forfeitures, licenses, prizes, and escheats. These could be claimed by the king for his own use or given over to the colonies to help make up their civil lists. Both practices were resorted to. Revenues arising under the Act of Trade of 1673, the so-called plantation duties, were also the king's, but these were remitted to England and were in no sense ever regarded as provincial, nor were they in any way involved in this question of the royal audit. Local revenue was that which was raised by acts of the assemblies and was voted annually or for a brief period of time. It was administered by the local treasurer, who was responsible to the assembly. Since, in no instance, was it true that the quit-rents or the casual revenues were sufficient for the ordinary expenses of a province, it was necessary to find some supplementary source. England could have provided for the deficit herself, but this would have raised too great a parliamentary opposition. As a matter of fact, England had no desire to pay even the governors' salaries, to say nothing of those of the lesser officials. The alternative, therefore, was to compel the royal provinces to pass permanent revenue acts, or such as would extend over a period of years, out of which the civil lists and the regular military needs of the colonies could be met.

This was the problem which English colonial administrators had been facing in all of the royal colonies since the Restoration. Efforts to find some solution for it had been vigorous for a few years after 1660 and had met with considerable success in two of the colonies. In 1663, Barbados had passed the famous four and a half per cent. export duty on all dead commodities. The following year a similar duty was enacted in the Leeward Islands, each of the four local assemblies giving their assent. The revenue was, technically, to be in lieu of all other sources of income which the king might demand, and it replaced an earlier system of quit-rents which had proved unremunerative. As we know, the four and a half per cent. reve-

nues failed to yield the anticipated profits. Prior claims
on the part of the original proprietors hampered matters.
Collection of the revenue also turned out to be very difficult, and in 1670 England resorted to a system of farming,
under which the farmers agreed to collect the duty for a
period of seven years at an annual rental of £7000, in Barbados, and of £700, in the Leeward Islands. The farming
of the revenue also proved unsatisfactory. At the end of
the seven years, England had realized only £20,975.19.8 of
the £49,000 which she had anticipated from the Barbados
farm, while that of the Leeward Islands had proved
equally disappointing.[1] Nevertheless, since no better solution offered, the farms were renewed for another seven
years, but at a reduced rental in Barbados, £5300 instead
of the original £7000.[2]

In other ways the fund failed to satisfy either England
or the two colonies, especially Barbados. It had been
agreed that the ordinary expenses of the government, including the governor's salary and the military needs of
the islands, were to be met out of the four and a half per
cent. Any amount in excess was to be at the disposal of
the king, although the Barbadians understood that it was
to be spent in the colony. The king, however, regarded the
revenue as peculiarly his own, to be disposed of as he
chose. A wrangle with the Barbadians ensued, which continued during Blathwayt's period of activities. Not until
one hundred and seventy-five years after the passage of
the act, did the quarrel come to an end, and then only because the act was repealed.[3] The Barbadians were especially enraged because the four and a half per cent. duty
raised in their island was used to defray the military ex-

---

[1] *Cal. Treas. Papers*, 1557–1696, pp. 12–13.

[2] *Ibid.*, p. 14; Beer, *The Old Colonial System*, Pt. I, Vol. I, 171–192. When
that farm lapsed, in 1684, it had yielded only £22,000.

[3] Beer, *The Old Colonial System*, Pt. I, Vol. I, 181.

penses of the Leeward Islands; the £700 available in these islands was sufficient only for the governor's salary, making it necessary to use part of the Barbadian revenue to pay the two companies of foot, stationed there at an annual expense of £2778.10.8. The Lords of Trade ignored the unpopularity of the four and a half per cent. as long as possible, but the passage of an act in Barbados repealing the duty without providing any substitute convinced them that the time was ripe for an investigation, and in 1679 they reported the matter to the Treasury.[4]

In Jamaica and Virginia there had been no early attempts to secure permanent revenue acts. Both colonies were for a time partly dependent on England. In 1663, £2500 had been settled on Jamaica, £1000 of which was to pay the governor's salary. Quit-rents were presently resorted to, and it was hoped that these, with the fines, forfeitures, and license fees, would provide an adequate civil list. Although this hope was not realized, England withdrew her subsidies in 1670 and instructed the governor to secure the passage of an annual revenue act. The act was not passed, and in 1677 more rigorous measures were planned. Not only was Jamaica to be compelled to provide a revenue, but that revenue was to be permanent, and the act providing for it was to be drafted in England. This was only one of a ready-made set of laws which were to be forced on the colony; Poynings' Law was being adapted to Jamaica. The plan met with the spirited opposition that might have been expected. The assembly refused its assent to the whole program, even to the revenue bill, which read nearly word for word with the act passed in Jamaica in 1675.[5] By October, 1680, the Lords of Trade,

4 C. O. 391: 3, 30–37.

5 Beer, *The Old Colonial System*, Pt. I, Vol. I, 208–212. The main objection in England to the law of 1675 was that it substituted a local collector for the royal receiver of the revenue. Needless to say, that point was corrected in the bill drafted in England.

after consultation with the Jamaica merchants, the agents of the island, and the law officers of the crown, decided that their stand was impolitic, if not untenable. They retracted even on the question of a permanent revenue, since the agents had convinced them that the passage of an act for a longer period than seven years was impossible.[6] Accordingly, Sir Thomas Lynch, the new governor, persuaded the assembly to pass a seven-year act, and it was confirmed by the king in February, 1683.[7] That same year the assembly agreed to extend the seven-year limit to twenty-one years.[8]

In Virginia, too, the attempts to secure the enactment of a permanent revenue met with opposition. During the Commonwealth, the province had been thrown on its own resources. By a temporary provision made after the Restoration, England agreed to pay Governor Berkeley's salary, but as early as 1662 decided that Virginia must resume the burden. Berkeley succeeded in having his salary made payable out of the local export duty of two shillings per hogshead of tobacco, an annual levy. England was determined that this must be converted into a permanent grant and instructed Lord Culpeper, Berkeley's successor, to that effect. Accordingly, in 1682, the required act was passed, providing a permanent revenue from the two shillings duty, a tonnage duty of 15d., and a poll tax of 6d.

---

[6] C. O. 391: 13, 107–109, 114–115, 224–225.

[7] *Cal. S. P. Col.*, 1681–1685, pp. 309–310, 386. Before Lynch's arrival, the lieutenant governor, Sir Henry Morgan, triumphantly reported the passage of a seven-year act, which was disallowed, however, because it stipulated that the governor was to give an annual account to the assembly of the way in which the funds had been disposed of. (*Ibid.*, pp. 125, 132, 315–316.)

[8] *Ibid.*, p. 518. In 1704, on its expiration, the act was renewed for another twenty-one year period. England did not, however, abandon her efforts to secure a perpetual revenue act and always included the proposal in the governors' instructions. Not until 1728, a decade after Blathwayt's death, were her efforts successful. (*Ibid.*, 1702–1703, pp. 211–212; 1704–1705, pp. 27–28, 147, 241.)

on every immigrant. It was calculated that these sources would bring in £3000 annually.[9]

Once a permanent revenue was secured in the royal colonies, the next step was a royal audit. The idea of such supervision was not new, either for the royal revenues accruing in the colonies or for the money which had been payable out of the Exchequer.[10] In Virginia an auditor, presumably with jurisdiction over the crown revenues of a casual nature, as well as over the levies granted by the assembly, had been appointed by local act within a few years after the Restoration. The office had subsequently been made a patent office under the crown. Thomas Stegg, a Virginian and a member of the council, had been the first to hold it. On his death, in 1670, a dispute arose with regard to the method of appointment. There were two claimants, John Lightfoot, an Englishman, who had secured his nomination under the great seal, and Edward Digges, a resident of Virginia, who had been appointed by Governor Berkeley. An investigation of the counter-claims followed, and on the basis of priority, Digges's right to the office was upheld.[11] No rule, however, was laid down for the future (in characteristic English fashion during this period), but the creation of Blathwayt's office, so shortly after, afforded a remedy. Some activity was manifested by the various Virginia auditors, as the books

[9] Beer, *The Old Colonial System*, Pt. I, Vol. I, 192–199; Osgood, *The American Colonies in the 18th Century*, I, 25–26; also C. O. 391: 2, 283–284.

[10] It may be that England had some idea of audit in mind when, in 1663, she created the office of receiver general of plantation revenues, although the use of the term, *receiver*, renders such an explanation difficult. Too little activity was manifested by the patentees for any conclusions with regard to its purpose to be drawn. (Andrews, *Guide to Materials . . . P. R. O.*, II, 143; Beer, *The Old Colonial System*, Pt. I, Vol. I, f.n., p. 200.) The office was granted to Chiffinch and Brown, but sublet to Blathwayt's uncle, Thomas Povey.

[11] Osgood, *The American Colonies in the 18th Century*, I, 24.

and papers in the Treasury and plantation office indicate, but practically nothing was accomplished.

During the time Jamaica had been dependent on English bounty, England had demanded a declaration of accounts from the governors, and the Declared Accounts reveal that the governors, in the main, complied with their instructions.[12] Here we have the germ of the royal audit, since the accounts of Sir Thomas Lynch, lieutenant governor from 1671 to 1675, include the proceeds not only of the quit-rents and the casual revenue but also of the tonnage duty, a local levy applied to the support of the government.[13] These accounts were secured most unwillingly from the governors, partly because it took so much time and effort to make them out. Lord Vaughan, Lynch's successor, made no similar declaration, and attempts to force him to do so proved unavailing. Nevertheless, he did transmit a few accounts to the Lords of Trade.[14]

Evidence that England was resolved to hold the royal colonies to stricter account appears for several months prior to the creation of the office of auditor general. In session after session, the Lords of Trade dealt with the whole range of colonial finance, while the Treasury manifested the same activity. Blathwayt was associated with their investigations at every step, hence he was the logical choice for the new office. On February 3, 1680, the secretary of the Treasury board ordered him to give what information he could of the various "revenues and profits arising or due to the King from or in any of his Majesty's

---

[12] Accounts running from 1662 to 1675 are to be found, although there is a gap from January, 1669, to June, 1671. It is noteworthy that they extend for four years beyond the time when England withdrew her support except for an annual grant of £600 for defense. (A. O. Declared Accounts, Nos. 1274: 248D, 250, 251, 252, 253.)

[13] Ibid., 1274: 253.

[14] Cal. S. P. Col., 1675–1676, pp. 341–344.

Plantations.''[15] On March 22, 1680, he instructed the attorney-general to draft a commission authorizing "Mr. Blathwayte to *receive* the revenue arising to the King from the Plantations, . . . in Africa and America; consulting Blathwayte thereon and leaving blanks for the term and the salary.''[16]

By Blathwayt's patent, certain revenues were definitely excluded from the royal audit. Blathwayt was not to "intermeddle in or with the customs, imports, or duties arising here in England on anything imported from said colonies or with any [plantation] bonds or obligations taken in pursuance of Any act of Parliament heretofore made or with any rates payable to the King for goods transported from one Plantation to another under the Act of 25 Car. II. [7]''[17] The exclusion was natural, for the custody of such revenues was in the hands of the commis-

---

[15] *Cal. Treas. Bks.*, 1679–1680, VI, 420.

[16] *Ibid.*, p. 487. The use of the words, *receive* and *Africa*, was unintentional. The patent was issued on May 19, 1680, and stated that a privy seal had been issued "for erecting and establishing an office of general inspection, examination, and audit of all and singular accounts of all moneys arising or accruing or which shall arise or accrue to the king from any of his foreign dominions, Colonies, and Plantations in America." The purpose of the office was "to make some better provisions for the due payment to us and our heirs and successors of our said revenues and for the due and orderly taking, examining and stating the accounts of all and every the collectors, auditors, treasurers, sub-collectors, and other inferior officers, ministers, and persons to whom the collecting, levying or receiving of any such moneys may appertain. The chief officer of said office is to be hereby styled the surveyor and auditor general of all his Majesty's revenues arising in America, and William Blathwayt is hereby appointed thereto with full power to inspect, examine, state and audit, and, with the consent of the Treasury Lords, to determine all accounts of all such rents, revenues, prizes, fines, escheats, forfeitures, duties, and profits whatsoever accrued since the beginning of his Majesty's first war with the Dutch and not before and all such as shall at any time hereafter accrue . . . to hold during good behavior." Blathwayt's Journal, Treas. 64: 88; the patent is entered in full at the beginning of the volume; *ibid.*, pp. 544–545.

[17] *Ibid.*, pp. 544–545.

sioners of the customs. Blathwayt was careful never to violate this injunction. It meant that, from the outset, one colonial collector was outside of his jurisdiction,—the agent appointed by the customs authorities in England to collect the plantation duty of 1673.[18]

Until satisfactory civil lists had been secured in each colony, England intended to hold them accountable for their local levies and argued that such revenues were as truly royal as the casual revenues.[19] The instructions given to Lord Carlisle, newly appointed governor of Jamaica, in November, 1680, indicated this determination. It was declared that public money could be issued only on the governor's warrant and was to be subject to royal audit, although "the assembly may be nevertheless permitted from time to time to view and examine the ac-

[18] Many of these officials, however, were also the receivers of the quit-rents and the casual revenues, for, with the scarcity of officials in the colonies and the small salaries paid, such pluralism was inevitable. In this second capacity, they came under Blathwayt's control.

[19] As has been stated, the collection of the local levies was in the hands of the provincial treasurer, but as these levies were made permanent or periodic, rather than annual, England frequently gave to the royal receiver of the casual revenues authority to collect them. Thus at the beginning, and, in many colonies, throughout the entire period, the provincial treasurer was as much under Blathwayt's orders as the royal receiver. When Blathwayt, many years later, made the following statement he was referring not to the revenues appropriated by the colonial assemblies for the ordinary uses of the government but to peculiarly local levies, granted for some local emergency. In his report to the Treasury in 1701, Blathwayt stated: "There are diverse other Revenues or Levies granted and raised annually in the respective Plantations by the respective Assemblies there under the denomination of Country Revenues, for which they appoint particular Treasurers with Directions that those Revenues be not issued without warrant from the said Assemblies, and for which these Treasurers do not hold themselves accountable to any other than the Assembly who take to themselves the sole Cognizance and disposal of what is so raised for uses relating to themselves and presents to their governors as particularly in New York during the late war and elsewhere at several times and upon several occasions, whereof no regular account is returned from thence." (Treas. 64: 89, f. 52. For the entire report, see ff. 45–53. The report is repeated in large part in March, 1703, *ibid.*, ff. 78–84.)

counts of money or value of money which is paid off by virtue of such laws as they shall make, which you are to signify unto them as occasion shall arise.''[20] This was a confusing distinction which some of the colonies could not, or would not, understand. The point was never clarified in the Leeward Islands or in Barbados. Had the four and a half per cent. and the casual revenue there sufficed to meet the annual expenses of the government, the question would, of course, never have been raised. As it was, England kept calling for accounts of the local levies.

Blathwayt's patent was so worded that it included all the colonies from which royal revenues were, or might be, derived. This made it easy to enlarge Blathwayt's province as new colonies came under the direct supervision of the crown. Originally, it had applied only to Jamaica, Barbados, the Leeward Islands, and Virginia, and according to his patent, Blathwayt could command a salary from these colonies only. Since the original patent was never altered, new colonies being absorbed into the system by royal order transmitted through the Treasury, it was possible for a colony to argue that it was not obliged to pay Blathwayt anything. Both Maryland and New York did so, in order to escape an annoying financial obligation and to challenge the existence of an office which they maintained was unnecessary.[21]

The office of auditor general was created within the Exchequer, but Blathwayt's position as secretary to the Lords of Trade made it convenient for him to administer it within the plantation office. He continued to do so until the dissolution of the Lords of Trade, in 1696. Until his dismissal from the Board of Trade (1707), he had mail

---

20 C. O. 138: 3, 450.

21 By the patent, Barbados and Jamaica were to pay £150 each; Virginia and the Leeward Islands, £100. For a discussion of Blathwayt's salary, see *infra*, pp. 451–456.

relating to the audit addressed to the plantation office, so that for twenty-seven years the auditor generalship was so closely related to the plantation office as to be almost indistinguishable from it. His immediate superiors, however, were the Treasury Lords, and he always turned to them for instructions. Once the office was created, the Treasury issued very few new instructions and did not call for a periodic account of the revenues until the beginning of the eighteenth century.[22]

Letters drafted by Blathwayt, but reading in the name of the king or the Treasury, were dispatched on June 30, 1680, to the governors of the four colonies affected, apprising them of Blathwayt's appointment.[23] The governors were given strict injunctions to lend the new system their unfailing support. On July 5th, letters were sent to the collectors of the revenue.[24] The letters all indicated

[22] Blathwayt also complied, however, with orders given him by the secretaries of state, the Lords of Trade, or the Board of Trade. After 1689, he was liable to investigation by the parliamentary commissioners of accounts who were appointed from time to time, and some of the most informative material on the working of the office is to be derived from his reports to these commissioners.

[23] *Cal. Treas. Bks.*, 1679–1680, VI, 597–598.

[24] *Ibid.*, pp. 598–600. The letter dispatched to Thomas Martyn of Jamaica was more or less typical. Martyn collected the quit-rents, the casual revenues, and the assembly levies for royal purposes. He was enjoined "to immediately transmit to Blathwayt a particular catalogue or ledger book of all persons answerable to the King for any quit-rents or other payments whatsoever by reason of any lands held by them of the Crown or by virtue of any concession or obligation whatsoever, as also the particular sums or value of money for which such persons stand charged or indebted to the King; together with copies of all laws and public acts concerning the revenues, to the end Blathwayt may be the better enabled to allow or disallow of such accounts as shall come before him and take care for the more effectual charging such persons as shall be found in default; and in general to follow said Blathwayt's directions. We are resolved to take a very exact account from time to time of your observance thereof." The Virginian auditor, Nathaniel Bacon, was also notified, for the patent stated, "whereas there is an auditor general established in the Colony of Virginia, the latter is, from time to time, to transmit to said Blathwaite the full and particular state of all ac-

that the retroactive clause of Blathwayt's patent was to be taken seriously.

With the dispatch of these letters, the first step had been taken toward launching Blathwayt as auditor general. The gravest concern was the reception which the office would have in colonies even then engaged in a heated struggle with the crown on the question of permanent revenue acts. It may have been on this account that Blathwayt tarried for several months before appointing any deputy auditors. Not until April, 1681, did he make an appointment in Jamaica, and his choice then fell upon Reginald Wilson, a resident of the colony.[25] Wilson served until the Revolution of 1688.

In October, 1681, a deputy, by the name of Doughty, was appointed in Barbados, but nothing can be learned about him.[26] In February, 1683, he was superseded by Archibald Carmichael, who served for the rest of the decade.[27] He must have been satisfactory, for in 1687 Blathwayt obtained for him the post of naval officer in Barbados.[28]

No deputy was appointed for the Leeward Islands, where the governor apparently assumed full responsibility for transferring the accounts.[29]

In Virginia, the presence of an auditor prior to the

counts of money arising [to his Majesty] in the said Colony.'' Both the king and the Treasury took care to inform Bacon of his new accountability, and the Treasury in its letter implied that Bacon had been deplorably negligent of his duties. A letter was also directed to the surveyor general of Jamaica, to investigate thoroughly the state of the quit-rents and to assist the receiver in collecting those that were over-due.

25 Wilson was also the naval officer there, until, as he claimed, he was unjustly set aside by the governor, Lord Carlisle. (*Cal. Treas. Bks.* 1681–1685, Vol. VII, Pt. I, 111–112; *Cal. S. P. Col.*, 1681–1685, 305–306.)

26 Treas. 64: 88, f. 88.

27 *Ibid.*, f. 109; *Cal. Treas. Bks.*, 1681–1685, Vol. I, Pt. II, 719.

28 Porlock MSS.; Carmichael to Blathwayt, Sept. 14, 1687, a letter thanking him for the favor.

29 Treas. 64: 88, f. 88.

creation of Blathwayt's office made it unnecessary to make any immediate appointment, but the Virginians at once raised the question of how future auditors were to be appointed. They demanded that they continue to be nominated by the governor, without reference to Blathwayt or the Treasury. To this the Lords of Trade, to whom the matter had been referred by the Treasury, objected. They recommended that the Virginia auditors be appointed in precisely the same fashion as the deputy auditors, and their recommendation was adopted.[30]

The first responses to the letters of June 30th and July 5th, 1680, were sufficiently gratifying. Even "Panama Morgan," deputy governor of Jamaica in Lord Carlisle's absence, expressed his pleasure over the creation of the office. "We have received yours of November 12 last," the Treasury lords wrote to him in April, 1681, "and are glad to find you have set so good a precedent to all the superior officers in relation to the office of Auditor of his Majesty's revenue in America."[31] Such gracious acceptance on the part of the local officials meant nothing, as England was soon to learn. Within a few months Morgan had struck a defiant attitude on the question of the king's share in piratical seizures. "Nothing surprised me like Sir Harry's denying the pirate's money and telling the auditor he might go look [for] it in the King's Bench," Sir Thomas Lynch, the newly arrived governor, reported in September, 1682.[32]

Sir William Stapleton's reserve was preferable to Morgan's glib acquiescence. That excellent executive of the Leeward Islands wrote: "I shall use all diligence possible to execute his Majesty's royal pleasure in his mandamus to me relating to the office of surveyor and auditor

[30] *Cal. S. P. Col.*, 1681–1685, p. 100; August 16, 1681; C. O. 391: 3, 276.
[31] *Cal. Treas. Bks.*, 1681–1685, Vol. VII, Pt. I, 111.
[32] *Ibid.*, Pt. II, 781.

general of his Majesty's American revenue. I hope to give all the satisfaction which can be expected from me in order thereunto; only I must pray your lordships' excuse if the accounts cannot be transmitted so immediately as you are pleased to require, it being a work of time, little or no care having been taken therein hitherto, some parties accountable being dead and insolvent, the islands or members of this Government not being entire but dispersed and several alterations being made in the several particular governments and for other reasons now tedious to be inserted in favor of time. I beg of your Honors to think that I only urge this for no other reason and that you will be pleased to believe that as I have not hitherto given any just cause of complaint (that I know of) to any particular, I shall be very cautious how I give any occasion to his Majesty's ministers to find fault with me in not giving my assistance in all I can or may depend upon my duty and service in respect of His revenue.''[33] To Blathwayt he wrote that the retroactive requirement—for the accounts were to begin with the Dutch War of 1672—made the task more difficult.[34]

The first accounts to be received came from Jamaica and Virginia, and on October 4, 1680, Blathwayt made a report on them to the Treasury. Those from Jamaica had been brought back by Lord Carlisle on his return to England and were the ones which, in the normal course of duty, he should have remitted.[35] The actual accounts have been lost, but we know from the digest which Blathwayt drew up that he found them unsatisfactory, because no vouchers accompanied them. Apparently they were never de-

[33] Treas. 64: 88, ff. 63–64; October 26, 1680.

[34] *Ibid.*, f. 65; letter dated October 22, 1680.

[35] His predecessor, Lord Vaughan, however, had failed to present any accounts, so Blathwayt stated in his report. Carlisle's accounts covered one year, July, 1678, to July, 1679. (*Ibid.*, ff. 46–48; Blathwayt to the Treasury, Oct. 4, 1680.)

clared.[36] Unfortunately, Blathwayt was never able to impress on colonial officials the importance of the *voucher*. The first Virginia accounts met with his criticism for that reason. Blathwayt's report stated: "There is come to my hand from Virginia, by order of my Lord Culpeper, four Accompts, from the year 1676, to 1680, of the receipt of the Two Shillings per Hogshead on Tobacco for the support of the Government, Which Accompts are not so particular nor so attended with Vouchers as may be fit for the future when all persons concerned shall have understood His Majesty's Pleasure lately signified to them in that behalf. I have nevertheless drawn them separately into such a form as may be fit for your Lordships' View and also contracted them into one General Accompt with my Exceptions to some particulars which I shall take care to transmit to the Auditor there, in order to further satisfaction or redress therein."[37]

Stapleton's accounts were an unconscionable length of time in putting in an appearance. Finally, in March, 1683, he wrote that they were about ready for transmission, and a few months later they arrived.[38] Blathwayt found

---

[36] The digest was entitled: "A state of an accompt of his Majesty's Revenue arising in Jamaica by virtue of an act made there for raising an Impost upon Liquor and the Commodities imported and for granting of Wyne Licenses as also by Quit Rents of Land granted unto the Planters and for Prizes, Fines, Escheats, and Forfeitures and other Dutys belonging to his Majestie in that Island for one year ended the 18th of July 1679." The digest is to be found among the Hyde Papers, Add. MSS. 17019, f. 37. Blathwayt's chief objection to any of the items included in the accounts was that they belonged to an earlier period. He wanted to know whether they had been included in earlier accounts, and if not, why not. In this instance, Sir Henry Morgan was ordered to have Carlisle's accounts done over again and was instructed to warn the receiver that he was in danger of forfeiting his position if he did not obey the order promptly. (*Cal. Treas. Bks.*, 1681–1685, Vol. VII, Pt. I, 111; April 18, 1681.)

[37] Treas. 64: 88, ff. 46–48; *Cal. Treas. Bks.*, 1679–1680, VI, 699; 1681–1685, Vol. VII, Pt. I, 76. The accounts have disappeared altogether.

[38] C. O. 1: 51, 67; Stapleton to Blathwayt, March 20, 1683. Some supple-

them unsatisfactory and sent them back to Stapleton. He noted the lack of vouchers, and the absence of certain specific items of information. His digest of the accounts contains a series of neatly written queries, with answers in Stapleton's sprawling hand. The chief query was by what acts the levies were raised, and to this Governor Stapleton answered: "By the Acts and orders of the then Council and Assembly being made for no other purpose but to defray and satisfy the debts of the island by a levy, which being done the Acts were expired." Another query asked by whose orders the payments were made, to which the governor replied: "The Governor, Council and Assembly orders." Blathwayt also asked for more specific information with regard to the recipients, and dates, of payments.

The additional information which Stapleton vouch-

mental accounts appeared in 1684. Like the Jamaica and Virginia accounts they have all disappeared from the official records, but copies of some, for the island of Montserrat, for the years from July, 1672, to February, 1674, and from February, 1678, to March, 1681, were discovered a few years ago, among the family papers of the descendants of Sir William Stapleton. Included with them was a summarized account, in sterling, of the receipts in all the islands for the period of Stapleton's administration, a digest which had doubtless been drawn up by Blathwayt, since it resembled those for the Jamaica and Virginia accounts. They included a statement of receipts from the annual imposts on liquor, negroes, or whatever local levy had been passed to make up the deficit in the four and a half per cent. and the casual revenue. These accounts, and Blathwayt's digest of them, were discovered by Mr. C. S. S. Higham, formerly of the University of Manchester. They are now in the John Rylands Library, in Manchester, having been lent by Sir Miles Stapleton. For a brief article on them, by Mr. Higham, entitled ''Some Treasurer's Accounts of Montserrat, 1672–1681,'' see the *English Historical Review*, January, 1923, pp. 87–90. The receipts in Montserrat reflected the social and economic life there; they were derived from annual levies on Christians, slaves, rum works, waste lands, thatched houses. Fines had been imposed for many offenses, but chiefly for making ''corrupted'' indigo. Among the expenditures are to be found the items of so many pounds of sugar paid to the deputy governor, and the other officials of the island in salaries; for repairs to the public buildings and the fortifications; for food and drink for the governor's meeting with the council and assembly.

safed failed to satisfy either Blathwayt or the Treasury, and accordingly, when the governor returned to England in 1685, he was called upon to make further explanations. His disclosures were of little value. Since he disclaimed all knowledge of the accuracy of the accounts, there was no point in asking him to take an oath upon them. He told Blathwayt, in fact, that he was quite a stranger to the accounts, and for good reason; thus, he said: "Whatever I have received I am ready to take oath of it; but the public Accompts of those Islands have been kept by a Receiver in each Island, which are delivered in, and sworn to by them respectively before the Deputy Governor of each Island, which I hope will be Satisfactory, for I can no more swear to any public Accompts than he that never was there. I am accomptable for any Seizure I ordered the Marshal or any else to receive. Indeed were the Leeward Islands entire as Barbados or Jamaica, it might be as easy for me to give an Accompt upon Oath as not, but being remoter and more separate by the sea than England, Scotland, and Ireland, I am as ignorant of the Receipts and disbursements in the respective Islands as any man."[39]

Stapleton's assertion that accounts could be more easily secured from Barbados was not borne out by the facts. For several reasons, no accounts could be expected from Barbados for some time. The four and a half per cent. duty, which provided the major portion of the revenue, was already undergoing investigation in England under Blathwayt's direction. Otherwise there was really no revenue to report on. The casual revenues of the island were so slight that steps had to be taken to improve

[39] Treas. 64: 88, f. 173; October 20, 1685; also Stapleton's letter of October 10, 1684; *Cal. S. P. Col.*, 1681–1685, p. 695. Stapleton's accounts were apparently prepared for declaration, but owing to his death in 1686, the process was interrupted and the accounts were not passed until 1701, when Lady Stapleton succeeded in having final action taken. (A. O. Declared Accounts, 1236: 312; Treas. 64: 89, f. 95.)

them before there was any necessity for an audit, and, as
Sir Richard Dutton, the governor who went out to succeed
Sir Jonathan Atkins in the fall of 1680, reported a few
months after his arrival, there had been no local duty
levied on imports for the preceding eighteen months or
two years.[40]

As events in all of the four colonies proved, Blathwayt
had no easy task on his hands. Promises of accounts were
easier to extract than the accounts themselves. It is impossible to ascertain the regularity with which they were
transmitted, for the originals in almost every instance
have disappeared. From the records in the Treasury and
the plantation office, it is apparent that Virginia was the
most regular in transmitting them.[41] From the steady

[40] *Cal. S. P. Col.*, 1681–1685, p. 72; June 11, 1681. Both Sir Jonathan
Atkins and Sir Richard Dutton were called upon to give an account, after
their return to England, of the money each had received from the assembly
while governor of Barbados. Henry Guy, the secretary to the Treasury, ordered Blathwayt in July, 1682, to send immediately to Atkins for the accounts, which Blathwayt did, but with no apparent result. (*Cal. Treas. Bks.*,
1681–1685, Vol. VII, Pt. I, 533.) In 1683, when Dutton returned to England
temporarily, he was obliged to present a statement to Blathwayt, which the
latter presented to the Treasury on December 4, 1683. (Treas. 64: 88, f. 147.)
In 1685 when he came back permanently, a similar request was made of him
by the Treasury, and he replied: ''According to my Lord Treasurer's commands I have herewith sent you an account of what money was given by the
assembly of Barbados to his Majesty for my use, and my general account
lyeth before Mr. Blathwayt in which this is likewise expressed, which I am
ready to make account of it.'' (*Ibid.*, f. 169; see also ff. 176–177.) The details of his accounts are to be found in Blathwayt's Journal; receipts included the four and a half per cent. duty as well as other sources; not, however, despite his statement, the levies which had been granted him in the
form of gifts by the assembly. (*Ibid.*, ff. 186–188.) The accounts ran from
October 21, 1680, to September 29, 1685, and showed a balance, Dutton being indebted to the crown several hundred pounds. Part of the four and a
half per cent. was, of course, being diverted to the use of the Leeward Islands. The Treasury was satisfied with the accounts and on March 18, 1686,
ordered that they be passed.

[41] *Cal. Treas. Bks.*, 1681–1685, Vol. VII, Pt. II, 1045; a letter from the
Treasury, announcing to Bacon the receipt of his accounts, sent in July,

complaints of the colonial executives, we know that deficits existed in all the colonies. This rendered the governors' salaries uncertain and led to the "presents" to which Blathwayt and other English officials objected so strenuously, and of which the governors were not eager to give account. Lack of evidence in the public archives does not necessarily mean that Blathwayt was making no reports to the Treasury on such accounts as appeared, since such reports, like his digests of 1680, may have passed into the private papers of one of the Treasury officials.[42]

As far as we can ascertain, Blathwayt made only one declaration of accounts prior to the Revolution—that of the first farm of the four and a half per cent. In his general statement to the Treasury, on June 15, 1680, on the condition of plantation revenues, he had reported the deplorable situation which existed in the four and a half per cent. revenue.[43] Letters were accordingly dispatched to the farmers, ordering them to attend Blathwayt at their earliest convenience, with a statement of their accounts. Strode, the farmer in England of the first farm, appeared within a few days and announced that he would comply with instructions as soon as possible. The others were less willing.[44] The investigation proved very vexing and occupied a great deal of Blathwayt's attention until

1683. By mistake Blathwayt's name instead of Bacon's has been inserted in the *Calendar*. Bacon's first accounts contained the usual flaw, the lack of vouchers.

[42] See *supra*, f.n. 40, for evidence that the accounts of one governor were passed.

[43] The farmers of the first farm had given no account of the Barbados receipts for the last three years, and for seven years in the Leeward Islands. Three years' accounts, Blathwayt stated, were wanting on the farm of 1677, which had never been called for. (*Cal. Treas. Bks.*, 1679–1680, VI, 573–574.) This statement was in response, no doubt, to the query which had been put to him on February 3, 1680. (*Ibid.*, p. 420.)

[44] *Ibid.*, p. 581; June 19, 1680.

1684, when the second farm came to an end. In October, 1681, he reported to the Treasury that there were two accounts ready of the revenue of the farm from 1670 to 1677, and that as soon as he had instructions from the Treasury, he would have them declared before the Exchequer.[45] The Treasury ordered him on July 3, 1682, to engross these accounts on parchment and present them to the chancellor of the exchequer.[46]

The farm of 1677 occasioned him more trouble. Letters were dispatched to both the governor and secretary of Barbados to prod the farmers' deputies into activity, but Stede, the secretary, reported that the deputies refused to open their books to him.[47] Finally, in December, 1684, Blathwayt presented a report, the outstanding feature of which was the appalling deficit in the revenue.[48] Under the circumstances, there was no necessity for declaring the accounts. Nor is there any evidence to show that Blathwayt made any attempt to declare the four and a half per cent. revenue after that time, until the beginning of the eighteenth century.[49]

[45] Cal. Treas. Bks., 1681–1685, Vol. VII, Pt. I, 271–272; Treas. 64: 88, ff. 82–85.

[46] Cal. Treas. Bks., Vol. VII, Pt. I, 514–515; also Cal. Treas. Papers, 1557–1696, p. 10.

[47] Cal. Treas. Bks., 1679–1680, VI, 599; 1681–1685, Vol. VII, Pt. I, 111–112, 514; Treas. 64: 88, ff. 75–76. Royal orders were thereupon issued to the farmers to command their deputies to open their books.

[48] Cal. Treas. Papers, 1557–1696, pp. 12–14. References to a salary paid Blathwayt, in spite of the deficits, are to be found. While it may be true that these items were simply references to Blathwayt's regular salary from Barbados and the Leeward Islands, they appear to be special payments. For a reference to £125 in unpaid tallies, see Cal. Treas. Bks., 1681–1685, Vol. VII, Pt. I, 49; for another, to £1062.10.0 for three years, on the second farm, see the same. See also ibid., pp. 36, 478–479, for references to similar work done by Mr. Aldworth, one of the regular members of the audit office. He was recently dead in 1680.

[49] In 1684, the collection of the duty, partly as a result of Blathwayt's efforts, was turned over to the commissioners of the customs, who were to act through local collectors appointed by the Treasury. These collectors were

Although accounts were slow and irregular in putting in an appearance, and few declarations of them were made, Blathwayt's determination with regard to his office continued. He made strenuous efforts to improve the quit-rents and the casual revenues. He attacked the problem of the quit-rents in Virginia as early as 1680, and in his statement to the Treasury, on June 15th of that year, he gave a *résumé* of the situation. England, he stated, was reaping the result of her folly in lavishly granting control over the quit-rents to private individuals—Lord Arlington and Lord Culpeper, in particular.[50] As early as 1650 a collector of the quit-rents, Henry Norwood, had actually been appointed, but he had never been brought to account, even though he was living close at hand in England. Blathwayt, therefore, recommended two things; first, that in accordance with the wishes of the Virginian assembly, as well as for England's own good, some attempt be made to come to an agreement with Culpeper,

to transmit either semi-annual or annual accounts to the commissioners of the customs, while duplicates together with the vouchers, were to be sent to Blathwayt. (*Cal. Treas. Bks.*, 1679–1680, VI, 720; 1681–1685, Vol. VII, Pt. I, 113; Pt. II, 1173, 1306–1307, 1314.) From this provision we may infer that Blathwayt's right to audit the four and a half per cent. revenues continued under the new arrangement, but apart from a more or less desultory correspondence which he carried on with the collectors, there is no special evidence of his activity. (Add. MSS. 38714, ff. 70–71. The entire volume deals with the four and a half per cent.) Carpenter served as collector in the Leeward Islands, and Stede in Barbados. Carpenter reported on September 9, 1685, and May 28, 1686, that his predecessor, Mr. Nagle, had been very remiss about sending his accounts, but before his death, had turned over his bills of entries to him. Stede's and Carpenter's letters are now at Porlock House. Yet Carmichael, Blathwayt's deputy auditor in Barbados, denied in 1687 that he had any control over the four and a half per cent. revenues. (Porlock MSS., letter to Blathwayt, September 14, 1687.)

50 In 1669, that section of Virginia known as the Northern Neck had been granted to the Earl of St. Albans, Lord Berkeley, and others, with power as lords of the soil to collect the quit-rents for themselves. Four years later the same power over all of Virginia had been granted to Lord Arlington and Lord Culpeper, to enjoy for a period of thirty years.

who by 1680 had succeeded to Arlington's share of the profits and was willing to relinquish his claims, provided he secure adequate compensation; and second, that Norwood be required to render an account.[51]

England succeeded better on the first than the second point, for Norwood, despite all of Blathwayt's efforts to force him, refused to give an account, stating that he was not required to by his patent, nor had any of his predecessors in office done so.[52] In 1684, however, a settlement was reached with Culpeper, and in the same year, in response to petitions from Virginia, England agreed that the proceeds from the quit-rents were to be spent in the colony.[53] The problem then became that of improving the collection of the quit-rents, so that they could be made to yield a fair amount of income. What was needed first of all was a satisfactory rent roll, but in all the years of Blathwayt's service as auditor, despite frequent injunctions to the surveyor general of Virginia, this was never obtained. The problem of how best to collect the quit-rents was equally urgent and was complicated by the fact that the quit-rents were paid in tobacco—for the Virginians steadily ignored the injunction that the rents be paid in coin. These were local problems over which Blathwayt had no real control, but he did what he could to bring about an improvement and the steady increase in the proceeds of the quit-rents indicated that his efforts were availing.

Jamaica offered the same difficulties when it came to the quit-rents. There, moreover, a sharp dispute arose be-

[51] *Cal. Treas. Bks.* 1679–1680, VI, 573–574. For a *résumé* of the entire situation in Virginia, see Beer, *The Old Colonial System*, Pt. I, Vol. I, 193–197. The grant of the Northern Neck was in perpetuity.

[52] *Cal. Treas. Bks.*, 1681–1685, Vol. VII, Pt. I, 304–305; C. O. 391: 3, 274, 276; *Cal. S. P. Col.*, 1681–1685, p. 100. Obviously Norwood did not regard himself as the first collector of the quit-rents.

[53] *Treas.* 64: 88, ff. 11, 124–133, 380.

tween the governor and the royal receiver over the best
way to collect them. Jamaicans were notoriously remiss
when it came to paying their rents. Martyn, the receiver,
argued that it was advisable to have object lessons made
of some of the offenders by bringing suit against five persons in every parish.[54] Governor Lynch declared that matters would never remedy themselves until local receivers
were appointed in each precinct.[55] Blathwayt upheld the
latter in this, and in 1683, after a hearing before the
Treasury, it was agreed upon.[56] No adequate rent roll,
however, could be secured in Jamaica any more than in
Virginia, and in the former there was never any great increase in the quit-rents, primarily because of lavish
grants of land made to governors on which little or no
quit-rent was ever paid.[57]

Efforts to bring about an increase in the casual revenue
were more or less futile. In Virginia such revenue was regarded as local, not royal, despite all of the orders in
council to the contrary, and was never included in the accounts remitted to Blathwayt.[58] Spirited attempts to improve the casual revenues in the West Indian Colonies
met everywhere with much the same response. The es-
cheator in the Leeward Islands, although he had been
warned to be zealous, accomplished almost nothing.[59] In
1688 the attorney-general of the islands drew up a report
stating that, if the collection of fines and forfeitures were
only prosecuted, the casual revenue could be made to

54 Porlock MSS.; Martyn to Blathwayt, July 25, 1682.

55 *Cal. S. P. Col.*, 1681–1685, p. 302; Lynch's letter of Sept. 29, 1682.

56 *Cal. Treas. Bks.*, 1681–1685, Vol. VII, Pt. II, 737, 779–781.

57 The proceeds varied from £20 to £2000 in later years. Blathwayt's Account Book (Lib. Cong.), ff. 496–607; Huntington MSS., Blathwayt Papers
relating to America, 1680–1741, no paging.

58 *Cal. S. P. Col.*, 1685–1688, pp. 149–151; 1689–1692, p. 142.

59 *Cal. Treas. Bks.*, 1679–1680, VI, 599.

yield considerable sums;[60] but the demoralized condition of island justice continued, and neither fines nor forfeitures increased.

The situation was more hopeful in Barbados, although Edwyn Stede, appointed collector of the casual revenue in 1682, reported that his duties were bound to be light.[61] He was ordered to levy by distress proceedings in cases where his attempts at collecting casual revenue of any sort were thwarted.[62] Some of his accounts were actually transmitted to Blathwayt, and, while Stede apologized for their form, saying that the exchequer method was unfamiliar to him, Blathwayt and the Treasury were satisfied with them and wrote to commend him.[63] One point in their favor was the fact that they were accompanied with the vouchers.[64]

Governor Lynch reported from Jamaica in 1683 that no casual revenues had been collected in eleven months and

[60] *Cal. S. P. Col.*, 1685–1688, pp. 530–532.

[61] Treas. 64: 88, f. 121; *Cal. Treas. Bks.*, 1681–1685, Vol. VII, Pt. II, 799.

[62] *Cal. Treas. Bks.*, 1681–1685, Vol. VII, Pt. I, 673. England, at the time, was outraged because she had received a law from Barbados giving a local commission power to examine and acquit of debt any persons they chose. (C. O. 391: 3, 281; meeting of the Lords of Trade, Sept. 30, 1681.)

[63] Porlock MSS.; Stede to Blathwayt, August 19, 1685; Carmichael to Blathwayt, September 14, 1687, saying that he was sending Stede's accounts. In his letter, Stede said that, as casual revenue receiver, he had no control over the local levies, which were under the direction of a treasurer appointed by the assembly, whereupon, on Blathwayt's injunction, a royal letter was dispatched to him, telling him to be as regular in giving an account of them as of the casual revenue. There is no evidence to show that he complied. (Treas. 64: 88, ff. 121, 169–170.)

[64] Like all the other accounts of these years, they have disappeared. From Stede's letters we know that the casual revenue reached fairly large proportions; in a single grand session, as much as £1300 was collected in fines and recognizances. Stede wrote, in 1687, that he had on hand £2000 sterling, in casual revenue, which he would disburse as the Treasury directed, while in 1689 he was asked to remit what remained on hand of the revenue, which was no less than £1409.7.9. (Treas. 64: 88, ff. 241, 242, 256–260, 323.)

implied that his predecessor, Morgan, had been very lax.[65] The royal receiver echoed his complaints and said that the greatest abuses were practices in the passing of escheated estates. "But there is not one escheat in 40 hath passed through my hands—whereby no bonds have been given according to the act of assembly to pay to the king the value at three years' end; nor pay me my fees. But which is worse any one that knows of an estate escheatable goes to the governor and begs it, promising to pay to the king the value; then goes and takes out a writ of escheat, and carries it to the marshal who summons what jury he pleaseth, and many times there hath not been returned the tenth part of the value. And of that the king has no account of either."[66] It was quite apparent that the revenue was casual.[67]

In only one of the four colonies was there a local contest over the royal audit. Evidences of malingering on the part of officials were plentiful, but in one case, that of the royal receiver of Jamaica, there was actual defiance of Blathwayt's deputy, Reginald Wilson. Personal politics probably played a larger part in the mind of the receiver, Thomas Martyn, than any real desire to challenge Blathwayt's position, or even that of his deputy; but without any doubt Martyn was encouraged in his pretensions by the fact that he was a patent officer, whose appointment antedated by several years Wilson's nomination by the Treasury. Lynch wrote to the Treasury of the difficulties

[65] *Cal. S. P. Col.*, 1681–1685, pp. 391–397; Lynch to Blathwayt, Feb. 22, 1683. Lynch, however, had hopes of their improvement, and that they might then be applied to his salary.

[66] Porlock MSS.; Martyn to Blathwayt, March 8, 1682.

[67] Treas. 64: 88, ff. 111–115; Lynch to the Treasury, Sept. 16, 1682. Molesworth, who succeeded Lynch as deputy governor, achieved the signal success of having an account drawn of estates escheated since the time of Lord Vaughan, but the amount realized in that period of a decade was no more than £1062. (*Cal. S. P. Col.*, 1685–1688, p. 306; December, 1686.)

he and Wilson were having in bringing Martyn to account. "Nor have we yet been able to bring the Receipts, since my Lord Vaughan's time, into any method, though the Auditor General's Deputy has your Honors' Orders, about three or four orders of the Council and as many of mine to command the Collector to show him all Accompts, but he has still objected that my Lord Carlisle, Sir Henry Morgan and the Council having seen them and approved them, there ought to be no retrospect, and that some of the Accompts were before the date of our Auditor General's Commission. This has made me often tell him, and something angrily, that, being the King's and your Honors' Officer, he was accomptable to you and to obey your orders without respect to the date of our Auditor's Commission; that the Council and the Governors' allowing his Accompts would make them pass if they were not surprised; that all Accomptants in England gave their Accompts to an Auditor; that it was a conveniency he had one here who was to examine and control his Accompts, then give them to us, and after remit them to your Honors as the ultimate Judge and final Tribunal."[68]

Reginald Wilson was so angered by Martyn's contempt for his authority that he referred the matter to the attorney-general of Jamaica, to see whether the statute of 7 Edward VI, c.1, could not be made to apply, thus forcing Martyn to obey or pay a severe penalty.[69] The attorney,

[68] Treas. 64: 88, ff. 111–113; *Cal. Treas. Bks.*, 1681–1685, Vol. VII, Pt. II, 780–781.

[69] This statute applied to officials in England who received the royal revenue; it was entitled, "An Acte for the true Answerings of the Kinges Majesties Revenue." (See also 20 Car. II, c. 2; also Wilson's letter to Blathwayt, April 28, 1684; Porlock MSS.) Curiously, Wilson had himself raised this very point in October, 1682 when he stated to Lynch, "As Mr. Blathwayt's deputy I cannot well inspect the account of the King's Receiver." This may, however, be a misprint in the *Calendar*, for, by Blathwayt's patent, Wilson's position was clear. (*Cal. S. P. Col.*, 1681–1685, pp. 305–306.)

however, was inclined to sympathize with Martyn.[70] Wilson meanwhile wrote to Blathwayt that it was not principle, but fear, that motivated the receiver, since he had been guilty of seizing piratical money for his own use and of including his personal expenses in his accounts.[71]

Martyn in his letters to Blathwayt gave his side of the story, complaining bitterly that Wilson refused to pass his accounts, not that he had refused to let Wilson have sight of them.[72] "Wilson," he wrote, "studdyes mischeif and writes you storyes."[73] Both Wilson and Martyn remained in office, however, although the rift between them was never mended. Wilson sent in Martyn's accounts in 1682, without passing them, and in 1684 he repeated the performance.[74] Martyn continued to protest his honesty, and since he sent in Blathwayt's salary with commendable regularity, the latter doubtless was satisfied.

Martyn's successor, Thomas Ryves, who produced his appointment in 1685 and was sworn in by the council, was no better than he should have been. Actual dishonesty was proved, in his case, by Wilson, who refused to audit his accounts and was upheld in his stand by the council. Even then, Ryves did not mend his ways, and in 1689 he was ordered to produce his accounts at his peril.[75] He complied, but the exceptions taken to them were so numerous that it was impossible to do anything except return them to him, with strict orders that he was to correct them and under no circumstances to send them to Blathwayt until

[70] Porlock MSS.; Wilson to Blathwayt, April 28, 1684.

[71] Ibid.

[72] Ibid.; March 8, 1682.

[73] Ibid.; letters of October 9 and November 14, 1682; July 23, 1683.

[74] Ibid.; letters of July 25, 1682, and April 28, 1684.

[75] Cal. S. P. Col., 1685–1688, pp. 6–7; 1689–1692, pp. 189, 191; Porlock MSS.; Ryves to Blathwayt, March 6, 1686, complaining of Wilson; Wilson to Blathwayt, March 21, 1687, saying that Ryves's peculations amounted to £375.

Wilson and the governor in council had passed upon them. Since Ryves failed to do anything about the matter, the council finally decided to send the accounts to Blathwayt with their comments enclosed, as evidence that their efforts had been futile.[76] Ryves was suspended from office, and two commissioners were appointed by the council to examine his accounts; they presently reported that he was in debt to the crown more than £1200.[77]

Whether Ryves was ever brought to justice and forced to clear his account with the crown, does not appear. Lack of evidence makes it impossible to trace his case to its final outcome, as is too often true in the relationships between colonial officials and the English government. These two instances of Martyn and Ryves were unfortunately indicative of what was to become a common occurrence among the colonial collectors. Blathwayt's office of auditor general was perhaps hampered more by acrimonious relations between collectors and deputy auditors, and by the peculations of the former officials, than by any other single cause.

In the meantime, four other colonies passed under the system of royal audit before the Revolution. The first was New Hampshire, which passed from a proprietary to a royal colony in 1679.[78] The history of the royal audit there, up to 1688, is almost a complete blank. Control of the local revenues, slight though they were, was hotly con-

[76] *Cal. S. P. Col.*, 1689–1692, pp. 207, 249.

[77] *Ibid.*, pp. 296, 315, 393. Governor Inchiquin reported to the Lords of Trade, in 1690, that Ryves's debt was £1600, not £1200. (*Ibid.* p. 315.)

[78] The revenues of the province consisted of an assessment on polls and estates as the primary source, of imposts and excises levied by the assembly, and of such casual revenue as came in from fines and forfeitures. England strongly desired the passage of a permanent revenue act and Governor Cranfield introduced one, in accordance with his instructions, which met with some response in the council but was bitterly opposed by the assembly. (*Ibid.*, 1681–1685, pp. 373, 575.)

tested by the province. Blathwayt's interest in the revenues of this province seems to have been personal.[79] He appointed Richard Chamberlain as his deputy and a statement of accounts running from 1679 was ordered.[80] All Chamberlain's efforts met with sturdy opposition, although in May, 1681, apparently prior to Chamberlain's appointment, the provincial treasurer submitted some accounts.[81] In 1683 Chamberlain had not yet succeeded in accomplishing anything, because, as Governor Cranfield wrote, the local receivers of the revenue refused to bring in their accounts to be audited, on the ground that the money which had been raised was for use in the towns and not for the support of the government as a whole. This excuse, Cranfield declared, was only a "trick to avert the discovery of their malversations."[82] The only further evidence of activity on Chamberlain's part is a reference to accounts rendered by two of the local receivers, Richard Martyn and Elias Stileman, in November, 1686.[83] Clearly the period was too embroiled for anything so stable as an audit.

Official dissatisfaction with the trend of events in Massachusetts led the Treasury to introduce the royal audit into that province even before the loss of the charter.[84]

[79] See *infra*, pp. 464–467.

[80] *Cal. S. P. Col.*, 1681–1685, pp. 307, 413.

[81] *Ibid.*, pp. 38–46; May 7, 1681. The council's report included a general statement on New Hampshire finances and indicated that the provincial treasurer was indebted to the government £131.13.4.

[82] *Ibid.*, pp. 412–413; Cranfield to the Lords of Trade, March 27, 1683. More, perhaps, might have been said of Cranfield's own trickery.

[83] *Ibid.*, 1685–1688, p. 279. When Andros was made governor of New England, in 1686, and Edward Randolph, Blathwayt's deputy auditor, New Hampshire was specifically excluded from Randolph's province, though it was otherwise absorbed into the union.

[84] The revenues of Massachusets were comparable to those of New Hampshire. Money was raised by annual grant, and the principal sources were an impost on all goods imported; a duty of twelve pence, or one pound of powder, on every ton of foreign shipping; an excise on liquor, which was

On October 15, 1681, Blathwayt issued a deputation to
Edward Randolph. His commission was read in the general court in February, 1682, and emphatically rejected.[85]
For the time being, the matter was allowed to drop, but
as soon as the temporary government under Dudley's
presidency was set up in 1686, Randolph's appointment
was renewed.[86]

As we might expect, he was an active and persistent
deputy, very eager to bring the former treasurers of
Massachusetts to account.[87] More of his energy was expended, perhaps, in an attempt to secure a satisfactory
salary arrangement for Blathwayt, and incidentally for
himself, and in disputes with Andros on the question of
their relative authority over certain revenues, than in the
actual work of auditing.[88] Although Randolph disclaimed
any real knowledge of accounting, he succeeded in transmitting one excellent set of accounts, which began with
Andros' administration. They came accompanied with

farmed out; and an assessment on polls and estates. Receipts from fines and
forfeitures were inconsiderable, although Governor Andros and Randolph
made vigorous attempts to improve them. (Goodrick, *Edward Randolph*, VI,
225, 229.) There were no quit-rents, although during the Confederation an
attempt was made to introduce them. Prior to 1685 revenues were in the
care of a treasurer appointed by the assembly, but under Dudley and Andros a receiver, or treasurer was appointed by royal commission. (*Cal. S. P.
Col.*, 1685–1688, p. 364.) John Usher was given the appointment in May,
1687.

[85] *Massachusetts Records*, 1674–1686, V, 333, 521–529. In May, 1682, in
presenting his charges against the general court of Massachusetts, Randolph
listed as one of the offenses, the fact that it had refused to recognize Blathwayt's office and his own deputation. (*Cal. S. P. Col.*, 1681–1685, p. 239.)

[86] Treas. 64: 88, ff. 238–240. His commission was dated in October, 1685.

[87] He had been instructed to make a statement on the revenue collected
since the Dutch War of 1664.

[88] Goodrick, *Edward Randolph*, VI, 220, 221, 250, 251, 257; like Stede, of
Barbados, Randolph apologized for the form of his accounts; saying that he
was "altogether unacquainted in forming and passing Exchequer Accounts,
further then [sic] what we have been instructed by his Excellence [An-
dros]." (*Ibid.*, p. 232.)

the necessary duplicate copy, the required vouchers, and certain annotations.[89]

In Bermuda and New York, the system of audit was barely introduced before the outbreak of the Revolution of 1688. It was adopted in each as soon as they passed into the category of royal provinces. In Bermuda, instructions were dispatched to Governor Robinson in November, 1686. Blathwayt took no steps to appoint a deputy auditor, for the small revenues of the colony scarcely warranted the additional expense.[90]

Local quarrels imperiled the course of the royal audit here, and the same difficulties presented themselves as

[89] Treas. 64: 88, ff. 250–252; C. O. 5: 904, 360–363; Cal. S. P. Dom., 1685–1688, p. 422; Goodrick, Edward Randolph, VI, 231–232. A second set was in preparation in 1688, but the oncoming crisis prevented its dispatch. (Goodrick, VI, 265; October 2, 1688.) In May, 1690, however, Blathwayt acknowledged the receipt of these accounts, which ran from December, 1686 to April, 1689. (Huntington MSS., Blathwayt Papers relating to New England, 1680–1714, no paging; Blathwayt to Andros, May 31, 1690.)

[90] The island was in debt at the time the Bermuda Company lost its charter, and England entertained little hope that the government could be made self-supporting for many years to come. Attempts to introduce a quit-rent system failed, but an agreement was reached whereby sixty shares of land of twenty-five acres each, and valued at £5 per share, were set aside for the support of the government. Of these shares, twelve were to be applied to the governor's salary, the rest being used for other official salaries and the various current expenses of the government. (Cal. S. P. Col., 1681–1685, pp. 270, 663, 664, 751; 1685–1688, pp. 258–259, 295.) The profits from whaling licenses were also to go toward the salary of the governor, and it was anticipated that these would amount to £100 per annum, although in 1687, according to Governor Robinson's statement, they amounted to only £15. (C. O. 1: 60, 88.) He also reported that the crown lands, the twelve shares of which were to yield £60, had only brought in £25. Since the salary of the governor was set at £400, and only £160 were raised in Bermuda, £240 had to be provided out of the English exchequer. The Bermuda Company had imposed a duty of 1d. per pound on tobacco, an export duty which was very unpopular, but which was continued by the king until 1687. (Beer, The Old Colonial System, Pt. I, Vol. I, 199–200; Cal. S. P. Col., 1685–1688, pp. 49, 101, 157, 394.) It was then replaced by an import duty on liquor, which the Board of Trade later contended was permanent, since the act providing it contained no clause of limitations. (Cal. S. P. Col., 1704–1705, p. 219.)

elsewhere. The collector, Samuel Trott, declared that he held a commission from the customs board in England and was not required to produce any of his accounts for Governor Robinson's inspection; this leads us to suspect that both the governor and the collector misunderstood Blathwayt's powers and thought they included control over the plantation duty of 1673. Robinson dismissed Trott in arbitrary fashion and appointed a favorite, Richard Ashworth, in his stead, but was subsequently required to re-instate Trott.

The assembly maintained that the import duty on liquor was a local levy, for which they were not required to give account to England. Robinson reported: "I can give no account of the public money, for it is still maintained to be the country's, and the collector has a commission from the custom-house, so that I cannot pay the poor workmen for the fortifications."[91] He wrested some accounts from Trott, but he made the cardinal error of sending them to Blathwayt before securing the council's sanction.[92] Hordesnell, the attorney-general, made haste to report this to Blathwayt, even though he declared he was so ill he could scarcely lift his head. "Your accounts sent home by Sir Robert Robinson were not seen by any of his council. I would have had them sign them, but they refused. He never yet called me to a council, but does everything without his council and uses their names unknown."[93] Blathwayt could hardly congratulate himself on the progress of the audit, but since he had regarded Robinson as an unfortunate choice for governor, he felt, no doubt, that events had vindicated his opinion.

[91] *Cal. S. P. Col.*, 1689–1692, p. 301; Robinson to the Lords of Trade, July 26, 1690.

[92] *Ibid.*, 1685–1688, p. 558; these accounts ran from July, 1687, to May, 1688.

[93] *Ibid.*, p. 565; letter of June 27, 1688.

The financial history of New York never once ran smooth, throughout the entire period of Blathwayt's activities as auditor general. Governor Dongan, the first royal governor, was apprised of the audit in June, 1686, and promptly wrote to express his willingness to comply with orders.[94] No deputy auditor was immediately appointed, but Lucas Santen, appointed collector of the revenue in 1683, by royal patent, was ordered to make a semiannual account to Blathwayt. His accounts were to begin, not from 1686, but from the year he entered office.[95] Santen proved not only ineffectual but also dishonest, according to the governor and council. Almost immediately after the audit had been announced, he was summoned before the council. He had fallen behind in his weekly statement to them and was suspected of defalcations. Asked to give a specific account, he flew into a rage and declared that he was responsible only to the English Exchequer.[96] Ultimately, however, he produced two accounts, which ran from 1683 to 1686. These were audited by a committee of three councillors, who discovered shortages amounting to nearly £3000.[97] The accounts were accordingly brought to England by the secretary, Spragg,

[94] Treas. 64: 88, ff. 189–190; Cal. S. P. Col., 1685–1688, pp. 207–208. The revenue of the colony consisted of export and import duties; duties on trade on the Hudson River; duties on Indian goods; weight duties; an excise on liquor, which, as in Massachusetts, was farmed out; the quit-rents, and casual revenue from fines, forfeitures, and escheats. Except for the money it provided for the defence of New York, the English exchequer expended no revenue on the province. The duties levied by the assembly were granted for a period of one or two years. England desired to have them made permanent, or for a longer period than two years but did not succeed in this until 1699, when their collection was assured for a decade. Osgood, *The American Colonies in the 18th Century*, I, 240–243.

[95] Treas. 64: 88, ff. 190–191; Cal. S. P. Col., 1681–1685, p. 387.

[96] Osgood, *The American Colonies in the 17th Century*, III, 364–367; Cal. S. P. Col., 1685–1688, pp. 249, 265, 269, 270, 279, 301, 303.

[97] Cal. S. P. Col., 1685–1688, pp. 321, 324.

who turned them over to Blathwayt.[98] Santen was in the meanwhile sent a prisoner to England.[99] To replace Santen, Mathew Plowman was appointed in November, 1687.[100] At the same time, Blathwayt appointed a deputy auditor, Stephen Van Cortlandt—according to Randolph, "an able man."[101] He fell into difficulties with the governor over the military appropriations which were levied by the assembly to make up the deficit in the amount England allowed, saying that by his commission he had no power to audit them.[102] Before any agreement could be arrived at, the Revolution and Leisler's rebellion occurred. The first episode in the royal audit in New York, therefore, was not auspicious, although the province had not objected to the introduction of the system. Such objections were reserved for a later period.

On the whole, the first eight years of Blathwayt's accountancy produced as much in the way of results as could be expected. Except in New England, there was no persistent attempt to deny his authority, and under Andros and Randolph, even Massachusetts was brought into line. All the latent dangers in the system were revealed,

98 Treas. 64: 88, f. 272.

99 Ibid., ff. 261–266, 273–278. Blathwayt after examining the accounts reported a deficit of £2701, but stated that Santen claimed an allowance of £1849.5.11, which his imprisonment kept him from collecting. Suit was begun against Santen for the collection of £1758.15.3, and the latter in vain solicited Blathwayt's favor. (Add. MSS. 38694, f. 103; Cal. Treas. Papers, 1557–1696, p. 223.)

100 Treas. 64: 88, ff. 261–266.

101 Ibid., ff. 267–269; Cal. S. P. Col., 1685–1688, p. 523. He had been one of the three commissioners to examine Santen's accounts. In October, 1688, there was talk of Van Cortlandt's succeeding Plowman, and Randolph then asked Blathwayt if he might secure the deputyship, saying that it would be to Blathwayt's financial advantage. (Goodrick, Edward Randolph, VI, 273; October 16, 1688.)

102 Goodrick, Edward Randolph, VI, 269; Randolph to Povey, October 7, 1688.

particularly, the dire consequence which followed in the train of inefficient governors, reluctant assemblies, and dishonest and quarrelsome collectors. Blathwayt's persistent efforts unfortunately could not cure those ills.

CHAPTER VII

A BRIEF INTERLUDE—SECRETARY TO THE EARL OF CONWAY, 1681–1683

THE brief interlude which Blathwayt spent as secretary to the Earl of Conway, secretary of state for the northern office from January, 1681, to March, 1683, is the least significant in his career. Had circumstances shaped themselves differently, he might have passed from clerk to secretary of state, as Sir Joseph Williamson had done before him. According to Lord Godolphin, his name was brought up for consideration by Charles II in 1684, when there was a vacancy in the office as a result of Sir Leoline Jenkins' death.[1] Nothing came of it, and Blathwayt went on instead to become secretary at war.

Sunderland's vote on the Exclusion Bill, late in 1680, was the reason for the Earl of Conway's elevation to the office. Sunderland was dismissed from the southern office in disgrace, and Sir Leoline Jenkins, the junior secretary, succeeded him. In choosing a secretary for the northern office, Charles turned to the triumvirate[2] which had replaced Sunderland in his favor, and accordingly the Earl of Conway was invested with the seals. In the general estimation, this was a ridiculous choice. Only the fact that Conway was the cousin of the great Edward Seymour could explain it. Those who read the signs of the time, realized that the disgrace of the adroit and crafty Sunder-

---

[1] *Clarendon Correspondence*, I, 94–96.
[2] Edward Seymour, the Earl of Ranelagh, and the Earl of Conway.

land was temporary. His reinstatement in Charles's good graces took, as a matter of fact, two years.

In many ways Conway was reprehensible, but the surprising feature is that he did not make as bad a botch of his office as was expected. True, he was ignorant and, in the beginning, had so slight a conception of the north European situation and of his duties in general that he did not know what was meant by the "circles of Germany."[3] He was too gay for the position and too often in his cups. Recently widowed, a disproportionate amount of his time in office was spent in courting the lady who was to be his second, and extremely youthful, wife. He was continually dashing off to his country estate at Ragley, whence he sent letters to his secretaries at Whitehall, full of reports on the charms of country life but very barren of instructions. Conway was always pleased when the Newmarket season came round, and he usually managed to be the secretary of state who attended Charles on the royal visit to the races. Nevertheless, he regarded his official duties with great gravity, when he did set his mind on them, and, like most stupid men, he felt that his services were almost indispensable to the king. When rumors of his dismissal began late in 1682, he displayed great perturbation, and once out of office, wasted a good deal of time trying to get in again.

That Conway cut no worse a figure than he did, may be attributed to various saving circumstances; for one thing, there was a spark of decency in him that was not wholly extinct. Fortunately, too, he served during a period which was crucial neither in domestic nor foreign affairs. Moreover, he had a colleague who could be trusted to act when he failed, for Sir Leoline Jenkins, the southern secretary, was a conscientious and able man, very learned and cul-

[3] Burnet, *History of His Own Times* (London, 1857), p. 348; Evans, *The Principal Secretary of State*, pp. 147–148.

tured, though not exactly brilliant. Finally, he had the
good sense to entrust the greater share of his work to his
clerks!

Under ordinary circumstances, there would have been
no opening for Blathwayt in the secretarial office at this
time. It was customary for an incoming secretary to take
over the staff of his predecessor, making only one new appointment, that of confidential secretary. This office was
usually conferred upon a relative or close friend. The
first secretary of the permanent staff was almost on a par
with the private secretary, as far as responsibilities and
dignity were concerned, and always knew more about how
the office was to be run. Such a man was John Cooke, who
had been in the secretarial office when Blathwayt was at
The Hague and was still presiding over Jenkins' office,
assisted by Owen Wynne, the political and personal favorite. Sunderland, however, had preferred to make of
his office a one-man affair. His trusted secretary was his
kinsman, William Bridgeman, who seems to have served
him both in a political and a bureaucratic capacity, com-
bining the functions performed by Cooke and Wynne in
the other office. Had Sunderland's disgrace in 1681 been
less complete, Bridgeman would doubtless have continued
in office, and Conway would have had only one appointment at his disposal. But Bridgeman was required to
share in his master's disgrace and, for the time being, resolved to "appear no more in public business."

Sir Robert Southwell little realized in 1679, when he
sold his clerkship of the council to Francis Gwyn, the extent to which he was furthering Blathwayt's fortunes.
Gwyn was the Earl of Conway's cousin, and the latter now
decided to make him his confidential secretary. Since
Gwyn shared Conway's fondness for pleasure, it would
never do to entrust the sole charge of the office to him. A
year's association with Blathwayt, in the plantation office

and at the council board, had convinced Gwyn that Blathwayt was not merely a good, but an indispensable, working mate. He, therefore, suggested that Conway make him
his second secretary, to whom could be entrusted all the
tasks which Gwyn knew he would find irksome beyond endurance. The bargain was struck and was mutually satisfactory, for Blathwayt welcomed any recognition of his
services.

In order to arrive at the duties of Conway's secretaries, it is necessary to examine the work which the
northern office had to perform. By 1681, its jurisdiction
was perhaps somewhat more clearly defined than it had
been in 1668, when Blathwayt was in Temple's office.
Technically, as already stated, it had no control over
colonial affairs, except as colonial governors occasionally
dispatched thither duplicate copies of the letters sent to
the southern secretary, or some northern secretary, such
as Sir Joseph Williamson, invited a correspondence. Irish
affairs were always in the hands of the southern secretary. Immediately after Conway took office, word was
sent to the Duke of Ormonde, the lord lieutenant of Ireland, that his dispatches were henceforth to be directed to
Secretary Jenkins.[4] Domestic and foreign affairs were
divided between the two offices, the line of division in the
latter being that which had been resorted to after 1660,
and which had become more or less fixed by 1668.[5] Thus,
Conway wrote to Jenkins from Newmarket, in Septem-

[4] *Hist. MSS. Com., Ormonde MSS.*, n.s., V, 569; the Earl of Arran to
Ormonde, February 1, 1681. John Cooke apparently fell heir to the Irish
agency, which usually went to the senior clerk in the southern office. On the
question of the Irish agency and service at the Irish committee of the Privy
Council, see *ibid.*, VI, 328; also Evans, *The Principal Secretary of State*, p.
165. Gwyn and Nicholas, as clerks of the council, waited on the Irish Committee during 1680; but, if Gwyn's letters to Ormonde are to be trusted,
Gwyn's attendance there ceased when he entered the secretarial office.

[5] Evans, *The Principal Secretary of State*, pp. 132–134.

ber, 1681: "His Majesty wonders he has had no French news since he came here, and asked me if I had received any French letters. I told him I never received any, but I mention it, that you may know it will be acceptable to him."[6]

The division of duties between Conway's secretaries cannot be easily or finally determined.[7] Technically, responsibility for the transaction of foreign affairs should have fallen more heavily on Gwyn, as senior clerk;[8] in practice, Blathwayt assumed the larger portion of it. Evidence that Gwyn was expected to carry on a correspondence with the foreign envoys is apparent from their letters to Blathwayt, in which they complained of Gwyn's neglect. Skelton, the English resident at Hamburg, wrote to Blathwayt in February, 1682, that he had decided to take Gwyn's advice and write to the latter only once a month. He added, "I feare his frequent visits to the toothless Captains [?] makes him forget his other friends."[9] Envoys recognized a division of duties between Blathwayt and Gwyn and regarded the office as a two-man affair. In 1683, when Conway was leaving office and the news of Sunderland's return had reached the envoys, one of them wrote to Blathwayt that he was glad to hear, "that my Lord Sunderland hath divided his office, and that honest Mountstevens hath so good share in it, besides you know *divide et impera* is an excellent modern maxim, and will

6 *Cal. S. P. Dom.*, 1680–1681, p. 453.

7 No account of office arrangements within Conway's office has been discovered, but they were doubtless very much like those in the Earl of Middleton's office, in 1684, a contemporary account of which is extant. (All Souls College MS. 204, f. 119 *seq.*, reprinted in Evans, *The Principal Secretary of State*, pp. 192–193.) There were six clerks, all of whom had various duties assigned them; of the four minor clerks, three were primarily engaged in translating, while one was a writing clerk and special assistant to John Cooke, the senior clerk. For a contemporary account of Arlington's office staff in 1673, see Stowe MS. 549, f. 18, also reprinted in Evans, pp. 191–192.

8 Evans, *The Principal Secretary of State*, pp. 192–193.

9 Add. MSS. 37983, ff. 82–83.

keep the office from being above the secretary, but all this
amongst friends for I would not by any means anger my
friend Mr. B[ridgeman]."[10] Such comments certify to the
fact that a dual system existed within Conway's office,
even though Blathwayt was the harder working member
of it.

A part of the foreign correspondence was actually assumed by Conway himself, and some of his letters appear
in the entry book, which Blathwayt kept. Envoys corresponded with him, though not very regularly. "You will
judge by my writing to my Lord Conway this post that I
have some extraordinary news, I being unwilling to
trouble him but upon such occasions," one of them wrote
to Blathwayt.[11] Conway's frequent absences from Whitehall with Charles II aroused the anxiety of one of the envoys, who had been ordered to direct his letters to Whitehall, instead of to Conway at his lodgings at Windsor. He
protested that the news he was sending of Dutch intrigues
was of too delicate a nature to be entrusted to any save
Conway. But the latter reassured him, saying that perfect secrecy would be maintained. "To satisfy you upon
the score of secrecy which you require, I shall only tell
you that I suffer them not to go out of my hands, that is, I
trust none in the office to keep them but myself, nor are
they communicated to all whom the King entrusts his se-
cretest affairs with, but only to one or two in whom you
confide as well as I."[12] Either Conway was pacifying
what he regarded as unwarranted concern, or else Blathwayt was among the two or three to be trusted, for all the
envoy's letters, including the one just quoted, are to be

10 *Ibid.*, 37987, f. 306 *dorso;* Poley, resident at Ratisbon, March 15,
1683, s.n.

11 *Ibid.*, 37979, ff. 85–86; Plott, the consul at The Hague, December 5,
1681.

12 *Ibid.*, 35104, f. 59; Windsor, May 2, 1682, a letter addressed to Chudleigh, diplomatic representative at The Hague.

found in Blathwayt's files.[13] Most of the representatives expected Blathwayt to see the letters they sent to Conway, and one of them declared on a certain occasion that he would not write Blathwayt at any length for fear he would simply repeat what he had already told Conway— and he knew that Blathwayt saw all of the latter's letters.[14]

The court was "much in motion" during the two years that Blathwayt was in the secretarial office. Conway, as we have stated, was usually called upon to make the royal progress, while the painstaking Sir Leoline Jenkins was required to carry on the work of the secretariat that could be done only in London. As might be expected, Gwyn rather than Blathwayt accompanied Conway on these excursions. Envoys commented on the way in which Blathwayt was left to drudge at Whitehall. "By the newspaper which I received this day from Mr. Benson," wrote Skelton, from Hamburg in March, 1682, ". . . I conclude the court removed to Newmarket, and you left in the office at London."[15] Another commented, "I found by your last, you were designed this Newmarket season, for business, and not for pleasure, consequently this will more probably find you at the office than anybody else."[16] Blathwayt, however, did go down occasionally to Newmarket, and in one instance Skelton wrote with candor that he was relieved to hear it, for now he could expect an account of events at the races, which he was never able to extract from Gwyn. Business, however, went on for the secretarial office even while it was temporarily stationed at Newmarket. In the fall of 1682, Blathwayt wrote that both

---

[13] See Add. MSS. 37980, a volume of Chudleigh's correspondence which Blathwayt kept in his possession after leaving the office.

[14] *Ibid.*, 37979, ff. 17–18; a letter from Plott at The Hague.

[15] *Ibid.*, 37983, ff. 90–91; March 17, 1682, s.n.

[16] *Ibid.*, 37985, ff. 169–170; see, however, *ibid.*, 37987, ff. 208–209.

Conway and he had come down, and "though this place seems more proper for sports than business, yet his lordship will always be very punctual in giving you the best satisfaction he can in all the parts of your negotiations."[17]

The division between the northern and southern provinces was, in a sense, set aside during the royal progresses at Newmarket and elsewhere, for Blathwayt while he was at Newmarket was expected to send news to the representatives in France.[18] In as far as it was possible, however, business was suspended while the court sought relaxation in such pleasures. Envoys grumbled and expressed their fears that they would get no satisfaction as long as the court and their "provincial," Conway, were away from Whitehall.[19]

For the dispatch of the foreign news-letters neither Blathwayt nor Gwyn was responsible. *The Gazette,* Sir Joseph Williamson's project, was still issued, and from the bills of profits which appear among Blathwayt's papers, it seems that the initial arrangement for a division of the proceeds between the senior clerks of the two secretarial offices still obtained.[20] In addition, a double system of news-letters was being used, and time and again the envoys would comment, "Mr. Benson writes me very regularly, but I have not heard from Mr. Yard yet."[21] News of the king's illness, in the spring of 1682, reached Skelton from three sources—Blathwayt, Benson, and Yard.[22] Again Skelton complained of having had no news of what

17 *Ibid.,* 35104, f. 70.

18 *Hist. MSS. Com.,* VII. Report, Grahame MSS., p. 359b.

19 Add. MSS. 37983, ff. 128–29; *ibid.,* 37979, ff. 61–62.

20 Porlock MSS.; see also Evans, *The Principal Secretary of State,* pp. 290–295. The division of the profits dated back to 1672. Whether Blathwayt or Gwyn was the senior clerk in this connection, is a question; it may be that they divided their share of the profits.

21 Add. MSS. 37983, ff. 23–24.　　22 *Ibid.,* ff. 210–211.

was happening in London except what he received through the news-letters, "which I fear I shall not have so regularly hereafter by reason of Mr. Benson's having an ague."[23] Blathwayt's letters to the envoys, containing instructions to the various English representatives and such news as he thought might interest them, went out on an average of once a week.

The frequency with which Jenkins' name appears on official papers shows that much of the domestic business was being done in his office, although Conway, no doubt, demanded his share of what was of a profitable nature, such as the issuance of commissions. While he was in attendance on the king at Windsor, Hampton Court, or Newmarket, much of the work that demanded the royal signature passed through his hands. Conway also received the various deputations, from London and elsewhere, which came down for audiences with the king.[24]

The royal progresses sometimes brought up difficulties with regard to the seals. The signet seal, Conway always kept in his immediate possession, but the cachet and his own private seal were often left behind in the office in Whitehall. Thus Gwyn wrote to Jenkins from Newmarket, "I have just received your packet, but you forgot to send me one of those letters which came out on Saturday in answer to Lord Shaftesbury's, which I desired you. The seal my Lord means is his private seal with his cipher with which you sealed my cousin Seymour's letter on Sunday night, since which my Lord says he has not had it, but you mind me of one thing I had forgot, that is, the King's small cachette seal. You have one of them and I would desire you to send it down, for there may be occasion, though it is used very seldom. I will dispatch the affairs recommended very speedily and by to-morrow's

23 Add. MSS. 37983, ff. 232–233.
24 *Cal. S. P. Dom.*, 1680–1681, p. 276; *ibid.*, 1682, p. 203.

post send you two warrants for the reprieve for man-
slaughter of Berrisford and Woodhall in Hertford-
shire."[25]

The Earl of Ailesbury made an interesting comment on
the share which Conway's clerks had in the investigation
of Shaftesbury's alleged treasonable intrigues. As was
customary, the earl, who disliked Blathwayt for his subsequent loyalty to William III, impugns Blathwayt's ability
and good sense. His comment, however, casts light on the
police powers in the hands of the northern secretary.
"The king having just reasons to suspect that this lord
[Shaftesbury] was unwearied in his contrivances, commanded Mr. Francis Gwinne, and Mr. William Blathwayt, the chief secretaries under the Earl of Conway,
Secretary of State, and I being continually with him as
my friend and kinsman, I came to the greater knowledge
of this matter. These two gentlemen went by orders signed
by the King to Thanet House in Aldersgate Street, where
that lord resided. On strict search they found nothing of
consequence, save a large folio book stuffed with receipts
of all sorts for kitchen, still-house, and for curing diseases
of horses, etc. [sic]. These gentlemen retired for to make
their report, but one of them, and as I take it, Mr. Gwinne,
who had a more quick discernment, told the other that
they should be received ill at Court, and persuaded the
other to go back again; and looking over the book from
one end to the other, they found the kingdom numbered,
and by alphabet, and of consequence the County of Bed-
ford led the dance. The two parties were distinguished,
'Men worthy,' and 'Worthy Men'; the former, worthy to

[25] *Ibid.*, 1682, pp. 119–120; also p. 112. Conway, in sending a letter to
Jenkins which was addressed to Chief Justice North, wrote, "I send it open
that you may read it and Mr. Blathwayt has my seal and can seal it."
Blathwayt always retained the ciphers at Whitehall, and this occasionally
caused delay. (*Ibid.*, 1680–1681, p. 394.)

be hanged, and the latter, he described as men of worth according to his sentiments. My father and myself had the honour to be of the former rank and at the head."[26]

In connection with his office, though often outside the immediate range of his work, Blathwayt lived close to some of the most important events of the time. He was in Oxford during the days of the ill-fated, short-lived parliament that sat there, and he reported events at first hand to the foreign representatives. The alleged intrigues and misdeeds of the Earl of Shaftesbury were often on his tongue, and he watched with alarm the growing power of that lord in the City of London. On July 5, 1682, came the celebrated election of the sheriffs of London. The interest which Charles and his court took in the outcome of events is well known. Jenkins and Blathwayt, who had been ordered by Conway to attend, were excited onlookers and every quarter of an hour sent curt reports from the Guildhall to Conway, on the way in which the hustings were proceeding. Blathwayt's dispatches, telegraphic in form, are full of photographic detail; the opening of the courts of aldermen and common hall in the morning, the coursing in and out of the people, the agitated reports of the lord mayor's reputed seizure with an attack of the stone, the attempts of the sheriffs to badger both the mayor and the electors, the arrival of various famous Londoners on the scene—all these pass before the reader's eyes in modern radio-announcement style.[27]

Blathwayt's correspondence with the English residents abroad, both diplomatic and consular, is our most complete record of his activities in Conway's office.[28] His dis-

---

[26] *Memoirs of Thomas, Earl of Ailesbury*, I, 63–64.

[27] Porlock MSS.

[28] Blathwayt's office methods are dealt with elsewhere in this study. His entry book is now in the British Museum, as are also the letters he received from the envoys. (Add. MSS. 35104, 37979–37990.)

patches were based on minutes from the committee of intelligence, some of which are to be found among his papers.[29] The letters which passed to and fro were largely stereotyped in content, yet they reveal incidentally many homely details with regard to both Blathwayt and his correspondents. Most of the latter had axes to grind and, finding it fairly easy to work on Blathwayt's good nature, bombarded him with requests to have their privy seals passed and to have included in them various exorbitant and extravagant items. Blathwayt found most of them too fond of expensive coaches and costly equipages and frowned away their requests.

He was a rigid though kindly taskmaster. He reproved envoys who used the pen of a clerk instead of writing themselves. He took Warwick, the Swedish envoy, to task for using too free and easy a style and for exceeding his instructions. He scolded whenever he detected any diplomatic leakages, but even his harshest criticisms were not very caustic.

The envoys liked him and showed their appreciation in various ways, although the desire to stand in well at Whitehall, no doubt, prompted their occasionally fatuous attentions. "Yesterday Alderman Dackwell with some other friends of yours dining with me," wrote one of them, "we did not fail to remember Mr. Blathwayt in our best liquor, as I always do on all other occasions." They kept Conway and Blathwayt well supplied with wine and fish and bore criticism patiently when either of them objected to the flavor. Poley, at Frankfurt, ordered periwigs for Blathwayt; Chudleigh, at The Hague, was on the watch for stallions for Conway, whose specific instructions in the matter are in marked contrast to some of his diplomatic orders. In return, Chudleigh begged Blath-

[29] Porlock MSS.; these are primarily for the spring of 1681. Gwyn may have been the clerk in attendance on the committee.

wayt to find him a good English cook; he had endured
Dutch cooking for six months and could stomach it no
longer! Weaknesses both of the spirit and of the flesh
come out in the course of this diplomatic correspondence.

Blathwayt, the colonial enthusiast and lover of rare
books, appears frequently in these letters. Envoys at The
Hague and Amsterdam were commissioned to keep their
eyes always open for books of interest. ''I am perpetually
enquiring for books of politics for you and concerning our
country of America,'' Plott wrote from The Hague, ''but
I can find nothing as yet that can be new to you.''[30] A little later he wrote, ''I have found a French book in folio
with maps and figures, printed in the year 1640 intituled
*L'Histoire du nouveau monde ou description des Indes
occidentales contenant dixhuit livres par le Sieur Jean de
Laet d'Anvers;* if you have it not already I shall send it
you, bookes of America being very scarce here, their genius as well as interest lyeing most towards the East Indies.[31] . . . The books you write about I shall be able
to furnish you with, except the Witsens Schaepsbow, that
being now so very rare that I could not get it in one shop
at Amsterdam, I having been told that 'tis only to be got
sometimes at auctions. Others have assured me there is to
be a new impression of it this winter, you may be sure I
shall look out sharp for it, and shall procure it if possible.''[32] Presently he reported that he had heard of a man,
who had recently died in Zealand, who had possessed a
copy of the coveted Witsen, and though he was having a

[30] Add. MSS. 37979, ff. 25–26. Plott was a colonial, with plantations in
the Leeward Islands and a Creole wife who often sent her respects to Blathwayt.

[31] *Ibid.*, ff. 41–42. The de Laet was one of the volumes in Blathwayt's
library, sold at Sotheby's in 1912.

[32] *Ibid.*, ff. 37–38. The Witsens Schaepsbow was the very famous work on
shipbuilding, by Nicolaas Cornelisz Witsen, entitled *Aeloude en heden-
daegsche schoepsbouw en bestier*, published at Amsterdam, in 1671.

friend make inquiries, his efforts so far had proved of no avail. Three booksellers at The Hague were on the watch for it, and several in Amsterdam. Finally Plott's zeal was rewarded, "I shall send you some books . . . and among the rest your beloved Witsens Schaepsbow, which at last I found, having left no stone unturned to get it."[33]

Chudleigh, Plott's successor at The Hague, was commissioned to buy lexicons and Bibles in "high Dutch," for Blathwayt. He wrote graciously; "There are no more but two of Moreri's dictionaries to be found in all Holland and those I desire you will give me leave to make you a present of, together with one Dutch book you will find in the box; the other books I sent for to Amsterdam are not to be had either."[34] The tables had been turned since Blathwayt's days at The Hague, and he was now being repaid in full and in kind for all the favors he had done the exacting Sir Joseph.

Blathwayt never neglected his diplomatic duties, but we can see the obvious relief with which he welcomed those which took a colonial cast. Chudleigh wrote of the Dutch discriminations against English beef and butter, but said that the impost on French brandies had been removed; eagerly Blathwayt made note of this, for immediate reference to the Lords of Trade.[35] His anger can well be imagined when he learned that Carr, the consul at Amsterdam, had so inadequate an idea of the Acts of Trade that he could write calmly of ships from the colonies docking at the Dutch ports. "As to the list or calculation of the

33 *Ibid.*, ff. 71–72.

34 *Ibid.*, 37980, ff. 265–266. The dictionary Plott referred to is that of Louis Moreri, *Le Grand Dictionnaire Historique, ou le mélange curieux de l'histoire sacrée et profane*. J. Collier, "the nonjuror" made three translations of the Moreri, the first in 1701, another in 1705, and a third in 1716.

35 Add. MSS. 37980, ff. 285–288; Blathwayt made a careful memorandum of this information and included the eighteenth article of the Dutch treaty of 1674. (*Ibid.*, ff. 289–290.)

duty payable by English ships," Blathwayt replied, "you send me no authentic or true written copy of it; in one I find for ships coming from Cadiz, etc. [*sic*] the sum of 18; and in another for the same *81* [*sic*]. Besides that you do not distinguish whether it be gilders or anything else. And further I must needs take particular notice (as it is besides relating to my other business of plantations)[36] that you settle a duty for ships coming from Virginia, New England, and other of his Majesty's colonies in America, when it is most strictly provided by several acts of parliament that no ships shall bring goods from thence to any other parts of Europe than England or Ireland."[37] Such ignorance and carelessness might well have reduced Blathwayt to tears of rage, and he must have rejoiced at, if indeed he was not instrumental in bringing about, the subsequent recall of Carr, who had proved so wretched a guardian of England's trade interests.

In the late fall of 1682, rumors of Conway's dismissal began to spread thick and fast. Sunderland's readmission into the royal counsel could have but one meaning,—a crash in Conway's political fortunes. The latter took his dismissal with outward calm and wrote to Chudleigh, "I do not go out as a discontented person being continued in all his Majesty's councils with a pension of £1500 per annum and a promise in writing of a considerable station when it falls, as also of £2500 ready money and *some other little things*. I need not say much to you that the king hath declared in council he was never better served nor better satisfied with any man in my station than he hath been by me, but his service did require this alteration. I wish it may stop there, but I fear it will not."[38]

This dismissal, manoeuvred so smoothly, though it cost the English treasury dear, did not put an end to Con-

---

[36] Blathwayt crossed out the parenthetical statement in his letter draft.
[37] Add. MSS. 37981, ff. 25–26.   [38] *Ibid.*, 35104, ff. 86–87.

way's hope of reinstatement in some public office. From Ragley, whence he and Gwyn betook themselves somewhat hastily, came letters which showed that he was fuming over the changes that had been made at court. He sent out letters of supplication to Dartmouth and Rochester and begged Blathwayt to interview them in his behalf.[39] His concern, however, was temporary and before the spring was over he succumbed to the delights of life at Ragley.

Blathwayt, meanwhile, was left to round out the work in the northern office, for Gwyn relieved himself of all obligations. Blathwayt dispatched the necessary formal letters telling of Conway's dismissal.[40] He refused to be enticed down to Ragley, where Conway was urging him to come, even by tales of the charms of Mrs. Basset, Lady Conway's friend and companion. Conway's letters were full of trifling nonsense. "Your kissing Mrs. Basset's hand hath made my wife give her many a rap on the fingers. I had no way to make Mrs. Basset bear up against her raillery, but by showing her the letter you sent me from Mr. Skelton, wherein he makes a great compliment to my wife."[41] Lovemaking was often on Conway's mind, as when he wrote with seventeenth-century allusiveness; "Can you with all your skill explain what this signified, that Mrs. Basset hath this year heard the nightingale before the cuckoo?"[42]

Fate had another fortune in store for Blathwayt than Mrs. Basset, and his heart was not to be stirred. He was

[39] *Hist. MSS. Com.*, XI. Report, App., Pt. V, Dartmouth MSS., p. 81; Conway to Dartmouth, Ragley, April 7, 1683: Add. MSS. 37990, ff. 30–31, 50–51; Conway to Blathwayt, March 22 and May 22, 1683.

[40] See especially Add. MSS. 37987, ff. 304–305; Blathwayt's letter to Poley, offering to carry on an unofficial correspondence with him, February 14, 1683.

[41] *Ibid.*, 37990, ff. 36–37.   [42] *Ibid.*, ff. 38–39.

preoccupied with thoughts of advancement at Whitehall.
An office had been lost, another must be gained. He played
his cards well, for by the end of the summer he had taken
over the war office.

CHAPTER VIII

AT THE WAR OFFICE, 1683–1688

IN August, 1683, six months after the dismissal of the Earl of Conway, Blathwayt decided to hazard the fortunes of the war office and purchased the position of secretary at war. Again he seems to have been indebted to his erstwhile patron, Sir Robert Southwell. The incumbent of the war office was Mathew Lock, an Irishman and a distant relative of Southwell.[1] Blathwayt must have met Lock frequently in the course of his official duties prior to the transaction of August, 1683, and may have been on terms of intimacy with him, but the bond which originally drew the two men together was unquestionably their mutual regard for Southwell.[2]

The status of the office of secretary at war at this time offers ample ground for speculation. A little more than a decade before, it had been merged with, and almost lost in, the office of commander-in-chief. By Blathwayt's time,

[1] Lock was a cousin of Sir John Percival, later Lord Egmont, one of Southwell's favorite nephews. See *Hist. MSS. Com., Egmont MSS.*, Vols. I, II, for numerous references. Also *Cal. S. P. Dom.*, 1677–1678, pp. 151, 287–288, for a reference to Blathwayt in connection with Southwell and the Percivals and some Irish land holdings. Lock was also related to the Davys family, prominent in Irish annals of the late seventeenth century. Sir Paul Davys, principal secretary of state for Ireland, 1672, was an uncle of Lock. The Davys and Southwells were well known to each other. (See *Cal. S. P. Dom.*, 1672, pp. 527–531; 1672–1673, pp. 315, 435.)

[2] The agreement between Lock and Blathwayt was among the Blathwayt Papers preserved at Dryham Park. (See item 115, Sotheby catalogue, April 25, 1910.) The details with regard to the sale are lacking; not even the sale price is known.

it was so closely bound to the office of secretary of state
that Blathwayt was sometimes spoken of as a member of
the secretary's official staff.[3] The abeyance of the office of
commander-in-chief was largely responsible for this
transfer of authority to the secretary of state, who thus
secured an increase in power destined to continue even
after the revival of the former office in the case of the
Duke of Monmouth, 1674 to 1679, and of Marlborough in
the reign of Anne.

As long as the office of secretary at war existed, it never
lost its joint responsibility to the secretary of state and
the commander-in-chief, though, many years later, Palmerston, as secretary at war, was to outdo himself in an
attempt to deny the authority of the latter official.[4] Why
was it that the office of secretary at war never escaped its
subservient position? In many ways it was an abortive
office from its very inception. There is reason to think,
however, that under Blathwayt it might have escaped its
inferior status and achieved a position of such near equal-
ity with the secretary of state that there would have been
created, in the late seventeenth century or early eighteenth century, the *secretaryship for war,* the establishment of which instead was actually to be postponed for

---

[3] See Lord Monmouth's statement on this in Burnet, *Memorial to Mary,
Princess of Orange,* with its appendix containing the letters Mary sent to
William, June–September, 1690, pp. xxi–xxii.

[4] For Palmerston's memorandum on the powers of the secretary at war,
see Sir Henry Lytton-Bulwer's *Life of Viscount Palmerston* (London, 1871),
I, 335–365. Also Clode, *Military Forces of the Crown,* Vol. II, App. CXXIX.
Palmerston, in 1811, was engaged in a quarrel with Dundas, commander-in-
chief, on the question of whether by his patent, Palmerston was to take
orders from Dundas. The argument seems to have rested on the question of
whether the term, *captain-general,* was the same as *commander-in-chief,*
Palmerston maintaining that it was not. He went over the records of the war
office from 1660 to 1811 and proved, to his own satisfaction at least, that he
was free from Dundas' jurisdiction. His line of reasoning was, of course,
quite beside the point.

another hundred years. They were critical and formative years in which Blathwayt held the office. The tremendous increase in the size of the army, the vast amount of interest which James II and William III felt in the forces, and the open admiration for the French system of control, where the position achieved by Louvois attracted a great deal of attention, might well have had a definite effect on the secretaryship at war. James II once expressed his belief that the office was of cabinet rank. Among his notes of advice to his son, dated in 1692, is to be found what he then considered the correct composition of a cabinet: "Two Secretarys of State, Secretary of War, of Admiralty, first Commissioner of Treasury, and two others."[5] He may have been thinking of a glorified secretary at war; at any rate, he himself made no known effort to include Blathwayt in his secret councils, though there are numerous evidences to show that the latter had admission to the royal closet and was often in conference with the king.

The fact that Blathwayt combined the two offices of secretary at war and secretary of state for so many months, in the decade between 1692 and 1702, would perhaps have reacted favorably on the former office had he served any other monarch than William III. William had no great admiration for powerful secretaries of any sort, and the position of subserviency in which he kept Blathwayt during the years of attendance in Flanders was little calculated to enhance the importance of the office of secretary at war. It might be argued that a man more politically able than Blathwayt could have accomplished more, but such a man would not long have continued in the service of William. As it was, the office increased in importance under Blathwayt, but this was largely a result of circumstances over which Blathwayt had no control: such as the promi-

5 Clarke, *Life of James II*, II, 642.

nent part played by military affairs; the resulting increase in the size of the army in the years from 1683 to 1704; and the consequent monetary possibilities of the office of secretary at war. Parliamentary interest in a standing army, and the financial control which parliament exerted after the passage of the Mutiny Act in 1689, required that body to take an interest in the secretary at war and to depend upon him and the paymaster-general of the forces for the presentation of the estimates.

Blathwayt in the war office had a distinguished line of successors, and immediately after his occupancy the office began to be a nursery for rising politicians. The number of men illustrious in England's political annals who held the post early in their careers is strikingly large. The office became a stepping-stone to greater things rather than a bureaucratic appointment in which the first clerk of the office automatically succeeded his superior, a scheme which represented the sum total of Blathwayt's ambitions. His immediate successor was St. John, later Lord Bolingbroke, who intended to make political as well as other capital out of the office. Then followed in rapid succession men such as Robert Walpole, George Granville (later Lord Lansdowne), Sir William Wyndham, and William Pulteney (afterward Earl of Bath).[6] Adam Cardonnel, the man whom Blathwayt trained as his successor, and who became Marlborough's secretary in attendance beginning with 1702, made an effort to get into the office in 1710, on the ground that it had been promised him, but the duke's political prestige at the moment was not sufficiently strong to accomplish this.[7]

[6] See the list in Andrews, *Guide*, II, 31–32, which is more accurate than that given in Hadyn's *Book of Dignities*, p. 233 (3rd ed., 1894); the short tenure in office of Blathwayt's successors is noteworthy. Blathwayt's former colleague, Francis Gwyn, was incumbent in 1713–1714.

[7] S. P. Dom., Military Papers, III, 40; Cardonnel to the secretary of

Blathwayt's political influence as secretary at war was not great enough to win him admission to the Privy Council. It is doubtful whether he ever asked to be admitted, but one of his successors attempted it. In November, 1710, Granville wrote to Harley: "If my little services in this part of the world have been acceptable to her Majesty, methinks it might not be difficult for you to obtain a mark of distinction for me which I know you would have readily yielded to my friend Mr. St. John if he would have again accepted his old post, that is to be added to the Privy Council. 'Tis a favour that will cost the Queen nothing, and 'twill give me a great deal of ease in my correspondence with the General when he comes home, by putting me above the servile attendance which he may expect by having been used to it by my predecessors in the same post."[8] Granville failed to realize his ambition, but within a few years Wyndham achieved it.[9] The office never attained cabinet rank, and after 1783, when it was reduced to the status of trusteeship over army finances, it sank to a level of subordination from which it never rallied.[10]

The history of the office prior to Blathwayt's tenure deserves some comment. The position developed as the standing army itself came into being. It had its genesis in that of scrivener of the army, or secretary to the commanding officer. The Civil Wars and the Restoration quickened its development, along with the establishment of standing armies. The tradition that it was a civilian

state, September 22, 1710, saying that he had kissed the hand of Queen Anne for it in the spring before his departure for Flanders. Cardonnel made a statement in his letter which Palmerston would not have relished, for he said he hoped he would have the office "out of consideration to his Grace [Marlborough], on whom, besides, the office in some manner depends." See also Luttrell, *Brief Relation*, VI, 535; January 14, 1710.

8 *Hist. MSS. Com.*, Portland MSS., XV. Report, App., Pt. IV, 627.

9 Wyndham secured admission to the council in 1716.

10 23 Geo. III, c. 50, §§ 20, 22, 26, 27, 28, 29, 35, 37, 38.

post dates from the very beginning.[11] At first the office was so closely associated with that of commander-in-chief that it was impossible for it to have any public significance, but by 1657 it had achieved the dignity of a patent office.[12] At the Restoration, even though the army was reduced almost to the vanishing point, the office of secretary at war was retained and was put on a public fiscal basis, remuneration coming directly from the Exchequer instead of out of the purse of the commander-in-chief. The duties of the secretary at war were gradually defined, until, by Blathwayt's time, there was little doubt where his powers began and where they left off. Office space had been provided in which he was to transact his business and house the official archives, which had begun to accumulate a decade before.

Blathwayt had some rather interesting, even illustrious predecessors. The first to be mentioned is Henry Parker, who was secretary to the parliamentary forces in 1642.[13] The corresponding agent of the royal forces, also known as secretary of the army, was Edward Walker, who followed Charles into exile.[14] John Rushworth succeeded Parker (who subsequently became secretary to the forces in Ireland, dying in 1652), and served in a dual capacity, as secretary to the lord general, Sir Thomas Fairfax, and also to the council of war.[15] After Fairfax's resignation

[11] Military leaders, particularly military historians, have regarded this as the great cause of weakness in military administration, but there was apparently never any real effort to change it.

[12] Patent issued to Charles I's secretary at war, during a part of his exile. See *infra*, p. 213.

[13] *Dict. Natl. Biog.*, XLIII, 240–241; together with Thomas May, Parker published *The King's Cabinet Opened*. His name appears in Peacock's *The Army Lists of the Roundheads and Cavaliers. . . . 1642*, p. 20.

[14] *Dict. Natl. Biog.*, LIX, 48–51; also Hadyn's *Book of Dignities*, p. 233; Harleian Catalogue, No. 6802.

[15] *Dict. Natl. Biog.* (article written by Sir Charles Firth), XLIX, 419–422; Firth's bibliography is of value for Rushworth's military activities.

Rushworth attended Cromwell, accompanying him on the invasion of Scotland. His name appears frequently in State Papers Domestic in a military capacity.

Rushworth's successor was William Clarke, who had served an apprenticeship as clerk in the office. Under Clarke, the war office rapidly took shape. Like Rushworth, he served in a double capacity. When Cromwell withdrew from Scotland, Clarke remained behind to serve the generals who succeeded in command. When Monck assumed control in 1654, Clarke became his secretary and invaluable attendant. Official records were compiled by him, but he unfortunately followed the prevailing tendency and carried them off with him when he left office.[16]

Meanwhile Edward Walker, Charles's faithful secretary at war, had his position fortified as an office under the great seal, the patent being issued at Bruges, January 1, 1657. He was allowed a salary of twenty shillings in Dutch money, per diem.[17] It was a hollow gesture. On Charles's restoration Walker was set aside, and for a few months, Sir Edward Nicholas, secretary of the southern province, administered military affairs.[18] Finally Monck, now the Duke of Albemarle, demanded recognition for the faithful Clarke, who, on January 28, 1661, was made secretary to the forces.[19] For five years Clarke served Albemarle, virtually as his private military secretary. He carried on an active correspondence, however, with the secretaries of state and with the Admiralty. He must have abandoned his attempts to keep any adequate system of records, for there are practically no war office archives

16 See *The Clarke Papers*, Camden Society, 4 vols.; there is a valuable introduction by Firth.

17 Add. MSS. 15856; warrant for payment dated January 10, 1657; also Walton, *History of the British Standing Army, 1660–1700*, App. LXXXV, p. 842. For mention of another claimant to the office during the Civil Wars see a reference to G. Tryme, *Cal. S. P. Dom.*, 1660–1661, p. 295.

18 See references, *Cal. S. P. Dom.*, 1660–1661.

19 *Ibid.*, p. 490.

for his period. In June, 1666, during the Four Days' Battle, he fell mortally wounded on the deck of the *Royal Charles*, whither he had accompanied Albemarle.[20]

As if to establish a precedent, Clarke was succeeded by Mathew Lock, who had been his clerk for several years. Lock had accompanied Albermarle on the expedition to Scotland.[21] At the Restoration he had been made secretary at war to the forces in Ireland, an office which was frequently in abeyance during the rest of the century and was regarded as the perquisite of the secretary of the lord lieutenant.[22] On June 22, 1666, Albemarle wrote to Secretary Arlington from aboard the *Royal Charles*, saying that he wanted a commission for Lock, "long one of his secretaries, and well versed in army business, to be secretary at war in place of Sir William Clarke."[23] The request was granted, but Lock's patent, as well as that of Sir William, seems to have been lost.[24]

The office developed rapidly under Lock, although not as a result of anything that Lock himself did. Albemarle died in January, 1670, and Charles failed to appoint an immediate successor as commander-in-chief. This crystallized matters; within a few days after the duke's death, Lock was granted an increase in salary, presumably in recognition of the added responsibility which he was to carry.[25] He was likewise given an office in the old

20 *Cal. S. P. Dom.*, 1665–1666, p. 431; Clifford to Arlington, June 5, 1666.

21 *Hist. MSS. Com., Egmont MSS.*, I, 534; also Percival's letters to Sir Paul Davys, his uncle, pp. 547, 550, 552, 554.

22 *Cal. S. P. Ireland*, 1660–1662, p. 215; the appointment was made February 12, 1661. See also *Cal. S. P. Dom.*, 1673–1675, pp. 246–248, for a dispute which arose over the right of the secretary of the lord lieutenant to claim for himself the secretaryship at war of Ireland.

23 *Cal. S. P. Dom.*, 1665–1666, p. 438.

24 *Ibid.*, p. 448. References to it are to be found, and in them Lock is referred to as *sergeant at war*, rather than *secretary*, evidence, not of any technical difference, but of the looseness in expression then current.

25 *Ibid.*, 1670, p. 1; the increase dated from January 7, 1670. Lock had

Guards House, and was instructed to keep entry books of the orders issued.[26]

The official who really gained by the absence of the commander-in-chief was the secretary of state. His power over military matters was already considerable. The establishments, which did not, of course, attain their real importance until after the Revolution of 1688, when they became subject to parliamentary control, were, by the order which Charles issued in January, 1669, invalid unless they were signed by the Treasury lords and one of the two principal secretaries of state.[27] Likewise, no military commissions could issue unless they bore either the sign manual and signet of the secretary of state or the signature of the commander-in-chief. Even during the temporary revival of the office of commander-in-chief, or captain-general, under Monmouth, the secretary of state continued to exercise this power over commissions.[28] Tech-

been receiving ten shillings a day; he was now to receive twenty shillings. In 1673, with the outbreak of the Dutch War he petitioned for a further increase and was granted one pound a day additional. (*Ibid.*, 1673–1675, pp. 82–83; W.O. 24:3.) By 1679–1680, his salary had dropped again to one pound. (W.O. 24:5.) As secretary at war in Ireland, Lock had been allowed one pound a day with five shillings extra for his clerk, Arthur Podmore. (*Cal. S. P. Ireland*, 1660–1662, p. 215.)

26 *Cal. S. P. Dom.*, 1671, p. 376; a letter dated from the old Guards House. This order has not been discovered, but Lock mentioned it in his petition for an increase in salary, 1673. (*Ibid.*, 1673–1675, pp. 82–83.)

27 W.O. 26:1, f. 4; January 24, 1669. The occasion for the issuance of this order is not apparent.

28 In Monmouth's office books appear numerous orders from him to the secretary of state for commissions to be made out. (See, for example, S. P. Dom., Military Entry Books, 41, 58.) This very matter involved Williamson in 1678, when he was condemned for countersigning commissions issued to Papists. His argument, that he had been ordered to sign and dared not refuse, was typical of him as a weak secretary of state. However, it is a question whether a secretary of state was, or was not, compelled to carry out an order of the commander in the issuance of commissions. (For Williamson's case, see Evans, *The Principal Secretary of State*, pp. 142–143: also *Hist. MSS. Com., Ormonde MSS.*, n.s., IV, 475–476.)

nically, the commander-in-chief still shared it and used it
at least in time of war, as Blathwayt himself testified
many years later.[29]

As the result of French influence and the prevailing admiration for Louvois' military administration, some men
at this time felt that the secretary of state should fall heir
to all the civil powers of the commander. Almost immediately after the death of Albemarle, Arlington, secretary
of state for the southern province, received a letter from
Montague, the English ambassador to France, which contained the following advice: "Your lordship ought, as you
are secretary of state, by the king's directions, give out
all the orders to the army as Mr. de Louvoy [M. de
Louvois] does here. Therefore look to it in time not to let
such a thing slip; the king will be better served by it, and
it will be an injury and diminution to your place to have
it done by anybody else."[30] A few years later, when Monmouth was banished, the Duke of York expressed great
joy that there was to be no successor: "As for the generalship, nobody will have it more. One of the secretarys,
which will be the Earl of Sunderland, is to manage that
affair as M. de Louvois does in France."[31]

More than a century elapsed, however, before the secretaries of state in England wielded anything like the
power exercised by Louvois. England's military administration was a long way from such complete centralization.
Although no contest arose between the incumbents of the
secretarial offices and the commander-in-chief during
Monmouth's occupancy, from 1674 to 1679, there was a
delineation of powers, which, in the end, was destined to

29 Add. MSS. 36860, f. 92; Blathwayt's testimony to the parliamentary
commissioners of accounts, October 14, 1702; he stated that generals on the
field had this power and frequently used it.

30 *Hist. MSS. Com., Montague House Papers*, I, 461; January 20, 1670.

31 *Ibid.*, XV. Report, App., Pt. V, Foljambe MSS., pp. 137–138.

enhance the influence of the secretary at war. In September, 1676, a royal warrant was issued which listed the powers the commander-in-chief might exercise without reference to the secretary of state, that is, with the countersignature of the secretary at war alone. The order had reference, primarily, to fairly trivial technicalities, such as the quartering of troops, marching orders, and convoys.[32] By this standing order the secretary at war gained the specific right of access to the crown and a position of partial independence of the secretary of state.[33]

This was the second time, as far as is known, when a specific definition was made of the powers of the secretary at war. The patent which had been issued to Walker, in 1657, had authorized him to "draw up, form, prepare, and present unto us for our royal signature all such commissions, warrants, letters, orders, and other institutions fit and proper for the government of our army and forces according to such commands as you shall receive from ourselves for the same or from any of our principal secretaries of state signifying our pleasure. We do likewise will and authorize you to be present at our councils of war to take the results thereof, and to cause all such directions as you shall receive thereupon to be duly executed and from time to time to give us an account of the per-

[32] W.O. 26:3, ff. 204–205; September 7, 1676. It stated specifically the point at issue: "And considering that Wee continue to Issue from Our selfe, some kind of Warrant and Military Orders which did belong to the office of our late Generall, and which hee was wont to dispatch and signe, Wee being desirous to distinguish such Warrants and Orders from the affaires of our Crowne passing our Signett and Signe Manuall, Have thought fitt . . . that all such kinds of Warrants and Orders as formerly issued from George Duke of Albemarle Our late Generall deceased (in regard of that Office) and which wee continue to Issue from Ourselfe; shall passe Our Signe Manuall onely, and shall be Countersigned by the Secretary to our Forces."

[33] There is plenty of evidence to show that the secretary at war had already exercised this right of countersignature, but this order clarified the situation by giving definite authority.

formance and to keep registers thereof.''[34] Since the patents of Clarke and Lock are not available, it is impossible to state whether they were as specific as that issued to Walker. Blathwayt's was far from being so precise; it simply stated that he was to serve as ''secretary at war to all my forces both horse and foote, which are now raised and of my forces and armies which at any time hereafter shall be raised in my kingdom of England, dominion of Wales, and town of Berwick upon Tweed and any other dominions and territories thereunto belonging.''[35] Blathwayt was to be allowed to appoint deputies, subject to the royal permission, and was to take orders only from the king, from the general in charge of the forces, or from the commander-in-chief.[36]

During Blathwayt's administration of the war office, no instructions were given him, comparable in scope and form to the elaborate instructions presented to certain other officials—for instance, to a colonial governor. When asked by the parliamentary commissioners, in 1702, whether he had specific instructions, he answered that he had not, many of his duties depending on the *lex non scripta*. From time to time, of course, royal and parliamentary orders were issued,[37] and despite the lack of definition in the office, the duties to be performed were

[34] Add. MSS. 15856; also Walton, *History of the British Standing Army*, App. LXXXV, p. 842.

[35] Add. MSS. 19519, f. 25; Patent Rolls, 35 Charles II, Pt. II, No. 25. See also Patent Rolls, I James II, Pt. XI, No. 17, for the reissue of the patent on James's accession.

[36] There was no specific mention of the secretary of state, though, of course, it was understood that the secretary transmitted the orders of the crown. Blathwayt was not called upon to serve as secretary to the councils of war. There is no evidence that he ever served as the council's secretary, though in the absence of evidence it may equally well be concluded that he did. One of the clerks in the war office served in this capacity while Blathwayt was in Flanders.

[37] Add. MSS. 36861; minutes of November 30, 1702.

sufficiently clear cut. Blathwayt was responsible for the movement of troops, and their levying, disbanding, marching, and quartering. He could issue all such orders under the royal sign manual and his own countersignature, without further reference to the secretary of state.[38] In performing these duties, Blathwayt exercised a greater independence than did Lock.[39]

The vast increase in the size of the army during Blathwayt's tenure meant that frequent orders were issued for recruiting. The actual service was performed by military officers, but, as Blathwayt stated, "No officer ought to beat up for recruits, without an order under her Majesty's own hand, or an authentic copy thereof, attested by the secretary at war, nor is it in the power of a sergeant or any officer under the degree of colonel, to discharge any man after being listed, or extort money for setting them at liberty."[40] Except for the disbanding that went on after the suppression of Monmouth's Rebellion, there was no real reduction in the size of the army until 1698, when the secretary at war was kept busy with the problems that necessarily arose on so radical a decrease.[41]

Since soldiers had no barracks provided for them but were quartered in inns and taverns, it fell to the lot of the secretary at war to see that such public houses as were required be notified. With his usual precision, Blathwayt

[38] See Blathwayt's entry books of such orders, W.O. 4:1–2; W.O. 5:1–11.
[39] A comparison of the books kept by Lock and Blathwayt in series W.O. 26:1–11 reveals this. It may be that Lock was diffident, or that the secretaries of state and Monmouth were assertive. (See Monmouth's books, S. P. Dom., Vols. 41, 58.) This was true even after the order of 1676.
[40] W.O. 4:2, f. 100; Blathwayt to the mayor of Nottingham, Whitehall, January 20, 1704.
[41] See W.O. 26:8, f. 106; Add. MSS. 38704, f. 79; Add. MSS. 9759, f. 13; and *Hist. MSS. Com., Bath MSS., Prior Papers*, III, 223, for some references to disbanding in 1698 and 1699, and the steps involved in the orders parliament had issued.

had a list of available places drawn up.[42] The problems of
discipline which arose as a result of this method of
quartering also fell within the purview of the secretary at
war. He based his orders on the articles of war. These
were drawn up from time to time by the council of war,
made up of the king and the general officers, the actual
drafting being done by the secretary at war, who then
submitted them to the council.[43] The articles of war were
supplemented by statutory regulations beginning with
the Mutiny Act of 1689. When completed, the articles
were dispatched by the secretary at war to all the commanding officers.[44] They attempted to cover every possible misdemeanor which a soldier might commit. When
quarrels arose among soldiers or cases of insubordination occurred, the matter was referred to the secretary at
war, who stated the rule of discipline that applied.

[42] W.O. 30:48. The list was apparently drawn up in the summer of 1686.
It is the only one of its kind among the war office files. There were, however,
the various garrisons, or castles, in which troops were stationed.

[43] Clode, *Military Forces of the Crown*, I, 144; quoting from the parliamentary investigations and from Lord Harding's evidence, 1837.

[44] W.O. 4:1, f. 10; the letter enclosing the articles of war made necessary
by Monmouth's Rebellion, July 4, 1685. See also Add. MSS. 38695, f. 179 for
an officer's acknowledgement of the copy of the Mutiny Act which Blathwayt had sent him. Blathwayt was also responsible for the removal of troops
on election days. The first order of such a nature that has been found is
dated 1695. (W.O. 5:7; October 13, 1695, issued by Blathwayt.) Luttrell,
Brief Relation (III, 531), cites one of September 28, issued by Clarke. However, a letter which Blathwayt dispatched during the election of 1695 proves
that the rule for the removal of troops was of long standing. He wrote to
Lord Cutts, then governor of the Isle of Wight, saying that he was surprised
to learn that Cutts had ordered two companies of foot from Portsmouth to
come and quarter at Yarmouth during the election there, ''where none or no
such proportion of men used to be at another time. I hope, my Lord, it is
quite otherwise, for that it is a constant rule, and His Majesty's express
pleasure that all soldiers do ever remove from a place where there is to be an
election, as it is absolutely necessary in this case, where the least intimation
of such quartering would set the House of Commons in a flame and make
void any election your Lordship should countenance.'' (*Hist. MSS. Com.,
Frankland Russell MSS.*, p. 85; dated March 26, 1695.)

Though the secretary of state's police power was here involved, he refused to have anything to do with the matter, except where the case was one which concerned civilians as well as soldiers, referring it instead to the war office.[45] When a court martial was necessary, Blathwayt's jurisdiction ceased, although there are rare instances when he issued orders for regimental court martials.[46] General court martials could be ordered only by the secretary of state,[47] and the actual trials themselves were under the jurisdiction of the judge advocate general.[48]

Disputes which arose over questions of precedency were constantly referred to Blathwayt, who cited the rule applying, and ordered compliance with it.[49] Except in time of war, his power never extended to the militia, which was under the sole control of the secretaries of state.[50] The royal guards and garrisons were under his jurisdiction, any evidence to the contrary notwithstand-

[45] *Cal. S. P. Dom.*, 1689–1690, p. 370; Shrewsbury to Colonel Foulke; also Porlock MSS., case of Colonel Kirke, April, 1689 (W.O. 4:1, ff. 20–21; a case of insubordination in which Blathwayt cited the rule applying). In case of legal technicalities, Blathwayt referred the matter to the attorney-general. (W.O. 4:1, f. 4.)

[46] W.O. 30:17, ff. 49–53; orders signed by Blathwayt during the encampment at Hounslow Heath, in 1686. See also ff. 1–2 for some minor orders bearing his signature, February, 1684; also f. 174 for one signed by St. John, August 8, 1704. George Clarke, judge advocate general in Blathwayt's time and son of Sir William Clarke, once complained bitterly that Blathwayt manoeuvered to get business away from him. (*Hist. MSS. Com., Popham MSS.*, p. 262.) But he seems in the case he cites to have been mistaken, for the order was signed by Sunderland. (W.O. 30:17, ff. 4–6.)

[47] S. P. Dom., Military Papers, III, 219. The orders were prepared for the secretary of state by the secretary at war.

[48] The formal reports on the trials were transmitted to the secretary at war. Only one such volume of entries appears in Blathwayt's period, W.O. 30:17, entries in which run from 1684 to 1704.

[49] Egerton MSS. 2618, f. 157; W.O. 4:1, ff. 37–38, 56, 85.

[50] W.O. 4:1, ff. 6–7. See also Egerton MSS. 1626, an entry book of militia returns drawn up in 1697, apparently for Blathwayt's use, since there are marginal insertions in his hand.

ing, since the term "guards and garrison" was the usual way of referring to the forces of the crown and was first applied when the army after the Restoration consisted of little more than the remnant of royal guards and the troops stationed in the various garrisons.[51]

One of the most important duties attached to the office of the secretary at war was the preparation of the establishments for signature by the Treasury and one of the secretaries of state. Establishments were drawn on the basis of the muster rolls, which were kept by the commissary of musters,[52] and the secretary at war had nothing whatever to do with them except to issue the various rules which applied.[53] He kept no muster rolls in his office, only muster books, in which were recorded the day on which musters were taken and information as to whether companies had been mustered complete.[54] When establishments were to be drawn up, he either made use of his muster books or called for the muster rolls and thereupon drafted triplicate forms, one copy of which went to the paymaster-general of the forces, a second to the commissary of the musters, while the third remained in the war office. The rule for the signing of the establishments was provided for in the order of 1669, and Blathwayt could never be persuaded to diverge from it, not even in the days when as secretary of state *pro tem.* he was in possession of the signet.[55]

[51] Andrews, *Guide to the Materials . . . in the P. R. O.*, II, 270.

[52] Add. MSS. 36859, ff. 25, 105, 126, 131, 138.

[53] *Ibid.;* also W.O. 26:1, f. 71; *Cal. Treas. Bks.*, 1685–1689, Vol. VIII, Pt. I, 272; Add. MSS. 38694, especially ff. 17–22.

[54] None of Blathwayt's muster books, however, is extant. See his testimony on the question of mustering companies to their complete numbers *infra*, p. 429. (Porlock MSS.; letter to the parliamentary commissioners, March 21, 1715.)

[55] George Clarke, Blathwayt's deputy secretary at war while he was in Flanders, urged him to sign some additional items to be inserted in the establishments of 1692, but Blathwayt refused. (Add. MSS. 9732, f. 27; Clarke to Blathwayt, Whitehall, April 29, 1692.)

Although the presence of the secretary at war in the house of commons is assumed to date from the Revolution of 1688, when army finances first came under parliamentary control, Blathwayt's presence in parliament antedated the Revolution by three years. James had a keen desire that as many of his military assistants as possible be members of parliament, and in consequence Blathwayt stood for Newton, on the Isle of Wight, in 1685.[56] Even after the Revolution, the rule was not strictly enforced. Blathwayt either failed to secure a seat in the house or felt that his presence there was not necessary, for it was not until December, 1693, that he was returned for Bath.[57] Ranelagh, paymaster of the forces, fell heir, in 1689, to Blathwayt's seat at Newton, and upon him fell the task of introducing the army estimates until 1693, when Blathwayt began to share the business with him.[58]

One of Blathwayt's most important duties was the payment of the forces. No money ever passed through his hands, but it was his task to sign the pay warrants which were based on the debentures prepared by the paymaster-general of the forces. The power which he exercised was far more extensive than that possessed by Lock, whose signature rarely appears on any pay warrants except those for the fire-and-candle money which was issued to the soldiers.[59] The question of how much the soldiers were paid, and of the various off-reckonings and deductions to which their pay was subject, has been adequately dealt with in military histories.[60] Blathwayt issued the various

56 *Members of Parliament* (1213–1885), p. 555; he was elected April 3, 1685.

57 *Ibid.*, p. 568; November 20, 1693. He replaced Sir William Bassett, deceased.

58 *Ibid.*, p. 561.

59 Several cases occur in W.O. 26:1–5; see, for example, W.O. 26:3, f. 211. Such money was issued only to the soldiers in the garrisons.

60 Walton, *History of the British Standing Army*, p. 646. One shilling

orders with regard to payment and respites of payment.[61] In 1702, when the parliamentary commissioners investigated the matter, Blathwayt gave some very interesting testimony on the various steps in procedure and the rules which applied, and showed how largely they rested on the binding force of custom.[62] His statements gave ample evidence of the opportunities for fraud which came to the paymaster, the muster master, and the commissary of the musters. Except through connivance with those officials, since no money passed through Blathwayt's hands, there was less chance for malpractices on his part. There is no evidence of Blathwayt's connivance, as far as we know.[63]

on the pound was always deducted for the army's contingency fund, and, after Chelsea Hospital was established, there was an additional off-reckoning, or stoppage, of a half shilling. The fees demanded of the soldiers and officers were, of course, tremendous and every official at Whitehall with whom they had dealings came in for his share. Soldiers were also granted subsistence money, amounting to 8d. a week. Blathwayt issued the pay warrants to the company agents who presented them to the paymaster for the issuance of their money.

61 Respites were made on an officer's or a soldier's pay if he was absent without leave. Such orders for respiting had to be signed by the king and countersigned by the Treasury. Blathwayt refused to countersign them while he was abroad, even though the Treasury tried to force his hand. He said he did not care to establish a dangerous precedent. (Porlock MSS., Hill correspondence; Blathwayt to Hill, one of the Treasury lords, August, 1700. See also Add. MSS. 9752, ff. 57, 73, for rules with regard to respites.)

62 He explained the steps with regard to the issuance of debentures, pay warrants, etc., saying that much of the procedure rested on the *lex non scripta*, and after 1689 on parliamentary statute. (Add. MSS. 36861; testimony of November 30, 1702.) For copies of debentures see Add. MSS. 9756–9757. For the rules with regard to stoppages for subsistence, etc., see Blathwayt's statement of August 20, 1702. (Add. MSS. 36859, f. 141.) He stated that most of them rested on common usage or the royal order of 1695. (W.O. 4:2, f. 79.)

63 Porlock MSS., Hill correspondence; letters of 1700 and 1701 at the time of the impeachments of the ministers involved in the treaties of partition, and the parliamentary investigations of public accounts. Petitions with regard to pay of the soldiers and officers were referred to Blathwayt, who drew up his report in conjunction with the paymaster-general. See the one

The rule with regard to the signing of military commissions was not altered during Blathwayt's administration of the war office. Commissions were prepared in the office of the secretary at war and transmitted to the secretary of state.[64] They were recorded in the books of both offices.[65] In the absence of a seal for the war office, the secretary at war was unable to issue commissions, and there is no reason to suppose that the secretary of state would have relinquished his power without a struggle, since he found it exceedingly remunerative. Blathwayt did, however, consider that the powers which he obtained as secretary of state *pro tem.* (1692–1701) enabled him to sign commissions, so that in the commission books appear numerous entries to which his countersignature is attached.[66] He relinquished this right immediately on his return to England in the fall and did not resume it again until his departure for Flanders in the spring. Even so, he used his power only in cases of emergency.

Because of the want of centralization in military administration, Blathwayt was constantly in touch with various departments and officials besides the Treasury,

volume in the war office, W.O. 30:88, which covers the period from 1685 to 1711; there are only 48 pages for Blathwayt, and these extend only to 1691.

[64] For the royal orders on this in 1687 and 1689, see the material on fees, *infra,* pp. 458–459. See also *Hist. MSS. Com., Ormonde MSS.,* n.s., IV, 475–476; also *Cal. S. P. Dom.,* 1691–1692, p. 504.

[65] See W.O. 25:1–7, and the secretarial books, S. P. Dom., Military Entry Books, Vol. II *et seq.*

[66] See, for example, W.O. 25:6. Some question must have arisen with regard to the power of a secretary at war in connection with commissions, for, in 1690, when Sir Robert Southwell, who was to attend William as secretary of state to Ireland in the campaign, drew up his memorial on the powers of the secretary of state, he included this query; ''Shall all commissions for the army be there signed by such secretary [i.e., of state], as now practiced by the secretaries here; or shall that branch be given to the secretary at war?'' (Add. MSS. 38861, f. 123 *dorso.*) St. John and Walpole, Blathwayt's successors, did not attempt to sign commissions. (See S. P. Dom., Military Papers, III, 9, 36, etc.)

the secretary of state, the paymaster-general of the forces, and the commissary of the musters. Chief of these was the Ordnance, which had control of military stores. Blathwayt had no control over the issuance of stores, and the Ordnance, as the more ancient department, refused to take orders from him, accepting only such as were signed by the king and countersigned by the secretary of state.[67] In 1693, and again in 1702, the Ordnance charged Blathwayt, whom they regarded as a sort of upstart, with irregular practices, a charge which Blathwayt stoutly denied.[68] Many of his communications with the Ordnance were on colonial matters, since military stores had to be sent to the colonial garrisons, and Blathwayt was constantly forwarding to the Ordnance news which he had received from the colonies as to the state of their stores.[69]

Blathwayt came into contact with the Admiralty in connection with the marine establishments which he and they prepared jointly.[70] Copies of these establishments were

[67] W.O. 55:333–334 are the Ordnance entry books for the issuance of stores; the orders bear the signature of the secretary of state, with occasional signatures of Lock on orders for drums, bandoliers, and barrels of powder. Blathwayt occasionally sent letters to them, ordering an economy in stores, but he always referred officers who appealed to him for stores to the Ordnance. (See W.O. 4:1, ff. 1, 4–5, 7, 12–13, 35.) The Ordnance drew up separate establishments. (See Add. MSS. 17771.)

[68] *Cal. S. P. Dom.*, 1693, pp. 141–142; this is an interesting letter, from the master of the Ordnance, with regard to Blathwayt's power to issue orders from the king which the Ordnance had to obey. William III was trying to force naval matters into the hands of Nottingham, southern secretary, whereas the latter contended that the army was his province, and the navy, his colleague, Trenchard's. The Ordnance upheld the right of Trenchard, even in the face of the order Blathwayt had transmitted from William. See also W.O. 4:2, f. 22; Blathwayt to the master of the Ordnance, Whitehall, March 24, 1703, contending that he had always used the proper medium, the secretary of state. Clode (*Military Forces of the Crown*, II, 222, 260) mentions 1715 as the earliest date of conflict he had discovered.

[69] Scattered references, *Cal. S. P. Col.*

[70] Add. MSS. 9755, f. 77; Admiralty 1: 4316; Cardonnel, Blathwayt's clerk, to the secretary of the Admiralty board, with regard to the establish-

left in the secretary at war's office, and data with regard to them were entered in the war office books.[71] In times of war the military agencies increased, and after the Revolution of 1688 at least three new boards appeared—the victualling board, the transport board, and the commissioners of sick and wounded. With these, Blathwayt, in common with the Admiralty, the Treasury, the paymaster-general, and the secretary of state, was in constant communication, transmitting the royal orders.

Now that some idea of the office which Blathwayt held has been given, we may turn to the narrative of his years in the war office prior to the Revolution. He received his commission as secretary at war on August 18, 1683.[72] Little public attention was given to his appointment, although the clerks of the secretary of state's office mentioned it in their letters to the envoys.[73] Blathwayt, who had no great knowledge of military matters, immediately set to work to gather information on his new duties. He wrote to Lord Preston, then minister to France, telling him of his appointment and begging him to send any printed books on the French army or any manuscript material of a similar nature.[74] In March, 1686, he dispatched a letter to Sir William Trumbull, Preston's successor: "I

ments for the marines, which he had been working on in Flanders and was transmitting to the Admiralty office, Loo, September 5, 1698, s.n.

[71] *Ibid.*

[72] Add. MSS. 19519, f. 25; it was countersigned by Sunderland. The patent is dated October 5, 1683, Patent Rolls, 35 Charles II, Pt. II, No. 25.

[73] *Hist. MSS. Com., Downshire MSS., Trumbull Papers*, Vol. I, Pt. I, 19; Owen Wynne, Jenkins' clerk, to Lord Dartmouth, August 27, 1683: "Mr. Blathwayt hath bought Mr. Lock's place of secretary of [*sic*] war."

[74] *Hist. MSS. Com.*, VII. Report, App., Pt. I, Grahame MSS., p. 368 b; Whitehall, Dec. 17, 1683. Among Blathwayt's papers are to be found some sheets marked, "Extracts out of the French Ordinances," notes which he made at the time he entered the war office. He had extracted the French regulations which bore on his duties as secretary at war. (See Add. MSS. 38694, ff. 17–22.) It is a fair copy with corrections in Blathwayt's hand.

am now reading a large description in folio of the *Hôtel
des Invalides,* which takes notice of several Edicts and
Regulations concerning the government and economy of
that place which are said to be published and observed
there, none of which are to be found in any of the volumes
of Military *Ordonnances,* and if by your means they could
be produced they would be of great use in the model of
government for Chelsea Hospital his Majesty is now ordering to be prepared. . . . I have one more favor to beg
of you,'' he added, ''which is an account of the rank and
command in all places of the marshals of France, lieutenant-general, *maréchaux de camp,* lieutenant-generals of
the artillery, and in short of all the considerable officers in
the French army or of as many of them as may be most
easily and suddenly procured.''[75]

Blathwayt immediately had to lend himself to Charles
II's schemes for the reorganization of the army. ''The
design of new modelling the army lies before the king,''
the Duke of Ormonde wrote at the very time Blathwayt
entered the war office, ''wherein he only scruples at
changing the foot the Scotch regiment is upon; but if that
may be not, I know not how the rest of the project will
subsist.''[76] No real increase in the size of the army came
during Charles's reign, except that the soldiers returning
from Tangier, in 1683, had to be absorbed into the regiments stationed in England.[77] James II had no scruples

[75] *Hist. MSS. Com., Downshire MSS., Trumbull Papers,* Vol. I, Pt. I, 140,
163; letters dated March 25 and May 6, 1686. Blathwayt had no jurisdiction
over Chelsea Hospital when it was completed; it came under the direction of
the paymaster of the forces.

[76] *Hist. MSS. Com., Ormonde MSS.,* n.s., VII, 106; Ormonde to the Earl
of Arran, St. James Square, August 16, 1683.

[77] W.O. 4:1, f. 4; on July 23, 1684, Blathwayt notified the colonels of the
Queen's and the Duchess' regiments that the troops were to be absorbed
into their companies. The same year, the order went out that no more English subjects were to enlist in the foreign service, and that those then serving in the French and Dutch armies were recalled. Blathwayt commented on

and used any excuse for enlarging the forces. Monmouth's Rebellion offered a convenient opportunity, and long after the danger had subsided he kept on adding to the troops. By this gradual increase, James II and Blathwayt were unconsciously preparing the minds of Englishmen, hitherto distrustful of any standing army, for the huge forces which William III was going to thrust upon them. The establishments of Charles II cost on the average £200,000 per annum for the guards and garrisons; those of James, even excluding the last half year, averaged £530,000. Three troops of guards, one regiment of horseguards, one troop of dragoons, and four regiments of foot guards, with one or two independent companies, were organized before the end of Charles's reign, but James had four troops of guards, eight regiments of horse, twelve regiments of foot, three regiments of dragoons, and fourteen independent companies. By the winter of 1688, there were 4,500 men in the army and 1,500 men in the garrisons, a total of 6,000, treble the number there had been in Charles's army.[78] The number was small when compared with the 50,000 who were to serve under William III,[79] ridiculously small, too, when compared with the size of modern armies; but even so, to meet these increases tested to the full the military administration then existing. Blathwayt took over a pygmy army in 1683; he saw it grow enormously within a few years and felt his duties increase in corresponding ratio.[80]

the fine condition of the returning soldiers and the excellent appearance they made. (W.O. 4:1, ff. 9–10; also *Cal. S. P. Col.* 1681–1685, p. 611; Blathwayt to Cranfield, March 24, 1684.)

[78] *Cal. Treas. Bks.*, 1685–1689, Vol. VIII, Pt. I, xciii–xcv.

[79] When the reductions of 1698 came, parliament allowed William to retain 10,000 men in the army, a larger number than James's had ever included.

[80] James's effort to popularize the army appears in his decision to have summer encampments of the troops at Hounslow Heath, where elaborate mili-

The events of the years which led up to the Revolution of 1688 are dimly reflected in the war office books. They do not mention Monmouth's Rebellion as such, but for that crucial first week of July, 1685, when the Rebellion reached its height and then as suddenly collapsed, they are full of dispatches, emergency recruiting orders, and emergency commissions. They show that *carte blanche* was given to many of the officers, that articles of war, prepared for this "present occasion," were hastily issued, and that after the flurry was over letters were sent ordering demobilization.[81] They contain Blathwayt's letter of July 9, 1685, to Colonel Mackay, announcing that James had received the news of Monmouth's capture, the night before, by the militia of Dorset; and bidding him speed the news to his various troops.[82] There are the letters of thanks to the various officers for the way in which they had conducted themselves; orders disbanding the militia;

tary parades would attract all types of onlookers. As early as the summer of 1685, Edward Randolph reported: "This day his Majesty with a great attendance and Mr. Blathwayt went to Winsor: to see fitt ground for the army to encamp upon during his Majesty's stay here." (Toppan, *Edward Randolph*, IV, 26; Randolph to Southwell, July 30, 1685.) The following order, which was issued by William III to Blathwayt in 1693, is typical of those which he had received under James: "The king intends to have an encampment of his forces here and wishes you to prepare a list of such regiments as will be most proper to be so disposed." (*Cal. S. P. Dom.*, 1693, p. 72; Nottingham, secretary of state, to Blathwayt, Whitehall, March 18, 1693. See also Add. MSS. 9722, f. 60.) In 1693, the foot were to be encamped at Hounslow Heath, the horse near Portsmouth, but not too near because the country in the vicinity had almost been eaten bare and still had to provide the navy with food. (Add. MSS. 24328, f. 3.) In drawing up the plans for the encampment, Blathwayt consulted the necessary officials, the Treasury and the commissary general in particular, before presenting his report to the king. (W.O. 4:1, ff. 41–42; Blathwayt to Captain Shales, commissary general, December 11, 1686, asking him to drop in to see Blathwayt the next morning and to invite the other gentlemen concerned in the matter to come too.)

81 W.O. 4:1, ff. 7, 9, 10.

82 *Ibid.*, f. 10; a letter curiously inserted in the margin of the page.

a circular letter announcing the reductions of certain troops, not because of any discreditable action on their part but in order to lessen the cost of the army, an illusory pretext.[83] They contain also, dated July 29, 1685, a circular letter to each colonel, bidding him make a careful report to Blathwayt of the state of his regiment;[84] and orders involving the trials held by Jeffreys and "Kirke's Lambs," especially the one wherein James admitted that the common law courts would, as a concession to public opinion, replace the extraordinary tribunals he had set up.[85]

The war office books become of increasing interest in the months immediately preceding the Revolution. All through the summer of 1688, Blathwayt's correspondence with the officers indicates preparation for William's threatened invasion. No word appears with regard to the Trial of the Seven Bishops, but we find the circular letter of June 10th, which Blathwayt dispatched to the colonels of the regiments and the governors of the garrisons, announcing the birth of the Prince and stating that a public thanksgiving day was set for July 1st.[86] During August and a portion of September, Blathwayt was with James at Windsor. Late in August he began to send out marching orders, together with news of the progress of the

[83] *Ibid.*, ff. 6–7. Chronological order was not strictly maintained when these letters were entered.

[84] *Ibid.*, ff. 11, 13.

[85] *Ibid.*, f. 12; Blathwayt to Kirke, July 21, 1685. "That in all cases where any differences arise between a soldier and another person, not in his Majesty's pay, the decision be left to the Common Law, which is to be done in all matters where any person not in pay shall be concerned. And that in all cases whatsoever where the punishment is to be by loss of life or limb, the trial of any offender in his Majesty's pay be left to the Common and Statute Law, the Articles of War in all those cases being only to take place during the rebellion which is now ceased." A similar order went out after the Revolution. (*Ibid.*, ff. 128–129.)

[86] *Ibid.*, f. 82; also Add. MSS. 38695, f. 15.

preparations in Holland. "There are great preparations making in Holland of ships, men, and warlick [sic] provisions which they say these are intended against England," one letter reads.[87] Meanwhile he drew up an abstract of "The Last and Present Disposition of the Troops," dated July, 1688, and based on the establishments of 1686, 1687, and 1688.[88]

From the correspondence on the order which stated that, in the emergency, troops on the march (who would ordinarily have been billeted only on the public inns and alehouses) would have to be lodged in private houses, some idea of the popular temper can be gained. Blathwayt said that these were the king's orders, and that in such perilous times it did not behoove the mayors and citizens of the towns to defy them, lest their loyalty be questioned. He approved of the conduct of the townspeople of Rochester and spoke of their "present scrupulous mayor,"[89] but Hull, he thought, was acting most peculiarly in what was expedient for the king's service.[90] When he heard that innkeepers were tearing down their signs rather than house the troops on the march, he instructed officers to pay no attention to them, but to force their soldiers upon the "hostelers" as though nothing had happened.[91]

Preparations were made for clearing the troops, to insure their continued loyalty.[92] Payments were made with

[87] W.O. 4:1, f. 93; Blathwayt to Captain Shakerley, governor of Chester, August 28, 1688. Duplicates were sent out to the other commanding officers.
[88] Add. MSS. 38695, f. 27.
[89] W.O. 4:1, f. 104; letter to Sir Thomas Oglethorpe, in command at Rochester, October 9, 1688; also ff. 96–99, for letters written in September.
[90] Ibid., f. 100, letter to Lord Langdale, Windsor, September 15, 1688. Sunderland, in his capacity of lord president of the council, also dispatched a letter. (See f. 102.)
[91] Ibid., f. 107; letter to Colonel Butler, Whitehall, October 25, 1688.
[92] Ibid., f. 103; letter to Captain Shales, commissary general, ordering him to send in an account to Ranelagh, paymaster-general of the forces, of

greater regularity than was usual, and in August subsistence money was handed over in advance to the agents of the companies—an unheard-of procedure.[93] Orders for biscuits for 20,000 men, for the first week of the march, went out to Captain Shales, commissary general, on October 16.[94] As late as November 22, Blathwayt transmitted a royal order to the Treasury Lords to provide shoes suitable to the season for 10,000 men—perhaps a last touch of royal effrontery.[95]

The great uncertainty as to the place where William would land can be followed very closely in Blathwayt's letters. On November 1, he wrote the Duke of Newcastle that, in all probability, it would be at Burlington Bay, or somewhere in the north. If this occurred, and if William approached Newcastle, where the duke was stationed, the latter was to march his troops to Berwick or to any other place of greater safety and await orders.[96] Reresby, governor of the garrison at York, wrote Blathwayt of the conflicting rumors he was receiving and said that he depended on Blathwayt to inform him correctly if news arrived.[97]

One of the most interesting orders which Blathwayt dispatched at this time was that for the transfer to London of the unruly Protestant officers, Colonel Beaumont

the forage and provisions for the several regiments during the late encampment, as the king wanted the regiments cleared at once (September 22, 1688).

[93] Add. MSS., 38695, f. 34; receipt signed by thirteen agents, of the amounts they had received in subsistence money to September 1, 1688, from Blathwayt's clerk, Adam Cardonnel. The amounts varied, but averaged about £18: 0: 0. The receipt was dated August 17, 1688.

[94] W.O. 4:1, f. 105; after the first week, soft bread, rather than biscuits, was to be supplied.

[95] Ibid., f. 110, November 22, 1688.

[96] Ibid., f. 108; November 1, 1688.

[97] Reresby, Memoirs (London, 1875), p. 410; also W.O. 4:1, letter of October 29, 1688.

and five of his captains. The conflict had arisen over the
Anglo-Dutch brigade, which had been in Louis XIV's pay
but had been recalled to England. All but forty or fifty of
the soldiers had been absorbed into Colonel McElligott's
regiment, the Roman Catholic regiment designed for
service in Ireland. The Duke of Berwick, then in command at Portsmouth and in charge of the matter, had
ordered Beaumont to take the remaining men into his
regiment, but the latter had stoutly refused to do so. Five
of his captains shared in his refusal. Their recalcitrancy
was reported to the king, and Blathwayt was thereupon
commanded to order Berwick to send up such officers "as
have behaved themselves disorderly towards you" to
London under heavy guard.[98] So far was Blathwayt willing to go in enforcing the Roman Catholic designs of
James II and Berwick.

Finally the "Protestant wind," the arrival of which
Blathwayt had repeatedly reported,[99] actually did arrive
and the invasion began. Whatever may have been Blathwayt's inward feelings and desires, his actions were out-
wardly entirely loyal to James. He dispatched royal
orders with alacrity. The week before the famous march
to Salisbury began, on which Blathwayt was scheduled to
attend James, Blathwayt kept busy reporting the supposed movements of various deserters to William—Lord
Lovelace, Tom Wharton, and others—and ordering their
apprehension if discovered.[100] On November 15, he announced their seizure by the militia at Cirencester.[101] On
the march to Salisbury, Blathwayt's conduct was punctilious, as far as outward evidence shows, and James did

[98] W.O. 4:1, ff. 95–96; letters of September 8, 1688. See the account given
by Sir Sibbald Scott, *The British Army*, III, 556–557.

[99] W.O. 4:1, ff. 103–104.

[100] *Ibid.*, f. 109; Whitehall, November 12, 1688.

[101] *Ibid.*

not suspect him. Blathwayt issued the circular letter regarding the royal nosebleed, which was in many ways the turning point of the revolution. "His Majesty finding the enemy like to remain in their present quarters, and being under some indisposition of health by a frequent bleeding at the nose, has thought fit to order the foot and cannon to march towards London whither his Majesty is going in person in a few days; the horse and dragoons being left in these parts to make head against the enemy as there shall be occasion."[102]

James's last desperate efforts to forestall disaster can be seen in the letters dispatched by Blathwayt before the royal party left Salisbury *en route* to London. They give no sign of the perturbation he himself must have felt, but they reveal the hopelessness that had settled down upon the situation. Kirke, who was awaiting the arrival of James at Warminster, was ordered to march toward London and to take every precaution against falling into the hands of William.[103] Orders went out that James was returning to London by way of Winchester, and Sir Henry Sheeres was ordered to keep the roads open.[104] A circular letter was issued that the articles of war were to be read to the troops, and soldiers and officers alike were to take the oath of fidelity.[105] James's attempts to compel loyalty by assurances of prompt payment and the granting of other favors are reflected in the dispatches. From Hartford Bridge Blathwayt wrote the Earl of Feversham, who was to prove so loyal to James: "The king commands me to let your lordship know, that all is well in these parts, his Majesty being ready to go in his coach for London, and

---

[102] Add. MSS., 28053, f. 357; the letter is in court hand, but bears Blathwayt's signature.

[103] W.O. 4:1, ff. 110–111; Salisbury, November 23, 1688.

[104] *Ibid.*, f. 111.

[105] *Ibid.*, ff. 110–111; also W.O. 5:4, f. 9; November 22 and 23, 1688.

that his Majesty has ordered Lord Ranelagh to send
money to Maidenhead to be ready for the forces when
they come thereabouts."[106] To Sheeres he wrote that he
could enlarge his quarters, spreading his troops over the
surrounding towns as he saw fit. "I have forthwith taken
care that you may be furnished with the £1000 you want
for the train which will be paid tomorrow in the usual way
by the treasurer of the army."[107]

By November 27, the royal party was back again in
London, and two days later the regiments of horse, foot,
and dragoons had arrived in their respective quarters.
Blathwayt wrote to Commissary Shales to take particular
care that they had the necessary provisions and, for his
better direction, enclosed lists of places where there were
troops quartered.[108] At the same time he wrote to Lieu-
tenant-Colonel Molineux of the king's regret that his
regiment had been guilty of insolent and reproachful language to the Protestants. His majesty wanted it understood that at all times his subjects, no matter of what per-
suasion, were to live peaceably and quietly together.[109]

One of James's last attempts at conciliation was his decision to call parliament. Writs were issued, and Blathwayt informed some of the officers on November 29 that
January 15 was the day set for the opening.[110] James
withdrew to Windsor, but Blathwayt apparently remained in London. Although he may have been torn by
doubts as to the course he was to follow, he continued to
perform his routine duties. As late as December 8, he
was still writing to the officers stationed in the provinces
and enclosing the king's orders. His letters give no indi-

---

106 W.O. 4:1, f. 112; November 26, 1688.

107 Ibid.; Whitehall, November 27, 1688. Blathwayt must have referred to
the paymaster-general, when he spoke of the treasurer, since such an official
was no longer to be found. He was a pre-Restoration official.

108 Ibid., f. 115; Whitehall, November 29, 1688.

109 Ibid., f. 116; same date.   110 Ibid.

cation of any perturbation he may have felt. "Sir," he wrote to Sir Henry Sheeres on the eighth, "I have laid your letters, dated this day, before his Majesty who does very much disapprove the placing the train of artillery at Brentford, and has therefore commanded me to signify his pleasure that you take care to have it removed tomorrow from thence to Hounslow, the Heath near it being very fit to encamp in. And that you may have more time to perform this I have sent you the present express."[111] This was the last letter in the letterbook under the old *régime*. Within a few days William was in possession of London, and the revolution was virtually over.

When, or under what circumstances, Blathwayt went over to William is a question, but it must have been almost immediately after William's entrance into the capital. It was shortly after James's first flight, according to Kennett, that William asked Blathwayt to furnish him with a list of James's forces.[112] Letters poured into the war office from the officers, particularly from the governors of the remote garrisons, such as York and Chester, begging Blathwayt to send them information and orders. Shakerley at Chester seemed convinced of Blathwayt's loyalty to James as late as the seventh of December, for he wrote to him that day, pledging his own allegiance to James and stating that he was doing all he could to keep his men at their posts.[113] By the thirteenth, news had reached him of Blathwayt's desertion, and panic-stricken he promptly followed suit; "Great Sir, the loyalty and fidelity I paid to my king will not, I hope, be imputed to

[111] *Ibid.*, f. 118. Although this was the last letter under James, there was no break in the entries; only a pencil mark, made by some one going over the book at a later date, indicates that a new *régime* had commenced.

[112] Kennett, *History of England*, III, 582; Scott, *The British Army*, III, 597–598.

[113] Add. MSS. 38695, f. 92.

me a crime by the victorious Prince of Orange, whose commands I now wait and shall steadfastly obey.''[114] Two days later, Shakerley acknowledged the news of James's first flight, "Honored Sir, I received yours last post bringing the sad account of the banishment of our king, which you will judge is very grievous to a loyal heart.''[115] The tone of Blathwayt's letter written immediately after James's flight must have been noncommittal, neither reassuring to Shakerley nor furnishing conclusive evidence that Blathwayt had thrown in his strength on the side of William. Subsequent dispatches, of course, proved that Blathwayt had indeed pledged himself to a new loyalty.

Blathwayt's conduct, cautious as it was, did not altogether save him. Somewhere he faltered in his balanced neutrality. Nor is it surprising that he aroused suspicions on both sides. There were those among William's followers who were ready to charge him with being a Jacobite and with a secret correspondence with James at St. Germain.[116] On the other hand, Berwick, James's natural son, brought charges against Blathwayt of traitorous conduct in 1688, and these appear in Berwick's *Memoirs*. Berwick claimed that Blathwayt had deliberately held back the marching orders which had been issued, instructing him [Berwick] to proceed to Salisbury on Thursday, November 8. "Le sieur de Blathwayt, secrétaire de la guerre, pour favoriser ce projet, avoit exprès différé pendant plusieurs jours de m'envoyer l'ordre du Roi.''[117] He maintained that Blathwayt was in league with Lord Cornbury, cousin-german of William of Orange, who, in Berwick's absence, was in command of the troops at Salisbury. With him also was Colonel Langston, in command of the fourth regiment of horse during the absence of St.

114 Add. MSS. 38695, f. 103; December 13, 1688.
115 *Ibid.*, f. 104.   116 See *infra*, p. 246.
117 Berwick, *Memoirs* (Paris, 2nd ed., 1780), I, 30; also pp. 29–31.

Albans in France.[118] It had been agreed that Cornbury
was to deliver the troops at Salisbury into William's
hands before the arrival of Berwick. When the mails arrived at Salisbury on November 11, Langston was to
open the bag and slip in false marching orders, commanding Cornbury to proceed at once to Exeter in the direction of William's army. This was done, but the ruse ended
in failure, for Berwick, on his alleged belated arrival in
Salisbury, discovered what had happened and went in hot
pursuit. He met the troops returning to Salisbury in
great disorder, they having for the most part deserted
Cornbury when they discovered the schemes he had contrived for turning them over to William.

Berwick's discomfiture and rage over this incident can
well be imagined, and he ultimately concluded that Blathwayt had connived at it by holding back the orders which
would have enabled him to arrive at Salisbury in time to
prevent Cornbury's departure. Whatever the truth of the
matter may be, the fact remains that Blathwayt did draw
up the orders for Berwick to march, and that this was
done, according to the date in the entry book, on November 6.[119] It is possible that he deliberately failed to dispatch them to Berwick in time for him to commence his
march on the eighth, but if this be so, it seems strange that
Blathwayt should have been in James's good graces during the royal progress to and from Salisbury a week later,
when Berwick's opportunity to reveal his treachery to
James would have been more than ample. Apparently
Berwick did not connect Blathwayt with the delayed or-

[118] Macpherson, *Original Papers*, I, 287–290. According to Macpherson,
Cornbury and Langston were both in sympathy and active coöperation with
certain members of the Treason Club, which met at the Rose Tavern, Covent
Garden, a center for followers of William.

[119] W.O. 5:3; no paging. Similar marching orders were dispatched to all
the other commanding officers. The volume ends with the entries of November 6, 1688.

ders at the time, but several years later, when seeking
some explanation for the incident, he hit upon the story of
Blathwayt's treachery as an excuse for his own bungling
in being outwitted.

For a few weeks after William's successful entrance
into London, Blathwayt continued in the war office. The
day before Christmas he wrote to Pepys, who was still at
the Admiralty, enclosing William's order for convoy for
the troops that were being dispatched to Jersey and
Guernsey as a result of their stand against William.[120] He
wished Pepys a pleasant holiday, so the prevailing gloom
had not crushed entirely the Christmas festive spirit. He
was still giving directions on January 10, for he wrote to
Sir Robert Holmes, who was in charge of the movement
of troops to Ireland and was seeking information on the
question of recruits there, that he could scarcely expect
much assistance from the Irish officers. "You cannot expect that the quarter masters of these Irish regiments
should be useful to you, since they are no longer in the
form of regiments, but in the nature of prisoners."[121] Undue optimism, however, on the Irish situation led him to
declare: "I cannot tell you when this trouble of guarding
the Irish will be over with you, but I imagine it will not
last much above a fortnight, so that the people of the
Island have the less reason to be dissatisfied with their
guests, and in the meantime I will take the best care I can,
that their subsistence be duly furnished to them, which is
all you represent as necessary on this occasion."[122] Such
a statement did not show much insight into the Irish temperament, but the transmission of the letter proves that
he was still in authority at the war office. He was also kept

[120] W.O. 4:1, f. 121; there is another for January 8.

[121] Ibid., f. 119; letters are entered with no strict adherence to chronological order.

[122] Ibid.

busy supplying the committee of the house of lords with information with regard to the state of the forces, and the minutes of the committee for March 9 contain a memorandum to the effect that Blathwayt had presented to the Duke de Schomberg a "Memorial of all that has been directed concerning arms to be immediately sent from Exeter to Liverpool, and from thence to Londonderry; 5,000 armes, 400 barrels of powder, etc."[123]

Altogether Blathwayt could not have felt very sure of himself, though he informed Shakerley, who from Chester was imploring his assistance and asking knowledge of the Prince's intentions, that while, for the present, William had no intention of disturbing any of the officers in their rank, there was no guarantee that they might not ultimately be reduced. Meanwhile he said that Shakerley had better keep in close touch with Churchill, whose influence might be of help, and take absolutely no liberties; a piece of advice which he was, no doubt, following himself.[124]

Sometime in January, or early in February, Blathwayt was ordered to give up his commission. We have his own testimony to that effect, for during the course of the investigations of the parliamentary commissioners in 1702, when asked to give certain information with regard to the events of the winter of 1688–89, he said he was in no position to do so: "Being asked what forces the Earl of Levens brought over at the Revolution, he said he could not give any account thereof. That things were in disorder at that time, that he himself was not in his place till two or three months after the Revolution, but that the

[123] *Hist. MSS. Com.*, XII. Report, App., Pt. VI, House of Lords MSS., p. 170; also pp. 167–172, 176, 178. Blathwayt here seems to have been acting in his capacity of clerk of the council, a position which he retained without any serious question being raised.

[124] W.O. 4:1, ff. 119–120.

Lord Portland for a month or two did most of the business belonging to the secretary at war's office with the assistance of the Dutch secretary."[125] Despite Blathwayt's testimony, it is difficult to discover just when he was out of the war office. The records for the period are none too complete, but apparently the only gap in Blathwayt's signatures to orders was from February 4 to February 23.[126] Orders during this interval were signed by a variety of persons, though, Blathwayt's declaration to the contrary, none of Portland's signatures appear. Schomberg was clearly in charge, and the Dutch secretary, von Huygens, was his assistant.[127]

William was evidently entrusting matters to the wise direction of Schomberg until he could find a suitable successor to Blathwayt. The latter must have understood what the situation portended, though he showed a coöperative spirit, fearful lest he fall into disrepute and lose his other posts. William's choice for the war office fell upon John Temple, son of Sir William. It was prompted rather by the desire on his part to reward the father's steadfast loyalty than by any great faith in the son's capabilities. Temple's commission was dated April 12, 1689,[128] and by the signatures in the entry books he assumed immediate charge of the war office. His tenure was destined to be tragically short. A week later he startled London by committing suicide and leaving behind the

[125] Add. MSS. 36861; testimony for November 30, 1702.

[126] See W.O. 4:1 for those weeks. See also W.O. 5:5 for the marching orders; there are a few signatures by Blathwayt. W.O. 25:3138, the entry book of pay warrants, contains no countersignatures for this period from January to the spring of the year. Blathwayt's do not begin until September, 1689 (see f. 39).

[127] W.O. 4:1.

[128] S. P. Dom., Entry Book, Military, Vol. 165, f. 238. Shrewsbury signed the commission; no patent was taken out, since the time was too short before Temple's death.

cryptic note: "My folly in undertaking what I cannot perform hath done the king great prejudice, which cannot be stopped any other way but this."[129]

It was his folly in connection with the Irish situation, rather than dismay over his new appointment, to which he referred. He and his uncle, the celebrated Irish Justiciar, had been determined to turn to William's advantage the state of affairs which had developed in Ireland. John Temple had put his trust in the ability of Major-General Hamilton to bring about the submission of Tyrconnel, and being a rather guileless youth, had taken Hamilton at his word and suspected no treachery. News of Tyrconnel's traitorous desertion to James was too much for his morose spirit, and he sought refuge in suicide. His action could have had no connection with the war office, for Blathwayt was giving him his assistance in order to initiate him the more easily. As a London correspondent remarked in trying to explain the mysterious event: "The discharge of the office of secretary at war is not a difficult task; besides, Mr. Blathwayt, knowing how well Mr. Temple was at Court, to gain his friendship did (I am very well assured) not only give him at present all the assistance he could to render it easy to him, but promised to continue it as long as he pleased."[130]

Blathwayt's timely assistance to Temple had its reward and may have been William's reason for reinstating him at the war office within a few days. The precise date of his reappointment is unknown, nor is there any entry of either his commission or his patent. Blathwayt himself did not possess a copy of the latter, as he said in 1702,

[129] *Hatton Correspondence*, (Camden Society, n.s., Vol. XXIII), II, 132; C. Hatton to Charles Hatton, April 20, 1689. See also Reresby, *Memoirs* (London, 1875), p. 458; Burnet, *History of His Own Times* (London, 1857), p. 512.

[130] *Hatton Correspondence*, II, 132–133; April 23, 1689.

since he lost it with various other papers in 1692, when his equipage was captured by a French privateer on the passage to Flanders.[131] From Temple's death until Blathwayt's reinstatement, Schomberg and Churchill did the work of sending out orders from the war office. By May 13 he had resumed his old tasks and had begun to send out directions for the campaign in Ireland.[132]

The first phase of Blathwayt's activity in the war office was now over. He had survived the unsettling consequences of the Revolution, although charges of Jacobitism were still to crop out against him. If James had presented a strenuous program to his secretary at war to fulfil, the tasks which William had in store for him were so much more rigorous that those under James must have seemed mere trifles by comparison.

131 Add. MSS. 36859, f. 123; testimony of August 8, 1702.

132 No letters appear in the entry book over Blathwayt's signature from April 6 until May 11. (W.O. 4:1, ff. 126–127, 129, 132–135.)

CHAPTER IX

ABSENCE FROM ENGLAND—SECRETARY OF STATE AND SECRETARY AT WAR TO WILLIAM III IN FLANDERS
1692–1701

BLATHWAYT finally emerged triumphant from the Revolution with all his offices still in his possession. When we consider the nature of the Revolution, this does not seem remarkable, although not all his colleagues at Whitehall had fared so well. All his actions in the disturbing events of the winter of 1688–1689 had been characterized by extreme caution. He had said very little, had been very assiduous, and had courted the favorable attentions of the right men, particularly of John Churchill, soon to be Duke of Marlborough. He had shown no resentment when Temple superseded him as secretary at war. On the contrary, he had appeared very eager to initiate the young man into the business of the war office and had governed his actions in such a way as to gain the notice of William, who had a shrewd appreciation of application to business. Life at last resumed its former even course, and three busy, and comparatively uneventful, years went by, during which Blathwayt was engrossed in the duties of the council board, the Lords of Trade, and the war office. Suddenly, however, the contingency which he had feared, and which he had tried to avert, presented itself. He was ordered to attend William on the campaigns into the Low Countries, and so peremptory was the order that he had no alternative short of resignation.

From the very beginning, William III's decision to conduct his campaigns in person raised an administrative problem with regard to the attendance of two important officials, the secretary of state and the secretary at war. As commander-in-chief of his forces, William quite naturally desired the attendance of so convenient an agent as his military secretary. Commanders-in-chief other than kings had expected and secured it—Fairfax, Cromwell, and Albemarle.[1] William was, therefore, making a perfectly legitimate request, quite apart from his royal power to compel attendance. As sovereign, he could not easily escape the less desired attendance of the secretary of state. The countersignature of that official was required on the royal sign manual to give validity to the countless orders which still must issue, even though the king was in a war zone outside of England. William had no objection to the attendance of a civil secretary, who would confine himself solely to the business of royal scrivener and custodian of the seals. What he did object to was the presence of a secretary of state who, as an official of considerable political prominence, might dispute the position of one of the Dutch favorites, William Bentinck, Duke of Portland, in particular.

By 1689, English secretaries of state had achieved a position of public dignity to which William never wholly reconciled himself. He spent his entire reign in attempting to nullify it and to limit it to the control of domestic affairs only, matters in which he had little interest and in

---

[1] When the Duke of Monmouth was commander-in-chief and the prospect of a foreign expedition arose as war with France loomed in 1678–1679, it was arranged that a special military secretary, James Vernon, was to attend him, not Mathew Lock, the secretary at war. S. P. Dom., Military Entry Bk. 44, f. 90; W.O. 24:5, the establishment of January 1, 1680.

which he concerned himself only as far as was necessary. It was not likely that he, who had every intention of serving as his own foreign secretary, would welcome the presence of a powerful secretary of state on his expeditions into the Low Countries, when more than ever he desired a free hand. Since he could not afford to endanger his own position by a careless disregard for constitutional technicalities, he sought to find some one docile enough to accept without protest a position of subordination and exclusion. He might have achieved this by appointing a bureaucratic secretary of state and compelling him to attend, and he did appoint such secretaries on occasion; but he preferred not to have even these with him, for he believed that the logical line of division in the duties of secretaries of state lay, not between northern and southern provinces, but between foreign and domestic affairs. William's ultimate solution of the problem was masterly. He decided to roll the offices of secretary of state and secretary at war into one, as far as the campaign was concerned, by conferring the signet on Blathwayt. In this ingenious arrangement he was aided and abetted by one important fact; no one, not even the most bureaucratic of secretaries of state, desired to undergo the hardships of a campaign. On the whole, it was agreeable to all concerned, with the single exception, perhaps, of the victim on whom the real hardship fell. Since William, as will subsequently be pointed out, made it financially worth while for Blathwayt to attend him, there was less opposition from that quarter than might otherwise have been expected.

This arrangement, which began in 1692, was arrived at only after two summers of experimentation. The first campaign which William conducted, that of 1690 into Ireland, allowed an easy solution; although, even then, questions as to administrative adjustments arose and had to be answered. At first William announced, to the horror of his council, or so at least his intimate counsellor, Lord Halifax, declared, that he intended to make the campaign without any secretary of state at all.[2] This position, though impolitic, was technically correct, since Queen Mary, as joint ruler, could, had she so chosen, have exercised all the powers which her husband possessed. William's announcement was prompted by a desire rather to escape his secretaries than to relieve the reluctant Mary of the burden of government. In the end, apparently because he could not help himself, he permitted an office which was falling into desuetude to be temporarily revived, that of secretary of state for Ireland.[3] Sir Robert Southwell, Blathwayt's friend and a man thoroughly conversant with Irish affairs, by reason of his extensive Irish holdings, was appointed to the office, and after making an interesting study of his duties, which he reduced to writing, he set out to make the campaign in close attendance on William.[4]

[2] Foxcroft, *Life . . . of . . . Halifax*, II, 249 (The Spencer House "Journals"). Halifax in recording his conversation with William on February 8, 1690, stated, "I told him of the unfitnesse of his going into Ireland without a Secretary of State, to which hee did not reply."

[3] The office of secretary of state for Ireland deserves further study. Miss Evans has something to say on it in her volume on *The Principal Secretary of State*, pp. 313–315. It seems, in our judgment, to have suffered at the expense of the office of private secretary to the lord lieutenant, but that is only conjecture based on an inadequate study of the documents. According to the *Calendar of State Papers Domestic*, a certain Dr. Robert George was filling the office under the Duke of Schomberg in the Irish campaign of 1689–1690. Some of his correspondence and comments on the office appear in *Hist. MSS. Com., Finch Papers*, I, 218–220; also *Cal. S. P. Dom.*, 1689–1690, pp. 440–441. Edward Southwell, Sir Robert's son, held the position under Queen Anne. There are numerous references to his activities in the *Calendar of State Papers Domestic*.

[4] *Cal. S. P. Dom.*, 1690–1691, p. 21. Southwell's warrant of appointment was dated May 29, 1690. The appointment necessitated the striking of new secretarial seals for him, both the signet and the cachet. (*Ibid.*, pp. 19, 21.) He was to receive a salary of five pounds a day and a contingency fund of

In the matter of a military adviser, the Irish campaign admitted an equally simple solution, for there was the office of Irish secretary at war to fall back upon. This office had apparently been in abeyance since the Revolution, for the commander-in-chief, the Duke de Schomberg, had depended on a military secretary of his own in the campaign of 1689–1690.[5] Originally William had no intention of reviving it, for his plan was to take Blathwayt with him, but the latter flatly refused to go.[6] Such boldness on

£600. Southwell made this the occasion for drawing up his interesting comment on the office. (See Add. MSS. 38861, f. 123.) This study is not to be confused with that which he made for the British office of secretary of state in 1689, evidently at the request of the Earl of Nottingham, the northern secretary. (*Ibid.* f. 46, reprinted in Evans, *The Principal Secretary of State,* pp. 364–365.)

See also Halifax's comment on the appointment of Southwell, Foxcroft, *Life . . . of . . . Halifax,* II, 251, (The Spencer House "Journals"): "He would carry Sir Robert Southwell with him, ask'd me if I knew anything to the contrary of his being an honest man. I said, not, confessed he was a weak man, but I took him to be entirely in his interest."

5 This secretary was James Cardonnel, a relative, and it may be the father, of Blathwayt's clerk, Adam Cardonnel. See references to his payment, W.O. 25:3145, Irish Pay Warrant Bk., no paging; warrant issued September 8, 1691. See also W.O. 24:884, f. 194; establishment for Ireland, 1689. He was paid fifteen shillings a day as a summer rate, ten shillings as a winter rate. Count de Solms, lieutenant-general of the forces in Ireland, had a secretary also, who was paid at the rate of ten shillings a day. (W.O. 25: 3145; warrants dated March 20, and May 30, 1690.) These warrants were directed to the Irish paymaster of the forces and were thus payable out of the Irish funds, but they were countersigned by Blathwayt.

6 Egerton MSS. 2618, f. 156. The commissary of the musters, Crawford, reported to Clarke, the judge advocate, on February 13, 1690: "Dear Judge, This is to tell you that Mr. Blathwayt is very soon to leave his employment of secretary; it has been talked of for this fortnight past, but with no public declaration till this day he told me of it, and that it was with the king's consent, and he believed that a person recommended by him might as soon procure the employment as any other; he asked me who [*sic*] I thought fit and truly for all our advantages as well as your own I could think of none so proper and so qualified as yourself. I wish you would come speedily to London to try what you can do. Your true friend Satan [?] has already spoke to my Lord Ranelagh who will give you his assistance. You know it is

his part was unusual and not at all in keeping with his wonted diffidence and docile obedience. Yet refuse he did, although it led to grave charges of Jacobitism against him on the part of Queen Mary and others, who marvelled at William's tolerance.[7] Evidently William valued Blathwayt's services, for he neither dismissed him nor accepted his resignation. Instead he decided on the easiest course that suggested itself—the appointment of George Clarke, son of Sir William Clarke, and judge advocate general of the forces, to the position of secretary at war for Ireland. The arrangement was not so satisfactory to Clarke as it was to Blathwayt, but Clarke was ambitious

three pounds per diem in salary and good salaries for clerks, two of which, Cardonnel and Thurston, understand the business very well, and you cannot doubt but you will be much more acceptable both to the king and the army than your predecessor. I would have mentioned it to a certain nobleman of your acquaintance, but upon second thoughts, I believe he would sell it by inch of candle if it lay in his power. Satan gives you his service to advise you not to neglect any time.'' Clarke went post haste to London and interviewed Blathwayt who indicated his willingness to have him succeed him. (See the ''Autobiography of Dr. George Clarke,'' *Hist. MSS. Com., Popham MSS.*, pp. 270–271.)

[7] Mary's suspicions of Blathwayt were based on the reports of the scandalmongering Earl of Monmouth, who spent the years after 1688 conjuring up Jacobite bogeys. He was largely instrumental in the so-called Fenwick disclosures. Thus Mary wrote to William: ''I had a conversation with Lord Monmouth t'other morning, in which he said what a misfortune it was that things went thus ill, which was certainly by the faults of those who were in trust; that it was a melancholy thing to the nation to see themselves so thrown away; and to speake plain, said he, do you not see how all you do is known, that what is said one day in the cabinet councill is wrote next day to France: for my part, said he, I must speake plainly, I have a great deal of reason to esteem Lord Nott[ingham], I don't believe 'tis he, but 'tis some in his office; then he fell upon Mr. Blaithwit. I owned I wondered why you wou'd let him serve here, since he wou'd not go with you, but I said I supposed you knew why you did it; and when he began to talk high of ill administration, I told him in the same freedom he seemed to speake to me, that I found it very strange you were not thought fitt to chose your own ministers.'' (Burnet, *Memorial to Mary, Princess of Orange*, pp. xxi–xxii; letter of July 17, 1690. See also Dalrymple, *Memoirs* (London, 1773), Vol. II, App. Pt. II, 133–134.)

to become Blathwayt's successor at the war office and felt that acceptance of William's offer would improve his prospects.[8]

In 1691, however, there were no offices which William could fill in order to settle the question of attendance. Flanders was not Ireland. In January, 1691, before the campaign opened, the king left England with a group of noble officials, among them Lord Nottingham, then secretary of state for the southern province, to attend a diplomatic parley of the allies. "But Nottingham, though, in matters relating to the internal government of England he enjoyed a large share of his master's confidence, knew little more about the business of the Congress than what he saw in the *Gazettes.*"[9] It is not clear whether or not Nottingham was intended to make the campaign with William. In the end it fell to the lot of the charming Lord Sydney, who had been appointed to the northern office in December, 1690.[10] Sydney was a more agreeable companion than Nottingham, who, though tractable, was somewhat dour. Sydney knew the Continent very well, particularly Holland, where a decade earlier he had served as minister, and, with his carefree nature, was not likely to resent the presence of Portland, whom he knew intimately and apparently liked. He was also used to cam-

[8] "Autobiography of Dr. George Clarke," *Hist. MSS. Com., Popham MSS.*, p. 275. "That I had offered him my service when those refused to come with him whose business it was, and that I hoped he would let me wait upon him back." So Clarke wrote, rather petulantly, when he discovered that his attendance was to bring him no particular ultimate reward. (For Clarke's warrant, see *Cal. S. P. Dom.*, 1690–1691, p. 20.)

[9] Macaulay, *History of England* (Boston, 1901), IV, 121. Norfolk, Ormonde, Devonshire, Dorset, Portland, Monmouth, Zulestein, and the Bishop of London were also in attendance.

[10] Nottingham went over with William on January 17, 1691, and returned with him on March 16, 1691. The king set out for Holland again on April 13 and Sydney followed him on May 2. See Luttrell, *Brief Relation*, for this information.

paigning and had shown himself a brilliant military officer. From the secretarial point of view, however, he was
not a success. He was never fond of arduous labor, and his
official duties bored him. One summer's campaign was
enough to convince both William and Sydney that the ex-
periment was not satisfactory. The latter was accordingly
transferred in February, 1692, on the very eve of the second campaign into the Low Countries, from the secretarial office to the lord lieutenancy of Ireland. Within a
few days came the public announcement that the northern
office was to be left vacant until the king's return in the
fall, and that Blathwayt, secretary at war, had been ordered to attend William as secretary of state for the
duration of the campaign.

It is not entirely clear just what provision was made for
the attendance of a military secretary to William in the
campaign of 1691. Blathwayt had apparently not been
asked to attend; Clarke seems to have been named at first,
since there is a record of a pass for him to go to Dover,
en route to Flanders, in May, 1691, and of special payments made to him while secretary at war in Flanders.[11]
His summer correspondence proves, however, that he was
in Ireland in attendance on De Ginckel, Schomberg's successor as commander-in-chief of the forces there.[12] William had evidently reached the conclusion that Sydney's
military experience was sufficient for the duties of both
military and civil secretary, if he had the necessary clerical assistance, and we learn from Sydney's correspondence with Blathwayt that he was playing the double rôle.[13]

Nottingham probably suggested the arrangement of
1692, or at any rate influenced William to make it. As

11 *Cal. S. P. Dom.*, 1690–1691, p. 370.
12 *Hist. MSS. Com.*, IV. Report, MSS. of Lord de Ros; numerous references.
13 *Cal. S. P. Dom.*, 1690–1691; numerous references.

secretary at war, Blathwayt was under the jurisdiction of Nottingham, since the army fell within the province of the southern secretary.[14] In all probability, Nottingham induced Blathwayt to accompany William by holding forth the prospect of appointment to the vacant secretaryship of state. He stressed the advantages to be gained from close proximity to the crown and graceful compliance with the royal commands.[15]

William was enthusiastic over the arrangement. He now had a thoroughly competent and very efficient political subordinate to attend him, who could be relied upon in matters of administration and ignored in matters of politics. Blathwayt had the secretarial training which made him familiar with the routine of business in a secretary of state's office, and he needed no initiation into his new tasks. He also knew Dutch exceedingly well and was familiar with The Hague as a result of his earlier service with Temple. There was probably no other official in England at the time who possessed quite the same happy combination of qualifications and experience. William was not in the least alarmed by the thought that he might be harboring a Jacobite. A sovereign who could restore to office such a man as Sunderland and retain the services of Shrewsbury during the months when Fenwick was making his charges against the latter, was not likely to be disturbed by a report about a political underling. William may well have believed that the charges against Blathwayt were true. At any rate he felt that there was a better method of disarming opposition than by dismissal from office.

What Blathwayt thought of his new task can only be

---

[14] See Monmouth's reference to him as belonging to Nottingham's office; Burnet, *Memorial to Mary, etc.*, pp. xxi–xxii: Dalrymple, *Memoirs*, Vol. II, App. Pt. II, 133–134.

[15] Add. MSS. 37992; Nottingham's numerous letters to Blathwayt.

conjectured. Family affairs engrossed him. Mary Wynter Blathwayt had died the preceding November, so he may have welcomed the change of scene. In any event, excuses were useless. So he began to brush up his Dutch, looked around for a clerk to assist Povey in the plantation office, saw Povey made clerk in extraordinary of the council (in order that the business of the Lords of Trade might not suffer in his absence), arranged the appointment of George Clarke as temporary secretary at war,[16] and then bade farewell to Whitehall. Since, even though he was in possession of the signet, he had not been made a true secretary of state, he was in a rather bitter mood; but he probably entertained the belief that on his return to England in the fall, the seals of the northern office would be conferred upon him. He was doubtless also buoyed up by the hope that his attendance would be temporary. No one anticipated that the war with Louis XIV was to prove so indecisive or to last so long.

The summer's campaign came to an end, and Blathwayt's hopes received their first blight. Although the rumor spread that he was to be made secretary of state, and his acquisition of the office was regarded by some as almost a foregone conclusion, nothing came of it. "But Mr. Blathwayt not being yet declared secretary of state puts all our business much out of order, and it will be worse if necessity of state should put him by," wrote Stepney, then the English resident at Cell, in Hanover, to another of the envoys.[17] In the end, William's personal feelings, as much as matters of state, prevented the ap-

16 Clarke objected to being thought of as Blathwayt's deputy and insisted on a separate appointment. He was very sensitive on the subject. See his autobiography, *Hist. MSS. Com., Popham MSS.*, p. 276. He was to receive three pounds a day. (See W.O. 25:3138, f. 212; *Cal. S. P. Dom.*, 1690–1691, p. 21.)

17 S. P. For. Archives, Vol. 84, no paging; Cell, November 16, 1692. See also Luttrell, *Brief Relation*, II, 601, entry for October 25, 1692.

pointment, for that astute monarch had no desire to overthrow an arrangement which seemed to him ideal. Perhaps because it would not do to destroy Blathwayt's
hopes entirely, and because he was satisfied to have only
one secretary of state, William waited the entire winter
of 1692–1693 before making an appointment. Finally, in
March, a month before the fourth expedition began, he
appointed Sir John Trenchard, whose chief claim to fame
was his introduction of the first Exclusion Bill. Macaulay
pronounced Trenchard a complete nonentity as a secretary of state; "little more than a superintendent of police, charged to look after the printers of unlicensed books,
the pastors of nonjuring congregations, and the haunters
of treason taverns."[18]

Disappointment over Trenchard's nomination must
have rankled in Blathwayt's heart; and, to appease him,
William III threw out the hint that if he chose to petition
for the emoluments of a regular secretary of state, his
efforts would, no doubt, meet with success. Blathwayt
acted upon the suggestion, but the subsequent delay of the
Treasury in granting his petition,[19] and the hardships of
another campaign, led him to express grave dissatisfaction that he should not be thought worthy of the reward
he coveted. "By the words I have marked," Stepney
wrote, in commenting on the matter, "methinks Mr.
Blathwayt is not in the humor he ought to be and I appre-
hended his resentment of not being made secretary of
state (as he expected and ought to have been) may make
him lay down his other employment or at least no more

[18] Macaulay, *History of England* (Boston, 1901), V, 480; also Burnet,
History of His Own Times (London, 1857), pp. 587–588. Trenchard's appointment was a political move to pacify the Whigs. He was the sort "with
whom he [William] could take freedom without disobliging him."
[19] Blathwayt submitted his petition in July, 1693; it was not acted upon
until February, 1694. (*Cal. S. P. Dom.*, 1693, p. 215; Treas. Ref. Bk., Index
4621, ff. 32, 35, 320–328.)

follow the king in Flanders which is as bad for those who are abroad. For certainly no other man can be found out who can acquit himself with such capacity, honesty, and diligence as he has done, which I apprehend his Majesty may perceive when it is too late.''[20]

In November, 1693, within a month after William's return from Flanders, Nottingham was sacrificed to the demands of the Whigs and dismissed from the southern office. Trenchard, though very ill, was ordered to take over the heavier burden of that province and removed his effects from the northern office.[21] Then, if ever, was William's opportunity to reward Blathwayt, but again he had no intention of appointing him and no doubt argued that the Whig reaction which was then sweeping over the government made it impolitic to do so. Blathwayt, deprived of the friendly support of Nottingham, probably decided that he cared to make no more campaigns with William; but in February, 1694, at an exceedingly psychological moment, the Treasury ordered that if he went he was to receive the salary of a junior secretary of state for his services in Flanders, and that payments were to be retroactive from the first year of his attendance.[22] Blathwayt, thereupon, not only decided to make the campaign but also wrote with some enthusiasm to Stepney, "But now I am further engaged by his Majesty's express commands that I give my attendance this next campaign in the same function as in the former years. . . . You will be so favorable as to believe that though this business which is laid on me is but a nurse child, I am too good natured

20 S. P. For. Archives, Vol. 60; Stepney to Stratford (the English banker at Hamburg), Leipzig, October 4, 1693.

21 Trenchard suffered from a lingering tuberculosis and was desperately ill during much of his secretarial tenure. He died in April, 1695, after repeated rumors of his death. Much of the work of his office was done by Bridgeman, his secretary.

22 Treas. Ref. Bk., Index 4621, ff. 320–328; February 7, 1694.

to starve it but intend to deliver it over to the true parents in as good plight as may be, besides, I may tell you that the king denies me no advantages that belong to the office during my execution of it which is more satisfactory to me in the present conjuncture than another tenure."[23]

The question of Blathwayt's salary is discussed elsewhere. It is quite clear that the financial advantage weighed very heavily in Blathwayt's estimate of the situation and, in the end, probably led him to put aside all thought of succeeding to the position of a regular secretary, although the opportunity to advance him, had William so desired, repeatedly occurred. Shrewsbury was persuaded to resume the seals of office in March, 1694, a month or two before William set out on his summer excursion, and, by dint of constant coaxing, was kept in office until December, 1698.[24] Blathwayt probably never thought of supplanting Shrewsbury and apparently scorned the thought of succeeding Trenchard, who died in April, 1695. We are indebted to Stepney for our knowledge of his state of mind. In the spring of 1695, Stepney wrote to a correspondent: "The king will certainly make the campaign, and, I believe, will declare as much to the parliament when he sees them next, to have in a manner, their consent, lest his crossing the water in this conjuncture be called abdication.[25] This is the talk of the Jacobites, who say likewise he will take Prince George over with him to

[23] S. P. For. Archives, Vol. 82; Whitehall, March 23, 1694.

[24] Shrewsbury's conduct in office is an interesting study in political evasion both on his part and on William III's. The latter had determined to keep the duke in office at any cost, for he intended to, and did, use him as a buffer against the attacks of the more ardent Whigs, headed by Wharton and Monmouth. Shrewsbury was unquestionably the most unifying force among the Whigs at the time and as a moderate was acceptable to William. (See Coxe's *Shrewsbury Correspondence*.)

[25] The situation prior to the expedition of 1695 was even more than usually critical, since Queen Mary was dead, and although sympathy was felt for William over his loss, there was still an undercurrent of hostility.

be sure of him. Poor Duke Shrewsbury will be quite blind, and Sir John Trenchard stone dead, very shortly. We have a weak ministry at present, and for aught I see, nobody brigues the employment. Mr. Blathwayt might have it, but seems to decline it, because, without envy, he is warmer as he is. The vogue of the town speaks of Lord Montague and Comptroller Wharton. I wish your lordship were at home to end the dispute, and be our provincial, instead of our correspondent.''[26]

The low estate to which the secretariat had fallen, as a result of William's intentional and continued disregard of it, made it an office little to be desired. Obtuse as he often was, Blathwayt realized this. The instructions which were issued to the French ambassador to England after the Peace of Ryswick disclose the opinions which were current, both among Englishmen and foreigners. ''When Count Tallard has lived some time in England, he will know, by his own observations, what we are to think of his [William's] real intentions. These he communicates to very few persons, and his confidence has hitherto been reserved for the Dutch alone, without admitting the English to share in it. The secretaries of state, with the exception of the Duke of Shrewsbury, have been, properly speaking, only clerks employed in writing the dispatches, without having anything to do with the secrets.''[27] As Montagu, William's able chancellor of the exchequer, put it, ''Formerly after a man had discharged a commission in foreign parts with credit he was called home, and made secretary of state, but that matter is a good deal altered and I believe we shall not see many more instances of

[26] *Lexington Papers* (Sutton edition), pp. 60–61; Stepney to Lexington, minister to Austria, February 13/23, 1695. Stepney's wish that Lexington might be made a secretary of state was shared by many.

[27] Grimblot, *Letters of William III and Louis XIV*, II, 249; instructions dated Versailles, March 2, 1698.

that kind, this king is so much master of all the foreign transactions, that his choice is directed by some consideration at home more than by their skill in the business abroad.''[28]

James Vernon, like Blathwayt, a mere foil for William, forced from his position as first clerk in Shrewsbury's office to a secretaryship of state, made the most pertinent comments of all on the situation. He took exception to William's careless way of letting one of the secretarial offices lie vacant for months at a time, even when he was in England and might well have made an appointment. In 1700, after the Earl of Jersey's relinquishment of the seals just on the eve of William's departure for Holland, Vernon wrote to Shrewsbury, his political father confessor, ''I waited on his Majesty this morning, who told me he would take time till his return from Holland, to consider of another secretary. I thought the deferring it so long might be indifferent, since if there were twenty Secretaries during his absence, they would be so many ciphers; but I begged it might be done as soon as he came back, or otherwise, his service must suffer extremely.''[29]

Vernon felt, and with reason, that William was being influenced in his treatment of secretaries by Sunderland, who, refusing to accept the seals again himself, enjoyed the prospect of controlling such tools as Vernon and Blathwayt, although the latter, since he was abroad, was

[28] S. P. For. Archives, Vol. 82; Montagu to Stepney, August 7, 1694.

[29] Vernon, *Letters Illustrative of the Reign of William III*, III, 95; June 25, 1700. Five times in the course of his reign William allowed the secretarial office to lie vacant for several months; after Shrewsbury's first resignation in June, 1690, until the appointment of Sydney in December of that year; after Sydney's resignation in February, 1692, until Trenchard's appointment in March, 1693; after Nottingham's dismissal in November, 1693, until Shrewsbury accepted the seals in March, 1694; from the latter's resignation in December, 1698, until Jersey took office in May, 1699. Jersey resigned in June, 1700, and Hedges was not appointed until November, 1700.

less subject to his influence.[30] "I found my Lord Chamberlain was looking for little men to make them Secretaries of State, and such as were framed for a dependence on a Premier Minister," Vernon wrote.[31] "I think I understand what sort of Secretary of State is intended as most suitable to our constitution and the present model of the court. He must be such an one as has more of the buckler in him than the sword, soft and stubborn within, where it is to be held, and yet so framed, as to receive all blows given from without; it is no matter how that is mauled provided those stand secure who are behind it. Parliaments are grown into a habit of finding fault, and some Jonah or other must be thrown overboard, if the storm cannot otherwise be laid. But if the great Leviathan will be amused by an empty barrel, it is a composition easily made. Little men are certainly the properest for these purposes; and if, like Pharaoh, they are raised to that end, and know the conditions they come in upon, they will have no great reason to complain.'"[32]

A person more amenable than Blathwayt to the wishes of those above him could scarcely have been found. He knew the terms on which he had accepted his appointment and observed them to the letter. Although there were subsequently some charges of inefficiency made against him, there was never a hint of insubordination. A more spirited soul would have found the situation intolerable. Not so Blathwayt, who had an overwhelming respect for men greater than himself. His position in the camp was

[30] Sunderland had known Blathwayt as James II's useful secretary at war and had wielded some influence over him in the years from 1685 to 1688. Though we have no comments on the matter, Blathwayt like others, no doubt, fell victim to mixed feelings of admiration and scorn for Sunderland's subtle power to reinstate himself in the royal favor.

[31] Vernon, *Letters Illustrative, etc.* I, 359; Vernon to Shrewsbury, September 11, 1697.

[32] *Ibid.,* I, 404–405; September 25, 1697.

little better than that of an automaton whose primary
business was the sending of the official dispatches. William was kind to him in a passive sort of fashion. After
all, there was nothing to be expected from a monarch who,
on hearing that one of his secretarial attendants had
been drowned, had no more in the way of comment to
make than, "Well, you must look for another."[33] Both
Portland and Albemarle, in their turn, treated Blathwayt
in a perfunctory, formal manner, realizing that they were
dealing with a good-natured, indispensable drudge. Portland thought so little of Blathwayt that his letters contain almost no reference to him, and a detailed study of
his activities during these years has been made without a
mention of the secretary at war.[34] Blathwayt did not enjoy the royal confidence, and William's more intimate letters were written either by himself or by the Dutch secretary who was in constant attendance upon him both in
England and abroad. Blathwayt's position can be judged
from the admonition which the Earl of Jersey, secretary
of state for the southern province from 1699 to 1700, dispatched to Matthew Prior: "When you write those things
to Mr. Blathwayt, I suppose you write them at the same
time to my Lord Albemarle, who is immediately about the
King."[35]

William himself showed in his letters that Blathwayt
had no share in his confidence. In 1696 he wrote to
Shrewsbury, apropos of the Duke of Savoy's lamentable

[33] Grew, *William Bentinck and William III*, p. 224; M. de Wilde, assistant to the Dutch secretary, who was drowned accidentally while boarding the
ship that was carrying back the royal party to England in 1694.

[34] *Ibid.;* an intensive study, based on the manuscripts preserved at Welbeck Abbey.

[35] *Hist. MSS. Com., Bath MSS., Prior Papers*, III, 374; July 24/August 3,
1699. Prior was then in Paris, in charge of the embassy, in the interval between Jersey's departure as ambassador and Manchester's arrival. He
served as secretary to both of them.

defection to Louis: "It is sometime since I wrote to you, having nothing agreeable to communicate, nor answer to give your letters, but what I could trust to Blaithwayt. I have now only bad news to impart; we have certainly lost the Duke of Savoy who has tricked us."[36] When the news of Fenwick's insinuations against Shrewsbury reached the king, the latter wrote hastily to reassure the duke: "I received last week by an express from Sir John Fenwick, which my lord steward forwarded to me, the paper annexed. You may judge of my astonishment at his effrontery, in accusing you. . . . I replied to my lord steward, that, unless he proved what he has written, and that he moreover confesses all he knows, without reserve, I will not permit his trial to be deferred, which is his only aim. It is necessary you should communicate this, on my part, to the lords justices, since I cannot employ Blaithwayt, who, as you well know, ought to have no cognizance of this paper."[37]

Blathwayt, of course, realized that a great deal was going on behind his back, but he showed no resentment. Though his apparent slowness of perception made him the butt of some of the wits who came in contact with him, there is some reason to think that he saw much more than was intended. Matthew Prior, who in the course of his various appointments came into direct contact with Blathwayt, dubbed him the "Elephant" and with characteristic irreverence used this sobriquet in speaking of him to the Earl of Jersey. "The Elephant is always the same, jocular and ignorant, disguising his want of knowing what is going on by affecting to keep it secret."[38]

---

[36] Coxe, *Shrewsbury Correspondence*, p. 127; Camp of Gemblours, July 23, 1696.

[37] *Ibid.*, pp. 145–146; Loo, September 10, 1696.

[38] Wickham-Legg, *Matthew Prior*, p. 315; letter dated, September 8, 1699. Wickham-Legg is probably mistaken in assuming that Somers is meant by the "Elephant."

Of Blathwayt's relations with the various members of the royal party, very little is known. What he thought of the Dutch secretary, who served in the capacity of private secretary to the king, can only be surmised, though it is probable he was incapable of nurturing a rancorous spirit toward M. Huygens, who was an older and very kindly man and had been in attendance on William for many years.[39] M. Huygens was a great favorite of the Duke of Portland, and died just about the time the latter's influence over the king was ebbing. Albemarle for a while served in the double capacity of royal favorite and royal scrivener, for no immediate successor to M. Huygens was named. During that interval Blathwayt probably enjoyed more of the royal confidence than at any other time, for his clerks declared that he viewed the appointment of M. d'Allonne, who ultimately succeeded M. Huygens, with considerable alarm.[40] According to them, Blathwayt feared that he would again be reduced to a mere news-agent. As a matter of fact, he probably never dropped back to his former status.

Except on matters of salary and certain unwarranted criticisms on the part of Whitehall officials, Blathwayt never exhibited any pique during these years. He accepted the prospect of "running about from one fortification to another" more or less stoically. He traversed bat-

[39] The diary of M. Huygens von Zulichem is preserved at Welbeck Abbey. Miss Grew has printed a portion of it, but there are only a few references to Blathwayt and these are most casual.

[40] Add. MSS. 28917, f. 286; Cardonnel to John Ellis, undersecretary in the northern office, Loo, November 4/14, 1698. Considerable surprise was evinced over d'Allonne's appointment. Thus Vernon wrote to Shrewsbury: "They write from Loo, that Monsieur d'Allonne is made Dutch secretary, and has got Monsieur Zalicherie's [Zulichem's] place. I must needs say that this is not what I expected, that a place which my Lord Albemarle has executed so long, should be given to a creature of my Lord Portland." (Vernon, *Letters Illustrative, etc.*, II, 208–209. See also *Hist. MSS. Com., Bath MSS.*, III, 287, 288.)

tle fields and witnessed encounters at so close a range that shot whizzed by him. He was standing next to Godfrey, the director of the Bank of England, who came over in 1695 to interview William, when that financier was killed by a cannon ball.[41] Though Blathwayt never exhibited any special heroism, it was something for a man who had never experienced warfare to keep his head and continue his routine work. Even under campaign conditions, he kept up his office establishment, which was not of the smallest, and he often worked until two and three o'clock in the morning, getting off dispatches. Occasionally a note of weariness sounds through his correspondence, though he took care to let it be heard only in the safest quarters. Even to Stepney, who more than others invited his confidence, he expressed himself very mildly: "You will allow me to be a little weary and the more willing to conclude since we march again to-morrow."[42]

Since it was necessary to begin the campaigns as early as possible in the spring and never to close them until late in the fall, Blathwayt was absent from England for the greater part of each year, from 1692 to 1698. Even in 1697, the first of the peace years, he was required to set out in April and did not return until the tenth of November. Campaigns were in every case prefaced by a stay of a fortnight either at The Hague or at William's favorite palace at Loo, where the atmosphere would have been restful had not every minute been taken up with dispatches announcing William's plans. In the fall, William usually indulged in a few days of hunting before crossing to England, and it was then that Blathwayt found his only real opportunity to relax. Often the winds kept the royal party on the Dutch side longer than was anticipated, and in a sense Blathwayt welcomed the delay. He was very busy

41 S. P. For., Military Expeditions, I, 72.
42 S. P. For. Archives, Vol. 59, ff. 194–195; July 20, 1693.

making purchases for Dyrham Park, which was rebuild-
ing, and it is clear that at such times his mind was more
taken up with the buying of rare china, velvets, and tapestries than with the sending of official announcements.

After 1697, with the cessation of hostilities, the expeditions became more leisurely, and until the summer of
1701, when hostilities were resumed, Blathwayt must
have found himself with a considerable amount of idle
time on his hands. The atmosphere, however, was electri-
cal, with every one awaiting the demise of the Spanish
king. The air of mystery which surrounded the actions of
William and his allies was unwholesome and in no sense
reassuring. Blathwayt, however, set about to enjoy himself. In 1698 he paid a visit with William to the Duke of
Cell, and his young son, who had accompanied him that
summer, went with him and partook of the various amuse-
ments which had been arranged for the court's entertainment.

Work rather than play, however, made up the bulk of
Blathwayt's program. In conducting two offices under
very difficult circumstances, he was carrying what, to one
physically weaker, would have been an intolerable burden. That he was serving as secretary at war for an unpopular monarch, who was waging an unpopular war, did
not improve matters; nor did the fact that, while he was
technically secretary of state and in possession of the signet, no one accepted his right to exercise the powers of
that office in their entirety. The arrangement was subject
to all the disadvantages from which any divided government suffers and was made worse by the prevailing lack
of confidence in the king.

Blathwayt's duties were sufficiently clear. He was to
keep in constant touch with Whitehall, with the various
naval and military bases, with the allies, and with all of
the envoys. His correspondence in the two offices was tre-

mendous, even though he had two distinct office staffs to carry on the work. All of Europe was his province, and he was expected to keep in constant communication with all the English representatives stationed abroad. That he did so, his correspondence reveals, but under circumstances which were far from favorable. Since he was in close touch with the king, he furnished envoys with their instructions; and as a result some of the latter neglected their correspondence with their regular "provincial." Secretaries of state in England complained from time to time that they were being ignored. Shrewsbury resented the way in which both William and the envoys kept him in ignorance of matters regarding which he should have been informed, even though he did admit that as long as William was on the Continent there was no avoiding it— envoys would have to receive their instructions either from Blathwayt or from one of the royal advisers.[43] On one occasion Wolseley, the representative at Brussels, begged that he might be excused from sending the news to Shrewsbury, since Brussels lay so near the camp and Blathwayt was transmitting the news thence. Shrewsbury answered in a manner that reveals his touchiness. "I am very willing you should ease yourself of the camp news, since Mr. Blathwayt takes care of that part. But upon other occasions it will be a satisfaction to me, to hear from you though you can expect no directions from hence, till his majesty's return."[44]

The envoys were instructed to send to the secretaries in England duplicates of their letters to the king and Blathwayt, and most of them must have complied, though a few of the secretaries were not satisfied with this way of do-

[43] *Lexington Papers*, pp. 40–41; Shrewsbury to Lexington, January 8, 1695, complaining that no one had bothered even to write to him of the proceedings which led to peace overtures with Louis, at Maestricht in 1694.

[44] S. P. For., Entry Bk., Vol. 198; Whitehall, June 7, 1695.

ing business and either implied or demanded that they should be treated in a more personal fashion. Although Nottingham does not appear to have taken exception to it, George Stepney thought he might, and once, after many months of silence, wrote him an apologetic letter, begging him not to interpret his conduct as neglect of duty.[45] Trenchard and Vernon never found fault with the system, but Sir William Trumbull was constantly complaining. Dr. Robinson, envoy to Sweden, answered that he was sending Trumbull duplicates of the letters he sent to Blathwayt—and what more could Trumbull desire?[46] Hedges told Blathwayt, in 1701, that he felt he was being neglected by the envoys, but Blathwayt retorted that he could not see why, since they sent Hedges duplicates of all the letters he (Blathwayt) received.[47] Reasonable secretaries of state suspected from the outset that William was so much his own foreign minister, that Blathwayt was as completely in the dark as they were. Sometimes the envoys, notably Stepney, who was Blathwayt's personal friend, enclosed friendly letters with their formal communications, as may be seen from the extant correspondence.

Except in the case of Sir William Trumbull, whom every one usually treated with the indifference which his unfortunate temperament invited, Blathwayt maintained an attitude of studied correctness in his relations with the envoys. His powers as secretary of state lapsed, techni-

---

[45] S. P. For. Archives, Vol. 50; Cleves, 2/22 [sic] July, 1692. According to the letters in this volume, Stepney had not written to Nottingham since May.

[46] For. Entry Bk., Sweden, Vol. 153, f. 300. See also the letter on ff. 329–330 in which Trumbull admitted that he received duplicates but expected letters addressed to him directly. Trumbull made similar complaints to Greg, stationed at Copenhagen, and Shrewsbury to Wolseley at Brussels. (For. Entry Bk., Vol. 197, f. 115, May 21, 1695; Vol. 198, June 7, 1695.)

[47] Add. MSS. 37992, ff. 268, 269; letters of September, 1701.

cally, the moment he set foot on English soil, though, of course, he could not regard his work as finished until he reached Whitehall and gave over the seals. Even then, it was not easy for him to drop the thread of business, for the envoys kept writing to him, particularly if they had some favor to ask. But, just as in the spring he had announced that he was resuming his duties, so in the autumn he replied that he was giving them up and that the envoys must apply to the regular secretaries, particularly if the matter was one of expediting the payment of their bills of extraordinary, the most common of their requests.[48] Stepney once asked that Blathwayt give him instructions on some point, but Blathwayt wrote from Whitehall that he could not, as long as the king remained in England.[49] In one instance, during Trumbull's incumbency, Blathwayt evidently had royal orders to continue his correspondence with Lexington at Vienna, and this led to trouble with Trumbull, for Lexington's secretary was careless in addressing the replies and assorting them into packets, so that some of them reached Trumbull's office and were opened there.[50] As secretary at war Blathwayt continued to correspond with certain of the envoys stationed in allied countries, as there were many military points to be settled, arrangements to be made for food and clothing for the allied forces, and details to be considered regarding the subsidies. On matters of this nature, for instance, Blathwayt was in constant touch with

[48] See S. P. For. Archives, Vol. 82; letters of March 4, 1692, October 2, 1693, and March 23, 1694.

[49] Ibid.; letter of March 3, 1693.

[50] Lexington Papers, p. 240; Blathwayt to Lexington, Whitehall, January 19/29, 1697; ibid., February 5/15, 1697: "Pray, my Lord, let your Secretaries be more careful in covering your letters, most of them coming quite open by the wearing out of the covers. Besides 'twere better, upon some considerations, that they did not come to me hither, under Mr. Secretary's packet, so perfectly open as they do."

Dr. Robinson in Sweden and with Stepney, who during this time was stationed in several of the German principalities.

Blathwayt had not only all Europe as his province but all Whitehall as well; and unlike the secretaries at home, he could not conduct his business in person, or by messenger, or through the writing of hurried notes of instruction or inquiry. It is true that he was relieved of any responsibility for the minutiae of domestic affairs, since he was not responsible for their transaction after he had dispatched the royal order; but no matter how hard William might try to turn over domestic questions to the government left in England, he was seldom successful, for business tended naturally to gravitate to royal headquarters. The outbreak of Jacobite plots; the crisis which came in colonial administration and resulted in the creation of the Board of Trade; the extended agitation over the land bank and the charter of the East India Company; and Scottish projects in Darien,—all raised problems to which William was required to give his attention while abroad. Queen Mary's unwillingness to manage the affairs of the kingdom increased William's difficulties, and he soon discovered that she neither would nor could govern without him. After her death, the lords justices showed much the same timorousness, so that matters were constantly referred to the king. William's repeated threat of abdication or the fear of parliamentary attack may have given rise to this deference on their part, but it was also due to a lack of able ministerial leadership, since there was no outstanding official who cared to challenge William's authority.

Blathwayt corresponded with the lords justices, the Treasury, the secretaries of state, the Admiralty, the paymaster-general of the forces, his own deputy secretary at war, and a host of minor officials, such as the commissioners of transport, the victualling board, and the various contractors for army supplies.[51] With Queen Mary, of course, he never had any communication nor with any of the household officials of the court, such correspondence being left to the king, Portland, or the Dutch secretary. With some of the ecclesiastical officials he communicated if occasion arose. His letters to the lords justices were read at their meetings, and their responses were transmitted to him by their secretary, Sir William Trumbull.[52] Blathwayt's letters to other officials, the members of the Treasury and the Admiralty boards, and the secretaries of state, were frequently read before the lords justices. Because of this fact, Nottingham found it necessary to warn Blathwayt to write separate letters to him if he had anything personal to communicate.

Blathwayt's communications were of an extremely stereotyped nature, taking the form of news-letters, in which were included royal commands on various matters. If the king chose to confer a special favor upon an official he wrote himself, for certain ministers took offense if they received their orders from Blathwayt rather than from the king; a justifiable attitude, since William always found time to write to his Dutch officials. Thus, in the late fall of 1694, Admiral Russell, later Lord Orford, stirred by the king's decision to winter the fleet in the Mediterranean, a project which Russell vigorously opposed, was distinctly angered by William's practice of ignoring him. He expressed his sentiments to Shrewsbury: "But I fear, my lord, you think my services deserve better than the

---

[51] For this correspondence, see *Cal. S. P. Dom.* and *Cal. Treas. Papers.* The bulk of it, however, is to be found in the Public Record Office, among the departmental papers or among the papers which Blathwayt removed to Dyrham Park.

[52] Sir William Trumbull served in the capacity of secretary to the lords justices, as well as secretary of state until 1697, when Robert Yard, one of the clerks in Shrewsbury's office, replaced him.

king believes. I ground this thought from never having the honour, in all this time of my being abroad, to have one single line from the king; nay, my orders for remaining here were handed to me under the cover of that never-erring minister, Mr. Blathwayt, without ever giving me the least hint of the king's thoughts upon so important a matter; when at the same time, under my cover, the Dutch vice-admiral was honoured with a letter under the king's own hand. This, you may please to believe, was no small mortification to me; but I have had the ill-fate in this war to meet with many.'"[53]

Not all officials were as testy as Russell, whose fits of temper caused the government considerable embarrassment, and it is remarkable, when we consider the high tension at this time, that Blathwayt for the most part escaped criticism. Every one was in a complaining mood, as to both delays and leakages, and since some one had to be blamed, Blathwayt was a convenient victim. The winds were contrary—he was censured for delays in the mails; if there was a bungling of orders, he was at fault! Because of the difficulties which arose over the ratification of the Treaty of Ryswick, he was charged with clumsiness, although, as it happened, the French and English representatives were themselves responsible. Naturally he was blamed for any news leaking out prematurely, no matter how much he denied the charge. When the Earl of Jersey was called to Flanders, in 1699, to assist in the drawing up of the second treaty of partition, Prior received orders to precede Jersey there and to be in attendance upon his arrival.[54] News of Prior's movements somehow seeped

[53] Coxe, *Shrewsbury Correspondence*, pp. 215–216. It seems William later declared the matter an unfortunate mistake, whether Blathwayt's or his own does not appear. Shrewsbury tried his best to pacify Russell and may have inspired the royal letter of explanation. (*Ibid.*, pp. 219–220.)

[54] Prior was proceeding to England in order to take up his work as under-

out, and Jersey took Prior to task for it, but the latter glibly denied all responsibility. "Not guilty as to have writ Mr. Mountagu word that I went by way of Holland. I never said one word of it to him or any man in England. The Elephant knew it, I presume, from something that might have been said at Loo, and according to his foolish manner, stuffed the great news into letters he wrote into England, at least as far as I can guess from the manner of his writing to Mr. Stanyan and I [sic]. The thing must be so. I am very glad you chid me upon a supposition. . . ."[55]

Blathwayt could scarcely have been as foolish as Prior made him out to be, or William would never have retained him in his service during those critical years. Fortunately we have evidence on the other side. James Vernon, who must have known Blathwayt very well, since he served under him on the first year's expedition in 1692, spoke of his extreme caution on a number of occasions. If Blathwayt used forceful expressions in letters which he sent transmitting the royal command, it must have been at the king's special injunction, since "Mr. Blathwayte is a cautious writer, and very sparing of harsh expressions."[56] Vernon knew well that it was easy to attribute misunderstandings growing out of the correspondence to any man's oversight or lack of comprehension, whatever the truth might be.

secretary in Jersey's office, and, as he was leaving Paris, was instructed to meet Jersey in Holland.

[55] Wickham-Legg, *Matthew Prior*, pp. 308–309; Paris, August 8, 1699, s.n. For an instance where Blathwayt stoutly denied the charge of having disclosed information prematurely, see Add. MSS. 9722, f. 88; Blathwayt to Shrewsbury, Camp before Namur, August 4, 1695. What the leakage was does not appear.

[56] Vernon, *Letters Illustrative, etc.*, I, 291; Vernon to Shrewsbury, June 26, 1697. The occasion for criticism was a heated memorial penned by Admiral Russell on the question of William's reinstatement of a naval officer whom the Admiralty had dismissed. (See *ibid.*, pp. 288–295.)

Vernon contradicted Prior on another occasion also. Prior had written: "I am almost ashamed to tell you that I have neither heard from my Lord Portland or Mr. Blathwayt since their arrival in Holland. My Lord indeed has a great deal of business, and I can only expect to hear from him when he has anything to command me . . ., but Mr. Blathwayt, I say, ought in conscience to let me have heard that the King was arrived in Holland, and when he went further, considering I am at a Court that is inquisitive enough and value those ministers that they see know their business, and can give an account of their own department. *Sed nobis non licet esse tam disertis,* because I have not the happiness to be one of his favourites; and a consul in any corner of Italy shall be certainly written to—no matter for the Secretary at Paris; for Lacrimae Christi and White Florence are very good wines; but this is too ill-natured a reflection."[57] In his reply, Vernon said: "I wonder you should not hear from Mr. Blathwayt; he does not use to be wanting in writing either long or short letters. Instead of your Lachrymae Christi and White Florence, can't you suppose that his letters have been opened at the French post-houses, and finding they were of consequence, they have been carried to Versailles instead of to Paris; or otherwise he might not think the news he uses to send fit to a minister in so polite a Court. What reputation would it give you for intelligence to be able to tell which way the stag ran such a day, and how long the chase lasted."[58]

Unless emergencies arose, a regular administrative procedure was adopted during the king's absence. Whenever possible, the signature of the regular secretary of state was used rather than Blathwayt's. The right of Blathwayt to countersign commissions came up for ques-

57 *Hist. MSS. Com., Bath MSS.,* III, 257–258; Paris, August 27, 1698, s.n.
58 *Ibid.,* p. 260; August 22/September 1, 1698.

tion and was apparently settled in his favor,[59] but no commissions were issued unless it was unsafe to postpone an appointment until the king's return. A ruse which Vernon successfully effected gives proof of the king's unwillingness to settle matters of that sort while abroad. An order removing Vernon's friend, Lord Haversham, from the Admiralty board was ready to be presented to the king just as the latter was leaving England. "This Mr. Secretary out of friendship to my Lord neglected to do till the King was gone, well knowing that his Majesty never signs any such thing out of the kingdom; and accordingly his sending it over afterwards proved to no purpose, and by that means Lord Haversham came to be continued all the summer in the commission to the great disgust of Sir G. Rook and the other admirals."[60]

From time to time commissions or letters were predated, and the regular secretary's countersignature affixed before the king's, so that they would appear to have been dispatched in England. Blathwayt accepted this method without protest. Thus he once wrote an urgent letter to Nottingham regarding the appointment of a successor to Harbord, the English minister at the Porte, who fell ill shortly after William arrived in the Low Coun-

[59] Trumbull was, of course, the secretary of state who chose to deny Blathwayt's right to countersign commissions. The matter did not become of any great consequence until after Mary's death, since she was able to sign commissions, if necessary, in England. Just after William went away in 1695, Trumbull demanded that some commissions which had not been ready for the royal signature at the time of William's departure, and were being sent over for him to sign, be sent back to England for countersigning. Blathwayt, somewhat annoyed, referred the matter to Vernon and Shrewsbury, saying that he knew it was a question of the fees for signing the commissions that was worrying Trumbull. He declared his willingness to abide by any decision reached. (Add. MSS. 9722, ff. 49–52; *ibid.*, 37992, ff. 94–95; *ibid.*, 28917, f. 48; *Hist. MSS. Com., Downshire MSS., Trumbull Papers*, Vol. I, Pt. I, 470; S. P. For. Military Expeditions, I, 15, 17.)

[60] *Hist. MSS. Com., Cowper MSS.*, Pt. II, 437–438; London letter of November 8, 1701.

tries in 1692. Paget was to be appointed and "because his dispatches as your lordship knows cannot be made from hence, his majesty directs that your lordship do take care that they be made in England with all speed to be transmitted hither in the proper forms, but to be signed here by his majesty; and because the affixing the great seal to the commission and the king's signing cannot be reconciled with the present dates, his majesty thinks fit that the dispatches be dated the first or the second of March which was before his leaving England and then no material difference will remain."[61] The logical Nottingham, however, objected to this procedure, since several months had elapsed since the king's departure. He decided that Paget's credentials would have to be dated from the camp in Flanders, although they would really be drawn up in England; "and because there is an art in sealing those gilded letters, the Q[ueen] must set the King's name to them."[62]

One irregularity had already occurred in 1692, in connection with the appointment of a secretary to Harbord. The commission was drawn up in Nottingham's office and then dispatched to Blathwayt. "I send it to you sealed and countersigned," Nottingham wrote, "though that is irregular in regard the business requires dispatch. If the king please to sign it, you will convey it to Mr. Harbord to be made use of pursuant to the limitations in my last letter to him, or according to such other directions as his majesty shall think fit to give. If his majesty should not sign this commission I must desire you will keep it by you and not let it be seen, this being a method which I should not have taken but that I think there is a necessity for it

---

[61] Add. MSS. 37991, ff. 85–86; June 6/16, 1692.

[62] *Ibid.*, f. 107; June 28, 1692. In either event, the warrant was to bear Nottingham's signature, not Blathwayt's.

in the present exigency."[63] As late as 1697 similar petty subterfuges were being resorted to, in order to obtain the semblance of official regularity. Some time previous to the king's departure, application for a pass had been made to Shrewsbury. The duke wrote to Vernon, still his undersecretary, to tell him the pass was to be made, and the latter answered: "If your Grace please to send his name [that is, of the applicant], a pass shall be prepared and sent to Mr. Blathwayte for the king's hand. . . . I suppose it must be dated the 23rd of April [two days before the king's departure] for your Grace's countersigning."[64]

Blathwayt made no attempt to oppose such arrangements and never assumed that he had the full power of a secretary of state. His deputy secretary at war, George Clarke, tried to persuade him from the first that, since he was in possession of the signet, he had the right to exercise the secretarial power of countersignature and could therefore countersign the supplementary establishments of the army.[65] Blathwayt was either too cautious or too diffident to be taken in by such arguments; he knew that if he followed this advice opposition would arise, particularly from the Treasury.[66] They would have rejected any establishment which bore Blathwayt's signature, for they denied his authority even in less important matters. He

[63] Add. MSS. 37991, f. 13; March 15, 1692.

[64] Vernon, *Letters Illustrative, etc.*, I, 249; May 15, 1697.

[65] Add. MSS. 9732, f. 27; April 29, 1692.

[66] Yet one of the envoys declared that it aroused Blathwayt's ire when he was not given all the recognition which a duly accredited secretary of state would have had. He was angered, however, by what he regarded as Blathwayt's shameful partiality toward Stepney, and he wrote to the undersecretary in Vernon's office: "I look upon everybody but the Secretary of State, my director [?], as an interloper in such matters, and am abundantly satisfied with Mr. Vernon's instructions without feeling for any other." Cresset, the resident at Hamburg, to John Ellis, June 7, 1698. (*Ibid.*, 28901, ff. 188–189.)

had received his first rebuff from them in 1692, when the board refused to recognize the validity of Stepney's bill of extraordinaries, "which," as Nottingham's clerk wrote to Stepney, "had been allowed by Mr. Blathwayt at the camp, but that was not a sufficient authority to the treasury to pay you the money."[67] The Treasury never changed its attitude on this point, though Blathwayt signed envoys' bills of extraordinaries several times after the Treasury's repulse of 1692, and Stepney complained in 1694 of the stupidity of a board that refused to see in Blathwayt a *bona fide* secretary of state.[68] As late as 1699, the Treasury and Blathwayt had not yet reached an agreement in the matter, for Vernon in a letter to Shrewsbury said: "The king has appointed Count Frize, a Saxon, to succeed Mr. Cresset as Envoy Extraordinary at the Court of Brandenburg. My Lord Lonsdale scruples at passing his Privy Seal; he has acquainted the Lords Justices with two exceptions he makes to it. One is his being a foreigner; the other, that his warrant was countersigned by Mr. Blathwayt."[69]

If Blathwayt knew that he could not take advantage of his position as secretary of state *pro tem.* in his dealings with the Treasury, that board learned that as secretary at war he could not be persuaded or tricked into any irregular practices unless he had their specific authorization. In 1700 he argued a point with them regarding a loan that had been negotiated several years earlier, in Holland. The Treasury had authorized the paymaster-general, Lord

67 S. P. For. Archives, Vol. 82; September 23, 1692.

68 *Ibid.*, Vol. 60; Stepney to Prior, Dresden, June 5/15, 1694.

69 Vernon, *Letters Illustrative, etc.*, II, 352. Cresset had earlier feared that his credentials might not be recognized because they had been signed by Blathwayt, but his fears proved unwarranted. However, credentials signed by Blathwayt were regarded as temporary and were set aside as soon as regular ones could be secured through the secretary of state in England. (Add. MSS. 28898, ff. 422, 473.)

Ranelagh, to refund the debt and to make provision for its immediate repayment, in order that the tallies might be recalled. Blathwayt knew of the warrant to Ranelagh and that it bore the Treasury's countersignature. He knew also that the Dutch ambassadors, who had helped negotiate the loan, expected to be paid for their services but did not care to have that fact advertised. He could appreciate their annoyance when they learned that their names had been stated in the warrant. Consequently he wrote to his friend, Richard Hill, who was then a member of the Treasury board: "I have also seen Mr. Geldermassen and his warrant. We have talkt it over and he is now unwilling to have it said that either their Excellencies have received money for their care and pains, etc. [sic] And we have agreed on an alteration which will not trouble you, the Receipts being only to be changed for others in the name of their secretaries."[70]

It was necessary, therefore, for Geldermassen to receive a new warrant, and Blathwayt argued that it could be issued only by the Treasury, even though the latter insisted that it could be issued equally well by himself. Blathwayt was so careful that he demanded a new order from the Treasury to Ranelagh, instructing him to draw up an entirely new agreement. He said that it made no difference whether the Treasury authorization was *ex post facto* or not, the important point being that the matter should be adjusted by the regular officials. Were he given the proper authorization, he would, of course, be willing to countersign a warrant of this sort himself. "Do in this matter as you please for I shall be brought to reason and further perhaps if it be necessary as you see demonstratively in the business of countersigning the respites, but I would have things done properly and with as little room for objection as possible which is nevertheless

70 Porlock MSS.; Dieren, August 17, 1700.

submitted.[71] . . . If it were one Act upon an extraordinary exigent, the secretary at war might play the dictator, but here is a sequel of winter and summer wherein the lords of the treasury might have been consulted to authorize the necessity of your proceeding.''[72]

When the Treasury argued that the matter was of no real importance, and that Blathwayt had consented to sign other similar warrants without consulting them, Blathwayt answered that this was true, ''but this last business having been so lately and so fairly transacted before them, why should they refuse their own warrant for it or why should Mr. Lowndes refuse his letter to me; nay, I will be satisfied with a minute of what passed at the treasury sign'd by Mr. Lowndes or Mr. Taylour. And if that can't be had, I will go further as I told you, provided the King and you be desirous it should go that way.''[73] He adhered steadily to his point, and his insistence was doubtless prompted by the temper of parliament and the suspicions resting on the Earl of Ranelagh. ''And for Mr. Geldermassen's warrant,'' he wrote to Hill, ''I beg you again to reflect that 'tis not *a minute or order of the treasury* [sic] that is propos'd for your warrant, but for my justification for doing a thing that belongs not to me without it. Pray consult Mr. Lowndes himself and he will tell you I cannot meddle without it or it shall be made a precedent against me ever hereafter when anything is to be done for the Army that carries any possibility of danger. 'Twas a cavill of mine said a great lord (and 'twas a hard word) when I said the respite warrants were to be countersigned by your lordships. And now the warrants for the general officers are turn'd upon my hands for want of an order or letter from Mr. Lowndes. I have

[71] *Ibid.*

[72] *Ibid.;* Blathwayt to Hill, Loo, September 23, 1700, s.n.

[73] *Ibid.*

known my trade too long, but it is hard for me to be always teaching it to others that have no mind to learn nor indeed is it worth this trouble. But to return to our point, the manner is all, the matter is already agreed.'"[74]

Such careful observance of accepted practices was not likely to enhance Blathwayt's popularity with the Treasury Lords, particularly as he was holding out at their expense. No one among the officials in England was eager to assume responsibility for William's dealings regarding loans or subsidies to the allies, if there was any trace of irregularity; nor were they eager to commit acts that might be interpreted as favoring William's hated Dutch advisers and soldiers. The difficulty of Blathwayt's position can be appreciated, as he attempted to steer a straight course through this sea of bewildering perplexities. He had to remember what he could do as secretary of state and what he must not do as secretary at war, lest he establish a dangerous precedent for his successors; or, what was perhaps more to the point, involve himself in difficulties. In general, he was at the service of every one who had the power to command him. That he was never involved in any serious altercation with any officials, and that none of his actions led to any troublesome consequences, are proofs of his good judgment and his knowledge of the situation.

The most important diplomatic events during the period of his attendance were the Treaty of Ryswick and the treaties of partition. If William did not inform Blathwayt of the desertion of the Duke of Savoy to Louis until it became impossible to conceal it any longer, it was not likely that he would inform him of anything else of major importance. Blathwayt was employed only in a minor way with the Peace of Ryswick. As for the treaties of partition, he would have been blind if he had not observed

[74] Porlock MSS.; Blathwayt to Hill, Loo, October 1, 1700, s.n.

something of what was going on. On the whole, however, he saw no more than he was expected to see.

In 1696, Matthew Prior paid Blathwayt the compliment of hoping that he would be appointed one of the commissioners of the peace, to be drawn in 1697, although it was a compliment of doubtful sincerity.[75] The aged Sir Joseph Williamson, who had been useful in earlier diplomatic negotiations, was ultimately selected to serve with Lord Villiers, soon to be made Earl of Jersey, and Lord Lexington. If Blathwayt was disappointed that he was passed by, there is no evidence of it. He remained with the king at Loo or in one or other of the camps throughout the summer and watched the interminable bickerings among the allies and with the agents of Louis XIV. He was in constant communication with Prior, who had been selected as secretary to the English peace commissioners, and he probably knew more than did the officials at Whitehall of what was in progress. Even the plenipotentiaries themselves did not always know precisely what was going on, since it was on Portland that William placed his real dependence. They learned in due time what had happened during the conversations which Portland had with Boufflers, but to no one except Portland did William reveal his true intentions. Even Shrewsbury, who undoubtedly knew more than any of his colleagues in England, complained of the ignorance in which he was kept.[76]

Under the circumstances, Blathwayt could not be expected to furnish much information in his letters to Whitehall. "Mr. Blathwayt refers it to those who are properly concerned, and I don't see anybody that under-

---

[75] *Hist. MSS. Com., Bath MSS.*, III, 98; Prior to Blathwayt, December 21, 1696.

[76] Coxe, *Shrewsbury Correspondence*, pp. 316–382; these are the letters which passed between Villiers, Williamson, Portland, and Shrewsbury. (See also Grimblot, *Letters of William III and Louis XIV*, I, 24–26, 38–39, 40–42, 52, 61, 70–71; *Hist. MSS. Com., Bath MSS.*, III, 108, 116.)

takes to do it," wrote Vernon, complaining that not only he but also the lords justices were kept in darkness.[77] Blathwayt himself declared it a shame that neither the lords justices nor Trumbull was better informed, though he doubted whether much was actually being accomplished by the peace commissioners. "For the general negotiations your progress is indeed retrograde, and till there be an inward desire in all of you to despatch, there will be none. There is nothing so easy as to hinder a treaty as well as to write against a religion: but to promise to propagate either in the present circumstances—Hoc opus, hic labor est," he wrote to Prior, a month after the peace conference had convened.[78]

Though Prior did not know it, Blathwayt was informed of the secret article which was to be attached to the treaty. When Prior heard that Blathwayt was aware of it, he was fearful lest the plenipotentiaries blame him (Prior) for allowing the matter to leak out, especially since Blathwayt seemed to be in possession of a copy of the article drawn in Prior's hand. But Blathwayt wrote to him reassuringly: "The project having been given me by the king with orders concerning it which I signified to their Excellencies [the plenopotentiaries]; so that so many clerks as I had, so many copies I might have taken of it without bringing you under censure or the imputation of discovering secrets, though, indeed, upon an English, Dutch, and German post-day my people were so employed that I rather chose to rely on your hands when they might be at leisure."[79]

The tortuous course of the negotiations annoyed every

[77] Hist. MSS. Com., Bath MSS., III, 116, 120.

[78] Ibid., p. 123; also p. 124.

[79] Ibid., p. 124; Cockleberg, June 8, 1697, s.n. Blathwayt also stated that Heinsius, the Pensioner, knew that Blathwayt was in possession of a copy of the article and had asked for it to use in conference with the king.

one, Blathwayt included. He was especially distressed over the way matters were going with regard to England's colonial claims in the Hudson's Bay region, and he lamented that no dependence was placed on his knowledge of the situation. His feeling over the slights shown him in that connection can readily be appreciated.

By September, 1697, the treaty was so far completed that preparations were made for the exchange of ratifications. Though Blathwayt's share in the activities was very small, there had been so much delay and confusion over the exchange that he fell a victim to severe criticism. Vernon declared that Blathwayt's conduct with regard to the ratification was so retrograde that it would probably cost him a secretarial appointment in 1697.[80]

The steps leading to the ratifications were as devious as those leading to the treaty itself. Difficulties arose over the way in which the documents were to be drawn that were to bear the great seal; should they be prepared in England or at Ryswick? The plenipotentiaries preferred the former course and accordingly sent Prior to London with a copy of the treaty on which to base the articles of ratification.[81] The lords justices somewhat pettishly decided, since the time set for ratification was brief (at most, three weeks) that it would be better to have the form of ratification drawn up by the plenipotentiaries, who were conversant with the treaty, of which they, the lords jus-

[80] It is not clear that Blathwayt was a secretarial candidate in 1697, although, with peace imminent, he may have argued that the campaigns were at an end, and it would be well to secure an appointment in England. In time Vernon discovered that he, himself, not Blathwayt, was slated for the position.

[81] A disgraceful quarrel arose between Trumbull, the lords justices, and Vernon over the treaty which Prior brought with him. It had to be printed and that involved a profit of forty pounds for the secretary, hence Trumbull's insistence that he be allowed to have possession of the treaty. (See Vernon, *Letters Illustrative, etc.*, I, 377–379.)

tices, were almost totally ignorant. The articles could then be sent to Loo, for engrossment and the king's signature, and thereafter dispatched to England, to have the great seal affixed. This course was decided upon, but in the meantime delays ensued. Fearful lest the articles might not arrive in time, William and the plenipotentiaries won the consent of the French to have a preliminary exchange of ratifications under the signet seal in Blathwayt's possession. When finally the articles arrived from England, it was found that the secret article with regard to the exclusion of James from the English throne was not included, and it became necessary to go through the same process again, in order to secure the necessary authority for its ratification. The French then took the opportunity to question the use of the phrase, "William King of France," which appears in the document. Prior reported their doubts to Blathwayt, who decided after consultation with William that a search for recent precedents in the use of the expression would be necessary.[82] Vernon and other officials in England were annoyed at this delay, although it was in no way the fault of either Blathwayt or the plenipotentiaries. Vernon exclaimed petulantly that, "The French if they are in earnest must think there is nobody amongst us understands what belongs to the king, for they may as well scruple the admitting the Great Seal because the arms of France are in it as the King's title."[83]

No one seemed to know what the final procedure was to be. Vernon blamed Blathwayt for failing to send directions. "But we think there has been some mistake some-

[82] Add. MSS. 37992, ff. 196–197. Trumbull was ordered to search the recent treaties with France and produced the Treaty of 1686, which revealed the use of the phrase in question. (See *Hist. MSS., Com., Downshire MSS., Trumbull Papers,* Vol. I, Pt. II, 766.)

[83] S. P. For., Military Expeditions, I, 134; Vernon to Blathwayt, October 5, 1697.

where on that side to keep the matter thus long in suspense. They at first neglected to engross the ratifications there, and send it over with the King's hand to it, which had been the most proper and expeditious way. Our Plenipotentiaries were under a prepossession, that the ratification of the separate article was not necessary till the French had sent theirs and were ready to exchange it. The ministers at Ryswick agree upon the times which the peace is to commence, and refer us to the directions we shall receive from Loo, and no such are sent, though there were time enough for it, so that no orders can be given here to the Admiralty, nor no proclamation be published, and we look like people that were neither in peace nor war. The Lords Justices do not much admire this conduct; this is not like to recommend Mr. Blathwayt to be Secretary of State. He writes to Prior to procure certificates of the peace, and papers to be sent to Newfoundland and other parts of America. Prior writes hither five days after, and is so far from giving an account what they have done in it, that he does not so much as mention that they have received such orders. And thus our negotiations are managed. We have put them in mind of these omissions, and perhaps may be chid for not knowing what to do without particular orders."[84]

Contrary winds and French objections to William's titles were responsible for the delay. Vernon, at the very time he was writing, spoke of the fact that "the wind has been so high and contrary, that we can never expect a mail or my Lord Portland."[85] Blathwayt's and Prior's correspondence reveals that they were sending off their dispatches regularly to England and that their letters

[84] Vernon, *Letters Illustrative, etc.,* I, 425–426; Vernon to Shrewsbury, October 9, 1697.

[85] *Ibid.,* p. 426.

were in transit at the very moment Vernon was complaining.[86] At Loo, and at the headquarters of the plenipotentiaries, the articles of ratification under the great seal were awaited with the same expectancy as was expressed in England over dispatches from the king.[87] The difficulties were very shortly brought to an end, and both Prior and Blathwayt wrote to explain to Vernon that they could hardly be held responsible for delays caused by the elements.[88] Peace was proclaimed at the cost of much possible misunderstanding, but the experience disclosed the highly nervous and tense state to which the various English agents responsible for its declaration were reduced.

The Peace of Ryswick did not terminate William's foreign expeditions, and Blathwayt, to his annoyance, was again summoned to attend in 1698. His mind was taken up with the disbanding of the army, and in the autumn he regretted that he had been kept so long on the Flemish side, for his absence was prejudicial to the king's interest in parliament in military affairs. He had a fair knowledge of what was going on behind the scenes regarding the Treaty of Partition, and in December, 1698, he wrote to Stepney, who he assumed was equally knowing, "But what do you think of the declaration the King of Spain has lately made of the Prince Electoral of Bavaria to be his successor. We ought to like it well. But how does it agree with—[sic]? What can my Lord Jersey say to—[sic], or rather what is to be done in case of the King of Spain's death? Untie this knot *et eris mihi magnus Apollo.* In the meantime I may tell you we are perfectly ignorant hereof—[sic] for what appears at least and 'tis well 'tis so. Though I must confess the warmth we show in

86 See Prior's and Blathwayt's letters, to be found in *Hist. MSS. Com., Bath MSS.,* III; also Add. MSS. 37992, f. 184, *et seq.*

87 *Hist. MSS. Com., Bath MSS.,* III, pp. 180–181.

88 *Ibid.,* pp. 180–182.

disbanding our army and all foreigners which seems to have almost a general consent argues very much.''[89]

Stepney eschewed all knowledge of what Blathwayt meant by his cryptic dashes but admitted his knowledge of the treaty. ''What you write with hyphens as to the Spanish negotiation is all riddle to me. Nor have I heard from Lord P[ortland] since he past Lingen and am satisfied, for I never liked the business; what excuses Lord Jersey may make to—[sic] is their concern, not mine. The disbanding of our army is certainly a proof that the negotiation has taken vent, and I perceive it by a clause in the pamphlet (The History of Standing Armies) [sic] that the author is not ignorant of such treaty, at least he guesses well.''[90]

It was clear that both Blathwayt and Stepney realized enough of what had happened to draw their own conclusions. They questioned Louis's good faith, and they accordingly decried the steps taken, at the insistence of parliament, to diminish the forces. England was enjoying only an armed truce. In February, 1699, came the death of the Electoral Prince of Bavaria, and immediately the question of the succession to the Spanish throne was thrown open again. ''The matter of the Spanish Succession is quick changed by Providence,'' wrote Blathwayt, ''and one good I think we have from it, that the former scheme is entirely vanished with the inconveniences attending it. Lord Jersey is perhaps at work upon another which may acquit him of those small obligations petty ministers are subject to,'' he added sarcastically. ''We of

---

[89] S. P. For. Archives, Vol. 52, no paging; Whitehall, December 30, 1698. The treaty had been drawn after the return of the royal party to England, so there was no occasion for Blathwayt's being employed in any connection with it. Jersey had been appointed ambassador to France after the Treaty of Ryswick.

[90] *Ibid.*; this was in answer to Blathwayt's letter of December 30, 1698. Stepney was then stationed in Berlin, an important diplomatic centre.

the council of trade desired to know of Mr. Secretary Vernon what had been done at Paris between the French and the Dutch about the tariff. Mr. Secretary answered that he had writ to the Lord Jersey, but that his lordship knew nothing of the matter. Mr. Prior, I suppose, follows the methods of his master or rather his master his."[91]

Negotiations for a second treaty of partition went forward just as Blathwayt had anticipated. Jersey was recalled from Paris and took up the seals of the southern office. Although there had been some talk of having Jersey instead of Blathwayt attend the king abroad, it was finally settled that the latter must make the trip again.[92] It was plain that William's mind was intent upon securing another treaty. Portland, as usual, was to be the agent, but the growing rift between him and the king made it very uncertain whether he would be retained long enough to complete the negotiations. Blathwayt watched the situation with a great deal of interest and reported his observations to Stepney. In August he declared that the rupture with Portland was virtually complete, and that Portland's share in the negotiations would have to devolve on the Duke of Albemarle, although, since "now it looks as if he had laid down the French affairs too and his negotiations with Count Tallard, who but Lord Jersey can take them up in the eye of the world at a time when they are so nice and critical, besides other considerations that may bring his lordship hither."[93]

As Blathwayt foresaw, Jersey after countless rumors and interminable delays was summoned to Loo. Meanwhile, Stepney's letters in the course of the summer in-

[91] S. P. For. Archives, Vol. 52, no paging; Blathwayt to Stepney, Whitehall, February 24, 1699.

[92] On June 6, 1699, Prior wrote to Jersey that he was glad to hear that it was the "Elephant" who was to swim to Holland, not Jersey. (Wickham-Legg, *Matthew Prior*, p. 288.)

[93] S. P. For. Archives, Vol. 53, no paging; Loo, August 4, 1699.

dicate that neither he nor Blathwayt were deceived by the clumsy attempts at secrecy. "The frequent meeting which Count Tallard has had of late with my Lord Portland and the Pensioner and the flying about of black boxes as last year, makes people think the Spanish project is again on foot. The Elector [of Prussia] speaks of it frequently, but with so little consistency that I am persuaded neither His Electoral Highness nor any of his Council are yet got to the bottom of it; however His Highness is resolved not to neglect the part of it at least which relates to his own interest, and for that reason has determined to send an envoy directly to Madrid who is to negotiate the arrears that are due His Highness from Spain. . . . Lord Jer-[sey] drives like Jehu; you observe I speak modestly of the Spanish project for I must not pretend to see into a millstone."[94]

To Stepney's inquiry whether Jersey was actually to be called over to Loo, Blathwayt made answer: "Lord Jersey's coming is yet uncertain and I suppose it will be somewhat late and yet time enough to sign what may be by others agreed upon."[95] He had no illusions as to William's willingness to make use of men as tools, nor any expectations that his own services would be called upon. Happiness, he took occasion to say at this time, did not consist in being a royal favorite. He was relieved, not disappointed, when at last Lord Jersey arrived on the scene.

Just before the earl's arrival, William ordered Canales, the Spanish ambassador to England, who had been angered by the reports of the treaty of partition, to leave the country, and Blathwayt was instructed to transmit the order to the lords justices. In his letter Blathwayt declared Canales's memorial of protest to William both "insolent and seditious."[96] He had already stated to

[94] *Ibid.;* August 1/11, 1699.   [95] *Ibid.;* Loo, August 5/15, 1699.
[96] Vernon, *Letters Illustrative, etc.,* II, 357–358.

Stepney: "I find nothing lies heavy upon the Elector but his not being informed of the Spanish affairs which you may easily turn off if you have anything more to say to him upon the want of maturity in the negotiations, or the coming of Count Frize, though you will judge the business far advanced by my Lord Jersey's being certainly expected very soon. In the meantime all the Spanish ministers thunder everywhere with their protest and our Canales has delivered memorials by his secretary to every lord justice in such a bear-garden and seditious style appealing to the lords and commons in parliament and to the whole nation against the present proceedings that the king cannot but highly resent such extravagant language and intentions."[97]

Blathwayt accompanied William on the two final expeditions very half-heartedly. He was annoyed, as we shall see later, over the financial arrangements which had been made and was filled with perturbation that there was never to be an end to his attendance. He realized the *débâcle* which would come in the wake of the death of the Spanish king. "But is the king of Spain to die and must all return to its former chaos? You thought perhaps of quiet and something like retirement," he wrote in whimsical despair to one of his friends as early as 1698.[98] A feeling of impatience over life's uncertainties possessed him, though he attempted to conceal it behind an ill-feigned jocularity. For one thing only was he grateful, that he had thus far escaped parliamentary attack. His insistence on observing the letter of official procedure during these years, because of the consequences which he felt might otherwise ensue, testifies to his uneasiness.

[97] S. P. For. Archives, Vol. 53; Loo, September 19/29, 1699.

[98] Porlock MSS.; letter draft of March 25, 1698, Blathwayt to Hill, who was then still deputy paymaster of the forces but presently took his place on the Treasury board.

Blathwayt's dispatches of 1701 were largely concerned with orders to the envoys regarding their conduct in the face of the complications which followed the death of the Spanish king and that of James II, soon after. One of his last acts as secretary of state was to order the recall of Lord Manchester, minister to France, thus announcing that war had been declared. Vernon was to have sent out the formal order from England, while Blathwayt was to have dispatched only the preliminary announcement; but William regarded the situation as so urgent that, when the news arrived that Louis XIV had actually recognized the Pretender, who had been crowned king of England at St. Germain, not a moment was lost.[99]

Thus far, more attention has been given to Blathwayt's duties as secretary of state than to those as secretary at war. The work of the two offices was equally engrossing. He had no immediate charge over any of the forces within the war zone, nor did he, during his absence from England, have any control over any of the soldiers at home. His primary concern was the transportation of troops, contracts for food, clothing and horses, and distribution of subsidies to the allied forces.[100] In so doing, he was sim-

[99] *Ibid.;* letter drafts of September 6/16 and 15/25, 1701. Also Add. MSS. 37992, f. 255; Blathwayt to Vernon, September 23, 1701.

[100] Blathwayt had a great deal to do with the various army contractors, most of whom were Flemish and Dutch Jews, of Spanish or Portuguese extraction; Pereira, Medina, and Machado were the three most important. Either Blathwayt was honest, or he was clever; at any rate, he never had to face parliamentary charges of accepting bribes from the contractors or sharing profits with them. Robert Walpole was expelled from the house of commons and sent to the Tower in January, 1712, for receiving the sum of 500 guineas and for taking a note for £500, in connection with army contracts. Marlborough and Adam Cardonnel were similarly involved, Cardonnel being accused of accepting a gratuity of five gold ducats, annually, from the contractors for bread and bread wagons. He, too, was expelled from the house of commons. Blathwayt was called upon to testify at this time, but no charges were brought against him. This was during the period when Marl-

ply transmitting the royal orders; endeavoring to see that schedules with regard to the movement of troops to and from England were maintained, and that, as far as possible, matters were facilitated by the prompt payment of money out of the treasury or by loans negotiated with Holland. It was a harrowing business, and Blathwayt was constantly at his wit's end to know what he was to do. Lack of ready money was the cause of all the trouble, and since it never became more plentiful, conditions never improved. Blathwayt was approached with tales of distress from all sides—by the generals on the field, the officers of the garrisons, the contractors for army supplies, and the deputy paymaster of the forces. All begged him to do what he could to force the hand of the Treasury. Money failed to arrive from England or came in exchequer bills or tallies, both of which suffered rapid depreciation. William, without the Treasury's knowledge, made agreements for subsidies to the allies and left the unpleasant task of informing the Treasury to Blathwayt. It also fell to Blathwayt to have ready for payment the subsidies to the allies, whose envoys thronged the camp. Not only did he have to endure their importunities but he also fell victim to attacks in England. "I cannot hear anything wherein your name is made use of," his friend, Robert Henley of the transport board, wrote to him in 1694, "but I think myself obliged to make you acquainted with it, be the thing in my opinion never so frivolous or improbable, that you may judge whether it deserves to be considered or despised. It is discoursed by some men very seriously that you occasion the carrying money out of England to be distributed to the Confederates whose agent you are in that matter, which they say shall be brought into parlia-

borough was being degraded, and political motives prompted the investigations. (See Boyer, *Political State of Great Britain*, III, 112–113, 276–296.)

ment. You will be pleased to use this advertisement so that it may not be known it comes from me."[101]

In the face of these charges, Blathwayt adopted an air of whimsical resignation. He had no other recourse. The situation in Flanders was bad enough, but the tales of distress among the soldiers were sufficient to drive a man to the point of madness. News came of similar suffering in England; of popular protests against further taxation; of the depreciation of coinage through clipping; of such ventures as the land bank, which threatened to endanger the security of the Bank of England; and of the tortuous politics played by parliament. His letters to Richard Hill, Ranelagh's deputy in Flanders, and to Charles Montagu, later the Earl of Halifax and at this time chancellor of the exchequer, reveal his despair, although he concealed his real feeling behind a mask of mocking raillery. All three workers realized the too-close dependence of England's military administration on the caprice of parliament.[102]

Blathwayt's winters were as busy as his summers. On his return in the fall, he immediately resumed charge of the war office in Whitehall and was responsible for the well-being of the soldiers in their winter quarters both at home and abroad. His chief task, however, was attendance at the house of commons. In 1693 he decided to stand for membership. "I have been for some time in Gloucestershire where my neighbors of Bath have made me a country gentleman," he wrote to Hill.[103] In answer to the latter's congratulations, he said: "I cannot guess half the twenty reasons you have to be glad I am come into the parliament. If there be one good one 'tis enough, for I am

[101] Add. MSS. 9729, ff. 102–103; July 17, 1694.

[102] Blathwayt's correspondence with Hill is to be found at Porlock House and also in *ibid.*, 9730; that with Montagu, in *ibid.*, 34355. Blathwayt and Montagu shared a solicitude for the welfare of George Stepney, who was in a sense their protégé.

[103] Porlock MSS.; December 8, 1693.

satisfied there were many against it, but I could not well see others run away with a burgership under my nose and to which I have secured an everlasting title if that can signify much."[104]

He proved an energetic parliamentarian, although he had fault to find with many of the actions of the house. When he wrote to Hill his criticisms took on a facetious character, though his frequent references to the parliamentary investigations of the period show that he was not wholly at his ease. "We have cut down our admirals again after hanging," he wrote, apropos of the inquiry which followed the naval disasters of the summer of 1693, "and yet the gallows is remaining, so variable are our proceedings and may be yet more."[105] "I told you we should be for hanging somebody to the seawards. My Lord Falkland is this day sent to the Tower by a vote of the house for misdemeanor and breach of trust in receiving money irregularly. The fault was indeed but small but the crime great, the house resenting his partial and furious animosity in the business of the sea admirals and his sudden turning upon the toe. And so they hanged Hamain[sic]."[106] In 1696, he reported that parliament was threatening to establish its control over colonial affairs and the administration of the Acts of Trade, by creating "a Councill of Trade by Parliament and of Parliament Men. Don't you fear it should extend to the Army too which is the only thing can relieve you."[107]

To both Blathwayt and Hill, the tactics of the house of commons on the question of supply were the chief concern. In 1695, Blathwayt reported that the elections boded

---

[104] Porlock MSS.; December 26, 1693. This was a by-election, to fill the seat left vacant by the death of Sir William Bassett. Blathwayt continued to sit for Bath until the election of 1710, when he was defeated.

[105] *Ibid.;* December 8, 1693.

[106] *Ibid.;* Whitehall, February 16, 1694.

[107] *Ibid.;* Whitehall, January 30, 1696.

well. "The choice of parliament promises very well, but
some of our friends are left out as well as others. There
will be one third of new men."[108] "You may judge by the
enclosed that our winter campaign will be answerable to
that of the summer, our temper and proceedings being
such as to give a prospect of success and dispatch."[109] He
was less optimistic in 1696, when the dilatory tactics of the
house in voting money drove him to distraction. "You are
so well informed by Mr. Yard of what we do, or rather, do
not in parliament that I have nothing to add."[110] The program for disbanding the army he regarded as short-
sighted. "I cannot and will not write our General [Prince
de Vaudemont] word our House of Commons has finally
pinned the basket upon the number of ten thousand men
for our whole army. The summ agreed on for this service
is £350,000, it and no more. I beg you lay this very gently
before His Highness and crave his pardon for our doings.
So the brave army late under his command is like a
shadow that fleeth away and is no more."[111] He was
cheered for a time by parliament's willingness to provide
money for other purposes. "You see the parliament are
fallen into better humor and think to make amends for
disbanding our army by providing a considerable fleet and
for the king's civil list during life."[112] He realized the
ineptitude of some of their acts in the winter of 1698.
"Our House was indeed very generous in voting or allowing the arrears of subsidies and forage money, but they
have since in some manner kicked down the milk pail in
postponing payments to the next parliament."[113]

[108] *Ibid.;* November 15/25, 1695.
[109] *Ibid.;* Whitehall, November 26, 1695.
[110] *Ibid.;* December 4, 1696. Blathwayt was referring to Robert Yard's
news-letters.
[111] *Ibid.;* Whitehall, January 11, 1697.
[112] *Ibid.;* Whitehall, December 24, 1697.
[113] *Ibid.;* March 8, 1698.

During these years Blathwayt argued like a true militarist. He preached a doctrine of preparedness, and in view of subsequent events, his stand was well taken. Whether his years of close association with James II and William III, both strong army men, had molded his views, or whether he was guided by conviction, is not easy to determine. He naturally objected to seeing the army he had helped to organize suddenly totter under the force of parliamentary attack, and his efforts to forestall reductions made him very unpopular with such men as Robert Harley and St. John, who led the movement for retrenchment. Neither had a high opinion of his military genius, although St. John, who served as one of the parliamentary commissioners of accounts in 1702–1703, could not find any actual flaw in his administrative methods.[114] St. John served, a few years later, as Blathwayt's successor in the war office, with no notable success; but though Harley as secretary of state and St. John as secretary at war probably reversed their opinion of the ease of administering an army, they never reversed their opinion of Blathwayt.

James Vernon declared that Blathwayt's attitude toward the disbanding of the army cost him needless trouble in the house of commons in 1698, though it is hard to see how Blathwayt could long have withheld the information which the house sought. Vernon wrote to

[114] Blathwayt had no knowledge of military strategy, to speak of, since that lay outside his purview. No one apparently ever gave him advice on how to conduct a campaign, except a certain intrepid Edward Littelton, who propounded schemes for military manoeuvres in the year 1696 and advised a march to Paris. His advice must have been welcomed by Blathwayt, since he continued his letters in 1697, when he had much to say about the peace terms England should accept. The correspondence was resumed in 1701, when war again threatened. Littleton's first letter of that year opened with the words, ''Your candid acceptance of my letters during the last war hath given me encouragement to presume now further upon you.'' (Add. MSS. 9726, ff. 18–19, 28; *Hist. MSS. Com.*, V. Report, Lord Hatherton MSS., pp. 296–297.)

Shrewsbury that on June 1, 1698, Sir Thomas Dyke moved that a list of the army, disbanded and to be disbanded, be produced before the house. "They say it was not intended to be carried farther, if Mr. Blathwayte had not happened to say he should be ready with the lists when he had orders for it. Upon that, Sir Christopher Musgrave said they saw now where it stuck, and therefore moved for an address. I know not whether those gentlemen will be the most forward in pursuing this matter much farther. Some suspect they are not very unwilling to make their court at other men's hazard."[115]

In January, 1699, Blathwayt argued against curtailing the number of guards and garrisons to 7,000, saying that 5,000 were needed in the garrisons alone. Robert Harley thereupon produced establishments from the time of Charles II, when guards and garrisons had numbered less than 7,000.[116] But as Blathwayt could well point out, it was a case of changed times and changed customs. He was relieved when, in the end, the number fixed upon was 10,000.

With William's death, in 1701, the need for Blathwayt's attendance on the summer expeditions came to an end. His clerk, Adam Cardonnel, was appointed military secretary to the Duke of Marlborough, and until the duke's campaigning ceased in 1710, he continued to perform the military duties which had earlier fallen to Blathwayt's lot. Blathwayt's ten years of arduous labor netted him perhaps less than they should have. There had been a rumor in December, 1700, that he was to be made Earl of Bristol "in consideration of his services to his majesty" but nothing came of it.[117] All that he had to show for his years of attendance were his increased

[115] Vernon, *Letters Illustrative, etc.*, II, 94.
[116] *Ibid.*, pp. 246–248.
[117] Luttrell, *Brief Relation*, IV; entry for December 14, 1700.

emoluments in the way of salary, for the receipt of which he had to put up a stubborn fight at the Treasury. He was not even made a privy councillor, for William had always regarded him as nothing more than a glorified clerk, unfit to be elevated to that dignity. He had lent himself to William's scheme of using unimportant men as his drudges in the secretarial office; he had simplified William's problem of protracted absences from England; he had done everything to win the gratitude of a monarch who, in view of his temperament, can perhaps be forgiven for thinking that he had done enough for Blathwayt when he provided him with a good salary.

Blathwayt had nothing to hope for from Anne and her government in the way of special recognition; but he was fortunate to retain his offices at the time new commissions were issued after her accession. As it was, his tenure of the war office was imperiled, and it was only a matter of time until he should have to relinquish it. Thanks to the support of Lord Nottingham, he retained his hold on it until the spring of 1704, when the crisis over the Bill for Occasional Conformity resulted in the resignation of that lord from the office of secretary of state and the appointment of Robert Harley in his stead.[118] Even then, Blathwayt's dismissal was not absolutely assured, according to the reports his friends sent out, until his own folly and fondness for a jest made it inevitable. Cardonnel wrote to Stepney: "You will now receive your Friday's letters from London which give you an account of Mr. St. John's succeeding Mr. Blathwayt. All of his friends agree that this happened to him perfectly through his own indiscretion. The first mention of it was merely in jest, on St. Taffy's Day [April 1], and if he had been quiet would have gone no further, but he saw no man alive from that

118 Luttrell twice reported Blathwayt's dismissal; once on January 27, 1702, and again on December 20, 1702. (See Brief Relation, V, 135, 251.)

day but whom he entertained with it, till it came really to effect, though no such thing was intended at first. He seems very easy under it, and I do assure you I am perfectly so, for if I may pretend to know anything of my own mind, I protest I think if I were free from my Lord Duke and it were offered to me, I should rather choose a retirement.'"[119] St. Taffy's Day or not, Blathwayt's dismissal could not long have been postponed. In the eyes of the moderate Tories who ruled England's destinies in 1704, Blathwayt found no favor; and his office they regarded as part of their legitimate political spoils.

[119] Add. MSS. 7063, f. 44; also Luttrell, *Brief Relation*, V, 411. Luttrell reported that dismissal was likely as early as April 6; Cardonnel wrote on April 22, 1704. For Stepney's answer and comment on the dismissal, see *Hist. MSS. Com., Duke of Buccleuch MSS., Montagu House*, Vol. II, Pt. II, 694. Luttrell in his earlier reports had named Cardonnel as Blathwayt's successor. (V, 251.)

CHAPTER X

MEMBER OF THE BOARD OF TRADE
1696–1707

THE year 1696 was a turning point in the history of England's administrative control over trade and plantations. It witnessed the passage of the last of the Acts of Trade, so called, and the unsuccessful attempt to transfer control over the colonies to a board constituted and named by parliament. It marked the culmination of a campaign which the merchant class in England, threatened with the loss of its trade, had waged for a decade. The leading writers on trade and economic polity had lent their support. The credit for the final passage of the act of 1696 must rest with Edward Randolph, who returned from Maryland in the fall of 1695 in ample time to impress upon such administrative agents as the commissioners of the customs and the Treasury the need of reinforcing that part of England's governmental machinery which controlled trade and the plantations. Few men in Whitehall opposed the bill, once the need for it had been seen, for Randolph was an effective "lobbyist." Preparations for its introduction into parliament were made, and on January 23, 1696, it was ordered "that leave be given to bring in a bill for preventing frauds and regulating abuses, in the plantation trade: and that Mr. Chadwick and Mr. Blathwaite do prepare, and bring in, the bill."[1]

1 Stock, *Proceedings and Debates of the British Parliaments respecting North America*, II, 155. Chadwick was a member for Dover, elected in 1689. See *Members of Parliament* (1213–1885), p. 578.

Blathwayt's influence in the house of commons and his attitude on the proposed measure can be seen from this parliamentary order. Randolph had counted on his whole-hearted support and was not disappointed. Beyond this one reference, however, Blathwayt's name does not appear in the parliamentary record. Mr. Chadwick presented the bill for its first reading on January 27, and we are left to conjecture how much of a part Blathwayt had in drawing up its various heads,[2] for he had meantime gone down to Dyrham Park. He was in constant touch with Randolph, however, who evidently depended on him for advice. By March 31, the bill had passed both houses, despite stiff opposition, and was ready for the king's signature.[3]

The bill for the creation of a parliamentary council of trade did not meet with the same success. The Act of Trade was acceptable to both the Whigs and the Tories, but this second measure was clearly a Whig proposal, made, according to one authority, at the suggestion of Lord Somers, the lord keeper.[4] It definitely expressed dissatisfaction with the lax administration of the Lords of Trade and was calculated also to embarrass the king, whose Dutch sympathies ran against the grain of most of his Whig attendants. That its proponents had worked out any very careful scheme of parliamentary control is doubtful; their purpose was far more destructive than constructive. Yet many took alarm. Blathwayt regarded the passage of the act as a foregone conclusion, for the

2 From Randolph's statements we should assume that Blathwayt's share had been very large. (Goodrick, *Edward Randolph*, VII, 504–505; Randolph to Blathwayt, Feb. 20, 1696.)

3 *Ibid.*, p. 536; Randolph to Blathwayt, August 25, 1698: "It was with great difficulty that the Act for preventing Frauds and regulateing abuses in the Plantation Trade was obtained."

4 Pownall, *Administration of the Colonies*, (4th ed., 1768), p. 20; Osgood, *The American Colonies in the 18th Century*, I, 118–159.

day before Colonel Granville reported the measure from
the committee of the whole house, he wrote to a friend
that the bill had actually been passed.[5]

Fears with regard to this encroachment on the royal
prerogative were soon set at rest. The bill was read and
committed, but it never emerged from committee. The
plot against the king's life had swung popular sympathy
in the opposite direction, and William III had decided to
rout his enemies by meeting them more than halfway. He
disarmed their arguments against the laxity of administration in trade and plantation affairs by admitting the
fact and appointing a new administrative board. On May
15, 1696, the commission under the great seal was passed
erecting the Board of Trade. A week earlier William and
Blathwayt had departed for Flanders. Any gloom which
the latter may have felt over the turn events had taken in
colonial administration was probably banished by the fact
that he was named a member of the board.

Except that the commission was issued and the members of the board named, the future was still uncertain
when the king left England. No meetings had been held,
and nothing had been determined as to the way in which
the board and its office were to be organized. No selections
had been made for the office staff. Blathwayt probably left
England regretful that his duties called him away from
Whitehall at such a critical time, but nevertheless he was
fairly confident of his ability to influence the situation. He
apparently assumed that John Povey would be named
secretary to the board. His complacency had a severe
shock when he learned, in July, after the first meeting of
the board had been finally held, that John Povey's claims
to consideration had been entirely disregarded, and an
utter stranger, without previous experience, named secre-

---

[5] Porlock MSS.; Blathwayt to Hill, Whitehall, January 30, 1696; also,
Stock, *Proceedings and Debates*, etc., II, 156.

tary instead. Robert Henley, Blathwayt's good friend on the transport board, reported the matter to him. "Having just made an end of scribbling to you what views of public matters, I shall now acquaint you of what's more essential to ourselves. I doubt not, but you have had an account of the meeting of the Council of Trade at Whitehall, and though, it may be, the majority of those lords, and others named in the committee were for Mr. Povey and Mr. Tollet to be secretaries, yet that was obviated by my Lord Keeper [Somers] who very early disclosed to the Board that one Mr. Popple was nominated thereto by his Majesty, and so there was no room to propose any other; and accordingly, I hear Mr. Popple, at this last meeting, did officiate as secretary. Although I hear there are several objections against him, as his long stay in France, after all other English merchants came away, and subscribing to some papers which the government, where he was, obliged him to do, if he would live amongst them. And that since his coming for England, he had not taken the oaths to his Majesty, unless he has done it on this occasion, and that he secured William Penn in his house till he made way to appear,[6] and is since married to a wife of £20,000 portion, by whose contrivance, probably, Mr. Popple comes to be taken notice of. I won't mind you of what William Penn said to a friend of yours about the plantation business, only to let you know when lately the same friend took occasion to say to an acquaintance of his that Mr. Povey, he thought, the most proper person in the world to inform that Board of what related to the plantations, Nay, said the party, he (and Mr. Blathwayt; though he be named in the committee) is the most improper person of all others to be concerned in it, for, said he, how

[6] The allusion to Penn is not clear; Penn had been a great opponent of the Act of Trade in 1696, and it may be that he had incurred a certain amount of dangerous unpopularity as a result.

will you come at the iniquities committed therein by them, etc. . . . [*sic*] I should tell you likewise, how I have been solicited by him, who is a philosopher,[7] and by his friends to give them a scheme, and if not that, to communicate my thoughts and observations about trade; on which occasion they have pretended great kindness for me. But I profess, Sir, I contend with every day greater difficulties in the transports, by clamors for want of money and that all my thought and time, is employed that way, and that is the reason I give, for not accepting of being concerned about trade, and leaving off all thought of it."[8]

Blathwayt was infuriated at the news. His chagrin can easily be appreciated. At a single stroke all his hopes for the perpetuation of his influence in the plantation office were swept aside. Was this to be his reward for twenty years of painstaking service in that office? He resolved not to tolerate it, though how he could honestly have believed that his influence would counteract that of Lord Somers is not clear. He approached the king, and he wrote to his various friends in England, principally Montagu, the chancellor of the exchequer, to see whether some change could be effected. He buoyed up the disconsolate Povey with the promise that something would be done to reinstate him, even though the latter feared that the decision of the board was conclusive.

Povey, meantime, had made up his mind to salvage what he could in the way of colonial perquisites from the wreckage of his hopes and wrote to inform Governor Nicholson, of Maryland, that he would be glad to continue as agent for the colony. In his letter he gave his view of the recent changes. "The Commission of Trade is now opened and Mr. Popple appointed by the king to be their secretary, a person who was but a merchant and had prac-

7 John Locke.
8 Add. MSS. 9729, ff. 140–141; London, July 3, 1696.

ticed it for some time, till the world frowned upon him.
Many of the Commissioners endeavored that there might
be two secretaries, that I might be continued in the service, without which they did me the honor to say they would
be in the dark; but the matter is not determined, though it
seems to be so with me; since in regard of my station at
the council board and the continuance of the business of
the revenue in my hands, together with the influence Mr.
Blathwayt must have, being the only Commissioner that
knows anything of the matter, I shall not be less able to
serve your Excellency.' '[9]

Blathwayt refused to take the matter so philosophi-
cally. He decided to undermine Popple's influence, and
meanwhile held out the hope that the board could make
use of two secretaries, a plan which could be legitimately
entertained on account of the increase in business. He was
convinced that within a few months the board would realize its inability to get along without his and Povey's services. When they came to him, as he was sure they would,
he would insist on the appointment not only of Povey but
also of George Stepney, who was then temporarily without a position.

Impressed by Stepney's ability, Blathwayt had called
him into his own service as a secretarial assistant, and,
in 1696, had him with him in Flanders. He had soon discovered that Stepney was pining for an appointment in
England and had resolved to use his influence in obtaining one for him, although Stepney had a more prominent
patron in Montagu. Knowing that Blathwayt had a poor
opinion of the members of the Board of Trade, Stepney
had begged that Blathwayt recommend him to the king
for a vacancy, should one occur. To this Blathwayt de-
murred, saying that Stepney had neither age, knowledge,

[9] Huntington MSS., Bridgewater Collection (Ellsmere 30:C29), Vol. 137,
Nos. 9625, 9626; Whitehall, July 4, 1696.

nor interest, three of the requisites for a successful commissioner of trade. However, he decided that Stepney might do as undersecretary to serve with Povey, particularly if Blathwayt gave him the benefit of his library and his vast accumulation of papers on colonial and trade affairs.

In August, 1696, therefore, Stepney wrote to Montagu: "I understand Mr. Popple gives not satisfaction in his new employment as secretary to the Commissioners of Trade. I am therefore inclined to offer myself for that station in case there should be any change and am apt to believe I may have his Majesty's approbation as a recompense for many years' service. 'Tis true this business of commerce will appear at first a new scene to me who have little experience or insight into things of that nature, but I hope soon to overcome those difficulties by much diligence and application. I humbly entreat you to favor me with your thoughts on this proposal if there be any ground for it. I should not have troubled you with it at this time, but that I suppose some other man step before me if I had neglected this opportunity."[10]

Blathwayt failed to place either Povey or Stepney in the office. He then fell back on the hope that the Board of Trade would prove only temporary, and that some change would be made in which his own and Povey's claims would be more fully recognized. He was not the only one to think that the future of the board was uncertain. Henley reported optimistically, "'Tis said 'tis forty to one

[10] S. P. For. Archives, Vol. 56, no paging; Camp at Attre, August 13/23, 1696. See his letters of August 31/September 10, 1696 and January 15/25, 1697, where he speaks of the assistance Blathwayt will give him. By 1697, Blathwayt had decided that Stepney was worth recommending to the board itself and secured him a seat. Stepney found the work there less to his taste than he had anticipated and was glad to return to the diplomatic service again, although he retained his seat on the Board of Trade—and a salary of £1000! *Cal. Treas. Papers*, 1697–1702, p. 53.

but it will be again controverted in the next session of parliament, of which they make a jest on the Exchange.''[11] James Vernon had similar doubts and expressed them in 1696, when answering the plea of Matthew Prior for a seat on the Board of Trade.[12]

All of Blathwayt's hopes were, of course, frustrated. Far from being temporary, the Board of Trade was destined to endure for eighty-six years. William Popple, Povey's "mere merchant," and a "business failure," according to Henley, proved to have secretarial ability of a high order. Somers's confidence in him was, therefore, not misplaced. Popple succeeded in ingratiating himself so completely at Whitehall that he easily established the dynastic control for which Blathwayt struggled so vainly. Unlike Blathwayt, moreover, he was a man of a single interest; he was content to be the secretary to the Board of Trade, and he made no excursions into politics. As a result, he aroused much less enmity than Blathwayt, both at home and abroad.[13]

Eventually Blathwayt resigned himself to the situation, convinced that further protest was futile. No one in that period of Whig ascendancy appeared to back his claims. He was living in a much less friendly court than that of James II, and unity of interest in colonial policy had disappeared. Moreover, Blathwayt had laid himself open to charges which easily account for the desire of his enemies

[11] Add. MSS. 9729, ff. 142–143; June, 1696.

[12] *Hist. MSS. Com., Bath MSS.*, III, 82; July 24/August 3, 1696. Prior hoped to replace Methuen on the board. He did ultimately replace Locke, but not until 1700. Prior was very bitter over the fact that he could not get a seat any sooner than he did, and he spoke with some bitterness of the fact that Stepney was serving *in absentia*. (See *ibid.*, p. 351.)

[13] Popple resigned his secretaryship in 1707, the same year in which Blathwayt was dismissed from the board. Popple's son, William, succeeded him and held office until 1722, whereupon in spite of some opposition on the part of Bryan Wheelock, the deputy (or assistant) secretary, Alured Popple, William Jr.'s son, was given the office. (Basye, *The Board of Trade*, p. 15.)

to discomfit and humiliate him. His devotion to England's trade interests was now challenged. Men were beginning to talk of his mercenary disposition and even to charge him with encouraging piratical governors. Enemies of Randolph and Andros were at work to discredit him. Penn, who hated Blathwayt as an opponent of proprietary colonies, was busy distilling his poison with a craftiness that became the diplomat better than the Quaker. The struggles which were racking New York, in the conflict of Leislerite with anti-Leislerite, were reflected in English official circles, where party lines seem to have been drawn clean and close on the basis of it. Whigs in 1696 and 1697 were not likely to forget that Tories, Nottingham and Blathwayt in particular, had been responsible for the appointment of Governor Fletcher, whose name became a term of opprobrium among the followers of his Whig successor, the Earl of Bellomont.

Lord Somers and Admiral Russell were apparently quite convinced by current tales about Blathwayt. Even the mild Shrewsbury was persuaded. It is clear that these men had secured the ear of William III even before his departure from England in 1696. The grant from the English Exchequer to fit out a ship for Captain Kidd's pursuit of pirates proves this, for the warrant for the issue of £6000 to that notorious Scotsman was drawn after William had set out. Comparison of dates indicates that Shrewsbury sent it over for the royal signature at the very time when Blathwayt was engaged most vigorously in trying to discountenance Popple. On August 15, 1696, Shrewsbury wrote cautiously to the king that he was transmitting the warrant: "They [that is, Somers and Russell] have desired it may be inclosed to yourself, being not willing Mr. Blaithwayt should have knowledge of it, some of the governors in the plantations, who are his friends, being greatly suspected to have made considerable advantage by conniving at these pirates. For the same reason the warrant is dated from the time of your Majesty's being here, that he might not countersign it. There is a blank for the names of the persons, to whom this grant is to be made, because we are not agreed what names to make use of. . . . Your Majesty may remember I mentioned this to you, when the ship was getting ready, and you were then pleased to say we should not want your favor.''[14] Blathwayt's state of mind, on learning that this bit of official folly had been negotiated without his knowledge, may be imagined. Possibly, however, history might have been robbed of one of its most picturesque ruffians had Blathwayt's opinion on Captain Kidd been solicited before William III affixed his signature to that famous grant.

The current of dissatisfaction with Blathwayt was constantly being fed by reports which came in from certain colonial governors, who now viewed Blathwayt's discomfiture with natural pleasure. One of these was Colonel Nicholson, in 1696 governor of Maryland. A few years earlier, he had been superseded in Virginia by Andros, under circumstances which left him highly disgruntled. He was an able man, whose services to the colonies were invaluable, but his judgment was warped by his hatred for Andros, under whom he had formerly served in the Dominion of New England. Blathwayt seems to have set great store by him, and for a long while was ignorant of Nicholson's true feelings toward himself. Povey was so sure that Nicholson was Blathwayt's friend that he wrote to Nicholson in the summer of 1696, offering to continue as agent to Maryland.

Nicholson was enraged over what he regarded as Povey's and Blathwayt's effrontery, and, more or less

14 Coxe, *Shrewsbury Correspondence*, pp. 136–137, 138; William III's letter enclosing the warrant is dated August 24/September 3, 1696.

convinced that his attack would meet with favor at White-hall, he began (1696–1697) to send in scurrilous reports of the two men. He enclosed Povey's letter in one he dispatched to the Earl of Bridgewater, president of the Board of Trade. "I am apt to believe that Mr. Blathwayt and Mr. Povey have endeavored to insinuate that his Grace, the Duke of Shrewsbury, is none of my friend, but I had the honor to be known to his Grace before I came to Virginia, he being secretary of state and whenever I had occasion to wait upon him, his Grace was pleased to express himself very kindly. And I hope your lordship will pardon me for sending to you a copy of his letter and Mr. Vernon's to me, as also one which I had from Mr. John Povey by which your lordship may please to see how those sparks would have affairs managed. So that if I had not known you, I might have been led into the error of not doing my duty to your lordships of the new Council of Trade and Foreign Plantations, etc., and of corresponding with your lordships' secretary. And I don't doubt but that they will take it very ill of me, that I don't follow the method what [sic] they have presented. I think they have been too long the engrossers of all his Majesty's and his governors' affairs in these parts of the world; but now I hope in God, that other methods will be taken by your lordships. I remember to have heard your lordships say that too much credit was given to some sort of men that were in their employment, even against an order of council or of the lords of the committee.[15] With submission I think Mr. Blathwayt and Mr. Povey pretend to have the same credit, but I hope they will fail of it, as also of a

[15] There may well have been some foundation in fact for this charge against Blathwayt and Povey, but no absolute evidence has been found. It was often difficult to get enough of the lords together for business to be transacted, so Blathwayt may have gone ahead in some instances and made his own decision. Frequently there could be no council meeting because there were not lords enough in town. (Vernon, *Letters Illustrative, etc.*, II, 185.)

great many bribes from these parts of the world. Though
I will not pretend in the least to be infalliable [*sic*], or
not to have done amiss, yet I thank God that I was never
forced to bribe myself off from punishment. I cannot expect those gentlemen to espouse my cause, unless I am
taxed of some crime and misdemeanors, then perhaps they
would bring me off for money, as they have done others.
For 'tis the governors and others who justly deserve to be
punished, that are their favorites, because they get the
most by them. . . . I think he [Ingoldsby] and I were
kicked alike out of the government of New York and Virginia by my Lord Nottingham. And it is much wondered
at in these parts of the world that Sir Edmund Andros
and Colonel Fletcher should now keep their governments,
when they came in upon such interest.''[16]

Bridgewater, who apparently admired Blathwayt, said
in his reply that he doubted whether Blathwayt was as
black as Nicholson had painted him.[17] Nicholson, however,
was prompted by an ulterior motive. He was determined
to wrest the governorship of Virginia from Andros, no
matter at what cost. It was this he had in mind in writing
to Bridgewater and Shrewsbury. He even resolved to
curry favor with Blathwayt for this purpose, after taking
counsel with Commissary Blair, who had recently come
from England and was full of information about matters
at Whitehall. Blair took a very practical view of the situation, considering his reverend profession. He urged
Nicholson to secure the Virginia governorship, ''even if it
be necessary to launch out any money'' for the purpose.
Blathwayt, he said, was Andros's supporter, but was so,

16 Huntington MSS., Bridgewater Collection, Vol. 138, No. 9722; Annapo-
lis, March 30, 1697. Apropos of Ingoldsby, Nicholson made the statement
that he had indeed been an excellent commander-in-chief in New York, but
that ''his living so generously (which no doubt was for his Majesty's service) I fear was to his prejudice.''

17 *Ibid.*, No. 9733.

no doubt, only because of the money Andros paid him.[18] Nicholson thereupon bestirred himself to have the Maryland assembly pay Blathwayt's arrears of salary as auditor general. Even Povey's services as agent were not to go unpaid.[19]

The whole affair was a rather unpleasant episode in personal politics. Blathwayt was unquestionably supporting Andros in his Virginia governorship, but he already anticipated the storm of local opposition which, as a result of Nicholson's and Blair's machinations, was soon to burst upon the Virginia executive. Vernon's letter to Shrewsbury indicates that Blathwayt was prepared with a pre-arranged letter of resignation from Andros. "Some complaint has been brought to his Majesty against Sir Edmund Hudros [misprint for Andros], whereupon Mr. Blathwayt has produced a letter from him, describing his revocation. It is supposed he has had it for some time, with an intention to make use of it only when it could be delayed no longer. His Majesty has thereupon given direction that a new commission and instructions be prepared for Colonel Nicholson, upon the recommendation of the Archbishop and Lord Chancellor."[20] Blathwayt informed Stepney of what had happened, giving his own version of the state of affairs: "We of the council of trade are very diligent and are now falling on the report about Virginia. I should think it a sin while I take the king's money to agree to it, and after all I believe there will be but a very little of it represented to the king, Sir Edmund Andros desiring to come home by reason of sickness having taken off the edge of the persecution."[21]

18 *Cal. of Hist. MSS. in the Office of the Secretary of State of New York*, 1664–1776, p. 342; Blair to Nicholson, February 15, 1697.

19 *Maryland History Magazine* (1917), XII, 119; Nicholson to the Bishop of London, February 13, 1697.

20 Vernon, *Letters Illustrative, etc.*, II, 92; May 31, 1698.

21 S. P. For. Archives, Vol. 51, no paging; May 31, 1698.

Blathwayt's timely presentation of the resignation of Andros had, of course, saved the latter from further embarrassment, but of that he said nothing to Stepney. Time was to show that Blathwayt was fairer in his judgment of Andros than Nicholson was, though in 1698 the result was only another blow at Blathwayt's prestige. The whole incident furnishes further evidence of Whig supremacy over colonial patronage. At least Blathwayt's enemies could never bring the charge against him that he was disloyal to his friends.[22]

Blathwayt now had to put by all thought of colonial patronage until Tory prospects improved. Not until 1699 and 1700 did the situation brighten. Meanwhile he had to meet the attacks of his most vehement opponent, Lord Bellomont, who seems to have held Fletcher directly, and

[22] Needless to say, Blathwayt had no voice in the selection of Nicholson's successor in Maryland. There is some evidence to show that he was advancing the claims of Joseph Dudley, whom later he was to assist in securing the governorship of Massachusetts. Lord Cutts, Dudley's patron, made the actual advances, but he was encouraged in his efforts by Blathwayt. Vernon gives an account of how high competition ran for the appointment: "My Lord Cutts has been asking me whether you had writ anything about his friend Dudley. He may expect to prefer him to Maryland; but I think the King has no such intentions. There are three competitors [who] have appeared lately, Sir William Russell, whom my Lord Fauconberg has recommended, and the whole family of the Russells are solicitors for him! But the King thinks he has no talent for this sort of business, and he considers of what consequence it is, to have governors in the plantations proper for their employments, and therefor he has civilly excused himself to Sir William. My Lord Scarborough solicits for one Colonel Blakeston who has been in the West Indies, and both he and his father, who lives at Newcastle, are very zealous for the government. I have heard Ben Overton speak of this Thom Blakeston as a man of courage, probity, and great ingenuity, which are all qualifications very necessary for a governor. The King mentioned to me a third, named Parker; I know not who he is, or by whom recommended. It seems he has a good character given him. I suppose he has the most powerful friend, and therefore may carry it." (Vernon, *Letters Illustrative, etc.*, II, 96–97; June 7, 1698; see also II, 93.) Blakiston was the man ultimately selected. See an interesting reference by Vernon to the younger Codrington as a governmental choice for governor. (II, 178.)

Blathwayt indirectly, responsible for everything that went wrong in New York during these years. If Blathwayt's reputation had to stand only on Bellomont's estimate of him, it would fall low indeed, for Bellomont's attacks, which antedate his arrival in New York, pass all bounds of scurrility. Blathwayt had vigorously opposed Fletcher's recall. At the time the matter came up, he was abroad with William III, and when news reached him that the lords justices had decided to appoint Bellomont to a governorship, he at first assumed that it was to the governorship only of Massachusetts. When he learned that a union of New York and Massachusetts was in contemplation, and that Fletcher was to be displaced in Bellomont's favor, he was up in arms. To him the idea was absurd. Fletcher had proved a good military governor, such as the occasion demanded. Their lordships were to remember, he wrote, that "the king by his own choice and in consideration of his services during the late war in Ireland, [had] taken him [Fletcher] out of Colonel Beaumont's regiment where he was a major and sent him to New York as a person fit to direct the war there."[23]

Blathwayt no longer advocated the union of New York and Massachusetts, for he was convinced that the plan was not as feasible as it had been under Andros. He wrote to the lords justices to explain his point of view: "But as to the uniting those two governments at present his Majesty has commanded me to observe to your Excellencies that since the time of Sir [Edmund] Andros, the two provinces or colonies of Rhode Island and Connecticut have been and do remain disjoined from the province of the Massachusetts Bay upon account of their distinct charters by which they [blank in MS.] so that his [blank in MS.] latter were now to be united in government to

---

23 Add. MSS. 9722, ff. 89–90; Camp before Namur, August 8, 1695, s.n. A draft of this letter is to be found in *ibid.*, 37992, f. 101.

New York, there would be an entire separation of great distance between the colony of Massachusetts Bay and that of New York which would make the communication the more difficult to the governors in the province of Massachusetts and those in New York, being very much different, the one depending entirely on his Majesty [blank in MS.] while the other is very much less subordinate. The government would be carried on with great difficulty by one person, and further his Majesty takes notice that the salary in New York not exceeding £600, it would be of little help to the Earl of Bellomont, since in the case of such a union there must necessarily be in New York a lieutenant-governor as there was in the time of Sir [Edmund] Andros who must be a person of experience and bred up a soldier by reason of the neighborhood of the French, and his command of the standing forces, which lieutenant-governor cannot be supported with much less than that sum of £600, the salary of the present governor, Colonel Fletcher.''[24]

Blathwayt's arguments were unquestionably sound, even though Bellomont was at the same time to serve as captain general of the forces in Connecticut and Rhode Island. The area was far too large for a single individual to govern unless he had not only a sufficient military force to keep invaders at a distance but also autocratic power to deal with hostile colonial legislatures, whose attacks could be just as embarrassing and paralyzing as those of the French and Indians.

Urged on by Penn and the New England agents, the lords justices nevertheless persisted in their views.[25] William III, removed from his close dependency on Blath-

---

[24] *Ibid.*, 9722, ff. 89–90; August 8, 1695, s.n.; *ibid.*, 37992, f. 101. This was his letter draft.

[25] Osgood, *The American Colonies in the 18th Century*, I, 268–271.

wayt in Flanders, fell in with their wishes when he returned to England. Fletcher was removed, not, as care was taken to express, because of any disservice on his part but because he had already enjoyed four years in office and ought to be content![26] Bellomont was appointed to succeed him and was given the governorship of Massachusetts Bay and New Hampshire as well. Bellomont went to America feeling that Blathwayt was his enemy, but an impotent one since he was in high disfavor with the Whig leaders at court. Probably nothing could have altered his feeling toward Blathwayt, not even the fact, had he known it, that Blathwayt had attempted to do him a service by guaranteeing the payment of his salary out of the English Exchequer, in case the people of Massachusetts failed to provide one for him.[27]

Feeling against Blathwayt and Fletcher was running high when Bellomont left England, and the situation in New York only heightened it. The details of that interminable conflict between Leislerite and anti-Leislerite, which now took the form of a bitter partisan controversy between the followers of Fletcher on the one hand and those of Bellomont on the other, do not call for discussion here. Many of the charges which were made against Fletcher were unquestionably true. He had connived at piracy, he had made criminally extravagant grants of land, and he had disported himself in a ridiculous fashion, what with his coach and six and his pompous boasting of

26 Add. MSS. 9722, ff. 89–90.

27 *Ibid.*; also *Cal. S. P. Col.*, 1696–1697, p. 448; Bellomont to Popple, April 14, 1697. In this letter he made a great point of salary; he wanted a guarantee that he would be paid out of the English exchequer, in case the assemblies failed to provide for him; also that he be allowed not only the £1200 salary which Massachusetts granted and the £600 in New York, but £200 additional, to be paid out of the royal revenues in New York. He also wanted an independent salary for his lieutenant-governor in Massachusetts.

"his great interest and credit at Whitehall, which would baffle any complaints against his administration." The truth is, that while he did possess the military skill with which Blathwayt credited him, he was an exceedingly poor civil governor. Bellomont, with his fairly high social standing both in England and in Ireland, and his strong Whig propensities, could dismiss Fletcher socially with the scornful comment that he was only a poor Tory commoner who had been "an under-actor on a stage in Dublin," advanced to be a barber or *valet de chambre* to an Irish lord, afterward a cornet of horse, then captain of foot, and finally major in Colonel Beaumont's regiment, which was a laughingstock and not worthy of the name of regiment.

The miserable plight in which Bellomont found the four companies which had been stationed in New York for several years, increased his anger.[28] Their condition was being investigated at the time Bellomont left England for New York, and he had been ordered to make the matter his special concern.[29] He boldly charged Fletcher and

[28] There had at first been only two companies there, even before New York became a royal province; in 1693 they were augmented to four.

[29] Since 1696, the matter had been in the hands of the Board of Trade, the Duke of Schomberg, and others of the general officers. It was finally referred to Bellomont on his departure for New York, but no ultimate action was ever taken. (*Cal. S. P. Col.*, 1696–1697, pp. 80, 82, 252, 271–285, 325–331, 377–378, 395–396, 445–446, 504, 505, 506; *ibid.*, 1697–1698, 450, 530; also Stock, *Proceedings and Debates, etc.*, II, 234–235, f.n.) Stock refers to the three lieutenants, who were most active in pressing the charges of gross neglect, as men who enjoyed the patronage of Blathwayt and the Duke of Bolton, a conclusion which he reached from inference rather than direct evidence. The three men, Shanke, Sydenham, and Wright, were bitter in their charges, and their reports may have influenced Blathwayt considerably in his subsequent disavowal of Fletcher. One of them had a very forcible comment to make on John Povey, when reminded that a certain order had come through him. "Mr. Povey! S'blood, Mr. Povey! What's he? Damme, I know him well enough. He is but a little inconsiderable supernumerary clerk of the Council." *Cal. S. P. Col.*, 1696–1697, p. 275.

Blathwayt with the entire blame for their wretchedness.
The thirty per cent. deduction from their pay, which had
really been decided on because of the difference in the
rate of exchange between English and New York cur-
rency, was, according to Bellomont, an arbitrary act of
Fletcher's, based on a pretended order in council. Many
of his other reports were, like this one, the result of a too
lively imagination; but when he stated that the thirty per
cent. deduction was a piece of folly, and that "things
both for the belly and for the back were very nearly treble
the rates" in England, he was undeniably right. It was
equally true that the soldiers were starving and unpaid.
Bellomont was probably wrong in assuming that this was
the result of Blathwayt's wilful neglect. Blathwayt himself had no control over the funds of the army. While he
might implore the paymaster-general of the forces, as
well as the Treasury, to hasten payment, he could not
compel them to do so.[30] Nor could he make sure that the
various orders which he issued to the officers of the four
companies were carried out.[31] Preoccupied with all the
difficulties which faced the army in England and the Low
Countries, and at his wits' end to provide money for
them, Blathwayt had, no doubt, overlooked the soldiers
in New York. This is not to be wondered at, though it cannot altogether be condoned. Bellomont's feelings against
Blathwayt and his conviction of the latter's rapacity were
too deep-seated, however, for him to admit any excuse for
either Blathwayt or Fletcher.

Many months were to elapse before Bellomont's

[30] Ranelagh made a report on the arrears of the four companies in
February, 1699, but gave no reason for the fact that nothing had been paid
them since 1693. (Stock, *Proceedings and Debates, etc.*, II, 278–279.)

[31] Lieutenant Wright spoke of landing orders which Blathwayt had issued, but which had been disregarded by Captain Hide. (*Cal. S. P. Col.*,
1696–1697, p. 275.)

charges against Fletcher were finally acted upon. Meanwhile Fletcher was sent to England, a prisoner, and a lengthy investigation of his case was begun. He immediately communicated with his "good friends," Blathwayt and Southwell. He was distressed to learn that Blathwayt was in Flanders, and he wrote to him, begging for his aid in refuting the false incriminations of the "persecuting" Bellomont.[32] "Age comes and my estate is not improved 18d. a year after twenty-nine years service."[33] "Sir Robert Southwell is gone into the country and obliged me to send you his service, and desires you will put my Lord Athlone in mind of his promise of mentioning me to the king, according to the opinion his lordship had of me and the character I bore in the war of Ireland, under his lordship's command. . . . The Lord Bellomont has writ over to stop what money is due me as captain and taken all measures to embarrass me, both my fortune and good name, the last of which is dearest to me."[34]

Unfortunately no letters from Blathwayt to Fletcher remain to show his attitude toward the latter's misconduct. Only once, in a letter to Stepney, did Blathwayt make a reference to the investigation: "Colonel Fletcher," he wrote, ". . . is upon the anvil with us and takes up most of our time."[35] Blathwayt's and Southwell's influence probably saved Fletcher from criminal prosecution but could not save him from ignominy. Blathwayt must have thought the charges at least partly true, for he signed the reports to the king, denouncing Fletcher's con-

[32] Add. MSS. 9747, f. 5; London, August 5, 1698; also *N. Y. Col. Docs.*, IV, 361–362.

[33] Huntington MSS., Blathwayt Papers relating to New York, I, no paging; letter of November 19, 1694.

[34] Add. MSS. 9747, f. 5.

[35] S. P. For. Archives, Vol. 52, no paging; December 30, 1698.

duct. It is hardly conceivable that his only reason for so doing was the desire to save his own face.[36]

Blathwayt was not embarrassed on his own account by Bellomont's attacks. His attitude seems to have been one of amused contempt, as if he were sure that sooner or later the folly of some of Bellomont's assertions would be revealed. Thus he wrote to Stepney: "Lord Bellomont drives furiously and has turned out all the council of New York but one and will soon lay the province desolate, I mean as to men of substance, for now Masaniello's Party,[37] I mean Leisler's, entirely prevail, but how am I justified in my opinion that New York and New England ought not to be put under one governor when my Lord Bellomont in a whole year has not been able to set his foot out of the former."[38]

Bellomont himself was soon convinced that Blathwayt's power in colonial councils was far from dead. As his hope for spectacular changes in New York, as the result of his own administration, faded away, he began to talk more and more frequently of a hostile influence at work against him in England. His suspicions were confirmed by the long silences of the board, which, curiously enough, he attributed to Blathwayt. In a lengthy letter to Bridgewater, in 1700, he brought thinly veiled charges against Blathwayt, speaking of him as an evil man, so sinister that he could "countermine and traverse all the honest endeavors of a number of men."[39] Bellomont's death was soon to put an end to the controversy, but not

[36] See especially *Cal. S. P. Col.*, 1699, pp. 95–98; March 9, 1699; also Add. MSS. 37992, ff. 142–143; Blathwayt to Vernon, November 1/11, 1698.

[37] Masaniello, the Neapolitan insurrectionist, often mentioned in this period in reference to Leisler. (*N. Y. Col. Docs.*, III, 661; also Michelangelo Schipa, *Masaniello*.)

[38] S. P. For. Archives, Vol. 52, no paging; December 30, 1698.

[39] Huntington MSS., Bridgewater Collection, Vol. 138, No. 9782; June 22, 1700.

before Blathwayt, as a result of ardent effort and timely party changes, had succeeded in reinstating himself almost completely in colonial circles. Meanwhile everybody, Bellomont included, had become convinced that the troubles which agitated New York lay far beyond the power of any one man either to create or to cure.

Once Blathwayt was convinced that further protest against the arrangements for the office staff of the Board of Trade was futile, he settled down to regain the ground which he had lost. He was too sincere in his devotion to England's trade interests to let his personal feelings interfere with what he regarded as the national welfare. Moreover, his vanity had been pricked, and he was determined to prove that the success of the board rested with him. Whatever may have been the opinion of his opponents on his work in the plantation office under the Lords of Trade, Blathwayt himself saw nothing in it to be ashamed of. He was constantly referring to the fine array of accurately kept office books, without which, he declared, the work of the Board of Trade would have been hampered at every turn. As for his new colleagues, he regarded all of them—with the exception of the Earl of Bridgewater, with whom he had earlier been associated as one of the Lords of Trade—as poor Whigs, with a most pathetic lack of any practical knowledge of the colonies and trade. His attitude, based as it was on personal and partisan pique, strikes an amusing note; but to Blathwayt there was no humor in the situation. He had no respect for the profundities of the aged Locke, or for the views of John Pollexfen, the pamphleteer, whom he considered an academic trifler. Training and experience in the actual administration of England's trade laws and the government of her plantations were the only qualifications that he valued. With his view that he was himself the great pillar of strength of the Board of Trade, many men agreed—

either to humor him in his disappointment or to curry favor. Thus a correspondent at Rotterdam wrote to him, in 1697, that he was really the sole person at court who was well versed in colonial affairs, while others referred to him as an "oracle."[40] Such opinions gave Blathwayt a great deal of satisfaction at a time when he was inclined to self-pity.

He regretted exceedingly that circumstances took him away from England during so crucial a period, even though attendance on the king gave him an undeniable advantage when it came to negotiations with foreign powers. He decided that he needed some one on the board whom he could regard as an intimate and friendly consultant, and with whom he could advise freely. His friend Charles Montagu, who shared this opinion, was an *ex-officio* member of the board in his capacity as chancellor of the exchequer, but other work prevented him from attending regularly. "As to the committee of trade I attend it as much as I can," he wrote in 1698, "but I am of your mind that the secretary is a bold man, and will have more business than he can go through with and we every minute want the assistance of somebody that is conversant in the affairs of the plantations."[41] Since Povey was an impossible recommendation for membership on the board, "a mere supernumerary clerk of the council," for whom, at best, Blathwayt could secure nothing more than a regular clerkship, he and Montagu now agreed on Stepney as a wise and tractable man for the position.[42] For the

[40] Huntington MSS., Blathwayt Papers relating to Canada, Darien, Hudson Bay, 1687–1699, no paging; a letter from a certain Mr. Nelson to Blathwayt, June 21, 1697. Blathwayt suspected Nelson of being a French spy, however, and ordered his arrest. (See Vernon, *Letters Illustrative, etc.*, I, 304, 309.) For references to Blathwayt as an oracle, see Bellomont's assertions, Huntington MSS., Bridgewater Collection, Vol. 138, No. 9782.

[41] Add. MSS. 34355, f. 15; July 17/27, 1698.

[42] On July 29, 1698, Blathwayt wrote to Stepney, begging him to come

same reason Blathwayt supported the appointments of
Matthew Prior and Lord Lexington, his friends in the
diplomatic service, for whose opinions he had a high regard. As time went on, he had the satisfaction of seeing
the board become preponderantly Tory.

His absence from England during the summer of 1697
was particularly trying. It was a critical period. The
Treaty of Ryswick was being negotiated; the question of
the Scottish East India Company, and its attempted settlements at Darien, was coming up for investigation; and
Peter the Great was in western Europe, indicating to the
powers that he was willing to make trade concessions in

home to take his position on the board. See S. P. For. Archives, Vol. 51, no
paging.

In 1697, as a result of a good bit of wirepulling, Blathwayt succeeded in
having Povey made a clerk in ordinary of the council. Since Povey was the
senior clerk in extraordinary, Blathwayt's claim for his elevation was, in the
light of existing practices, perfectly valid. The matter, however, was dis-
puted by none other than Sir Robert Southwell, who advanced the claims of
his son, Edward, also a clerk in extraordinary. It was a heated contest, in
which Blathwayt called in the aid of Montagu, Shrewsbury, and the latter's
secretary, James Vernon. That a point so trivial, for it was after all nothing
more than a tempest in a teapot, should have aroused so much discussion, indicates the high value set on the clerkships. Southwell based his claim on
the fact that Povey, while a senior clerk, had been appointed, in 1692, only
to enable him to wait on the Privy Council when matters of trade and
plantation came up; by 1697, the Lords of Trade had ceased to exist, therefore Povey's right to serve was no longer valid. Povey, however, claimed
that he had continued to serve the council in other matters. Blathwayt meanwhile was deeply grieved to offend his good friends, the Southwells. In 1699,
another timely death among the clerks in ordinary made way for Edward
Southwell's admission. The matter is of special interest because Edward
Southwell made it the occasion for some interesting research work on the
status and the duties of the clerks of the council and drew up a brochure on
the subject. His own attitude toward Blathwayt, which was very bitter, seems
to have been a reflection of the feeling then current. (See Add. MSS. 38861,
especially ff. 64–66, 72–75, for Edward Southwell's notes; also *Hist. MSS.
Com., Buccleuch MSS.*, Vol. II, Pt. II, 483–485, 486, 488, 494; Add. MSS.,
37992, f. 266; Add. MSS. 34348, ff. 70–71; Vernon, *Letters Illustrative, etc.*,
I, 289–290, 310.)

Russia. Blathwayt was keyed up to a high pitch of excitement, fearful lest any trade advantage be lost to England. His proximity to the king presumably put him in a position of vantage; on the other hand, it kept him from the meetings of the Board of Trade.

The peace commissioners at Ryswick, in drawing up the articles of the treaty relating to trade and the colonies, seemed to take it as a matter of course that the secretary of state, Sir William Trumbull, and the Board of Trade should first be consulted. This procedure filled Blathwayt with despair. He could hardly imagine more ineffectual agents than Trumbull and the board. Early in the summer, the commissioners drew up a preliminary treaty to be submitted to the king, with a view to presenting it to the French as a basis for negotiations. The two clauses dealing with trade and plantations (articles four[43] and seven) were based on material furnished Lord Pembroke, one of the commissioners, by Sir William Trumbull, shortly before the former went over to Holland. The fourth article dealt with restitution to be made for damages committed during the war; the seventh, with the restoration of the *status quo* of 1689, the year the war broke out—in other words with the settlement made at the Treaty of Breda, in 1667, when the previous encounter with the French had come to an end. Trumbull, in compiling his report, made use of the Board of Trade, which was, as John Ellis, his clerk, said, ''our oracle in matters relating to that other world.''[44]

Blathwayt received a copy of the treaty and reported his views to Matthew Prior. He took immediate exception to the seventh article. He argued that this was too easy a surrender, since France was discouraged over an unfavorable balance of trade. The uncertain outcome of

43 The fourth article of the draft is the third article of the finished treaty.
44 *Hist. MSS. Com., Bath MSS.*, III, 127.

Pointis's expedition to the West Indies could also be turned to advantage, Blathwayt thought. The report of its failure would make France even more tractable, while news of its success would render her exceedingly high-handed. England must therefore strike while the iron was hot and not let matters drag on until the French knew more definitely where they stood.

The settlement made for the Hudson's Bay Company, which provided that all places belonging either to the French or to the English at the beginning of the war were to be restored, greatly disturbed him. He said that this arrangement was absurd. "Although the Hudson's Bay Company do now tell you in the papers remaining in your hands that they are the masters in fact as well as by right of all that Bay, and consequently of the peltry trade, the French upon signing our treaty will come in for their share, and show a new title to their imaginary pretensions."[45]

However, since Prior and the commissioners still chose to depend on Trumbull and the Board of Trade, Blathwayt made the gesture of washing his hands of the whole business. "I have already told you the clause about Hudson's Bay is not only useless but hurtful to us; but that, you know, is not my fault."[46] It was not until Prior had admitted to Blathwayt that the papers which he had received from Trumbull were, if not inaccurate, at least incomplete, that Blathwayt offered to explain himself further.[47] His attitude of rather childish pique was based, however, on one sound argument; namely, that the account which the Board of Trade had submitted to Trumbull did not go beyond the date 1682 and therefore ignored

[45] *Ibid.*, p. 122; June 1, 1697.   [46] *Ibid.*, p. 124; June 8, 1697.

[47] Prior accordingly wrote to Trumbull to tell him that it was impossible to form any conclusion on the basis of the report he had submitted. (*Ibid.*, pp. 126, 127, 148.)

what had happened from 1682 to 1697. "I must observe to
you in particular that your 7th Article will be of the
greatest prejudice to the Hudson's Bay Company, as you
may have judged by the papers received from the Council
of Trade; for that by this article all those places taken
from that Company before the war, and retaken by them
during the war, must be restored to the French, whereas
we have not in nature a reciprocal to give us an equal advantage; for let me tell you, your 4th Article will not help
us in this case, but on the contrary, as I could explain to
you for your private satisfaction if the post were not going away, and show you that three words would have
mended the matter, I mean an exception of these evident
voyes de fait the French made use of before the war, and
which was a cause assigned for it in the declaration of
war, wherein we shall now have no remedy. But all this is
only by way of discourse with you, which your former letters have engaged me in; not doubting," he continued
with mock humility, "but their Excellencies have had
their superior reasons to word the treaty otherwise, so
that it could not be fit for me on a sudden to hinder the
progress of it by a single discussion with the king at so
critical a time."[48]

His tone had the proper psychological effect on Prior,
who immediately begged him to explain himself. "I send
you a copy of the treaty and the great article, and shall
think it abundantly returned if you write me three words
of explanation in the fourth article, and alter the form of
the seventh, so as to help the Hudson's Bay Company.
. . . We have not all the light imaginable from the other
side, Mr. Ellis having once more referred us to what we
had of my Lord Pembroke from the Commission for

[48] *Hist. MSS. Com., Bath MSS.*, III, 129–130; June 27, 1697. Blathwayt by
the "*voyes de fait*" was referring to the attacks which the French had made
on certain forts of the company in time of peace.

Trade, which paper is very imperfect; and . . . though
they would altogether labour to inform us, you can do it
something better.''[49] More than that, the commissioners
consented to add to the article the words, ''Except such
places as belong to His Majesty of Great Britain, which
the French seized during the peace immediately preceding this war,'' the very point Blathwayt had been insist-
ing upon.[50] Blathwayt knowing that the French would undoubtedly take advantage of the expression *belong to,*
since they declared that the whole region was theirs on
the basis of prior discovery, advised that it be changed to
in possession of His Majesty.[51] To this, however, the commissioners would not agree, fearing that the French
would raise such a storm of protest that England might
lose her point entirely.[52]

Blathwayt agreed to this more or less regretfully, and
also to the decision that the whole matter of Hudson's
Bay be referred to a commission to sit in London within
three months of the ratification of the treaty. The letter
in which he gave his assent indicates how thoroughly he
identified himself with the interests of the merchants:
''You see how ready I am to lay myself forth at their Excellencies' desire in the business of Hudson's Bay. The
matter is indeed very much perplexed, which I gave you
warning of, and told you how our West Indies suffered
heretofore for want of information and true measures.—
Nemo poeta nascitur [In other words, no one is born with
a knowledge of matters relating to trade and planta-
tions]. I do not see how you will get well out of the difficulty you are engaged in. There was room for a little arti-
fice, which the French Ambassadors and their Court

[49] *Ibid.,* pp. 130–131; June 29, 1697.
[50] *Ibid.,* p. 132; July 3, 1697; also p. 135.
[51] *Ibid.,* p. 151; Prior to Trumbull, quoting Blathwayt, August 23, 1697.
[52] *Ibid.,* p. 152.

would have hardly discerned, and then you would have had the applause of the merchants. We are now engaged to leave matters as they were before the war, but, thanks be to God, our American affairs are so well changed that I wish they were to be left *in statu quo nunc,* which would gain us St. Christopher's, worth a million without any probable hazard to ourselves. I can't tell if it be for the King's service that the French Ambassadors should be informed of the good news from Newfoundland, which will make them incline the more to restitutions, which is not to our advantage at present.''[53]

Blathwayt felt all along that the English commissioners were foolishly lenient in their treatment of the French. ''What the Council of Trade have sent you further about the West Indies is but 'whitewashes' and nothing to your purpose,'' he wrote to Prior. To this the latter glibly replied: ''You judge most truly of the worth of those papers relating to the West Indies which the Council of Trade has sent us; however, having laid them before the Lords Ambassadors, *liberavi animam meam.*''[54] Blathwayt was also annoyed that England was forced to consider the renewal of the treaty, and attributed this to the spineless attitude of the commissioners. However, there was nothing to be done about it, so he regretfully transmitted the letter conveying the royal assent to a conference by special commission: ''His Majesty does not think a neutrality in America convenient for us, but, as the referring the consideration of such a treaty to commissioners may induce the French to give their concurrence in other things that may be desired by us, is pleased to agree to such a proposal.''[55]

From the context of Blathwayt's letters at this time, it

---

[53] *Hist. MSS. Com., Bath MSS.,* III, 156–157; also pp. 179–180.
[54] *Ibid.,* pp. 140, 141.
[55] *Ibid.,* p. 148; August 19, 1697.

is clear that he had numerous conferences with William III on colonial matters and that he probably wielded an influence equal to that of the commissioners at Ryswick. His general dissatisfaction with the progress of events arose out of his error in thinking that the Treaty of Ryswick could be made to constitute a lasting peace, not merely a truce, in so far as the colonies were concerned. Had he been in direct communication with the French plenipotentiaries, he might have been affected by them as were the English envoys. As it was, he talked rather glibly of treating the French with a high hand.

In the meantime, the Scots were causing Blathwayt as much anxiety as were the French. An act incorporating a Scottish company to trade to Africa and the Indies had been passed by the Scottish parliament on June 26, 1695. Blathwayt was opposed to the company, even though it confined its activities to the East Indies, for he felt that if the monopoly of the English East India Company were to be broken, it should be by some English interloper. He was, therefore, very much alarmed when he learned, late in the summer of 1696, that the Scottish company had grandiose plans under way for establishing a factory at Hamburg or some one of the German Hanse towns, of building or buying ships there, and of floating a loan among the Germans. He was not inclined to compromise. At the time, he was with William in the Low Countries and hence in a position to write to the English representative at Hamburg, Sir Paul Rycaut, transmitting a royal order that Rycaut instruct the German towns to give the Scots no hospice, on peril of incurring the grave disfavor of England.[56] At some time during the winter of 1696–

[56] *Darien Shipping Papers* (Scottish Hist. Soc. Publ., 3rd ser., Vol. VI, edited by G. P. Insh), p. 13; Rycaut to Trumbull, February 16, 1697; see also pp. 7–12. Blathwayt was apparently aware of the Scots' intentions even before Rycaut. He kept up an animated correspondence with Rycaut during

1697 he may have learned, possibly through Randolph, that the Scots were turning their attention to America, in all probability to the acquiring of land belonging to some one of the proprietors.[57] Not until April, 1697, on his return to the Continent, did he discover through Rycaut's secretary, Orth, that the Scots were, in fact, diverting their attention from the East Indies to America, to a section of the Isthmus of Panama which they claimed did not belong to Spain.[58] He sent the news to James Vernon, who thereupon, according to the records, transmitted it to the Board of Trade.[59] The moot question became whether the land did, or did not, belong to Spain. According to Blathwayt, there was no doubt that it did, and he was out of patience with the Board of Trade for entertaining any doubt about it. The board had called upon two men who had visited the territory, and whom they regarded as reliable authorities—Dampier and Surgeon Lionel Wafer. Both said that, so far as they knew, the territory which the Scots planned to settle lay outside of Spanish bounds.[60] Blathwayt foresaw war with Spain if the Scots were allowed to persist. He wrote to Bridgewater that the board should have known that the territory belonged to Spain by papal bull,[61] and that England had admitted Spain's claim by the Treaty of Madrid, in 1670, definitely recognizing Spain's right to carry off trespassers as slaves to Mexico. He regretted, he told Bridgewater, that he could not have been present at the meeting at which the ques-

the entire period, and the latter usually sent him duplicates of the letters he wrote to Trumbull.

[57] Goodrick, *Edward Randolph*, VII, 517–520; Randolph's report to the Board of Trade on the matter, March 4, 1697.

[58] *Darien Shipping Papers*, pp. 34–35.

[59] *Ibid.*, pp. 35–36.   [60] *Ibid.*, pp. 48–54.

[61] The famous division of the New World by the Pope, leading to the Treaty of Tordesillas, in 1494.

tion came up for consideration, because he could have cleared up the difficulty in short order.[62]

Several years were to elapse before the Scottish ventures finally ended in hopeless failure and were permanently abandoned, and during this time Blathwayt continued his hostile attitude.[63] The Spanish, he maintained, were jealous of new settlements, and a rupture with Spain should be averted at all costs. "The Spaniards have fortified some places in the West Indies, but it remains nevertheless in his Majesty's Power to be Master of the greater and best parts of their Dominions in America. . . . It cannot easily be made to appear how it can be for His Majesty's service to weaken or disturb the Spaniards in America, they being already subservient in the course of trade to the English nation who reap the profit of their hazards and labour without any expense to the Crown."[64]

The opportunities of 1696 and 1697 for an increase in England's trade with the northern European powers aroused Blathwayt to great activity. He sympathized with the proposal of the English merchants to make Peter the

[62] Huntington MSS., Bridgewater Collection, Vol. 138, No. 9740; Loo, October 1/11, 1697.

[63] He always looked askance at any suggestion that the English attempt new settlements in the Caribbean or the Gulf of Mexico, and he strongly opposed the Board of Trade proposal of 1697, that an expedition be dispatched from Jamaica to take possession of Golden Island, off the Darien Coast. (Add. MSS. 37992, f. 183; Blathwayt to Vernon, October 3, 1697.)

[64] Huntington MSS., Blathwayt Papers, America, 1681–1741; an undated draft of a report on America, with special reference to Jamaica and Darien, obviously written in the year 1697. In 1701, when Scottish hopes for an American settlement were at an end, William Paterson, curiously, wrote to Blathwayt, asking that, as his good friend, he remember him in his adversity and assist him in a revival of Scotland's East India project. That Blathwayt offered him any aid or in any way altered his opinion in the matter of Scottish colonial and trading ventures of any sort, is improbable. (Add. MSS. 9728, f. 125; London, September 30, 1701.) Paterson and Blathwayt had been associated in the steps leading up to the establishment of the Bank of England. (Porlock MSS., especially for 1691.)

Great's visit to Holland, in the fall of 1697, the occasion for a renewal of trade relations with Russia, which had been broken off since the execution of Charles I. Indeed, it is possible that the original suggestion came from him. On August 4, 1697, he wrote to Trumbull to say that the Czar was coming and would in all probability be taken out by William to view the army. "In case he shall desire to see it as is most probable he will, on this occasion I leave it to you to judge whether we may not hope to obtain some advantages in trade or, at least, the restoring our former priviledges from the good nature of the Czar, when we shall have made much of him. I know, Sir, without doubt how these priviledges were taken away from us in resentment of the death of King Charles the 1st, which my Lord Carlisle nor any other minister from the Crown could ever recover; what seems most requisite at present is that the merchants would send me a state or a memorial of what they desire for the advantage of their trade in those parts. I will endeavor to negotiate further with the Czar if there shall be any good opportunity for it; at least such an application cannot be prejudicial to them."[65]

A memorial was presented not only by the merchants but also by the Board of Trade.[66] The latter reviewed the situation since 1556 and made a plea that a restoration of England's earlier advantages be restored. The desire to open up Russia to the tobacco trade was particularly stressed, since "our tobacco is much better than any the Dutch have, unless they buy it from us." Instructions were issued over Blathwayt's countersignature to the English plenipotentiaries at Ryswick to inform the Czar, when he arrived at The Hague, of England's warm feeling

[65] Add. MSS. 37992, ff. 193 *dorso*–194; August 4, 1697.

[66] *Hist. MSS. Com. Bath MSS.*, III, 149–150, 155. Blathwayt stressed the fact that the petition came from "the most considerable merchants of England."

of friendship and her desire for mutual trade advantages
with Russia. Blathwayt had no further part in the negotiations, but the incident reveals his keen anxiety to secure for England a wider market and his readiness to
make suggestions.[67]

He was also anxious to secure better trade relations
with the other Baltic powers and attempted to make the
conference at Ryswick his opportunity. The Hudson's
Bay Company was in difficulty with the Danes at Arch-
angel, where, it seems, the company's factors had been encouraging what the Danes regarded as illicit trade with
some of the Hanse towns.[68] Blathwayt hoped that something could be done to bring the Danes to reason. He objected to England's dependence on the Baltic states for
naval stores and hoped that this incident of ill usage at
the hands of Danes, as well as similar instances in the
case of the Swedes, might encourage the movement for
bringing naval stores from England's own colonies. The
English High Court of Admiralty was engaged at this
time in the trial of six or seven Swedish ships which had
been caught trading fraudulently with the colonies.[69]
Blathwayt was torn between his desire to make an example of the Swedes, which might lead to the formation of
a plan for the development of naval stores in the West
Indies, and his hope that reasonable treatment of the
Swedes might lead to further advantages for England in
the Baltic. He had already written Trumbull that it would
"not be amiss to turn all our thoughts toward resenting
the ill-usage our merchants meet with from the Swedes, I

[67] Add. MSS. 37992, ff. 194–196.
[68] *Ibid.*, ff. 194–195; Blathwayt to Trumbull, August 19, 1697.
[69] *Ibid.*, ff. 194–196; letters to Trumbull, August and September, 1697.
The Swedes' decision to make the incident the occasion for a memorial led
William to decide that the High Court of Admiralty was to be lenient, and
that "no hardships [were to] be putt upon the Swedish ships or effects which
might give that Court any just reason of complaint."

mean in our own defence, and I hope 'twill give occasion
to carry on vigorously the project I have many years labour'd to promote of bringing naval stores from our West
Indies, which will make the Northern Crowns more reasonable to us. . . . Great care has been taken in it by the
Committee of Plantations and a good foundation laid for
the bringing them from America where a great tract of
land has been reserved on purpose for the necessary supply, as will appear by the books of the office.'[70] He was
overjoyed at the rendezvous of the fleets of Holland, England, and Sweden, in the Sound, in 1700, and the resulting
recognition of free navigation in the North Sea.[71]

The first decade of the Board of Trade's existence
bears a striking resemblance to that of the Lords of Trade
from 1675 to 1688. The principles of administrative control which were laid down in both cases were the same,
and allowing for the lapse of twenty years, the problems
confronting the two bodies were in general identical. Enforcing the Acts of Trade was still the all-absorbing question, and both bodies were equally determined to do so. In
1675, the Lords of Trade were confronted with the problem of putting into effect the acts of 1660, 1663, and 1673;
in 1696, the Board of Trade was intent on working out the
act passed in that year to strengthen the earlier acts. The
machinery in the latter case was more elaborate, and the
great extension of vice-admiralty jurisdiction was expected to simplify matters. The corps of colonial officials
deputized to enforce the Acts of Trade had likewise visibly increased. The determination of the Lords of Trade to
compel subservience to England's policy resulted in the

[70] Add. MSS. 37992, ff. 134, 135.

[71] Blathwayt's correspondence with Dr. John Robinson, the minister to
Sweden during these years, indicates how eager he was to see an improvement in England's relations with the Baltic powers. (Add. MSS. 35105,
35106.)

quo warranto processes and the establishment of a united New York and New England. The Board of Trade, pursuing a similar course, was behind the bills of 1701 and 1706 for the annulment of the charters of the remaining corporate and proprietary colonies. There had never been any departure from this policy, save perhaps in 1681, when Penn received his charter, and in 1691, when the second charter was finally granted to Massachusetts. That in this second period the English colonial administration showed a greater dependence on parliament, is only indicative of the constitutional changes which had come over England since the annulment of the charters under Charles II and James II.

Blathwayt was certainly in large part responsible for this activity on the part of the Board of Trade in 1696 and the ensuing years. Time had sapped none of his energy or optimism. Until 1702, he was distracted by the war and by the European situation in general, but he never lost sight of the main thread in colonial administration. He was a constant attendant at the meetings of the board, except for his absence during the summers from 1696 to 1701, and at most he missed less than a fourth of the meetings, according to the records of attendance. Only indirectly can we gauge the part he played at these meetings, but knowing his assertiveness in such matters, we can assume that he adopted a rôle of leadership. Some of the Whig members may have grown weary of his *ex cathedra* pronouncements, and the Tory Matthew Prior, who found Blathwayt a dull fellow at best, no doubt yawned with boredom; but there was no denying that Blathwayt spoke with authority. All the members of the board were free to correspond with colonial officials, but Blathwayt did so more than the others, not merely because of his annoyance with Popple and the desire to be free from a dependence on him, but because of his work as auditor general of the plantation revenues. He was still some one to be reckoned with in colonial circles. The New England agents continued to hate and fear him, and in 1697 Sir Henry Ashurst was in a panic because he had heard that Blathwayt was conspiring to secure the agency of Massachusetts for himself.[72]

The close relationship which had always existed between Randolph and Blathwayt continued. Randolph alone, of the English officials stationed in the colonies to enforce the Acts of Trade, was Blathwayt's close friend, but all the others—Jahleel Brenton, George Larkin, Robert Quary, and Jeremiah Basse—were in constant communication with him, though their correspondence was of a stereotyped nature. Randolph drew the bond between Blathwayt and himself even closer, for one by one, his other friends in the English administration were deserting him. "I have no other freind [sic] but God and you to stand by me,"[73] he wrote to Blathwayt, in melancholy vein, in 1700—refusing to admit that it was his own bitter and uncompromising spirit that had brought about the desertion.

Randolph alienated the commissioners of the customs in this later period, just as he had done in the earlier, by sending Blathwayt and the Board of Trade copies of all communications that he dispatched to the commissioners. The preoccupation and indifference of the customs offi-

[72] This was the report of Joseph Dudley and Nathaniel Byfield, Ashurst's enemies. *Mass. Hist. Soc. Coll.*, 6th ser., V, 39; Ashurst to Wait Winthrop, August 25, 1697.

[73] Goodrick, *Edward Randolph*, VII, 641; November 23, 1700. Yet Randolph and Blathwayt did not always see eye to eye. Thus Randolph looked sceptically on Sir Edmund Andros' administration of Virginia; and when he returned to America, in 1697, he seems to have upheld Bellomont. He did, however, admit that Fletcher, at least on first meeting, impressed him as being a "reserved and retiring" gentleman; whether he subsequently changed his mind does not appear. (See *ibid.*, pp. 409, 431, 461, 547.)

cials were the excuses Randolph offered Blathwayt in exoneration of his action. "This evening I have a message sent me from a freind [sic] belonging to the Custome house: advising that the Commissioners are told I have discoursed reflectingly upon their Manage[ment]: I confess upon your directions as one of the Lords Commissioners for Trade I did lay before your Board a Narrative of my Journall; and also duplicates of the papers I transmitted in mine of the 17th past, which I have received from Mr. Popple and corrected them, but delay the returning them till your arrivall: I guess some of your Board may have discoursed accidentally with some person that has told some of the commissioners that my papers containe custome house business. 'Tis true, that I have attended with my papers twice or thrice every weeke, they are so busy that they have not tyme to heare one read. They made an entrance upon my Narrative: and some tyme after heard my paper shewing the losse his Majesty has in his customs upon tobacco shipped from the plantations on the Continent to the other plantations, but have not as yet read my proposals to prevent it and will perhaps lay me and them both aside: I expect that the Lords Commissioners for Trade will take care of me and hope my readiness at all tymes to lay before their Lordships all matters relating to Trade, to Customs and to improving the Revenues, shall not be my ruine whilst I have done my duty to preserve them."[74]

No better tribute to the Board of Trade's energy at this time could be desired, and it is clear that Randolph gave Blathwayt the chief credit. He and Blathwayt were both quite capable of handling the situation in a high-handed fashion, regardless of the authority of other branches of the government. It would be impossible to prove that Blathwayt was primarily responsible for the lengthy re-

[74] *Ibid.*, pp. 640–641; November 23, 1700.

ports which were drawn up in these years for presentation to the king and to parliament, for excellent reports were handed in during his absence in Flanders, such as the memorial on plantation justice, which was presented by Pollexfen to the Board of Trade in September, 1700, and which formed the basis for an elaborate representation on the subject.[75] Plainly Blathwayt served as the great spokesman for the board in parliament, even though some of his colleagues were also members of the house of commons. He brought in a majority of the reports presented, and he served on most of the parliamentary committees appointed to consider matters relating to trade and plantations.[76] Thus he presented the report on piracy in December, 1699, and later reported out of committee the bill for the better suppression of piracy. He was also delegated to carry the bill up to the house of lords, after its passage in the commons.[77]

He was enormously proud of these reports and of the impression they made, though he was willing to admit that they did not always meet with a cordial reception. Vernon might say, as he did in January, 1698, after Blathwayt had presented the report on the state of trade, "I have not heard much of the Commission of trade, not being able to come early to the House. I don't find people have generally any great veneration for them, and their accounts are more liable to be found fault with than otherwise"; but this was a Whig view of the matter.[78] The author's verdict was more optimistic than the critics'!

[75] *Cal. S. P. Col.*, 1700, pp. 508–513; September 4, 1700.

[76] Stock, *Proceedings and Debates, etc.*, II, 265–267, 314, 363, 364, 426, etc.

[77] *Ibid.*, pp. 314, 363–364. The bill itself was drawn up by Blathwayt's Tory friend, Sir Charles Hedges, then judge of the High Court of Admiralty but soon to be secretary of state as well.

[78] Vernon, *Letters Illustrative, etc.*, I, 481–482; Vernon to Shrewsbury, January 29, 1698.

Blathwayt, in commenting on the same report, was so jubilant that he regarded the matter facetiously, "Our general report of trade had gained applause in the world. That of the poor is less approved of. The one and the other has got us a name from Jack How of Commission, not of America, but of Chimerical affairs, but his tongue you know is no slander and we join not unsuccessfully upon the whole matter."[79]

Blathwayt and Randolph were largely instrumental in bringing in the bill for the revocation of the charters of the corporate and proprietary colonies, in 1701. Randolph had been sending in to Blathwayt a flood of evidence of their malpractices. He and Blathwayt, moreover, had been the authors of the clause in the act of 1696 which declared that the governors of the proprietary colonies must first be approved by the crown. Randolph had regretted Blathwayt's absence from London in February, 1696, at the time this bill was under debate and had written to him: "I know the pleasant entertainment at Durham will afford little time to consider of the proprietys: but since you are pleased to think it necessary that a clause should be provided for investing the Governments of the proprietyes [in the crown] be pleased to oblige Mr. Pen and the Jersey Gentlemen with a draft of such a clause, that I may have it ready against the next tyme I attend their Lordships; it will save a great deale of tyme and putt a speedy issue to their uncertain expectations. I had this day a general order to attend: and I hope not to loose [sic] my tyme or business. I will not faile to give you an account how matters go in my new province."[80] Penn's

---

[79] S. P. For. Archives, Vol. 51, no paging; Blathwayt to Stepney, February 18, 1698. Jack, or John How, one of the most active politicians and wits of his time, was, like Blathwayt, a Gloucestershire man. (*Dict. Natl. Biog.*, XXVIII, 89–90.)

[80] Goodrick, *Edward Randolph*, VII, 503–505; February 20, 1696.

failure to pay any heed to this provision became one of Randolph's many grievances against him.

Prior, not Blathwayt, was the member of the board instructed to present the report of that body, advocating the annulment of the charters, in 1701.[81] The bill, owing to the strenuous opposition of Penn, Ashurst, and Phips, was subsequently dropped, but not before deep fear had been instilled into their hearts lest Blathwayt, Randolph, and Dudley be successful in forcing its passage. Ashurst commented on Blathwayt's activities and his insistence that the crown was well within its rights in demanding the abrogation. The weight of Whig opinion in parliament, however, was on the side of the colonies, and, as Ashurst said, the attorney and the solicitor general were fortunately sympathetic. Ashurst also reported that Blathwayt had shown some desire to compromise and had said that if Connecticut, for example, would acknowledge the right of appeal to the king's courts, the government might take a more reasonable stand.[82] Further arguments were unnecessary, since the agents succeeded in having the bill dropped.

Ashurst and Blathwayt were to have still another passage at arms over the question in February, 1706, when the desire to consolidate the colonies was beginning to ebb. The preponderance of Whigs in parliament would seem to have made the failure of a bill to annul the charters a foregone conclusion. At the direction of the crown, however, Blathwayt introduced such a bill in February, but as Ashurst wrote the government of Connecticut, "I made such an interest against it with some of the leading men of the House so that it was thrown out at the 1st reading. I have the vanity to say that if you had not em-

81 Stock, *Proceedings and Debates, etc.*, II, 392–406.

82 *Mass. Hist. Coll.*, 6th ser., III, 76; Ashurst to Fitz-John Winthrop, July 10, 1701; also V, 86; Wait Winthrop to Fitz-John Winthrop, June 16, 1701.

ployed me, you would have been in a sad condition this day.''[83] Blathwayt's feelings in the matter have not been recorded. A little earlier, however, he had been successful in having passed what he regarded as a very constructive piece of legislation, an act providing bounties on the importation of naval stores into England.[84]

Blathwayt either identified himself with, or took the lead in proposing, all the measures for colonial consolidation during these years. He was exceedingly interested in the efforts to establish an effective postal system in the colonies, and he backed Edward Dummer's attempts to set up a smooth-working packet system to the West Indies. When, in 1707, Dummer protested that he could no longer bear the risks alone, and, despite his contract with the government, declared that the king should assume the losses, the Treasury referred his petition to Blathwayt as well as to the postal authorities. Blathwayt heartily supported Dummer's contention and made the occasion his opportunity for delivering a long report on the importance of the colonies to England's welfare.[85] He was also interested in the various schemes for further settlements in the colonies, and he favored the proposal to establish settlements of the German "Palatines" in the Carolinas and in Jamaica. In 1697, when the plans for disbanding the army were under way, he wrote to Bridgewater that he wished a large number of the disbanded sol-

---

[83] Root, *The Relations of Pennsylvania and Great Britain, 1696–1755*, pp. 360–361. Root's citation for the quotation, *Mass. Hist. Soc. Coll.*, 6th ser., III, 384, is erroneous, but for letters in the same vein as the one cited, see *Mass. Hist. Soc. Coll.*, 6th ser., V, 138–140; also Stock, *Debates*, II, 403, 405, 418, note 117. For the rough draft of Blathwayt's report, see Huntington MSS., Blathwayt Papers relating to America, 1681–1741, no paging.

[84] 3 and 4 Anne, c. 10.

[85] This is traced in Blathwayt's Journal, Treas. 64:89, 352–382; also *Cal. Treas. Papers, 1702–1707*, pp. 525–526; Blathwayt's report is dated September 6, 1707, and he was acting in his capacity as auditor general, since he had been dismissed from the Board of Trade in April, 1707.

diers could be encouraged to go to the colonies. "Their transportation gratis and other advantages that may be offered them in the several colonies will turn to a vast advantage for England and encrease of the revenue." He was careful to add that the suggestion was wholly disinterested on his part.[86] Such a plan obviously offered a solution for many of the problems which he was daily facing as secretary at war, for requests that he find new posts for officers and soldiers kept pouring into his office.

The return of the Tories to power, after 1700, temporarily afforded Blathwayt a more congenial working atmosphere. Nottingham, with whom he had been so closely associated from 1689 to 1693, returned to the secretarial office. This time Nottingham was insistent that he have a Tory colleague, and Sir Charles Hedges was accordingly continued in the Northern office. Lord Godolphin accepted the position of Lord High Treasurer and proved as earnest in his efforts to improve the colonial revenue as Blathwayt himself. The accession of Anne meanwhile afforded wide opportunity for dispensing patronage in the colonies. The governorship left vacant by the death of Lord Bellomont, in 1701, had to be filled. Again the question arose, should New York and Massachusetts be governed by one or by separate governors? Needless to say, Blathwayt's desire for a separation, expressed so earnestly in 1695, was fulfilled. The selection of Dudley as governor of Massachusetts was clearly Blathwayt's, and was one which he had been advocating for years.[87] Dudley's appointment as governor was made in the face of

---

[86] Huntington MSS., Bridgewater Collection, Vol. 138, No. 9740; Loo, October 1, 1697.

[87] Dudley's position in England in 1702 was powerful; he was a member of parliament, sitting for Newton, the Isle of Wight (the constituency which Blathwayt had earlier represented), a seat which Dudley owed directly to his patron, Lord Cutts, the governor of the Isle of Wight.

bitter opposition from Ashurst and Phips, the New England agents, who now more than ever regarded Blathwayt as a spy and a tool of New England's worst interests. It seems curious that Blathwayt should have continued to support Dudley, who, from having been a friend of Randolph, had become one of the latter's enemies. It simply shows, however, that Randolph's opinion was not necessarily Blathwayt's. Blathwayt, to his discredit, would not lend his support to Thomas Byfield, whom Dudley wanted appointed lieutenant-governor. He had already resolved on the post for his own cousin, Thomas Povey.[88]

Povey was, in fact, a relative for whose official security Blathwayt had always felt more or less responsible. Ten years earlier, when Nottingham and he had been dispensing offices, Povey had been given the position of naval officer in Jamaica, to the annoyance of the Admiralty who claimed the appointment as their own.[89] That Povey ever served in Jamaica is unlikely. His appointment as lieutenant-governor caused the inhabitants of Massachusetts considerable surprise. Samuel Sewall wrote in his *Diary*, "I was startled at two or three things: viz., the Lieutenant-Governor, a stranger sent whom we never knew nor heard anything of before."[90] Timothy Woodbridge identified him, however, as "Captain Thomas Povey, cousin to one of that name knowne to yourself; he

[88] *Trans. Col. Soc. of Mass.*, X, 382; also *Mass. Hist. Soc. Coll.*, 6th ser., V, 109, 110, 218–219. Phips, however, became Dudley's friend.

[89] *Cal. S. P. Dom.*, 1691–1692, p. 496; also pp. 432–435; *Cal. S. P. Col.*, 1689–1692, p. 736.

[90] *Diary of Samuel Sewall*, 1674–1720, II, 58; entry for June 1, 1702. In a footnote is a quotation from Palfrey, *History of New England* (Boston, 1858–1890), IV, 247, to the effect that the selection was made without reference to the Board of Trade, which was, of course, technically correct. Povey was also governor of the castle. (See Journal of the Board of Trade, April 21, 1702.)

is a souldier, was nine years in the army in Flanders."[91] He was a poor choice as lieutenant-governor and proved more or less of a laughingstock. No doubt he was glad to escape from the province in 1705, when he returned to England. The only people in Massachusetts who regretted the loss were the struggling members of the Church of England in Boston, who wrote to the Board of Trade begging that he be returned on a good and substantial establishment.[92]

Dudley had no reason to allow his disappointment over his failure to secure the lieutenant-governorship for Byfield to alter his attitude toward Blathwayt. He had already recommended Byfield for another position, that of attorney-general and in this Blathwayt supported him. When, a little later, the post again fell vacant, Blathwayt agreed to the appointment of Dudley's son, Paul.[93] Blathwayt also bestirred himself to have Dudley paid the arrears due him for his services in raising the two companies sent to Massachusetts Bay—an incident which shows that Blathwayt could, if he desired, arouse the paymaster-general and the Treasury to action. Chamberlayne, Dudley's London agent, told Dudley how kind Blathwayt had been, and said that he thought the latter deserved a present of twenty pounds, though he dared not make it until he had directions from Dudley. "I suppose your Excellency intends him some furrs, or the like, and I wish they may turn to as good account as those you sent to Lord Weymouth, a copy of whose letter I send enclosed, because nothing can describe his friendship to you so well as his own words."[94]

[91] *Mass. Hist. Soc. Coll.*, 6th ser., III, 99; also pp. 97–98. Woodbridge's letter was addressed to Fitz-John Winthrop.

[92] *Cal. S. P. Col.*, 1706–1708, p. 36; February 4, 1706.

[93] *Mass. Hist. Soc. Coll.*, 6th ser., III, 546–547, 551.

[94] *Ibid.*, 539; July 24, 1703. Weymouth was also a member of the Board of Trade. See also pp. 545–546, for a letter in which Chamberlayne sent

For New Hampshire, over which Dudley was also in charge, Blathwayt successfully supported John Usher as lieutenant-governor, a distinct triumph over Ashurst, who supported William Partridge.[95] The appointment of Lord Cornbury, a scion of the house of Clarendon, to the governorship of New York, can hardly be attributed to Blathwayt, though Cornbury occasionally referred to him as his friend, especially during the preparations for his departure to the province. Cornbury and Blathwayt had been associated in 1688, during the march of King James to Salisbury, when, according to Berwick, Blathwayt had aided Cornbury to desert to William. Whether or not Blathwayt assisted Cornbury to secure the governorship of New York, he certainly did not uphold his high-handed rule.

In the West Indies, Blathwayt supported Sir Beville Granville for governor of Barbados, and Major Handasyd, the Earl of Peterborough's deputy-governor, for Jamaica. Handasyd pleased Blathwayt, for in 1706, when Handasyd begged to be relieved of his post and allowed to come home, Blathwayt answered that it was out of the question; he had served too short a time and was far too satisfactory a governor in the eyes of the ministry and "Our Board."[96]

Granville got into serious trouble with his council and

Dudley the compliments of the Archbishop, the Bishop of London, Weymouth, Sir R. Worseley, James Vernon, and Blathwayt. He added: "The Archbishop and Mr. Vernon thank you for all their letters; to which I only add, they are not yet ciphers." Vernon and the Archbishop were both Whigs, hence the statement. The letter was written in August, 1704, when the Whig reaction was beginning.

[95] Belknap, *History of New Hampshire* (1831), I, 152, 153. Belknap reported that in 1696 Ashurst had succeeded in getting Usher ousted from the lieutenant-governorship and William Partridge installed in his place. He had wrested the appointment from the lords justices in the absence of William III. Usher was subsequently reinstated, however.

[96] Add. MSS. 38712, f. 80; May 1, 1706.

assembly over alleged arbitrary and illegal acts. They said that he "encouraged" the Jews and the Scots by advancing them to civil and military posts; that he accepted presents which he tried to conceal; and that he violated the Acts of Trade to his own advantage. The leading merchants of the island and the members of the Royal African Company supported him, and the matter was referred by petition to the consideration of the Board of Trade, who reported to the Privy Council, upholding Granville. The petitioners and the agents of the islanders asked to see a copy of this report, but they were told by the board that it had already been sent to the council. They subsequently tried to secure a copy from the council and were refused, so they said, whereupon they petitioned parliament.[97] Their importunity amused, rather than annoyed, Blathwayt, who reported to Granville: "Your Excellency will understand by this conveyance what lengths the angry gentlemen have gone, not only against yourself but even against the Commission of Trade before the House of Lords and how unsuccessful they have been in all their unwearied endeavours."[98] Blathwayt's tone of bland self-satisfaction probably indicates that he knew more about the transaction than the records show.

A successful candidate for a governorship needed, of course, other support than Blathwayt's. Competition for the office was keen and a tremendous amount of wire-pulling went on. The man who had greatest family influence or the strongest friend at court was usually selected. The support of the secretary of state was almost essential, since the governor's commission was issued over his countersignature. A weak secretary of state could sometimes be bullied into compliance, and both Trumbull and James Vernon, no doubt, signed warrants for candidates

97 *Hist. MSS. Com., House of Lords MSS.*, n.s., VI, 363–380.
98 Add. MSS. 38712, f. 75; February 25, 1706.

not of their choosing. No commission for a governorship was issued over Blathwayt's countersignature during his *pro-tem.* secretaryship.[99] The presence of two secretaries of state sometimes made it easier for a candidate, particularly when one was a Tory and the other a Whig, as when Nottingham and Shrewsbury were in office, from 1689 to 1690. The candidate then applied to the one whose party views fitted his own, although, since colonial affairs supposedly lay in the province of the southern secretary, this could not always be managed.

It is rash to conclude, as Osgood does, that Blathwayt dispensed a patronage comparable to the Duke of Newcastle's in a later period, even if more quietly and in a narrower field.[100] Blathwayt had actually not a single office at his disposal; even the appointment of a deputy auditor was subject to the sanction of the Treasury. Though we find no instance where the Treasury Lords refused to accept his nomination of deputy auditor, the fact remains that they could have done so if they had wished. Blathwayt, no doubt, had a good deal of influence, but the picture of him as a baleful figure behind the scenes rests on the statements made by the New England agents, especially Ashurst, at a time when they were smarting under defeat. Blathwayt's real power depended on a Tory administration, and even then he needed a friendly secretary of state. From Nottingham's dismissal, in 1693, until the Earl of Jersey took over the southern office in 1699, Blathwayt exercised little patronage. Ashurst then accused Blathwayt of stealing a march on him. He wrote Wait Winthrop: "Mr. Bl[athwayt] hath got one Atwood that My Lord Belamount desired might bee Chiefe Justice of

99 For Blathwayt's declaration that he preferred to waive his right to sign commissions rather than raise an argument, see his letters to Vernon, June, 1695, S. P. For., Military Expeditions, I, 17.

100 Osgood, *The American Colonies in the 18th Century*, I, 136.

New York to bee Judge Advocate in your place while I was in the countray. But I sopos I shall er long get you in the same post againe.''[101]

The New England agents hated Blathwayt mainly for his support of Randolph, Andros, Fletcher, and Dudley, but none of the latter seems to have been aware of any great influence in Blathwayt's hands. Randolph, applying for the governorship of Bermuda, went to Clarendon, Ormonde, and Beaufort for help, though he made the application at Blathwayt's suggestion. Fletcher, while he willingly acknowledged Blathwayt's coöperation, made his acknowledgments equally to the Earl of Athlone and to Sir Robert Southwell. Dudley tried for years to get a governorship, preferably that of Massachusetts; but he was not successful, even with Blathwayt's friendship and aid, until 1701, when he gave thanks to Lord Weymouth as well as to Blathwayt.

The feud over the power of recommendation to appointments which developed later in the eighteenth century between the secretary of state and the Board of Trade did not appear during Blathwayt's tenure at the board. The secretary of state guarded his control over appointments very jealously and resented any interference with his authority, but at this time, his resentment was directed, not against the board, but against other officials in the government. A warning, however, of what was to develop, can be seen in the letter which the Earl of Sunderland, secretary of state for the southern department, sent to the board in January, 1707, expressing surprise that a report had been sent to the Privy Council without his knowledge.[102] Since Blathwayt was a clerk of the council, the only member of

---

101 *Trans. Col. Soc. of Mass.*, X, 382; May 5, 1701; *Mass. Hist. Soc. Coll.*, 6th ser., V, 84.

102 *Cal. S. P. Col.*, 1706–1708, p. 353; Sunderland to the Board of Trade, January 3, 1707.

the board in that position, we can assume that he was the sinner. Sunderland was a Whig, and as the Tory Blathwayt's dismissal from the board was imminent, the latter's eagerness to rush business through without Sunderland's knowledge was only to be expected. Sunderland demanded most peremptorily, however, that in the future all such papers be brought to him first.

Blathwayt's admission of the secretary of state's right to control minor colonial appointments was shamelessly partisan. Two cases illustrate this. In 1692, as already noted, Blathwayt wanted his cousin, Thomas Povey, appointed naval officer in Jamaica and applied to the Earl of Nottingham, who accordingly prepared a warrant. Apparently neither Blathwayt nor Nottingham was disturbed by the fact that this office fell technically within the patronage of the governor of the colony. In this instance, not the governor, but the Admiralty made the challenge. William III referred the matter to the Privy Council, and Nottingham wrote to Blathwayt, then in Flanders, that he had better secure some one to appear for him. He evidently did, for Povey secured the position.[103]

On another occasion, Blathwayt took precisely the opposite stand and sought to uphold the rights of the Admiralty over those of the secretary of state, with regard to an appointment in Jamaica. Shrewsbury, however, not Nottingham, was then secretary. The question arose over the secretaryship of Jamaica, a patent office. Shrewsbury and Vernon were supporting a certain Mr. Baber. In drawing up his commission, they vested him with authority to fill minor offices. The warrant was dispatched to Blathwayt, then in Flanders, for the king's signature. "Mr. Blathwayte," Vernon wrote to Shrewsbury, "has at

[103] *Cal. S. P. Dom.*, 1691–1692, pp. 432, 496; 1693, p. 31; *Cal. S. P. Col.*, 1689–1692, p. 731.

last sent Mr. Baber's warrant, and it is signed. As he went from hence he has suffered himself to be convinced that nothing extraordinary was intended to be imposed; but few men will ever own themselves in the wrong. He still maintains, that upon his knowledge the Treasury and Admiralty appointed officers for executing many employments that are mentioned in Mr. Harris's patent. If they did so, they will do it again, and I suppose Mr. Baber will acquiesce as Mr. Harris did. In the meantime he [Baber] has received your Grace's kindness entire; he has his warrant, and my Lady Sunderland has taken notice of it, who is so much the more pleased with it, as it is not curtailed by Mr. Blathwayt's gainsaying."[104]

On the question of patent offices, deputyships, pluralities, and the authority of the governors to make appointments as opposed to the officials in England, Blathwayt's views were equally inconsistent. Himself an undisguised pluralist—though it is only fair to say that none of his offices were either sinecures or mutually incompatible— he was more consistent than Randolph, who objected to the fact that in the colonies the offices of collector of the customs, receiver of the royal revenue, and naval officer were often combined in a single individual. Blathwayt saw nothing amiss in making a man who was already collector of the four and half per cent. duty in Barbados also deputy auditor of the casual revenue. His acid test—if he

104 Vernon, *Letters Illustrative, etc.*, I, 281; June 22, 1697. The stand that Blathwayt took on another claim made by Nottingham is not so important, since the matter came up prior to his attendance on William as secretary of state. The incident is, however, illustrative of the questions that arose over this petty patronage. Luttrell reported in September, 1690: "The provost marshal of Jamaica being lately dead, the Earl of Nottingham as secretary of state, pretends a right to dispose of the same, and has accordingly recommended Mr. Warr, his lordship's secretary, to that employment; the Marquis of Caermarthen putts in for the same on behalf of Mr. Paston, the Earl of Yarmouth's brother. He has not disposed thereof, but has referred it to the king." (Luttrell, *Brief Relation*, II, 98.)

had one—seems to have been the man's character. If an officeholder was honest, let him have more offices. If he was dishonest, take away the office he already had. Blathwayt rigidly applied this test to his dishonest cousin, Robert Gibbs, of Barbados, who had been serving as his deputy auditor and wanted to be made prize commissioner, collector of the customs, and also a councillor.[105]

As far as deputyships were concerned, we have Blathwayt's own statement that he disapproved strongly of governors holding offices *in absentia,* and he apparently disapproved, with fair consistency, of this system for lesser officials as well. Surely the letters which poured in from the colonial governors—James Kendall of Barbados and Francis Nicholson of Virginia, in particular—must have impressed him with the folly of the deputy system. George Larkin presented the case well, when he wrote in 1702: "Patent offices are so frequently disposed of to persons wholly unacquainted with business, and officiated by Deputys' Deputys' Deputy, some of which are scarce capable of writing six words of sense."[106] Theoretically, at least, both the Lords of Trade and the Board of Trade were opposed to the system. The former put on record, as early as 1680, their disapproval of the holding of patent offices in Barbados by deputy.[107] In February, 1699, an order in council, which had been favored by the Board of Trade, stated that all holders of patent offices should be in actual residence and execute their offices in their own persons.[108] Needless to say, the order went unheeded. To the

---

[105] See *infra,* pp. 367–369.

[106] *Cal. S. P. Col.,* 1702, p. 305; Larkin to the Board of Trade, May 11, 1702.

[107] C.O. 391:3, f. 197; September 16, 1680. On December 4, 1679, the Lords of Trade approved a report to the Privy Council, in which they ordered that the colonial governors should not dispose of public offices for profit.

[108] C.O. 391:20, f. 235; also Basye, *The Board of Trade,* p. 25.

officeholders, colonial offices were as much a business proposition as the colonies were to the merchants. Blathwayt probably was no grave offender, except in the case of his cousin, Thomas Povey. He had relatively few kinsmen holding colonial offices, and with the exception of Povey, they seem to have been actual residents.[109] Yet he never took a determined stand in the matter, and in any event it would have been futile to attempt to thwart powerful political leaders, intent on securing appointments for their friends.

Blathwayt was entirely inconsistent in his attitude toward patent offices and the governor's power to make appointments. He regarded the governor's office as the mainspring of the colonial system and lamented the governor's isolation and powerlessness, yet he did nothing to free him from the strangle hold which the patentee officeholders and other independent appointees had upon him. Presumably he could have done nothing to change a system so firmly entrenched in the official mind, even if he had desired it. Few offices which had once become patent ever changed their character. The auditorship of Vir-

[109] Thomas Povey, Robert Gibbs, George Clarke, and Samuel Barwick are the only relatives of Blathwayt whom we have found holding colonial offices, with the exception of Trefry, who was an officer in the New England regiment under Andros. Gibbs and Clark are discussed in the chapters on the auditor general. Barwick was a councillor in Barbados, who came over with the fleet, sometime before 1708. He was declared to be the friend of Governor Crowe, upholding him in his supposedly nefarious schemes. Barwick served as a collector of the revenue in Barbados. For a reference to him as the son of a former deputy governor of Barbados, see *Cal. S. P. Col.*, 1708–1709, pp. 430–431; also pp. 124–129.

The only other relative for whom Blathwayt secured an appointment in connection with the colonies was John Povey who for a while served as agent for Virginia, Maryland, and New York, the appointments having been made either at the time of the Revolution or shortly after. (See *Cal. S. P. Col.*, 1689–1692, p. 692; *Md. Archives, Proceedings of the Council*, 1698–1731, XXV, 45; *Executive Journal, Council of Virginia*, I, 187, 255, 331, 383; II, 34, 138, 278, 317.)

ginia, a patent office until Blathwayt became auditor general, passed then, like the other deputyships, under Treasury warrant; but it is one of the few exceptions. The secretary of state had no desire to relinquish his hold over the colonial patronage, and Blathwayt let the matter rest. In common with other English administrators, Blathwayt felt that governors easily got out of hand, and that they too often fell in with the wishes of colonial assemblies or became mercenary and yielded to temptation. In spite of this, he was usually tolerant when a complaint came in about a governor and generally supported him when the quarrel was with the assembly. He knew that much could happen in a colony without the governor's knowledge, and he was even willing to admit that piracy could go on quite extensively with the governor wholly unaware of it.[110] He never supposed that appointment to a governorship equipped a man with an all-seeing eye or with all-pervading common sense. He was inclined to agree with Codrington, the younger, that "in respect of governors who come abroad to make their fortunes, . . . Acts of Trade, Instructions and all your Lordships' wise and good orders to them are *verba et praeterie nihil.*"[111]

Osgood, in referring to Atwood, who replaced William Smith as chief justice of New York, after Bellomont had suspended the latter from office, on December 25, 1700, makes a curious statement with regard to what he calls Blathwayt's "theory of colonial appointments."[112] According to this story, Bellomont failed to apprise Smith of his removal, with the result that the latter still regarded himself as in office when Atwood arrived to take

[110] Huntington MSS., Blathwayt Papers relating to America, 1681–1741, no paging; draft of a report on the colonies.

[111] *Cal. S. P. Col.*, 1701, p. 467; Codrington to the Board of Trade, August 25, 1701.

[112] Osgood, *The American Colonies in the 18th Century*, I, 156–157.

up his duties. Ashurst attributed the appointment of Atwood to Blathwayt's insidious influence, and Osgood
accepts the view, at the same time holding Blathwayt
responsible for the state of affairs which resulted from
Bellomont's failure to inform Smith. The case is hardly
a good one to select as illustrating Blathwayt's indifference to the cause of colonial justice. He could not be held
responsible for a system which he did not invent, and he
could not be expected to clarify a situation already complex and destined to become more so. In this instance,
neither Blathwayt's inconsistency nor his indifference
can be proved; in supporting Atwood, he was acting for
what he regarded the best interests of the provinces, and
he was doing it for Bellomont, who ordinarily did not expect favors from him. There was really no theory of colonial appointments involved; the incident appears to have
been a simple case of negligence on the part of the governor.

Like the English administration in general, Blathwayt
desired to make the governor financially independent. He
supported, with fair consistency, the rule that the governors must not accept presents from the colonial assemblies. Of course he knew, as did most sensible administrators, that it was idle to protest against such gifts unless
the government had some more satisfactory alternative to
suggest.[113]

Attempts by colonial assemblies to interfere with established salaries or fees of colonial officials and to displace
patent officials, annoyed Blathwayt. In the long-drawn-
out Maryland quarrel over Sir Thomas Lawrence, the
patentee, who held the position of secretary to the province, Blathwayt evidently accepted Randolph's opinion

---

[113] See the board's report on the matter in 1703. (*Cal. S. P. Col.*, 1702–
1703, pp. 317–321, 348; also a statement by Blathwayt in the same year,
Cal. Treas. Papers, 1702–1707, p. 186.)

that Lawrence was a "man of worth." In April, 1705, the Board of Trade sent a letter to Governor Seymour of Maryland, ordering him "to preserve the ancient rights of his Majesty's Patent Office and Officers," to give all due encouragement to Sir Thomas Lawrence, and to refuse to sign an act whereby the just and usual fees of such patent officers might be diminished.[114] The next year the board recommended the disallowance of an act passed by the assembly of Nevis, which settled the fees to be paid the secretary and the marshal, the act "intrenching upon your Majesty's prerogative and diminishing the rights of Officers holding under your Majesty's Letters Patent."[115]

Party organization was so perfected that the return of the Whigs to power in 1707 rendered inevitable Blathwayt's dismissal from the Board of Trade. He had nearly lost his seat in 1704, when he was deprived of his office of secretary at war, but for some reason or other he was allowed to continue on the board, though Luttrell, with his characteristic tendency to anticipate events, announced in April of that year that Blathwayt had lost his seat to Sir Thomas Cook, of Derbyshire.[116] On April 22, 1707, however, Luttrell quite correctly announced: "The Earl of Stamford, Lord Herbert of Cherbury, Robert Monckton, and John Pulteney, esquire, are to be commissioners of trade in the room of Lord Weymouth, Mr. Blathwayt, Mr. Pollexfen, and Mr. Prior."[117]

Blathwayt relinquished his post with great bitterness, and he went away feeling that the great merit of his services had not been recognized. From that time forward, his relations with the board became acrimonious. He was bound to keep in touch with it, through his work as au-

[114] *Cal. S. P. Col.*, 1704–1705, p. 483; April 12, 1705.
[115] *Ibid.*, 1706–1708, p. 129; May 2, 1706.
[116] Luttrell, *Brief Relation*, V, 414; April 15, 1704.
[117] *Ibid.*, VI, 163; April 22, 1707.

ditor general, but petty jealousies were always cropping out. The board refused him ordinary courtesies and became angry when Governor Seymour wrote his letters to Blathwayt in care of their office. Seymour apologized, saying he had done so simply because it seemed more expeditious and safe: "Mr. Blathwayt being often out of towne on his own affaires, as well as Her Majesty's service."[118] When Colonel Lloyd, who served as governor for a short time after Seymour's death, told the board that he had not sent them a copy of the accounts of Maryland because he was sending them to Blathwayt, the board wrote to him: "You tell us indeed . . . that the accounts will be transmitted to Mr. Blathwayt; that is nothing to us, you are required by your instructions, to transmit those accounts to us half yearly or oftner, and therefore wee do expect that the same be punctually complyed with."[119] In the investigation of colonial finances which parliament made in 1711, Blathwayt's attitude toward the board displayed itself repeatedly, and he complained bitterly that the archives of the plantation office were closed to him.

In 1711, Blathwayt had an additional grievance. The Tory revival to power, which had come in 1710, had not carried him back into office with it. Worse than that, he had lost his seat in the house of commons. This was because he had offended his patron, the Duke of Beaufort, who controlled Gloucestershire. Blathwayt wrote to Dartmouth, the secretary of state, explaining what had happened. The Duke of Beaufort had seen a "false print," which stated that Blathwayt had voted against Dr. Sacheverell, and as a result he had opposed Blathwayt's reëlection at Bath. Blathwayt declared the report a gross falsehood; he had been so ill at the time of the crisis that

[118] *Cal. S. P. Col.*, 1706–1708, p. 762; also pp. 674, 758–763; February 13, and June 23, 1708.

[119] *Ibid.*, 1712–1714, p. 211; July 23, 1713.

he had been unable to attend any of the debates, much less take part in the division on the subject. He begged Dartmouth to use his influence to secure his reinstatement in the duke's good graces and to remember him in case there were any alterations made in the membership of the Board of Trade.[120]

But Blathwayt's days at the board and in the plantation office were over forever, and his voice was rarely again to be lifted in colonial councils except in connection with his work as auditor general. It was a pity that he left office a disappointed man. No one, however, could have spared him the vicissitudes of party politics. He had pursued a straight course throughout his entire tenure of office. As far as we know, he never once swerved from his original tenets in matters of trade and plantations. One of his last statements on colonial questions came in 1711, when he was asked to report to the secretary of state, Lord Dartmouth, on the question of whether Maryland should revert to Lord Baltimore and be under his absolute control. He answered that he felt the arrangement of 1691 should continue, otherwise Maryland would again become a "nest of Papists."[121] It is clear from this that his views with regard to proprietary and corporate colonies had not undergone a change; that he still viewed the colonies through the eyes of the merchants and the great corporate companies; and that in 1717, the year of his death, he was as ardent a supporter of the Acts of Trade as he had been in 1675.[122] He was always the firm upholder

120 *Hist. MSS. Com.*, XI. Report, App., Pt. V, Dartmouth MSS., p. 297; Gloucestershire, August 14, 1710.

121 *Cal. S. P. Col.*, 1710–1711, pp. 421–423.

122 It would be interesting to know what would have been Blathwayt's reaction to the anonymous proposal made in 1715, to the effect that the Board of Trade, since it lacked a personal knowledge of the colonies and trade and industry in general, should have included in its membership two merchants and two ex-governors. Another suggestion was that the efficiency of the board

of the royal prerogative in the colonies, and while his knowledge of the plantations and of trade had grown with the years, it brought no alteration in his original principles. If consistency be meritorious, then Blathwayt was a man of great merit. In any event he was a stalwart guardian of England's growing commercial interests.

would be improved if a single colony were assigned each member as his special charge. This, it will be remembered, had been a plan resorted to in 1697, but apparently never adhered to. Blathwayt had been given the West Indian colonies, while New York, New England, and Newfoundland had been assigned to Abraham Hill, a good Whig. (*Cal. S. P. Col.*, 1696–1697, p. 303; 1714–1715, pp. xii–xiii.)

CHAPTER XI

SURVEYOR AND AUDITOR GENERAL OF PLAN-TATION REVENUES. THE SECOND PHASE, 1689–1717

It would be natural to conclude that the years of almost continuous warfare from 1690 to the conclusion of the Peace of Utrecht, would have a shattering effect on the royal audit of plantation revenues. As a matter of fact, the war did have a disastrous effect, but the results were by no means so demoralizing as might be expected. Colonial revenues decreased; copies of the accounts were delayed or lost at sea; yet, except in the colonial war zone, particularly the Leeward Islands, there was no actual falling off in the accounting. It is surprising to discover that in 1711, when Blathwayt made his report to the Treasury and the commissioners of accounts, he had complete statements to present for most of the colonies. Since, in 1702–1703, he had already given in similar statements for the previous decade, there is a continuous record for most of the provinces from 1689 to 1711.[1]

The difficulties encountered were in general those already discussed and grew out of conditions peculiar to individual colonies. Factional disputes, conflicts between local assemblies and councils over the right of the latter

[1] The actual accounts in most instances have been lost, but the references to their receipt and the summaries based upon them, which Blathwayt drew up, not only point to their existence but also in many cases give a clear idea of their content.

to amend money bills, and quarrels between the provincial treasurer (an official to be found in most of the colonies) and the royal receiver, caused much more trouble than the war. England's policy was precisely the same as it had been prior to 1689, and was very little affected by the general conflict. Except for occasional reference to levies for defense, the records give no indication of hostilities. The English government was still intent on securing permanent revenue grants in the colonies where such efforts had been unsuccessful, and in obtaining a satisfactory commutation of the perpetual revenues where they had fallen short of original expectations. Thus, governors going out to Virginia, the Leeward Islands, or Barbados were instructed to secure new revenue acts which would be an improvement on the two shillings per hogshead grant or the four and a half per cent.[2]; while the governors of New York, Massachusetts Bay, or Jamaica were ordered to have acts passed to provide revenue in perpetuity. In not a single colony, however, did England succeed in having her wishes carried out. Interest was still felt in the improvement of the quit-rents, and there was talk of their introduction into colonies where they had never existed before or had been abandoned for some other form of revenue, as in the Leeward Islands. Efforts were made to increase the casual revenues in all of the colonies. On the whole, therefore, the records of the post-revolutionary period read very much like those of the earlier years.

There was no structural change in the system. Gover-

[2] *Cal. S. P. Col.*, 1704–1705, pp. 737–742; 1706–1708, pp. 62, 213–216, 625–626; 1710–1711, pp. 408–411. Governor Nott succeeded in having such an act passed, but like its predecessor it discriminated in favor of Virginia shipping, with the result that the act as a whole was disallowed, not merely the offending clause, as in 1682; the act likewise gave exclusive control over the revenues to the assembly, not to the crown. In 1711, Spotswood succeeded in having a more satisfactory measure introduced into the assembly, but no final action was ever taken on it.

nors were still required to see that semi-annual accounts of the revenue were sent to Blathwayt.[3] Blathwayt continued to appoint his deputies as in the earlier period, and his nominations were seldom opposed by the colonies. No new instructions were given to the deputies, except in rare instances where Blathwayt drew up a form for the accounting. His instructions were then so obvious that we are inclined to question their necessity. Some of the deputies and collectors must have possessed very elementary notions of bookkeeping if they required Blathwayt to tell them that they must keep a double column, one of receipts and another of disbursements. It would have been more to the point if he had explained the complicated "Exchequer method," which Stede and Randolph had found so baffling. The earlier difficulties with regard to vouchers recurred, and the tendency of collectors to send their accounts without first securing the attestation of the governor in council caused Blathwayt a tremendous amount of vexation. In one case, not only a second, but a third set of accounts had to be demanded from the collector in Barbados.

Two more colonies were included in the system: Maryland, in 1690, when Lord Baltimore lost his governmental rights, and New Jersey, in 1702, when the control of the proprietors came to an end. According to Randolph, whom Blathwayt had just appointed his deputy, Governor Copley, of Maryland, was prepared to set the audit aside in a most arbitrary fashion. "I made my visit to Coll. Copley," Randolph wrote to Blathwayt in June,

[3] Duplicate copies were still to be sent to the Lords of Trade—after 1696, to the Board of Trade. Most governors observed this order faithfully, although accounts were rarely sent oftener than once a year, since many of the provincial revenue systems did not lend themselves to the half-yearly basis. Governors kept up a regular correspondence with Blathwayt, and after Blathwayt lost his seat on the Board of Trade, that body began to complain that it was being neglected; but the governors protested their innocence of any deliberate desire to slight the board.

1692. "He gave me a faint reception, he allowed my deputation from the Custome house, but speaks very coldly of yours. He entertained me with grave discourse but nothing to the purpose but advised me to write to you: that he would serve you. Once in his drink he said you were a Jacobite and a great enemy to their present Majesties: that your commission of Auditor ought to be renewed upon their Majesties' coming to the Crown. I told him my deputation was allowed of and signed by the Lords of the Treasury, and pressed him that it might be registered, but refused saying it was not a proper tyme, I discoursed him about the treasurers and receivers of the publick money of the Province, whether he found any of itt at the tyme of his arrival, he told me he was especially commanded to take care of it and give their Majesties an Account and was very unwilling to do anything about the Deputation till he had done his business with the Assembly."[4]

Copley's strong affection for William and Mary may have prompted his attitude. Blathwayt was too tolerant of him. "I have forborn to make my complaint to the Lords of the Treasury whose subordinate I am for the very reason you mention—which is my respect for your family and consideration."[5] Naturally Copley's studied defiance continued. He refused to bring the question of his deputation before the assembly and encouraged the two collectors of the royal revenue, Nehemiah Blakiston and George Plater, in their attempts to thwart Randolph. The latter had scandalous reports to make of these two, whom he encountered in his capacity of surveyor of the customs.[6] Copley thus succeeded in nullifying the royal

---

[4] Goodrick, *Edward Randolph*, VII, 373; June 28, 1692.

[5] *Ibid.*, f.n., p. 354; Copley prided himself inordinately on his family connections.

[6] *Ibid.*, pp. 373–374, 432. Blakiston and Plater were the collectors of the

audit, and it was not until Governor Nicholson's time that any conscientious attempt was made to introduce it. Copley, moreover, had inculcated a defiant spirit in the assembly, which, in turn, challenged Blathwayt's office and pronounced it a luxury they could ill afford, thus rendering Nicholson's efforts almost futile.[7]

In New Jersey the introduction of the audit was little more than a gesture. The years until Blathwayt's death were spent in wearisome wrangling between the governor and the proprietary members of the council and assembly, who refused to provide any establishment for the government.[8] Under Cornbury, the attitude of the members was more or less justified, but Governor Hunter's efforts at conciliation were equally resisted, until, in 1715, after years of frustrated effort, peace was finally made.

To trace the course of the audit in each of the provinces would be to write a financial history of each of them and would go far beyond the bounds of this study, which merely intends to point out where the system met with conspicuous success and where with dismal failure and to indicate its inherent weaknesses. The audit would never work of itself, and its delicate balance could be completely upset by the local political situation. Everything depended on the governor—on his willingness to carry

plantation duty as well as of the royal revenue. Maryland's royal revenues were very much like Virginia's. By an act passed in 1679, a two shillings per hogshead duty on tobacco was collected, and this, under the arrangement of 1691, was divided between Baltimore and the king. The quit-rents were Baltimore's, but after some dispute the casual revenues were assigned to the king. In 1692, the assembly granted an additional levy of 3d. per hogshead on tobacco. (Treas. 64:89, ff. 48–49; Osgood, *The American Colonies in the 18th Century*, I, 370–373.)

[7] *Infra*, pp. 455–456.

[8] New Jersey's revenue system was comparable to New York's. As long as the legislature refused to pass a revenue act, there was virtually nothing for Blathwayt or his deputy to do in New Jersey, since the revenues arising from the quit-rents and casual sources were too slight to take notice of.

out orders and his ability to compel obedience from the collector, the deputy auditor, and the assembly. Blathwayt's work might have been facilitated if a surveyor of the royal audit had been appointed to range over the colonies, investigating conditions in much the same way as Randolph did, as surveyor of the customs. Some such appointment may have been intended in 1712, when Sir Francis Nicholson was given a roving commission to survey plantation revenues, but he apparently made no report until 1719.[9] The definiteness of the plan, therefore, may be questioned.

Randolph, as a matter of fact, took upon himself a certain responsibility for the general welfare of the audit, even after he had ceased to be Blathwayt's deputy in Maryland. He reported what he regarded as the gross laxity of the New York collector in 1692, although he subsequently retracted his statements.[10] When in Bermuda, in 1699, he was so appalled by the financial practices of the then governor, Day, and his predecessor, Richier, "two broken linnen Drapers" as he called them, that he wrote to Blathwayt: "I know not wheither these Islands are included in your Honor's grant of Auditor General of his Majesty's Revenue in the plantations. If

[9] The appointment was made on the basis of Blathwayt's report to the Treasury in 1711; it may be, on Blathwayt's particular recommendation. Nicholson, as governor of Maryland and Virginia, had been a watchful guardian of the royal revenue and had enforced the audit. His failure in 1712 was due to the fact that his appointment was incidental; he was first and foremost military governor of Nova Scotia and his two appointments were mutually incompatible. (Osgood, *The American Colonies in the 18th Century*, II, 239; Bond, *The Quit-Rent System in the American Colonies*, pp. 394–395.)

[10] Goodrick, *Edward Randolph*, VII, 400–402, 403, 409, 426–429. Randolph declared Brook, the collector, to be as "proud as Lucifer and negligent in his busines," but he seems to have been influenced by the fact that his enemy, Joseph Dudley, and Brook had been friends. Brook wrested a retraction of his statements from him and enclosed it in a letter which he sent to Blathwayt, March 7, 1693.

so: Tis absolutely necessary that you appoint a Deputy to inspect and audite all Mr. Dayes accounts: which, by the inclosed Copy of part of his Majesty's Instructions to the Governor of those Islands, he is to transmitt home, etc. [*sic*]: as also what publick money has been raised and how disposed of, by the former governors. I cannot inform my selfe how the present Governor has observed that part of his Instructions: but know that he has such an awe upon those appointed amongst themselves to that purpose that they will allow and passe any accounts that he proposes to them."[11]

After fifteen years, the royal audit had taken so slight a hold in Bermuda that Randolph did not even know whether the system applied there; from this the paralyzing effect which a succession of obdurate governors could exert, may be appreciated. Of course, even with more cooperative governors a surveyor general who was less of an irritant than Randolph would have been needed, in order to make the system what Blathwayt and the English government desired it to be.

If much depended on the governor, a great deal also depended on the deputy auditors. Whether Blathwayt had any guiding rule which he constantly employed in selecting them, is not apparent. He often consulted the governor before making his choice, but only when the governor was a man of whom he approved, or one whose opinion carried weight in Whitehall. Needless to say, Blathwayt had not consulted the wishes of Governor Copley in appointing Edward Randolph his deputy in Maryland.[12] In 1699, when he first appointed a deputy in Bermuda, he followed Randolph's recommendation in nominating Samuel Spofferth, "a man of integrity and of a very good

[11] Goodrick, *Edward Randolph*, VII, 613; Randolph to Blathwayt, Bermuda, February 22, 1699.
[12] Treas. 64:88, ff. 412–416.

estate in these islands.''[13] Plainly he had not consulted the wishes of Governor Parke of the Leeward Islands in appointing Edward Perry. Blathwayt met Parke's initial objections to this choice by implying that he did not have a free hand in making appointments, but was responsible to the Treasury. He later tried to smooth over Parke's ruffled feelings by saying that Perry had ''the character of a diligent and honest man and he will I verily believe do nothing to displease you.''[14] Parke could not have been convinced by this, or he would not have written to the Board of Trade two years later: ''Mr. Blathwyte has made this Perry his Deputy Auditor, which is just nothing, for the Queen has no revenue here butt the four and a half per cent., the Queen has no Quitt-Rents, nor has there been any fines since I came or any other Revenue.''[15] In appointing a successor to Van Cortlandt, of New York, who died in 1701, Blathwayt selected Abraham De Peyster; but he wrote to the new governor, Lord Cornbury, that if the appointment did not meet with his approval, he would be glad to consider another, which would.[16]

In the case of two appointments, one in Virginia and one in Jamaica, frustrated governors attempted to raise legal objections to Blathwayt's nominations, by declaring that the latter had failed to secure the Treasury's sanction. Thus Governor Spotswood held up the appointment of John Grymes, the son-in-law of Philip Ludwell, whom Spotswood had just deposed from the office of deputy auditor, by complaining that the Treasury had not attested

[13] Treas. 64:89, ff. 43, 58–60, 170–176; Goodrick, *Edward Randolph*, VII, 613–614.

[14] Add. MSS. 38712, f. 79; April 30, 1706.

[15] *Cal. S. P. Col.*, 1706–1708, p. 694; letter of March 8, 1708. Parke declared Perry to be the creature of his predecessor in office, the younger Codrington.

[16] Huntington MSS., Blathwayt Papers relating to New York, I; letters of August 22, 1701, and July 12, 1703.

it.[17] Colonel Peter Heywood challenged the right of Edward Pratter, in 1716, in Jamaica, for the same reason. In each case, however, personal motives prompted the governor's stand. Naturally, Spotswood had no desire to see an appointment given to the relative of a man whom he had just dismissed for incompetence. Heywood had himself been deputy auditor and had, no doubt, come to regard the office as his own perquisite. Theoretically, the point was well-taken,—there was no question that Blathwayt's deputations required Treasury sanction,—but in neither instance was the objection sustained by the Treasury or by the attorney-general. Both reasoned that Blathwayt's neglect was unintentional; the consent of the Treasury was so much a matter of form that he was occasionally careless about securing it. Blathwayt supplied his deputies with the necessary endorsements of their appointment, and the governors had to admit defeat.[18]

[17] Spotswood had originally given Ludwell his hearty support and had granted him an *ad interim* appointment in 1711, when the previous deputy auditor, Dudley Digges, died. (*Spotswood Letters*, I, 69, 71.) For Grymes's case, see *ibid.*, II, 159–162. For Ludwell's dismissal and Spotswood's charges, see *ibid.*, II, 172–187; Treas. 64:90, f. 102; *Cal. Treas. Papers*, 1714–1719, CXCIX, No. 22, and CCVI, No. 9. Grymes's deputation was dated July 2, 1716.

[18] Pratter wrote to Blathwayt to tell him what had happened, whereupon the latter replied on June 14, 1717: "I have received the favor of your letter of the 20th November no sooner than the last month, by which I find my deputation has reached your hands, but I observe that Coll. Heywood made a difficulty of admitting you to act upon it because not witnessed: if the Governor means by his saying it is not witnessed that it hath not been confirmed or approved by the Lords of the Treasury as has been sometimes heretofore practiced, the enclosed copy of a letter from Mr. Lowndes as also of the opinion of the Attorney General lately sent to Virginia upon the like occasion will I doubt not remove the difficulty, which you will please to show his Excellency. But if it be meant that it ought to be witnessed, as Deeds or Letters of Attorney usually are, I can only say that I have never done it in such writings relating to the Crown, nor do I remember any such witnessing was used when the Governor himself was concerned for me upon the same occasion. Nor has my deputation been thought defective without it in

In selecting his deputies, Blathwayt, for good reason, usually took local men. As Governor Spotswood said: "I don't suppose the Sallary of this Office will encourage any Gentleman to come from England."[19] Randolph was, of course, an exception, although it is doubtful whether a deputy auditorship alone could ever have persuaded him to leave England. Another exception was the nefarious Edward Cranfield, who seems always to have had some personal claim on Blathwayt, and who was made deputy auditor in Barbados, in 1694.[20] George Clarke, who succeeded Abraham De Peyster in New York in 1703, was not only an Englishman but also Blathwayt's kinsman.[21] While Blathwayt was not opposed to the idea of securing offices for members of his family, he did not overwork the practice. The only other recorded instance of a deputy auditor who was also a relative was in Barbados, where Robert Gibbs, Blathwayt's cousin, was appointed to succeed Cranfield.[22] When it came to choosing local men, Blathwayt was careful to select those of substance, whenever possible. Thus Governor Parke reported that Edward Perry of the Leeward Islands, was one of the "greatest merchants in the island . . . and . . . had near £3000 cargo last from England which he sells by retail."[23]

It was not merely the desire to have his deputies represent the more prosperous and stable elements in the colony that influenced Blathwayt. His own monetary in-

any other plantation." (Add. MSS. 38713, f. 93.) For Spotswood's temporary acceptance of Grymes, see *Executive Council of Colonial Virginia, Journal*, III, 437.

[19] *Spotswood Letters*, II, 162; letter to Blathwayt, May 24, 1716.

[20] Treas. 64:88, f. 416.

[21] Treas. 64:89, ff. 78, 92; Add. MSS. 9732, ff. 262–263. This Clarke, subsequently governor of New York, is not to be confused with the George Clarke who served as Blathwayt's deputy secretary at war.

[22] Huntington MSS., Blathwayt Papers relating to Barbados; numerous letters from Gibbs to Blathwayt in 1704 and 1705.

[23] *Cal. S. P. Col.*, 1706–1708, p. 694.

terest was at stake, and, if possible, he disposed of no office gratis. He usually made the deputy pay for the appointment, and then struck as close a bargain as he could in the matter of the salary, which, except in Virginia, came out of Blathwayt's own pocket. In Virginia, Blathwayt demanded for himself a certain percentage of the deputy's salary, in addition to the regular £100 allowed by the patent. The financial negotiations with Ludwell, appointed deputy auditor in 1711, give an idea of Blathwayt's tactics. Ludwell's two intercessors were Blakiston, the Virginia agent in London, and Micajah Perry, "the great merchant," who served the colony in an unofficial capacity. They approached Blathwayt, who indicated that competition was running high. He set his first figure at £500, which Blakiston reported to Ludwell was exorbitant; the office was worth no more than £100, or possibly £200, and Blakiston believed he could secure it for that, since Blathwayt was indebted to him for a late service. "Though I joyn with you he is hard to make any impression upon, but by the method you mention, but I was determined to try my interest in him," Blakiston wrote to Ludwell, "I must doe him justice, he told me frankly that if I inclined to prefer you before any other friend or was pre-engaged to you that you should have it upon terms of allowing two and a half per cent. which I suppose is one moyety, and I am apt to - - - [sic] Colonel Diggs did not pay any such sume. I will not say there was nothing given for [it]. . . . He gave me a hint as to the way he had been applied to by several . . . but my advice shall be to play . . . [break in MS.] hand for you and part with noe money and take no obligation upon myself."[24]

[24] *Virginia Magazine of History*, IV, 16; see also pp. 19–23. Ludwell was fearful that Blathwayt might not appoint him, because his father had participated in Bacon's Rebellion, but Blakiston reassured him, "If Mr. Blath-

Although Blathwayt was on the whole successful in securing fairly competent deputies, very little is known about the majority of them outside their own provinces. The position was not of sufficient importance to attract men of very high calibre or of great ability, although there are a few notable exceptions. Virginia had some very distinguished auditors, probably because the office was more remunerative there than in Barbados or the Leeward Islands. Moreover, the two offices of auditor and receiver were for many years combined, which made it more profitable for the incumbent and may explain why the elder Bacon and the two Byrds were willing to accept the appointment.[25] Next to Virginia, New York had per-

wayt had any ill impressions of your Father, he never suggested the least hint to Mr. Perry or myself, when we applyed to him. Neither did we mention the old gentleman, and if Mr. Blathwayt had any resentment I hope he is too much a good orthodox Xtian [sic] to forget it, but the best way is not to put him in minde of them, but I hope he has too much generosity that he would not entaile the Crimes if any of the Father upon the Son, the best way is to let things of that matter keepe and not needlessly revive them.'' (*Ibid.*, p. 19.)

25 This union of the two offices was not peculiar to Virginia. We know that Samuel Spofferth, of Bermuda, was also the collector of all the revenue there; while in the Leeward Islands, Edward Perry was the collector of the four and a half per cent. duty and, no doubt, of the casual revenue as well. (Goodrick, *Edward Randolph*, VII, 615.) Randolph had Spofferth made collector against Governor Day's wishes. Perry was also commissioner of the customs in the Leeward Islands, an appointment separate from that of collector of the four and a half per cent. What he collected is a question; the appointment was clearly a political one, the work of Lord Weymouth of the Board of Trade, who needed a place for a kinsman, so Governor Parke declared. (*Cal. S. P. Col.*, 1706–1708, p. 694.)

William Byrd, the father, succeeded the elder Bacon in office, in Virginia, but not without some difficulty. Bacon had promised to turn the offices over to him, provided official consent could be secured. The assistance of the governor, Lord Howard, was successfully enlisted, and through him Byrd secured a letter of introduction to Blathwayt. On December 4, 1687, Byrd, who had in the meantime gone to England, secured his appointment from the Treasury as deputy auditor and royal receiver. He returned to Virginia in February, 1688. Meanwhile counterclaims to the office arose from Robert

haps the most outstanding deputy auditors; Stephen Van Cortlandt and Abraham De Peyster are both well known in the annals of the province. In Massachusetts, Paul Dudley, the son of the governor, secured the appointment, but his tenure of office did not begin until after Blathwayt's death.[26]

From the scanty evidence at hand Blathwayt's relations with his deputies seem to have been, in the main, extremely cordial. Only in one case, apparently, was there any hostility; the deputy involved was Blathwayt's own cousin, Robert Gibbs, of Barbados. Blathwayt became convinced of Gibbs's utter dishonesty and accordingly would have none of him, authorizing the governor to dismiss him on short order, but not until he had compelled him to make good his defalcations. Gibbs plied his cousin with sycophantic attentions, announcing pompously, in

Ayleway, who successfully proved that he had been granted the office of auditor for life by Charles II, in 1677. A legal controversy followed, in which Byrd trusted to the assistance of Blathwayt and John Povey. They could not prevent the attorney-general from upholding Ayleway's claim, but, together with Micajah Perry, they helped Byrd to buy out Ayleway.

The stand of the attorney-general is the more interesting since the Lords of Trade had decided a few years earlier that the Virginia auditor was to be appointed in precisely the same way as the other deputy auditors; it was a clear case of defiance of their wishes, although, of course, Ayleway's appointment antedated the creation of Blathwayt's office.

Byrd was willing to pay as much as £300 to Ayleway and hoped that Blathwayt and Povey were men of sufficient influence, so that with their assistance he could conclude the matter "without incurring any danger from the law against purchasing offices." (*The Writings of Colonel William Byrd*, pp. xxiii–xxv; *Cal. S. P. Col.*, 1685–1688, p. 477; 1689–1692, pp. 39, 69, 70, 72.)

Another Virginian, William Fitzhugh, hoped to be Bacon's successor, desiring the office because it was so remunerative. (*The Virginia Magazine of History*, II, 125.)

[26] He owed his appointment to Blathwayt, however, as his father's correspondence indicates. (*Mass. Hist. Coll.*, 6th ser., III, 551; the elder Dudley to Blathwayt, February 15, 1706; *Cal. Treas. Papers*, 1714–1719, p. 387.)

one of his letters, that he had named his infant son "Blathwayt"—but to no avail.[27]

Under ordinary circumstances, Blathwayt was very solicitous for his deputies' welfare and exceedingly patient with their mistakes. Young William Bladen, a deputy in Maryland (appointed, as Blathwayt rather naïvely admitted, because the youth's father had recommended him so highly),[28] met with the kindest of treatment, even when he sent in accounts so bad that the Lord Treasurer threatened a process if they were not amended. For Bladen's guidance Blathwayt drew up a form, according to which the accounts were to be made out. It was simple enough; first was to come the list of charges, then that of discharges; the whole was to be signed first by the collectors, then by the deputy auditor, and finally by the governor.[29] It seems incredible that Blathwayt should have borne with the youth's stupidity. There was probably a money motive, though Blathwayt always had a warm spot in his heart for young men without experience and enjoyed adopting a fatherly attitude. To Spofferth, in Bermuda, he wrote the friendliest of letters when the latter gave illness as an excuse for not sending in his accounts. He expressed his keen desire to retain him in office and did so, although Spofferth's illness continued for four years and ultimately proved fatal.[30]

[27] The collector of the casual revenue had deposited £500 in prize money with Gibbs, and Governor Granville had turned over to him £2000 in fines, which Gibbs had apparently turned to his own use! For this material and for letters indicative of his blandishments, see Huntington MSS., Blathwayt Papers relating to Barbados; letters of 1704 and 1705.

[28] We are led to think that the recommendation must have been monetary in its inducement.

[29] Treas. 64:89, ff. 126–128, 164–165.

[30] Huntington MSS., Blathwayt Papers relating to Antigua, Bermuda, etc., 1669–1709; various letters to and from Spofferth are to be found. *Cal. S. P. Col.*, 1706–1708, p. 667; Governor Bennet to the Board of Trade, February 10, 1708.

Blathwayt was always willing to secure for his deputies other appointments, as we have already seen in the case of Archibald Carmichael, of Barbados, for whom he obtained the office of naval officer, in 1687. Isaac Addington, of Massachusetts, who was also secretary of the province, owed both his appointments to Blathwayt.[31] After the union of New Hampshire and Massachusetts Bay, under Bellomont, Addington's province was extended to the former colony. Only one other deputy auditor served two colonies simultaneously: George Clarke, of New York, who also had the appointment in New Jersey, since the two provinces were under the same governor. The discredited Robert Gibbs's request to be made naval officer, collector of the casual revenue, customs commissioner, and member of the council met with a negative response from Blathwayt—but not because the advisability of plural appointments was being questioned. Most of the deputy auditors were also members of the council.

Only one combination of offices did Blathwayt oppose, and that not consistently: the union of the office of collector with that of deputy auditor. This combination seems to have been used in the Leeward Islands, Barbados, Bermuda, and Virginia,[32] and Blathwayt opposed the union only in Virginia. In the other colonies the revenues were so slight as to make the question unimportant.[33]

[31] Blathwayt Papers relating to New Hampshire (Lib. Cong., formerly Phillipps MSS. 35882); letters from Addington, October 4 and 11, 1692.

[32] See *supra*, f.n. 25.

[33] In Virginia, Blathwayt did not advocate any change, however, as long as Byrd I was in office. Two governors supported him in his views—Sir Francis Nicholson and Colonel Nott. (*Cal. S. P. Col.*, 1700, p. 458; 1704–1705, p. 624.) Blathwayt realized that it would be more expensive for Virginia to have two officers, since the salary allotted Byrd, seven and a half per cent. on his collections, would never suffice for two. Nevertheless, when Byrd died late in 1704, Blathwayt and the Treasury recommended the separation. This was effected and remained permanent as long as Blathwayt held office. (Treas. 64:89, ff. 34–40, 265–266) The younger William Byrd became

The receivers of the royal revenue were as much Blathwayt's subordinates as the deputy auditors, although he did not have the same control over their appointments. He did, however, have the power of recommendation. This he used freely, and in doing so, sometimes came into conflict with governors jealous of their right to control the patronage. Thus Governor Cornbury and Blathwayt found themselves working at cross purposes, the former dismissing from office Thomas Byerley, whom the latter had recommended, and replacing him with his own candidate, Peter Fauconnier. Byerley was the third New York collector to be displaced by the governor; his two predecessors, Chidley Brook and Thomas Weaver, had both been dismissed, one by Bellomont, the other by Cornbury. Both had fled to England with their accounts, to present their cases before Blathwayt and the Treasury. They had met with a fairly sympathetic response from the English officials, although in neither case had it led to their reinstatement in office.[34] In Byerley's case, Blathwayt and the Treasury gave him their vigorous support and sent him back to New York with an order to Cornbury to reinstate him.[35] They were convinced of Byerley's honesty and of

receiver, while Dudley Digges secured the deputy auditorship. (*Ibid.*, ff. 277–281.) Three per cent. on collections was the salary first allotted to Byrd, but in 1709 it was increased to five per cent., which was the percentage given the deputy auditor. (*Ibid.*, ff. 400–401.)

[34] Blathwayt audited both Brook's and Weaver's accounts (1699 and 1703) and in the main upheld them, though he criticized both for their lack of specific information with regard to disbursements. Since both sets naturally lacked the proper attestation, the signatures of the governors in council, they were returned, and the governors were instructed to have them checked. Both Bellomont and Cornbury proved very loath to take any further action and apparently never did. (Treas. 64:89, ff. 26–31, 73–76; Huntington MSS., Blathwayt Papers relating to New York, I, II; *Cal. S. P. Col.*, 1696–1697, pp. 487–488, 514, 524, 544; 1699, pp. 5–7; 1700, p. 12; *Cal. Treas. Papers*, 1697–1701/2, pp. 222–224, 449, 541–542.) New York governors, beginning with Fletcher, had the power to dismiss the collector.

[35] Treas. 64:89, f. 320; Huntington MSS., Blathwayt Papers relating to

his good intentions in opposing a thoroughly unscrupulous executive.
There is no evidence to show that Blathwayt ever upheld a receiver who was actually dishonest. The temptations of the office were numerous, and Blathwayt was relieved when the Treasury finally decided to demand security, which royal receivers must take out in England before their appointments were confirmed. Since many of the colonies also insisted on having them take out local security, the expense to the receiver was heavy. William Byrd, the younger, for instance, had to give security of £10,000—£5000 in England and £5000 in Virginia, an excessive amount, against which he protested unavailingly.[36]

Blathwayt frequently threatened processes against the receivers unless they remitted properly attested accounts. Too often his threats evaporated into thin air. Captain Charles Thomas, the royal receiver in Barbados, was a case in point. He sent in accounts which ran from 1698 to 1701, so illegible and unintelligible that neither Blathwayt nor the Treasury could make head or tail of them.[37] He was told to do them over again, but the second set was only a slight improvement on the first, for the inventories of appraisement on goods seized or forfeited were lacking, and the attestations were not in order. Called to ac-

New York, II; Clarke to Blathwayt, November 28, 1705; *Cal. Treas. Papers, 1702–1707*, p. 354; *Cal. S. P. Col.*, 1706–1708, pp. 622–623; Osgood, *The American Colonies in the 18th Century*, II, 80.

36 Treas. 64:89, ff. 247–248; *Cal. Treas. Papers, 1702–1707*, p. 417; *Cal. S. P. Col.*, 1704–1705, p. 624. The amount demanded, of course, depended on the collections in each colony; Virginia's was accordingly very high. The order was issued in 1704, under Lord Godolphin's vigorous administration of the Treasury; it was simply an indication of the general stringent policy which the trade act of 1696 had ushered in. Governors and customs collectors were under bond for the strict enforcement of the Acts of Trade.

37 Thomas collected only the casual revenue. For Blathwayt's and Godolphin's letters of reprimand, see Treas. 64:89, ff. 72–73.

count, Captain Thomas shifted the responsibility, first to
his two deputies and finally to a clerk who was dead.
What Gibbs, the deputy auditor, had been doing in the
meantime, does not appear, but in 1704, Blathwayt wrote
to him, instructing him to threaten Thomas with an
ouster. Gibbs reported that nothing better could be expected of Thomas, who was overburdened with work—
presumably his "arduous" duties as prize officer, an office of which Gibbs was exceedingly eager to relieve him.[38]
Such a tale could hardly have found credence in Whitehall. But Thomas was dead before a third set of accounts
could be procured. It was a clear case of Blathwayt's inability to make the system work, and his efforts to get results from Thomas' successor (Samuel Barwick, his own
kinsman) were no more successful.[39]

Samuel Trott, the collector in Bermuda, continued to
cause Blathwayt trouble, although, according to Randolph, the fault lay with the governors. In 1690, Governor
Robinson reported the following cheerful news to Shrewsbury: "I can give you still no account of the revenue, as
I can get no satisfactory accounts from the collector,
Samuel Trott. It is thought that he has spent it."[40] A suit
was accordingly commenced against Trott, who raised a
tremendous outcry—though he forthwith produced ac-

---

[38] Add. MSS. 38714, ff. 107–108; Treas. 64:89, ff. 57–58; Huntington
MSS., Blathwayt Papers relating to Barbados; correspondence between
Gibbs and Blathwayt, May, 1704.

[39] Colonel Wiltshire was appointed to succeed Thomas on Blathwayt's
recommendation, but he died very shortly thereafter, whereupon Barwick
took his place. The latter was a man of substance and the son of a former
deputy governor of the island. In January, 1719, we find that he was suspended from the council for failure to make up his accounts with the deputy
auditor. He was only restored in 1728, when he had at last closed his accounts. (Add. MSS. 38712, f. 75; Treas. 64:89, ff. 296–304, 329–330, 421;
Cal. S. P. Col., 1708–1709, pp. 124–125; Acts Privy Council, Colonial, 1720–
1745, p. 190.)

[40] Cal. S. P. Col., 1689–1692, p. 347; Sir Robert Robinson to Shrewsbury,
secretary of state for the southern province, November 17, 1690.

counts, which Richier refused to accept.[41] Several years later, Trott declared before the Bermudian council that the only reason he had been threatened with a process was because a bribe had been given by Governor Richier to three members of the Board of Trade—Shrewsbury, the Earl of Bridgewater, and the Earl of Stamford. When brought to book by Governor Goddard, Richier's successor, who declared that such noblemen were incapable of being bribed, Trott retorted resentfully that at any rate a bribe had been thrown into Blathwayt's office.[42] Neither the fact of the case nor its outcome is clear, for both are obscured by personal politics and animosities.[43]

Blathwayt's zeal for the king's revenue caused him to press the examination of William Byrd I's accounts, after the latter's death in 1704. Blathwayt was unquestionably convinced of Byrd's integrity, but the local situation in Virginia required the investigation. Charges had come to England from a faction headed by Commissary Blair and bitterly hostile to Governor Nicholson, that while the latter had been sending in with commendable regularity Byrd's accounts, not a one had been seen by the council. Since considerable sums, both in quit-rents and the two shillings revenue, were involved, the executors were required to open Byrd's books for public investigation. To assist in the work, Blathwayt ordered his deputy in New York, George Clarke, to proceed to Virginia.[44]

[41] His accounts were not accepted by Richier, hence the suit continued, although Trott was dismissed from office by Governor Goddard and a nephew of that official installed in his place. (Goodrick, *Edward Randolph*, VII, 612.) Randolph charged all three governors of Bermuda (Robinson, Richier, and Goddard) with thefts of the royal revenue.

[42] Huntington MSS., Bridgewater Collection, Vol. 138, Nos. 9725–9727; Trott's affirmations and various attestations, June, 1697.

[43] Goodrick, *Edward Randolph*, VII, 586–587, 612; Randolph examined Trott's books in 1699 and rose vigorously to his defense. Trott by that time was dead.

[44] *Cal. S. P. Col.*, 1704–1705, pp. 91, 403–406; *Journal of the Board of*

The royal receivers and collectors may have caused Blathwayt a considerable amount of trouble, but the provincial treasurers caused him far more. The question of whether, in certain colonies, the local levies were subject to royal audit still continued. Some colonies took a very tractable stand in the matter. Thus we find the query raised in Virginia, in 1692: "Whether Mr. Auditor Byrd should audit the duties arising by the imposition on liquors, skins, and furs?" To which the council made the obliging answer: "It is our opinion that if the honorable William Blathwayt, Esquire, Auditor General of Their Majesties Revenue shall empower him to do so, he ought to do it, otherwise not."[45] Maryland, despite the initial objections, consented to allow Blathwayt and his deputy to audit the additional levies granted by the assembly.[46]

In Massachusetts, where the principal revenue was in the nature of grants passed by the assembly and in the control of the provincial treasurer, no question was raised, and under the watchful eye of Governor Dudley the royal audit achieved considerable success. Less favorable was the situation in New Hampshire, where Blathwayt and his deputy encountered as dilatory a lot of provincial treasurers as could well be found. When informed that their original accounts were unsatisfactory, they all protested their unwillingness to draw them up a

Trade, 1704–1708/9, p. 19; Huntington MSS., Blathwayt Papers relating to New York, II; especially Clarke's letter to Blathwayt, November 28, 1705. The investigation resulted in Nicholson's recall.

[45] Executive Council of Colonial Virginia, Journal, I, 530; April 21, 1692. Ordinarily, however, the accounts contained nothing more than the quitrents and the two shillings revenue.

[46] Treas. 64:89, ff. 17–20; George Plater's accounts for the two years ending December 11, 1697. For such additional levies, of course, both in Virginia and Maryland, the collector and deputy auditor were equally responsible to the council and assembly if those bodies cared to audit their accounts. See also a statement by the Virginia agent, Henry Hartwell (Cal. S. P. Col., 1696–1697, pp. 606–608, 641–646).

second time or to secure the necessary attestation by the governor in council. The combined efforts of Blathwayt and Dudley ultimately forced from them at least a show of obedience.[47]

In Jamaica, the question seems never to have arisen, and when additional levies were granted by the assembly, as they were from time to time, these were collected by the royal receiver, and a statement of them was included in his accounts. Apparently the island did not have a provincial treasurer apart from the royal receiver. Much the same situation existed in Bermuda, where the collector seems to have held himself responsible for all collections of revenue. The Bermudian assembly, however, insisted on its right of audit.[48]

In the Leeward Islands, Barbados, and New York, Blathwayt encountered his real difficulties. Neither of the West Indian colonies was convinced that England was serious in demanding that they account to Blathwayt for the levies which the assemblies granted. Barbados continued to regard the treasurer as peculiarly a local official, in charge of local revenues. Thus Governor Kendall wrote in 1691: "You will perceive that there is an act annually passed here for levying an excise for repair of the fortifications and for other uses. The appointment of a treasurer under this act has given me great trouble, and will give me the like every year unless you intervene. The as-

---

[47] Treas. 64:89, ff. 94, 158–159; Blathwayt MSS. relating to New Hampshire (Lib. Cong., formerly Phillipps MSS. 11568); *New Hampshire Provincial, State, and Town Papers*, 1696–1722, Vol. II, Pt. I, 472–473, 571, 572, 573–575; *Cal. S. P. Col.*, 1706–1708, pp. 774–777. The accounts involved ran from 1694 to 1702; the treasurers who were being questioned were George Jaffrey, Major William Vaughan, and Samuel Penhallow. Their grievance, however, was not the royal audit in theory, so much as the fact that as the deputy auditor, Isaac Addington, lived in Boston, they were expected to make the trip to him in person with their accounts.

[48] *Cal. S. P. Col.*, 1706–1708, p. 667; Governor Bennet to the Board of Trade, explaining the assembly audit, February 10, 1708.

sembly claims this appointment as absolutely its own. The council says that it lies with the governor, council and assembly equally. I hope that the king will empower me to nominate the treasurer in the future. The assembly takes themselves to be notable politicians, and some coxcombs have made them believe that they have as many privileges as the Commons of England.''[49]

A constitutional issue was at stake, and the struggle in Barbados over the appointment of the treasurer continued throughout Blathwayt's day. Blathwayt reiterated his demand that the annual levies be accounted for to him, but he made no headway and never brought the matter to an issue.[50]

Governors of the Leeward Islands continued to take it as a matter for surprise that Blathwayt should demand an account of the assembly levies. Governor Codrington reported to Blathwayt in 1696: ''But the accounts from the treasurer is yet a new thing to them, although your new Deputy Auditor tells me he believes he apprehends you and has taken upon him to transmit you the accounts of disposals of the several sums of sugar and money raised by the Councils and Assemblies within my government since my being chief governor, as soon as it is to be accomplished, he being at present Treasurer of Nevis, and I doubt not but he will effect it to your satisfaction.''[51] Despite this, Governor Parke acted, in 1707, as though

---

[49] *Cal. S. P. Col.*, 1689–1692, p. 405; Kendall to the Lords of Trade, April 4, 1691.

[50] In 1710, the struggle between the council and the assembly over the way in which the treasurer was to be appointed still continued, the council making the repeated charge that the lower house tolerated dishonest treasurers in office. (*Ibid.*, 1704–1705, pp. 744–746; 1710–1711, pp. 115–117, 180–183.) The council threw out two excise bills because they objected to the assembly's choice of a treasurer.

[51] Add. MSS. 9727, f. 179; Codrington's letter of September 1, 1696, in response to Blathwayt's letters of inquiry, February 17, April 20 and 21, 1696.

the treasurers of the Leeward Islands were not responsible to Blathwayt. When instructed that he must hold them to account, he wrote, "As to the treasurer of Antigua he tells me he accounts with the assembly every year and has his discharge and is not obliged to have whole books transcribed. If I will be at the expense of doing of it I may which would cost me in this place at least fifty pounds."[52]

Governor Parke gave the reason for much of the laxity when he pointed out the relatively tremendous outlay in time and money which the accounts required.   Nevertheless, some of the treasurers in the islands did attempt to send a few accounts of the annual or biennial levies. Even Penny, treasurer of Antigua, drew up some, running from September, 1704 to September, 1705; but at that point his courage and zest seem to have failed him.[53] Just after Blathwayt's death, a series of accounts for all four islands was sent to his successor, Horatio Walpole.[54]

In New York, a battle royal arose over the question of the treasurer's responsibility to Blathwayt. The story is only one aspect of the province's complicated financial history during this period, an account of which has been presented with great clarity by Professor Osgood.[55] The struggle was constitutional rather than financial—a question of the royal prerogative against the rights of the provincial assembly. Into it was injected a party bitterness made so venomous by the Leislerian conflict that it

[52] C.O. 153:10, f. 208; August 7, 1708; see also ff. 181–183; *Cal. S. P. Col.* 1706–1708, pp. 567–569, 649–650.

[53] C.O. 152:6, f. 49; C.O. 153:9, ff. 267–269; C.O. 154:4, f. 140; *Journal of the Board of Trade*, 1704–1708/9, p. 260. Some accounts were sent from Nevis also which ran from 1702 to 1705. (*Ibid.*)

[54] C.O. 152:13, Nos. 26, 27, 28; C.O. 10:4; the accounts, which run roughly from 1713 to 1719, resemble those which Stapleton sent over in 1683. Deficits were more common than balances. They were transmitted on August 29, 1720.

[55] Osgood, *The American Colonies in the 18th Century*, I, 240–247, 258, 278–279, 281; II, 67–85, 95, 100–115, 412–425.

is almost impossible to tell which actions of the assembly
were prompted by factional hatreds, which by high constitutional resolve. Blathwayt's connection with the appointment of the hated Governor Fletcher made his name
a term of opprobrium among the Leislerites, who took up
the cause of Governor Bellomont. New York's unhappy
experience with royal collectors such as Santen, Brook,
and Weaver, had convinced many of the citizens that the
province was better able to administer its finances than
were the crown agents. Blathwayt's dismissal of Abraham De Peyster, his deputy auditor, was regarded as a
deliberate insult by the political group of which De Peyster was a prominent member. The appointment of
George Clarke, Blathwayt's cousin, as De Peyster's successor, did nothing to allay their resentment. Thomas
Byerley, who replaced Weaver, was an Englishman, and
being regarded as Blathwayt's tool, he met with little
favor. The assembly decided, therefore, to make political
capital out of the acute financial situation which confronted the province, and thereby to nullify the position
of both the deputy auditor and collector. In this they had
the support of the wretched Lord Cornbury, who hated
both men.

As a direct blow at Blathwayt, the assembly announced
that the colony could not afford to pay him a salary and
was under no obligation to do so.[56] They then proclaimed
their willingness to vote appropriations to make up the
deficit under which the province was laboring, provided
the revenue raised could be under the control of a treasurer named by themselves. The proposal, however, failed
in the council, which was already hotly contesting its right
to amend money bills. In 1706, however, Cornbury came
with a proposal which he trusted would meet with the consent of both the assembly and the council. He stated that

[56] *Infra*, pp. 454–455.

he had secured royal authority to allow the legislature to appoint a treasurer to collect the additional levies, but under the joint control of the assembly, the governor, and the council. The proposal was accepted; bills providing additional revenues, in particular for fortifications, were passed; and Abraham De Peyster was named the treasurer.[57]

Needless to say, the assembly had no intention of having De Peyster give account to Blathwayt of that additional revenue, and no accounts were sent in. Moreover, the position of the royal collector was distinctly imperiled. In less than three years, the revenue act, out of which the regular expenses of the government were paid, was to expire.[58] Under a new act providing for the civil list—if, indeed, one were passed—into whose hands would the collection of the revenue fall? If the treasurer secured control of it, it left the royal collector in an extremely ignominious position, for he would have only the casual revenue, the quit-rents, and the plantation duty to collect.

The threatened impasse occurred in 1709. The old revenue act expired, and the assembly refused to pass another, preferring instead annual grants under local control. Governor Hunter endeavored to effect a compromise, whereby the receiver would be allowed to collect the revenue but would be required to make monthly statements to the governor and would be equally responsible to that official and to the assembly. The assembly, however, was obdurate. The situation became so desperate that Blathwayt and the Board of Trade fell back upon the solution,

---

[57] Osgood, *The American Colonies in the 18th Century*, II, 71–74.

[58] In 1693, Fletcher had secured the passage of a five-year revenue act, which in 1699 was extended until 1709. (*Cal. of Hist. MSS. in the Office of the Secretary of State of New York*, 1664–1776, p. 236; *Cal. S. P. Col.*, 1699, p. 257.)

sponsored by the Privy Council, of having a bill introduced into parliament providing a standing revenue for New York. Nothing, however, came of this proposal, for parliament rose before it could be introduced.[59]

In 1714, however, Hunter succeeded in having a temporary compromise made; revenue acts were passed to run at longest for two years, but they settled nothing, since certain of the revenues were to be controlled by the royal collector and others by the treasurer, while only the former was to be responsible to Clarke and Blathwayt. Hunter succeeded in having some of these acts extended for five years, but they were unsatisfactory to the Board of Trade, which contrived to have them disallowed.[60] Matters were at this point when Blathwayt died. Within a few years the question was threshed out, through the vigorous efforts of Clarke, Walpole, and Hunter's successor, Governor Burnet, who claimed that he risked his official position in order to vindicate the royal audit.[61]

During the years from 1689 to 1717, Blathwayt's interest in increasing the casual revenues and the quit-rents continued. As far as the former revenues were concerned, his efforts were more or less futile. Usually the reports on them were like the elder Byrd's report of 1690: ''I have

[59] Cal. S. P. Col., 1710–1711, pp. 403–404, 424; 1712–1714, pp. 167–168, 174.

[60] Osgood, The American Colonies in the 18th Century, II, 101–103; N. Y. Col. Docs., V, 178.

[61] Osgood, The American Colonies in the 18th Century, II, 108, 111–114, 412–414; N. Y. Col. Docs., V, 764–766; Burnet's letter to the Duke of Newcastle, November 17, 1725. De Peyster's executors were forced to open his books to Clarke for the latter's inspection. By the compromise act of 1723, which was more truly a victory for the English government, Clarke was to have the right to audit the annual revenues, even though they were collected by the treasurer, and to audit the accounts in arrears since 1709. In 1725, in making his report to Walpole, Clarke stated that while his office was generally unpopular in New York, there were certain people who upheld its continuance. (Osgood, II, 412–425; N. Y. Col. Docs., V, 545–548, 770; Assembly Journal, I, 452, 454, 459, 467, 468, 481.)

several small bills for composition of escheats, but cannot yet get anything considerable in, but (God willing) all I can get shall be brought to the next year's account, as also some small fines which yet stand out.''[62] In Maryland, the casual revenue derived from fines and forfeitures in five years, 1692 to 1697, netted no more than £220, collected in money, and 27,780 pounds of tobacco, worth about £83.6.9. —in all, £303.6.9.[63] In Jamaica the casual revenue rarely amounted to as much as £500 per annum, and it was always extremely variable. In New York it was frequently no more than £60. Governor Parke reported from the Leeward Islands, in 1707, that the casual revenue collector had taken in not a farthing since his (Parke's) arrival in the island.[64] Even in Barbados, the hopes which had been entertained for an increase in the casual revenue proved disappointing. Up to 1702, a balance was reported which was often as high as £1377, but the peculations of Thomas and his successors reduced the balance to very near the vanishing point.[65] In 1714, when Blathwayt made a general report to the Treasury, he stated that the casual revenue of the island did not exceed £200 per annum.[66]

Little improvement could be reported in the quit-rents of New York or Jamaica. In the former, the early land system was too deeply imbedded to admit the successful introduction of quit-rents, and the lavish land grants made by governors like Fletcher rendered matters more difficult, even though, as in Fletcher's case, most of these grants were ultimately rescinded. Blathwayt did little to

---

[62] Porlock MSS.; Byrd to Blathwayt, July 30, 1690. From this it would seem that Virginia intended to obey the order in council of 1689 with regard to the disposition of the casual revenue accounts, but the subsequent accounts from Byrd do not seem to have included them.

[63] Treas. 64:89, ff. 49–50.

[64] *Cal. S. P. Col.*, 1706–1708, pp. 567–569; October 22, 1707.

[65] Treas. 64:89, ff. 45, 79; 64:90, ff. 34–37.

[66] *Cal. Treas. Papers*, 1708–1714, pp. 573–575.

insure the successful collection of quit-rents beyond giving what encouragement he could to governors, such as
Hunter, who were interested in bringing about an improvement.[67]

For Jamaica, Blathwayt harped constantly on the need
of a satisfactory and complete rent roll. The steps he had
advised in 1683, with regard to the acceptance of Governor Lynch's plan for sub-collectors under the royal receiver, led to an increase of the quit-rents up to 1691.[68]
The devastation caused by the earthquake in the island in
June, 1692, threw everything into confusion again, and
the accounts showed no real improvement until 1703,
when the assembly decided that quit-rents were to be paid
up within a year, on pain of forfeiture.[69]

Blathwayt never ceased to deplore the laxity of the
land system in Jamaica, although he seems to have been
helpless to effect any change in it. Through his deputy
auditor and the royal receiver, he was familiar with its
details, and, in 1709, on the request of the Board of Trade,
he made a fairly elaborate report.[70] In an earlier report
he stated: "Individuals take up large tracts of land in
Jamaica and have since the time of the first settlement
and are permitted so to do provided they develop the land,

[67] Bond, *The Quit-Rent System, etc.*, pp. 254–272; *N. Y. Col. Docs.*, V,
179–180; *Cal. Treas. Papers*, 1714–1719, pp. 462, 471.

[68] Treas. 64:88, f. 379.

[69] Bond, *The Quit-Rent System, etc.*, pp. 363–364; *Cal. S. P. Col.*, 1693–
1696, p. 597; 1702–1703, p. 564. The revenue act passed in 1704, however,
discharged the payment of quit-rents unpaid at Michaelmas, 1692, on account of the earthquake and the subsequent loss of the records. (*Cal. S. P.
Col.*, 1704–1705, pp. 147, 241; Board of Trade letter, August 25, 1704, asking
to have the provision explained since "the loss of the Receiver General's
books of accounts and of all papers relating to quit rents by the earthquake
does not seem unto us a sufficient reason for such a discharge.")

[70] *Cal. S. P. Col.*, 1708–1709, pp. 500, 506–507. Blathwayt had been asked
by the Board of Trade how much land was available for settlement in
Jamaica, since they were making arrangements for the migration thither of
some of the German "Palatines," who were refugees.

and are exempt from quit-rents. But better track of the state of land should be kept. It would be better if more places than Port Antonio were settled and fortified. Lands of Earl of Carlisle and Sir Thomas Lynch ought to be made liable to quit-rents—or forfeitures follow. The Proprietors not needy persons, no excuse for not developing their lands.''[71]

The quit-rents of Virginia caused Blathwayt most concern, since they represented by far the largest potential revenue. The revenue derived from them differed from that in New York or Jamaica, in that it was regarded as a special fund which could be issued only under royal warrant. The English idea—which was also Blathwayt's—was that it should be reserved for emergencies. Thus Blathwayt stated that the existence of such a fund in 1676 might very well have prevented Bacon's Rebellion, since the province would then have had ready money with which to suppress the Indian attacks out of which the rebellion grew.[72] He believed that the quit-rents should be reserved for local use, although, in 1697, he was not above recommending that they be used for the payment of his own clerk, John Povey, since there were no funds available at the time in the English Exchequer.[73] In 1709, he

[71] Huntington MSS., Blathwayt Papers relating to America, 1681–1741; draft of a report undated, but, from the context, drawn up about the time of the Darien ventures.

[72] Treas. 64:89, ff. 236–239, 243–244. This was stated in the report which John Povey handed in to the Treasury in 1705. Blathwayt was so firm a believer in the efficacy of quit-rents that he advised that they be introduced again into St. Kitts. (Hist. MSS. Com., Portland MSS., n.s. V, 108; recommendation to Lord Oxford, secretary of state, in 1711.) Both the Codringtons approved of this. (Cal. S. P. Col., 1689–1692, p. 540; 1693–1696, pp. 680–681; 1702–1703, p. 157; Bond, The Quit-Rent System, etc., pp. 356–357.

[73] Add. MSS. 38703, f. 43. The amount to be paid was £1000, in three annual installments. The revenue from the quit-rents was remitted to England. In 1705, as a result of the investigation of Byrd's accounts, the order was issued that the proceeds of the two shillings revenue were likewise to be sent

stated that the cost of drawing the boundary line between Virginia and North Carolina should be borne by the quit-rents.[74]

When the two shillings revenue declined in Virginia after 1689, largely as a result of the war and the deprecia-tion in the price of tobacco, Blathwayt was very loath to see the quit-rent fund used to make up the deficit. Such a use, he declared, was not in accordance with its original purpose. He recommended, however, in accordance with the wishes of the Virginian government, that some of the quit-rents be applied to the erection of William and Mary College, but on the report to the Treasury appears a mar-ginal note which may very well be his: "The solicitor for Virginia knows well that the assembly of Virginia can levy what taxes it pleases for the support of a college and for the better payment of the clergy without encroaching on the king's revenue."[75] He never ceased to argue that Virginia must find some other way out of financial dilem-mas than by dipping into the quit-rents, and he opposed even his good friend, the younger Byrd, who in 1715 peti-tioned the Treasury that Virginia be allowed to dispose of the quit-rents as she herself saw fit. The Treasury agreed with Blathwayt, but the Board of Trade favored the peti-tion.[76]

to England, but through the assistance of Blathwayt and Micajah Perry, according to Blakiston, this ruling was rescinded as early as January, 1706. (*Virginia Magazine of History*, XIX, 14–15.)

[74] Treas. 1:112, f. 114; Bond, *The Quit-Rent System, etc.*, p. 410. In 1710, Hunter, who was going out to Virginia as governor, was captured by the French. Blathwayt recommended that he be reimbursed for his losses out of the quit-rents. (Treas. 64:90, ff. 15–17.)

[75] *Cal. S. P. Col.*, 1689–1692, p. 672; also Treas. 64:88, ff. 346–363; 64: 89, ff. 414–419; 64:90, ff. 26–27, 31.

[76] By 1712, the quit-rent fund had become so depleted as a result of Eng-land's practice of dipping into it for military purposes, that an order from the Treasury that £3000 be transmitted to England could not be honored. It

The method of collecting the quit-rents and of enforcing their payment caused more difficulty in Virginia than in Jamaica, as the instructions to the governors disclose. Both Nott and Spotswood were ordered to see that the penalty of forfeiture be strictly enforced in cases where persons securing land failed, at the end of three years, to have three acres out of every fifty settled and cultivated. With this plan Blathwayt was wholly in sympathy. On the question of how the tobacco in which the quit-rents were paid was to be collected and disposed of, he took a less resolute stand. Under Nicholson, an attempt was made to replace the ancient practice of disposing of the tobacco by private sale (that is, auction by "inch of candle") by the more businesslike method of public sale. Why Blathwayt and the English government in general failed to support this plan is not clear, but in 1711 Blathwayt certainly stated that the tobacco was still sold by "inch of candle."[77] It is likely that he was influenced by the Byrds, who were both as far as is known, opposed to a change which affected adversely their profits.

Blathwayt likewise opposed Spotswood's vigorous steps to improve the collection of the quit-rents by making the sheriffs, who acted as the receiver's deputies, personally responsible for their collection, instead of depending on deputies of their own. Spotswood ordered—and he was upheld by the council though Byrd II made rigorous objections—that the sheriffs should be required personally to attend in designated places to receive the quit-rent tobacco; that they make their payments directly to the receiver; that the tobacco be sold at public auction; and that

was this which led to the Virginian petition and Byrd's resolute plea. (*Spotswood Letters*, I, 154–156, 157–159; *Journal of the Board of Trade, 1715–1718*, pp. 69, 70, 74; Bond, *The Quit-Rent System, etc.*, pp. 240–241; Osgood, *The American Colonies in the 18th Century*, II, 231.)

[77] Bond, *The Quit-Rent System, etc.*, p. 229; Osgood, *The American Colonies in the 18th Century*, II, 216–217.

a complete rent roll be drawn up.[78] This program was sufficiently businesslike to have won Blathwayt's approval, but instead we find him writing to Spotswood: "I am sorry that I have been obliged of late to commit neglect which has been occasioned by my indisposition. . . . I have withal received several accounts from my deputy and of late some mention . . . [illegible] inconveniences happened by a new method of taking those accounts of the quit rents and without advantage to the Crown, the difference of the advance of that revenue arising lately from the price of tobacco rather than the method of collecting and accounting. . . . [illegible] I desire that we may recur to the ancient method which 'tis averred was more easy and no less advantageous which if you shall judge otherwise upon further examination you will please to send me your reasons for the new method which I may be enabled to lay before the Lords Commissioners of the Treasury who have been seeking to present the condition of the colony to be such as to procure His Majesty freedom for disposing of what is remaining of the quit rents in the receiver general's hand toward the supplying the 2 . . . [illegible but referring of course to the two shillings revenue] with what is deficient on that account."[79]

The date of this letter is March 2, 1716, after the disagreement between Spotswood, Byrd, and Ludwell had reached its climax, although before Blathwayt had heard of the governor's removal of Ludwell as deputy auditor or of his stand on the reappointment of Byrd, whose appointment as collector had come to an end with the death

[78] Bond, pp. 230–231. Spotswood also ordered the sheriff's fee cut from ten to five per cent. on his collections. Blathwayt had upheld these very innovations in his earlier reports to the Treasury. (*Cal. S. P. Col.* 1689–1692, p. 601; Treas. 64:89, ff. 237–239.)

[79] Add. MSS. 38712, f. 25; letter draft in Blathwayt's own hand. For Spotswood's response, see *Spotswood's Letters*, II, 172–175; July 3, 1716.

of Queen Anne.[80] It seems incredible that Blathwayt, who up to this time had showed the gravest concern for the improvement of the quit-rents, should have expressed an opinion such as this. His failing health as well as his affection for Byrd may have been in part responsible for it, and also for the high-handed way in which he ordered Spotswood to discontinue his new method of collecting the rent, an assumption of authority on Blathwayt's part that defied both the Treasury and the Privy Council. Yet he did not wish to oppose Spotswood too strongly, for he said he would instruct Ludwell to be more prompt in his response to the governor's instructions. Ludwell, who in the meantime had been ordered by Spotswood to improve his bookkeeping, had denied that he was required to take orders from Spotswood, asserting that he was governed instead by the ancient practices of Virginia and by the instructions of Blathwayt and the Treasury.[81]

The question of Blathwayt's right to control and audit another troublesome source of revenue, that of the four and a half per cent., came up for consideration early in the century. This unpopular levy had been causing both the islands and England a great deal of difficulty since the settlement of 1684, in which Blathwayt had played so large a part.[82] It was not until 1702 that the matter came up again for investigation, and then only on an order of the house of commons demanding that henceforward an annual account of the revenue of the four and a half per cent. be given them. Local feeling in the islands had been running strong, particularly against the provision, made by act of parliament in 1697, that the proceeds of the revenue be applied to the expenses of the royal household and

[80] Blathwayt favored Byrd's reappointment, but the Treasury ignored his recommendation, appointing James Roscoe instead. (Treas. 1:189, f. 16; 64:90, ff. 100–101.)

[81] Add. MSS. 38712, f. 25.   [82] *Supra*, pp. 169–170.

that other resources be found for the support of the islands.[83] Barbados had petitioned that the duty be used as originally designed, to which the Board of Trade had answered somewhat angrily that the king spent far more on Barbados than the four and a half per cent. produced.[84] Consequently no change was immediately effected.

In June, 1701, the Treasury requested Blathwayt to give an account of the duty, whereupon he produced a statement of the receipts for 1700. This indicated that the gross amount collected in the two colonies was £10,234.3.2., showing that the four and a half per cent. had increased considerably since the days when it had been farmed out.[85] The revenue was examined also by the parliamentary commissioners of accounts, and a wholesale investigation was made. As a result, the order for expending the duty on the royal household was revoked, and the fund was again applied to the current expenses and the defense of the islands.[86]

Meanwhile, in 1703, the Treasury instructed Blathwayt to bring in his accounts for audit and declaration before them.[87] He forthwith wrote to the controller of the customs that he wanted an account of the proceeds of the four and a half per cent. revenue for 1701 and 1702, or any other accounts that had been received, proof that in the meantime no duplicate copies of them had been com-

[83] 9 and 10 William III, c. 23; *Cal. S. P. Col.*, 1701, pp. 111–112. Up to 1689 the duty had been remitted to the English Exchequer, usually in tobacco rather than in specie. In November, 1689, an order in council was issued, directing the retention of the duty in the islands, where it was put under the charge of Governor Codrington and was designed for military purposes primarily. It proved inadequate for all the demands made on it, and in January, 1692, the order of 1689 was revoked. (Treas. 64:88, ff. 378–379; *Cal. S. P. Col.*, 1689–1692, p. 171; 1693–1696, pp. 216, 221–222, 253.)

[84] *Cal. S. P. Col.*, 1697–1698, pp. 123–124, 233.

[85] Treas. 64:89, f. 45.

[86] *Ibid.*, ff. 78–79; *Cal. S. P. Col.*, 1702, pp. 188, 189, 243–246.

[87] Treas. 64:89, f. 78; order of March 9, 1703.

ing to him from the collectors.[88] He also sent a letter to his friend, Lord Halifax, auditor of the exchequer, saying that, in pursuance of the Treasury's direction, he wanted an account of all money from the four and a half per cent. brought into the Exchequer from 1701 to 1702.[89] To the receiver general of the customs he wrote on June 4, 1703, calling for the same reports.[90] In October, 1703, he repeated his requests to these three officials, this time calling for additional accounts from Christmas, 1702.[91]

These accounts were apparently transmitted, but in July, 1703, Holt, the controller of the customs, was called before the parliamentary commissioners of accounts to explain the procedure with regard to the audit of the four and a half per cent.[92] He was asked how far Blathwayt was concerned with the revenue, to which he responded that he did not know that Blathwayt had anything at all to do with it. He had never written to Blathwayt until two months before, when he had received the latter's request for a statement of the accounts. He said that he felt it would make a great deal of unnecessary trouble to bring Blathwayt into the accounting, since he had nothing to do with the revenue. Blathwayt nevertheless went ahead with his plans, though obviously with a somewhat unwonted timidity, since, as Holt stated, he was not familiar with the customs office system of accounting or auditing. He wrote to the Treasury on August 9, 1703, that he had prepared a statement of the four and a half per cent. revenue from March 24, 1701, to May 24, 1703, and would

---

[88] *Ibid.*, f. 103; May 24, 1703. [89] *Ibid.*, f. 104; May 25, 1703.
[90] *Ibid.*, f. 106; June 4, 1703. [91] *Ibid.*, f. 134; October 28, 1703.
[92] Add. MSS. 36859, f. 142. Some of the accounts which Holt sent to Blathwayt are to be found in Treas. 64:89, ff. 84–85, 100, 106. There are also some of Holt's computations of the revenue from 1691 to 1700. He complained that some accounts had been lost in transmission, naming those of 1694–1696, 1694–1698 and those since December, 1700. Those for 1694–1696 had been twice lost and sent for a third time.

continue further if they approved of the form he had used.[93] The inference is that he never got as far as a declaration. Walpole stated, many years later, that there had been no accounts of the four and a half per cent. passed since 1684, although some imperfect accounts running from 1684 to 1712 had been delivered to the auditors of the imprest by the controller of the customs.[94]

Clearly both the Treasury and Blathwayt were uncertain as to the latter's obligation to audit the four and a half per cent. revenue. In 1711, Blathwayt said that he was not concerned with it, since it fell to the commissioners of the customs to audit.[95] Nevertheless, in 1721, the Treasury issued instructions to the commissioners of the customs, directing them to order the collectors to transmit duplicates of their accounts to Walpole.[96] In 1732, the latter, in response to a Treasury order, made a statement on the four and a half per cent. revenue, although the commissioners of the customs also reported on its general condition.[97] In having duplicate copies of these accounts sent to the auditor general, the Treasury may have intended merely to keep him informed in regard to the four and a half per cent. revenue, in the same way as the plantation office was kept informed by the duplicates of the deputy auditor's accounts. As against this the fact that the *vouchers* of the four and a half per cent. disbursements were also ordered sent to the auditor, would indi-

[93] Treas. 64:89, ff. 118–121; August 9, 1703.

[94] *Cal. Treas. Bks. and Papers*, 1739–1741, p. 486; May 26, 1741.

[95] Huntington MSS., Blathwayt Papers relating to America, 1681–1741, no paging; here is to be found the rough draft of the report Blathwayt drew up in 1711.

[96] *Cal. Treas. Papers*, 1720–1728, p. 85; October 10, 1721.

[97] *Cal. Treas. Bks. and Papers*, 1731–1734, pp. 7, 260. The order was issued on January 14, 1731, but Walpole's and the controller's answers did not come in until August and November, 1732. The latter presented some accounts for 1685–1687.

cate that he was meant to have some definite control. The whole situation gives proof of administrative confusion. As long as no actual audit of the fund was enforced, the question of who was ultimately responsible remained more or less academic.

To return now to the main issue. Some of the great changes which were being made in the English constitutional system are reflected in the office of auditor general. The course of the royal audit of the plantation revenues may be traced not only in Blathwayt's correspondence with the colonial officials but also in the reports which he made from time to time to the Treasury and to the parliamentary commissioners of accounts. Blathwayt was summoned at least four times before the parliamentary commissions—in 1691–1692, in 1696, in 1701–1702, and in 1711.[98] His reports, as preserved in his Journal, are of a fairly searching nature, although the first two are less so than the other, perhaps because there was less to report upon, and because Blathwayt at the time had his attention taken up with William III's summer expeditions. The investigation of 1701–1702 was exceedingly thorough, and Blathwayt and his clerks appeared day after day before the commissioners to present the accounts that had come in from the colonies. Blathwayt made no effort in 1702, apparently, to draw up a report as comprehensive as that of 1711, when his accounts and his statement upon them filled a large folio volume. The report of 1702, however, undoubtedly roused the house of commons to investigate the four and a half per cent. duty and the question of the "presents" voted to the governors by the assemblies in the Leeward Islands and Barbados. Trying as the

[98] Treas. 64:88, ff. 378–381 (1692); 444–445 (1696); Treas. 64:89, ff. 63–69 (1702); Treas. 64:90, ff. 39–40, 46–58, 61–68. Blathwayt's account book of 1711 has the full copies of the accounts which he submitted. (See also Add. MSS. 36859, ff. 62, 93, 123, 141–142.)

demands of the commissioners of accounts were, there can be little doubt that their investigations had a wholesome effect and did much to stimulate Blathwayt to activity.

The Treasury used at first to order Blathwayt to report to them whenever they felt so inclined, but after 1689 their demands began to follow closely upon those of the commissioners of accounts. During the administration of Lord Godolphin (1702–1705), especially, the Treasury quickened its interest. A letter issued to Blathwayt on May 1, 1703, by the secretary to the Treasury, ordered him to submit a statement on the plantation revenues every six months and indicated the Treasury's intention of subjecting his office to periodic inspection.[99] It was a reasonable request to make, since semi-annual accounts were demanded from the governors, the deputy auditors, the receivers, and the local treasurers. Such attempts at periodicity were rendered futile by the great distances to be spanned, and by the fact that, as the treasurer of New Hampshire stated several years later, the revenues in some of the provinces were on an annual, not a semi-annual, basis.[100]

Under Godolphin, also, the first attempt since 1684 was made to have accounts declared before the Treasury. Not since Blathwayt made his declaration of the farms of the four and a half per cent. duty in that year, had any such thing been done. It is not clear whether the steps taken in 1703 were the result of the zealous activities of the parliamentary commissioners of accounts, of Godolphin, or of Blathwayt himself, who, since he had been released by the death of William III from making the summer campaigns, had time to apply himself with more vigor to his duties as auditor. At any rate, on the day when the order

[99] Treas. 64:89, ff. 117–118.
[100] *Cal. Treas. Papers*, 1714–1719, p. 387; June 20, 1718.

to make semi-annual reports to the Treasury was issued, Blathwayt was also instructed to declare the accounts of Jamaica, Virginia, Bermuda, Maryland, New York, Massachusetts Bay, and New Hampshire.[101] These accounts were those which Blathwayt had already produced, according to his instructions from the commissioners of accounts, on May 21, 1702; they roughly covered the colonies from 1695, when the commission of 1696 had ended its investigations.[102] Although Blathwayt himself criticized the accounts of the colonies which he presented, they evidently proved satisfactory to the authorities. Whether the actual declaration ever took place is not known, although it seems unlikely, in the absence of any entry of it in the Exchequer records. The Treasury was undoubtedly in earnest in its instructions, for subsequent accounts for

[101] Treas. 64:89, ff. 117–118; May 1, 1703.

[102] *Ibid.*, ff. 61, 63–69. On May 21, 1702, Blathwayt had been ordered to produce the following accounts by ten o'clock on the morning of June 17 :—

> Barbados, Michaelmas, 1690—December 25, 1701.
> Jamaica, Michaelmas, 1695—December 25, 1701.
> Virginia, May 31, 1695—December 25, 1701.
> New York, Michaelmas, 1695—December 25, 1701.
> Maryland, August 22, 1690—December 25, 1701.
> Massachusetts Bay, May 29, 1695—December 25, 1701.
> New Hampshire, May 16, 1695—December 25, 1701.
> Bermuda, August 25, 1689—December 25, 1701.
> Caribbean Islands, March 25, 1691—December 25, 1701.

He was also ordered to give account of any other revenue which might have arisen to the king in the colonies since November 5, 1688. Blathwayt accordingly sent in eight accounts from Jamaica, running semi-annually, from March, 1695, to March, 1700; eight from Massachusetts, from May, 1695, to May, 1701; twenty-six from New York, running quarterly, from Michaelmas, 1695, to midsummer, 1701; accounts for both the quit-rents and the two shillings revenue in Virginia, from 1695 to November, 1701; accounts from Maryland, from 1697 to 1700; accounts of the casual revenue in Barbados from June, 1691, to September, 1694; and certain reports on the four and a half per cent., for ten years, ending 1700. For further accounts from Virginia and New York, running up to 1704, see *ibid.*, ff. 132–136.

some of the provinces, notably Virginia, Jamaica, New York, New Hampshire, Maryland, and Massachusetts for 1702–1703, were ordered prepared for declaration on October 3, 1703.[103] In May, 1704, Blathwayt wrote to the deputy auditor for Massachusetts Bay and New Hampshire: "It will be very fitt that the Receiver General have some agent here in Relation to his Accompts, which are to be declared before the Lord High Treasurer."[104]

From 1705 to 1711, there was an abatement in the Treasury's activities, although Blathwayt was still at his post. In 1710–1711, the office took on renewed life as the result of fresh requests from parliamentary commissioners of accounts. The account book which Blathwayt and his clerks compiled for them in 1711 took two months to prepare, a period twice as long as the commissioners would have allotted him; its existence is proof that Blathwayt had never regarded his office as a sinecure and gives a striking evidence of his prodigious energy. The accounts for all the colonies under his control were included, with the exception of the Leeward Islands, New Jersey, and Maryland. Those from Maryland were omitted, Blathwayt stated, because both of the receivers, Muschamp and Plater, as well as the governor, had recently died. No accounts had been received from Maryland since August, 1703, although he had written for them repeatedly and was awaiting them daily.[105] Conditions in New Jersey were too chaotic for much to have been expected in the way of regular accounting. Scattered among Blathwayt's papers are references to New Jersey accounts sent or to be sent, but in the end all that were received were two years' accounts, from December, 1704, to December, 1706,

103 Treas. 64:89, f. 145; October 29, 1703.
104 *Ibid.*, ff. 157–159; May 20, 1704.
105 Huntington MSS., Blathwayt Papers relating to America, 1681–1741, no paging; comment by Blathwayt in connection with his draft report.

submitted by Fauconnier, Cornbury's appointee as receiver, which George Clarke, deputy auditor, had refused to audit.[106] As to the revenues of the Leeward Islands, Blathwayt reported that he lacked all information. This was his habitual answer regarding them, both to the commissioners of accounts and the Treasury.

Of the accounts rendered in 1711, those of Virginia, Jamaica, and Massachusetts were very comprehensive and included detailed information with regard to receipts and disbursements. Those which Blathwayt presented to the commissioners were probably exact copies of the ones he had received from the colonies, since each had a different form, showing that Blathwayt himself had laid down no uniform rules for drawing them up. The Massachusetts accounts covered nearly two hundred and fifty pages. The Virginia accounts of the quit-rents extended from April, 1701, to April, 1712 (the last year's were addenda), with the exception of the year 1709, which (because of some error on the part of the receiver) had to be sent for again. Blathwayt's clerk had left a gap in the accounts expecting to fill it up when the missing data arrived. In the case of Jamaica, the accounts of 1705–1706 were missing. Blathwayt stated that they had been lost in a shipwreck, and that he had sent for duplicates, which had not yet arrived.[107]

---

[106] *Cal. S. P. Col.*, 1708–1709, pp. 15–17, 516. Cornbury announced to the Board of Trade on July 1, 1708, that he intended to send the accounts, even though Clarke refused to audit them. Ultimately Lovelace sent them to England. The New Jersey assembly asked Fauconnier to let them see his accounts, but he refused, saying that by his deputation he was responsible only to Blathwayt and the Treasury. As a result, the assembly refused to extend the appropriation act, and the province was left without revenue. Osgood, *The American Colonies in the 18th Century*, II, 88–94.

[107] The Virginia accounts for both the quit-rents and the two shillings revenue cover only about forty-five pages. In the case of Massachusetts, the accounts for 1708–1709 for some reason or other were lacking. Blathwayt stated that the Jamaica accounts totaled 69 folio pages, but the final total

The accounts for New York extended only to 1709, when the revenue act expired. The receiver had apparently not bothered to send in the accounts of the quit-rents and the casual revenue since that time. Included in his accounts, however, was an elaborate list of all the ships which had entered the harbor, with detailed data regarding each.[108]

The New Hampshire accounts were nearly complete, extending from 1701 to 1712, with a gap for 1704. No explanation was given for this, but blank pages indicate that Blathwayt was expecting additional statements. Possibly a set had been received and had been returned for lack of proper attestation. The accounts as a whole were confused; obviously they had been drawn up in a hasty and careless fashion by the treasurer, although they had been passed upon by the governor, since they bore his signature.

Those from Bermuda, which ran from 1704 to 1711, were more or less negligible, although they indicated some show of activity on the part of the treasurer, John Tucker. No attempt had been made to list the receipts and disbursements by separate years, both being lumped together as a whole, yet items of expenditure were quite detailed. Small though the revenues of the island were, £271.6.10. had been paid to the London agent of the colony.

For Barbados, Blathwayt had only the accounts of the receiver, Thomas, which were worse than negligible. They consisted of three pages, two of receipts and one of discharges, covering the casual revenue for 1697, 1698, and 1700.[109] Discharges were indicated for 1697 only, and then for but two months, March and June. In partial explana-

in the account book is 111 sheets. (See his draft report, Huntington MSS., Blathwayt Papers relating to America, 1681–1741, no paging.)

[108] Probably included because the receiver was also a naval officer.

[109] For another set of Thomas's notes, the first he sent over, no doubt, and rejected by Blathwayt, see Add. MSS. 38714, ff. 102–106. The two sets of accounts do not tally, although apparently covering the same period.

tion, Blathwayt presented to the Treasury a statement from the island attorney-general, which dwelt upon the irregularities in the Barbadian courts and stated that these were so serious as to prevent any casual revenue accruing from fines and forfeitures.[110] No report on the four and a half per cent. revenue was included, since Blathwayt said he had nothing to do with it.

After 1711, Blathwayt seems to have made only one comprehensive statement on colonial revenues; this was in 1714, when he made a report to the Treasury, very much like his earlier ones. He stated that the object of the audit was to put the revenues of the colonies in such a condition that they would be made to support the entire charge of the government. He listed the various dependencies of England, those colonies which were included within the royal audit as well as those which were not; presented the approximate annual charge of the various colonial governments and their main sources of revenue; and indicated those colonies which were no burden to the crown and those which had a settled revenue.[111] He reviewed the financial situation in New York, where, since 1709, the attitude of the assembly had been ''derogatory to her Majesty's prerogative and authority.'' He also listed the proprietary colonies and described their financial status. He spoke of the negotiations with Penn for the surrender of Pennsylvania, Newcastle, and the Lower Counties, stating that the quit-rents, half of which belonged to the crown, were in arrears from August 24, 1682, the amount owing being equivalent to £6200. Penn had been called upon for this sum, but, as he was treating for the surren-

---

110 Treas. 64:90, ff. 35–37, 61–62.

111 He stated that the only colonies which were not self-supporting were Bermuda, where the governor's salary had to be made up in part from the English Exchequer, and New York, for which he advocated the introduction of a bill into parliament which would provide a standing revenue.

der of the property, there had been "no further prosecution." Should the surrender take place, there would be an annual expense for a governor and other officials, and since the assemblies might refuse to make an allowance, as was the case in New York, the expense to her majesty would be about £1000 per annum.[112] In conclusion, he classified the colonies according to type and drew the usual distinction between royal revenues accruing in the plantations and those which were to be regarded as strictly local in character. His report is an exceedingly clear and succinct statement of colonial finance and of colonial relationships to the crown; it indicates that its compiler was wholly alive to the various problems which confronted England in carrying out the royal audit.[113]

Blathwayt continued to perform his tasks as auditor until within a few weeks of his death. The question of his successor had been settled in October, 1715, when Horatio Walpole had secured a reversionary grant to the office.[114] This was a party arrangement; there is nothing to show that the two men ever met for Blathwayt to explain the

[112] In his earlier reports, Blathwayt had always listed the "proprieties" and the various forms of tribute which the crown required of them—from the Jerseys, with their yearly rental of ten nobles, and the Carolinas with theirs of twenty marks, to Hudson's Bay, with its annual acknowledgement of two beaver skins and Mount Hope with its seven. In 1703, as a part of the general movement at that time, steps had been taken to bring the proprietors to account. Blathwayt's dealings with the Carolina proprietors had been very vigorous. On June 5, 1703, he threatened the lord palatine with a process if he did not make prompt account. In January, 1705, he reported that at least a promise of payment had been made, but that the accounts stood open from 1697. At the same time, he declared that he was threatening the Jersey proprietors with a suit if they did not make up their accounts prior to 1702. (Treas. 64:89, ff. 106, 110, 208.)

[113] For the report of 1714, see *Cal. Treas. Papers*, 1708–1714, pp. 573–575.

[114] *Cal. S. P. Col.*, 1714–1715, p. 296; entry for October 7, 1715. His patent was dated October 15, 1716. (Patent Rolls, 3511, No. 28.) He was sworn before the Privy Council, (September 27) October 8, 1717. *Hist. MSS. Com., Polwarth MSS.*, I, 358.

duties of the office, nor have we any opinion of Blathwayt's on his successor. In August, 1717, Walpole had had news of Blathwayt's illness and was waiting impatiently for the outcome. On August 17, the day following Blathwayt's death (the news of it had not yet reached him), Sir Robert Walpole wrote to a friend: "We have received such accounts of Mr. Blathwait's desperate state of health, that we have reason to apprehend my brother's seat in parliament, to whom the reversion of Mr. Blathwayt's place is granted, may be immediately vacant."[115]

With Blathwayt's death, the first thirty-seven years of the royal audit of plantation revenues came to an end. How much had been accomplished in that period of nearly four decades? More perhaps than might have been expected; less, however, than was necessary if the security of the system was to be attained. The results had been discouraging in the Leeward Islands, Barbados, New York, and New Jersey, but even there some idea of conformity with the practice of royal control had been implanted. At this very time New York was approaching a crisis, in which the royal audit was to receive a vindication. Accounts were also in transit from the Leeward Islands, not of the casual revenue but of the levies granted by the assembly. There was not a colony, however, which was not more or less restive under the system and eager to give some expression of its independence in matters financial. The attitude of the colonial assemblies and of their financial agent, the treasurer, was always to be an uncertain quantity, even in colonies where a permanent revenue had been granted, and where, as in Jamaica, that revenue was in the hands of a royal receiver. Additional levies would always be needed, and the question was

---

[115] Porlock MSS. It is interesting to notice that it was a ministerial office, which called for resignation from parliament.

bound to arise whether the fund was to be under the control of the assembly or the crown.

Not a single problem with regard to the royal audit was settled during Blathwayt's tenure of office. He accomplished one very important thing when he kept the idea of accountability before the various colonies. No colony, however, made any financial gain as a result of his efforts, and it is difficult to see how, with his control of the system so imperfect, he could have done any more than he did. Had the royal receivers been Blathwayt's deputies rather than crown officers, and had the local treasurers been accountable to him, the system might have been workable. Of course, no real pressure could be brought to bear on the local treasurers, and the English administration probably thought that, by Blathwayt's patent, an effective control of the royal receivers had been secured.

Curiously, Blathwayt did not regard the royal audit as a failure, nor did any of the officials to whom he was responsible. They were all unduly hopeful, for the scheme was purely Utopian. Their optimism was more comfortable, if not more wholesome, than the pessimism of a later day.

CHAPTER XII

A SURVEY OF BLATHWAYT'S ADMINISTRA-TIVE METHODS

BLATHWAYT's administrative system was good, but there was nothing novel or original about it. Its value lay in its order, businesslike arrangement, and consistency. Blathwayt followed a method in general use at the time. He had been drilled in the simple duties of a clerk by Thomas Povey, and he had learned the niceties of public correspondence in the office of Sir William Temple. Sir Joseph Williamson and Sir Robert Southwell had put the finishing touches on his administrative technique. His own amazing energy and industry did the rest. Blathwayt had, in fact, the qualities which go to make a good administrator in any age. He was a bureaucrat by temperament and never at home on the political battle field. An impregnable Whitehall, free from the onslaughts of Westminster, would have suited his fancy. He loved order and dreaded the confusion of change. His work was founded on precedent, and he always demanded good authority before diverging from it.

In his neat way of thinking, he pigeonholed ideas; and office files almost automatically took orderly form under his precise manipulation. He never groaned or protested over work dumped on an already over-burdened office, so long as he thought it properly belonged there. He was singularly lighthearted about his duties, though punctilious to the last detail. Even in the days when his office was migratory in Flanders, and he was obliged to travel about bag and baggage with the army ready to take to the rear at the advance of the enemy, his official papers show less petulance and haste than many of those written from the comfortable permanence of Whitehall. His manuscripts rarely display any sign of undue haste. He wrote an excellent hand, very regular and clear, and he had a satisfying sense of the importance of paragraphing, margins, and proper spacing in general. His spelling was consistent in a rather inconsistent age, he knew how to punctuate, and his syntax was good. His imprint on an office was clearly one of quality rather than form. It was not so much what he did as how he did it that made him a better clerk or secretary than some of his associates.

Blathwayt probably never took on the work of an office without doing his best to master its details. Scattered among his papers are copies of the forms of the various official documents which he was called upon to draw up. He occasionally made historical investigations into the duties of his offices. His first correspondence after entering an office usually took the form of requests for information, in particular from Continental correspondents.[1] Even in the busy years of attendance in Flanders, he instructed many of them not to forget that he would welcome books and treatises on military administration or on colonial projects. He seems to have had the perfectly correct impression that he could not do a good job unless he kept up with the times.

It seems strange that, with his knowledge of adminis-

---

[1] For instance, while he was in Conway's office from 1681 to 1683, he deputized his correspondents to execute a variety of literary commissions and to send him any books on trade and plantations which they thought would interest him. (*Supra*, pp. 198–199.) After taking over the war office, he immediately wrote to the English representative in France for copies of French military regulations. (*Supra*, pp. 223–224.) He was equally interested in Prussian and Swedish military manoeuvers.

trative methods and his appreciation of an efficient office system, he should have followed the dubious practice then in vogue of carrying off many of his record books and official papers when he left office. The line of division between what constitute the public archives of state and what the private papers of an official was not so sharply drawn in Blathwayt's time as it is today, but every officeholder was aware that the demarcation existed. Blathwayt observed it as well as, if not better than, his contemporaries. In several instances he turned over the papers of an office to his successor with some formality. In 1681, he acknowledged the receipt of the current files of the secretary of state's office from the clerks of Sir Leoline Jenkins.[2] In 1683, he noted the transfer of similar files to his successor, William Bridgeman, Sunderland's clerk.[3] John Povey turned over to William Popple, in 1696, most of the office books and papers of the Lords of Trade, with the exception of letters addressed personally to Blathwayt.[4] In every instance, the transfer was so far from complete that it would never meet modern requirements, but Blathwayt apparently had no misgivings. In fact, from some of his statements, it is clear that he felt he had done more than his duty and had really handicapped himself by turning over as many of the papers as he did.

In spite of his numerous positions and his long years of service, Blathwayt actually organized only one office, the

[2] Porlock MSS.; Blathwayt received about 184 letters, and many of these he turned over to Sir Leoline Jenkins' estate, in March, 1686. A few, for some reason or other, he reserved for Sir Robert Southwell.

[3] ''Journal of all that Passes in the Office''; entry for January 19, 1684.

[4] Index 8307 and 8308; Popple's list of the books and papers he received. Some of these were papers belonging to the Shaftesbury council, 1672–1674. Povey's transfer was far from complete, for in 1703 Blathwayt turned over to Popple quite an additional collection. Even so, he kept in his own possession a great many which more properly belonged in the plantation office. Doubtless he regarded some of his papers as belonging to his office as auditor.

auditor general's. The plantation office ran on Southwell's system, and the war office, new as it was in 1683, when Blathwayt took it over, had already been organized on a very workable plan. Even in the case of the auditor general's, there was no necessity for pioneer work, for the system of audit used was that of the Exchequer, and the work was actually done within the plantation office until 1696. Blathwayt simply adapted the methods of the plantation office to his work as auditor.[5]

Except for the brief period when he was temporarily in charge of the embassy at The Hague and, later, left to his own devices in the office of Lord Conway, Blathwayt directed only two offices and office staffs—the plantation office and the war office.[6] In the case of the former, he was technically under the supervision of the Lords of Trade. No contemporary account of his office staffs or of the internal arrangements of his offices has been found, but we know that his clerks were few in number and his office appointments of the simplest.[7] Blathwayt may have required elegance in his domestic setting, but he felt not the slightest need of it when at work. Extravagance, moreover, was not encouraged at official headquarters, and Blathwayt made no objection to paltry economies. The two rooms which were fitted up for the plantation office in Scotland Yard were secured in 1676 at a rental of £7.10.0 per quarter. Less than £100 was spent to fit up the rooms. An item appears of £32.9.0 paid, "to a Joyner for fitting up the said two Rooms, making four large presses for

[5] After the dissolution of the Lords of Trade, in 1696, Blathwayt must have transferred the audit to Little Wallingford House, where he had set up the war office in 1689, and where he had his private London establishment.

[6] During the years when he was secretary of state *pro tem.*, he organized the secretarial office within the war office, which was then migratory.

[7] There is, for instance, no such contemporary account as exists for Arlington's office in 1673 or Middleton's in 1684. (Evans, *The Principal Secretary of State*, pp. 191–193. *Supra*, p. 190.)

The Prospect of Whitehall From the Park of S. James's

Engraving by J. Kip

WHITEHALL, FROM ST. JAMES'S PARK, 1720

Showing from left to right: Little Wallingford House, Great Wallingford House, the back of the old Guards House, the Banqueting Hall, the Holbein Gateway, the Cockpit, and several of the private mansions

papers, books, and maps, altering of doors, windows, making tables, seats, and partitions for the clerks, shuts [shutters?], shelves, etc. As also a large scrittore, lining and stands.''[8] £52.2.10 was paid ''to an upholsterer for hanging the two rooms and furnishing them with curtains, carpets, bed for a servant, chairs, stools, and table.''[9]

During the lifetime of the Duke of Albemarle, the commander-in-chief, the war office was housed in the Cockpit, where the duke had his palatial apartments; but within a few months after his death, it was transferred to Old Pall Mall, where Lock, no doubt, had his lodgings, and presently to the Guardhouse. By July, 1671 it was housed in the Old Guards House where it stayed until Blathwayt removed it to Little Wallingford House in 1689. The office records reveal almost nothing about the fittings of the office. In 1678, when this building was undergoing extensive repairs at the hands of Sir Christopher Wren, all the war office got, apparently, was a new bookshelf. The munificent sum of two shillings was spent for a ''wainscote shelve, 4 feet 8 inches long, 14 inches broad.''[10] As far as we know, that was the sum total of the expenditures for alterations in the war office during both Lock's and Blathwayt's administrations, although it is possible that Little Wallingford House underwent considerable repairs when Blathwayt moved in, in 1689.

Both the plantation office and the war office were allowed a chamber-keeper and a cleaning woman; each had an official messenger, the one in the war office drawing a salary of £30 a year, while the one in the plantation office had an assistant, and the two were allowed £50. The un-

---

[8] C.O. 391:2, f. 12. In 1679 two more rooms were added, at the same rental. (Add. MSS. 9767, f. 74.) Further alterations were made in the rooms in 1683, when the presses and the cases for keeping books and documents were enlarged. (*Ibid.*, f. 102.)

[9] C.O. 391:2, f. 12.   [10] W.O. 26:4, f. 412.

der-keeper of the Privy Council chamber provided the Lords of Trade with paper, pen, ink, and such accessories as were required by the committee during its meetings. For his services, he was given two shillings a day, or £36.10.0 a year. The two keepers of the Privy Council chamber were also allowed two shillings a day, out of which, presumably, they furnished the committee with fire and candles.[11] Extraordinary expenses of the plantation office varied considerably, but averaged £300 a year. The same was true of the war office, where in Lock's day the quarterly bills were often no more than £5,[12] while under Blathwayt they sometimes rose to over £250 a year.[13]

In both offices, considerable sums were expended for maps, books, and charts. From time to time, Blathwayt ordered military regulations sent him from abroad. Very little is known of the war-office library, but the plantation office had an impressive list of books. It was naturally supplied regularly with the Bills of Rates and the Price Current, as its account books show, and it had an extensive collection of maps and some fine atlases, which Southwell purchased for the committee within a few months after its establishment.[14] He also bought Hakluyt's *Relations of the West Indies,* Ogilby's *History of America,* Smith's *Voyages,* and a number of books on colonial exploration.[15] Bound copies of treaties were pur-

---

[11] In May, 1685, it was decided that they were to have compensation only for the days the committee sat. (Add. MSS. 9767; privy seal of May 3, 1685; also Add. MSS. 9768, ff. 18–19; *Cal. S. P. Dom.,* 1689–1690, pp. 133, 160.)

[12] W.O. 26:5, f. 330; also Clode, *The Military Forces of the Crown,* II, 472–473.

[13] W.O. 25:3138, f. 306; W.O. 25:3139, ff. 54, 174, 234, 279. There are no account books for the war office comparable to those of the plantation office, so that it is almost impossible to trace expenditures with any degree of accuracy. For the plantation office account books, see Add. MSS. 9767, 9768.

[14] *Cal. S. P. Col.,* 1675–1676, p. 427.   [15] *Ibid.*

chased. In 1678, when Blathwayt made his flying trip to Paris with Dr. Tabor, he purchased several volumes on the colonies and a number of maps. On his return he presented these to the committee, together with his bill, and their lordships seemed "well pleased with the collection and order[ed] that a list be made of all books, maps, and papers belonging to the committee, and that an authentic copy be lodged in the council chest."[16] The library was added to from time to time throughout the period of the committee's existence.

Blathwayt's clerks and his relations with them are more interesting than his office equipment. His office staff was small, partly because economy demanded it, but chiefly because Blathwayt did so much of the work himself. He was fond of being the general factotum, as his youthful colleague, Monsieur Jollyuet, had discovered in the early days at The Hague, and few tasks, apparently, were too menial for him to perform. The presiding clerk in the plantation office was Blathwayt's cousin, John Povey, who succeeded him as first clerk early in 1680.[17] In the war office, Adam Cardonnel officiated. Two assistant clerks were allowed the plantation office from the outset, and an additional one was added in 1677.[18]

[16] C.O. 391:2, f. 216; July 30, 1678; *Cal. S. P. Col.*, 1677–1680, p. 280; also C.O. 391:2, ff. 145–146. At the meeting of the committee on November 8, 1677, it was ordered that an "inventory be prepared of all books and maps belonging to the committee of which two copies are to be made, indenture-wise, the one to be left in the council chamber and the other in the office of the committee, signed by those that shall have them in custody."

[17] The precise date is unknown, but it could not have been long after the departure of Southwell from the office in December, 1679.

[18] The two assistant clerks were originally Bert Sergeant and Philip Madox. The name of the clerk added in 1677 is unknown, and it is impossible, and not important, to know who the clerks were at all times. As we have stated, Madox stayed in the office until the Revolution. Bernard Randolph was engaged for a short time in 1684. (*Supra*, pp. 107–108.) The organiza-

Chamberlayne took cognizance of the war-office staff, beginning with his 1682 edition of *Angliae Notitia,* and thereafter usually listed the clerks.[19] None of the names he mentions is of any particular importance. When Blathwayt went to Flanders to attend William III, the office staff which he took with him had a dual aspect, for he insisted on drawing a careful line of distinction between his military and civil duties. Cardonnel accompanied him as military secretary; but, lest the war office left in Whitehall under George Clarke's direction suffer, John Thurston, the second clerk, remained behind. Blathwayt had at least three chief clerks serving him in a civil capacity during the decade from 1692 to 1702, all of whom were fairly

tion of the plantation office under the Lords of Trade and the amounts paid the clerks, can best be traced in the account books. (Add. MSS. 9767, 9768.)

Blathwayt apparently used Povey and the other clerks of the plantation office to help him with the royal audit, at least until 1696. After that date, Povey continued to assist him for a while. Blathwayt had at least two clerks after 1696, for he always referred to them in the plural. In 1702–1703, at the time Blathwayt's accounts were undergoing investigation at the hands of the parliamentary commissioners, Charles Le Bas was his faithful drudge; in 1711, Thomas Dod is mentioned.

19 In 1682, Chamberlayne named John Perrot as clerk and Richard Plumpton as war-office messenger. (*Angliae Notitia,* p. 140.) If his list is correct, the war office had lost a clerk since 1673 when Lock had had two clerks as well as a messenger. (*Cal. S. P. Dom.,* 1673–1675, pp. 82–83.) In 1684, Chamberlayne listed John Povey as clerk, and it is possible that, during the first few months in the war office, Blathwayt did make use of Povey. Cardonnel was engaged shortly after, as the handwriting in the war-office books indicates. In 1690, Chamberlayne listed Cardonnel and John Thurston and continued to do so in his various editions from 1692 to 1702. (*Angliae Notitia,* 1684, p. 144; 1692, p. 272; 1694, p. 326; 1702, p. 553. See also Egerton MSS. 2618, f. 156.) Cardonnel left the war office in 1702, to serve as military secretary to the Duke of Marlborough. In 1702, Chamberlayne also mentioned Mr. Watkins, apparently a relative of Blathwayt, who also served him as steward. In 1702–1703, when Blathwayt was answering the interrogations of the parliamentary commissioners, his clerk was Sam Lynn, whose brother, Francis Lynn, had assisted John Thurston in the war office during Blathwayt's absence. (Add. MSS. 38712, f. 132; also numerous references, Add. MSS. 38710.)

distinguished. The first was James Vernon, who accompanied him the first summer and was intended for the campaign of 1693, till, at the last moment, what Vernon regarded as a kindly fate intercepted the plan.[20] Matthew Prior, the poet, was with Blathwayt for a part of the summer of 1696, when his diplomatic fortunes were at a low ebb; he spent much of his time inveighing against "cold Mr. Blathwayt" and sounding out opportunities of escape.[21] The third was George Stepney, like Prior, devoted to the poetic muse, but far less temperamental. He was easily Blathwayt's favorite, and his mild Tory outlook agreed with Blathwayt far better than Prior's high Toryism or Vernon's Whiggery.

Stepney was never so hypercritical of his chief as Prior was, yet even he entered somewhat unwillingly into service, emboldened only by the prospect of what might be in store for him at Whitehall.[22] He was more keenly aware than Vernon had been of the hard labor which service

[20] Vernon had been appointed, in 1678, as military secretary to the Duke of Monmouth for the French expedition, and that may have been the reason why he was mustered into service in 1692. At the time he entered Blathwayt's service, he was a secretary in the embassy in Vienna. (S. P. Dom., Entry Bk., Vol. 44, f. 90; W.O. 24:5; Luttrell, *Brief Relation*, II, 369.) Vernon came in with the understanding that there would ultimately be an opening for him in the secretarial office in Whitehall. (For. Entry Bk., 1689–1695, Vol. 194, f. 69; Lord Sydney to Vernon, February 26, 1692.) In the spring of 1693, his expectation was realized, and he was made secretary to Sir John Trenchard, newly appointed secretary of state. (S. P. For. Archives, Vol. 49, ff. 244, 259.)

[21] *Hist. MSS. Com., Bath MSS., Prior Papers*, Vol. III; correspondence of 1696.

[22] Like Prior and Vernon, Stepney was in the diplomatic service and was stationed in Germany, where he served in a number of the principalities. Blathwayt began to negotiate for his services late in 1694.

We hear occasionally of other clerks in Blathwayt's civil employ while in Flanders. A certain Mr. Kratchbull was mentioned as planning to accompany Blathwayt in 1696, should his health permit. He had apparently been absent on sick leave from the diplomatic service. (Add. MSS. 28898, f. 65.) Another, Mr. Egar, later heard of in the English service at Hamburg, was

with Blathwayt would involve, for he wrote that he had little desire to let Blathwayt "hook" him into a campaign; "after the manner I saw he used Mr. Vernon two years ago (who has merit enough beyond mine) and the slavery in which he keeps poor Cardonnel I am not resolute enough to embarque with him."[23] Although he said he preferred to be Mr. Blathwayt's servant at a distance, since he generally fell asleep before three in the morning, financial inducements finally persuaded him. He wrote to Cardonnel to announce his decision, saying whimsically, "For though we are both of a trade (brothers of the quill) I make no doubt but we may cross the proverb and agree very well, since the nature of our employment will be different, you being a man of war, and I only an underpuller at politics."[24]

With the possible exception of Matthew Prior—and even his jeremiads were usually voiced only in the safest of quarters—Blathwayt's relations with his clerks were

of Blathwayt's party for several summers, but dropped out after 1697. Egar regarded his training under Blathwayt as an excellent recommendation. (Add. MSS. 28901, f. 133.) From 1698 to 1701 Blathwayt's official family was reduced, owing to the general policy of retrenchment. In 1701 it was again increased, and Warre, one of the clerks in Secretary Vernon's office, attended Blathwayt as civil secretary. (Add. MSS. 7074, f. 214.)

Blathwayt usually had a fairly large number of attendants, for in 1692, when his equipage was captured by a French privateer, he stated that his official family of seventeen was being held captive at Dunkirk. He had replaced fourteen of them, and the new servants were with him at Loo. This "family" included personal attendants as well as clerks, among them his valet, his coachman, and possibly even his cook. (Add. MSS. 9732, ff. 11, 13; 9735, f. 52.)

23 S. P. For. Archives, Vol. 55; Stepney to his patron, Montagu, The Hague, November 9, 1694. Curiously, in 1692, Vernon had written to Stepney to say that time was hanging heavy on his hands, and that he had nothing to do in camp, because Blathwayt was too experienced and proficient in the dispatch of business to need much assistance. (S. P. For. Archives Vol. 82; April 19, 1692.)

24 S. P. For. Archives, Vol. 55; letter dated Dresden, May 21/31, 1695; also Stepney's letter of April 26/May 6, 1695.

very cordial. He drove them hard, but never at their expense rather than his own, and he set himself the same high standards that he set them. In a sense, he might be called a poor executive, since he did so much of the work himself. Cardonnel and Povey, who were longest in his employ, were apparently loyal to him in every respect, though we know very little about their personal relationships with him. Blathwayt was exceedingly loyal and generous to them, as far as outward appearances go, and sufficiently disposed to be friendly. He had no objection to having Povey as a brother-in-law; for Cardonnel he arranged the secretaryship to the Duke of Marlborough, which, in 1702, looked like a very enviable appointment. Subsequently, of course, Cardonnel had to bear the brunt of attacks directed against the general's maladministration of military affairs. He secured the agency for Maryland, Virginia, and New York for Povey, and military agencies for both Povey and Cardonnel, for one that of the New York companies, for the other that of the Newfoundland contingent. He went out of his way to see that Povey was compensated for his special services in the plantation office, while he himself was in Flanders.[25] A natural desire to have his work perpetuated was at the root of his ambition to have Povey succeed him in the plantation office, and Cardonnel in the war office. He had the pride in them which a father feels for his children, and he was certain that they would do him no discredit.

[25] No formal arrangement was made for an increase in salary for Povey in 1692, when he succeeded Blathwayt at the plantation board for the duration of the campaign. In 1697, therefore, Povey petitioned the Treasury for some sort of payment, and Blathwayt came to his assistance, ''the petitioner having not only for above twelve years past applied himself entirely to the business of the late committee of trade and plantations, but has had the whole care during my absence in Flanders, etc.'' (Add. MSS. 38703, f. 43.) The petition was granted, and at Blathwayt's suggestion was paid out of the quit-rents of Virginia. £1000 was the amount agreed upon and it was to be paid in three annual installments. (See *supra*, p. 383.)

On the whole, his feeling for all of his clerks, judging from the scanty evidence at hand, was very kindly and human and was to a large extent reciprocated.[26]

Despite small office staffs and unpretentious office surroundings, Blathwayt left behind him an enormous mass of office books and papers. He thoroughly appreciated the importance of records, and he prided himself on his success in compiling archives. While he was in Flanders, he was in a constant state of agitation lest some of his office files be lost. His feeling was justified and is probably explained by the capture, in 1692, of the ship in which he was crossing to Flanders.[27] He then lost his official family, but he managed to save his most valuable papers. A correspondent writing home to England, in 1693, of the rout of the English forces by the French, said, "The English horse have learnt of the Dutch to run away, and it is said were much too nimble for them and far outrun the Dutch. Mr. Blathwaite, the secretary at warre, was soe carefull of his papers, for fear of losing them, he never stopt till he came to Breda."[28] There was another story, to the effect that at one time Blathwayt fled so fast that he lost the king and did not come upon him again for hours, so great was his concern for his effects.

Blathwayt's vast pride in the archives he compiled in the plantation office came out clearly in 1711, when the parliamentary commissioners of accounts called upon him to supply them with a list of all the colonial officers, and the method for the payment of their salaries, from the time he first entered the plantation office. He had been

[26] We have already spoken of Blathwayt's strenuous efforts to find Stepney a post, first in the reorganized plantation office, then as a member of the Board of Trade. (See *supra*, pp. 301–302.) Stepney was with Blathwayt in Flanders two summers.

[27] Add. MSS. 9732, ff. 11, 13; Add. MSS. 9735, f. 52.

[28] *Hatton Correspondence* (Camden Society, n.s., Vol. XXIII), II, 195; August 3, 1693.

dismissed from the Board of Trade four years earlier, but, since he was still auditor general, he assumed that he could examine the files. His letter to the commissioners showed that he was mistaken; "I shall endeavor to comply with such part of the precept as may be judged possible for me who have not since my dismission of that Board had any admission to those [records] of that Board, though most of them of my own compiling, for the same reason which occasioned my discontinuance, though I delivered over at the first settlement of that Commission more than sixty volumes, many of them methodized by a Journall by myself or under my direction of which I cannot now have any inspection to supply or help my memory with them (after so many years past) in the exigency, besides that my present clerks are wholly ignorant of that part of the plantation business, wherein they have never been employed."[29] Considering the reason, it is no wonder that anger had temporarily robbed Blathwayt of his usual coherence.

The amount of work which Blathwayt did himself, particularly in connection with the correspondence, is almost unbelievable. To the very end of his tenure in each of his offices, his letter drafts appear with great frequency, often in instances where the task might equally well have been entrusted to a clerk. Either his conscientiousness or the notion that no one could do the work quite as well as he could, caused him to assume a burden which another would gladly have transferred to a clerk. Moreover, he scrutinized his subordinates' work very carefully. Their letter drafts and reports bear his interlinear corrections and his "blue pencil" was always actively employed. Povey's work, in particular, bears signs that

[29] Huntington MSS., Blathwayt Papers relating to America, 1681–1741; letter of August 15, 1711. Horatio Walpole, Blathwayt's successor as auditor, seems to have been an *ex officio* member of the Board of Trade.

Blathwayt felt his relative's style was too diffuse and his knowledge of correct usage limited.

When it came to the entry books, Blathwayt was willing to leave the burden of responsibility to his clerks, although, where the finished entries were based on preliminary rough journals, as was true of the Journal of the Lords of Trade, he checked their work carefully. However, he was simply following Southwell's methods, for in his early days at the plantation office his own work had been subject to the same close supervision.

The system used for the preservation of the records was the one in general use at the time. Papers were classified as they came into the office and filed away, and entry books were kept of such out-going and in-coming documents and letters as needed to be recorded. In every instance the plans were much more elaborate than the results achieved, but the preservation of rough drafts helped to fill in the possible gaps in the case of papers dispatched from the office. The entry books of the plantation office had been begun under Southwell and were classified according to colonies. General entry books were also kept, as well as some which applied exclusively to trade.[30]

In the war office, Blathwayt found a very presentable group of general entry books, which were of Lock's making.[31] No attempt had been made at the classification of war office orders in the entry books. Blathwayt began the work of specialization and succeeded very well, consider-

[30] For a careful study of the colonial entry books and a complete list of them, see C. S. S. Higham, *The Colonial Entry-books* (*S.P.C.K.*, 1921).

[31] In 1670, Lock had been ordered to keep an entry book of the orders issuing from the war office or from the secretary of state's office, but having a bearing on the army. (*Cal. S. P. Dom.*, 1673–1675, pp. 82–83.) Lock drew up five entry books of miscellaneous orders, with no attempt made at classification except that the chronological sequence was maintained. These are now classified as W.O. 26:1–5. Two volumes must have been lost, for there is a gap for 1677 and another from 1680 to 1683.

ing the handicaps under which he worked and the difficulties attendant on the rapid expansion of the army with no corresponding increase in the size of the office staff. His entry books amply reflect the variety of his duties; there were general entry books of out-letters,[32] miscellany books full of warrants and precedents,[33] volumes of marching orders,[34] registers of pay warrants,[35] commission books,[36] an entry book of orders for court martials,[37] another of reports on petitions,[38] and one which listed the inns and public houses available for quartering pur-

[32] W.O. 4:1–2. The first volume runs from March 22, 1684, to December, 1690; the second from January 2, 1703, to April 22, 1704. The intervening volumes have doubtless been lost. Entries consist largely of quartering and marching orders, points with regard to discipline and the articles of war, and a great many inter-departmental letters. Both volumes have alphabetical indexes. There are many blank pages.

[33] W.O. 26:6–11. W.O. 26:1–5 were Lock's; 26:8–9 were Clark's; 26:7, 10 were volumes which Blathwayt used while in Flanders. They contain all sorts of miscellaneous orders, many from the secretary of state's office. Here are found the actual orders, whereas in W.O. 4:1–2 are the letters with regard to them. There is a gap from 1689 to 1691.

[34] W.O. 5:1–12. W.O. 5:7–8 were used by both Blathwayt and Clarke; W.O. 5:9 was Clarke's. The volumes run from 1683 to 1704, except for a gap from 1692 to 1694. Marching orders, routes, and occasionally victualling orders are included.

[35] W.O. 25:3138–3140, 3145–3148. The latter are the Irish pay books. The volumes begin with the Mutiny Act of 1689, and there are numerous gaps. The pay warrants except in rare instances include only those not on the regular establishment.

[36] W.O. 25:1–7. The first volume belonged to Blathwayt's predecessors, but there are practically no entries from 1667 to 1681. After 1681, Lock made only four entries. Some of Blathwayt's commission books overlap because he tried to keep up a double system, one according to the type of commission, the other according to date. Entries were made from two to six days after the commissions had been issued. The sixth volume was for commissions issued while Blathwayt was in Flanders. There are also commission entry books in the secretary of state's office which begin with 1661. (See State Papers Domestic, Military Entry Books.)

[37] W.O. 30:17, 1684 to August 8, 1704.

[38] W.O. 30:88, 1685–1711; ff. 1–47 cover Blathwayt's period.

poses.[39] In addition there were the establishments, which Blathwayt was required to draw up in triplicate and according to set form.[40] These entry books in many cases fail to come up to Blathwayt's usual standards. There are omissions, deletions, entries out of chronological order. Many of the volumes are only partly filled. On the whole, however, they are excellent records and point to a facile and usable office system, which was continued by Blathwayt's successors. Cross references to other office books are frequently given; nearly every volume has a carefully alphabetized index, made simultaneously with the entries. The books are bound in brown russia, often elaborately tooled, and are identical in appearance with the plantation office books under the Lords of Trade.

The books which Blathwayt kept in his other offices are in the main of the same high standard. The entry book he compiled while in Conway's office is a model of its sort, although it failed to include all the out-letters.[41] Only the foreign entry books, which the secretarial office was supposed to keep, show a falling off of his usual quality; they were as much neglected under Blathwayt as they were under his predecessors and successors. The actual letters or letter drafts Blathwayt filed away according to the countries of dispatch, and then, with the exception of the more formal, carried them off with him to Dyrham Park.

Blathwayt made extremely ambitious plans for the sec-

[39] W.O. 30:48. The volume was drawn up in 1686, and Blathwayt's hand appears on several of the 660 pages of entries.

[40] W.O. 24:6–37, 1684–1704. There were five establishments drawn prior to Blathwayt's time according to the records; 1661–1662, 1668, 1673, 1679, 1680; see also W.O. 24:884–885 for some copies of establishments.

[41] Add. MSS. 35104. Francis Gwyn also kept an entry book, which he removed from the office. It was sold at a Sotheby sale, June 15, 1908, when many of the Gwyn papers preserved at Ford Abbey were disposed of. The foreign entry books were of course left in the office and were used by several secretaries of state.

retarial office, while he was with William III in Flanders
but these soon fell through under the pressure and hardships of war. His entry books of which there were two,
must have been compiled in England after the summer's
campaign was over. The first one covers the first year; the
second, all the remaining years; both contain only the out-
letters which Blathwayt directed to Whitehall officials.[42]
Apparently no attempt was made to enter the letters he
sent to, or received from, the foreign envoys.[43] A journal,
or sort of diary, was planned in 1697, but it degenerated,
after a few pages of entries, into a volume in which Blathwayt listed the letters he sent daily.[44]

The archives of the auditor general show that the excellent system of the plantation office had been carried
over. Blathwayt's effort to keep a continuous record of
the business transacted, resulted in the three volumes
known as his "Journal," extending from 1680 to 1717.[45]
They contain in-letters and out-letters, abstracts, petitions, and reports; they do not, however, contain any of
the accounts received. Most of the entries are in court
hand, with occasional marginal insertions and comments
by Blathwayt. Comprehensive as the Journal is, it is far
from a complete record of Blathwayt's work as auditor.
There exists a great mass of correspondence, now widely

---

[42] Add. MSS. 37991, 37992; these are large quarto volumes; the first is
the better kept and has in-letters as well as out-letters.

[43] That correspondence ultimately found its way to Dyrham Park.

[44] Add. MSS. 22031; large quarto with only 38 pages of entries.

[45] Treas. 64:88–90. There is a transcript in the Library of Congress. The
first volume extends from 1680 to 1696, with one entry for June 23, 1697.
Entries are least frequent while Blathwayt was abroad. The second volume
runs from 1696 to 1709, with entries most frequent from 1703 to 1705, when
Godolphin was Lord High Treasurer. The third, which extends to 1717, is
chiefly taken up with the report to the parliamentary commissioners of 1711.
The first volume is bound in brown russia like the books of the plantation
office up to 1696, the other two in the white vellum affected by the Board of
Trade.

scattered, which Blathwayt removed to Dyrham Park, and which he never had entered. The only other important record of the auditor general's office is the report, or account book, which Blathwayt drew up in 1711; this contains a comprehensive statement of the accounts received from the various colonies over a period of more than a decade.[46]

Blathwayt's most voluminous files were those of the plantation office and they best attest his administrative skill. We have already mentioned the pride with which he regarded them.[47] The basic record of the office was the Journal in which were kept the minutes of the meetings of the Lords of Trade. This Journal, at least after 1677, was based on a rough journal, some of the volumes of which are extant, full of interlinear corrections made either by Southwell or, after 1679, by Blathwayt.[48] In ad-

[46] This volume, unlike the Journal, never passed into the public archives, but became a part of Blathwayt's collection at Dyrham Park. It is now in the Library of Congress. Blathwayt evidently intended it for his own use, as a permanent record. It is curious that he did not turn it over to the Treasury when the Journal was given over.

[47] See *supra*, pp. 330, 352, 413.

[48] The first volume of the Journal was not based on a rough journal apparently, but was made from notes taken at committee meetings by the clerk of the council in attendance. On November 8, 1677, the committee issued the order, ''Their Lordships direct that the minutes taken at the committee be extended the next day and entered the third.'' (C.O. 391:2, ff. 145–146.) This order may simply have reference to the speed with which the Journal was to be drawn up, or it may be that their lordships preferred the more painstaking method of having a rough journal on which the finished Journal was to be based. Two volumes of the rough journal are extant and are in the Library of Congress; the first runs from March 31, 1677, to April 26, 1679, thus antedating the order of the committee by several months; the second runs from January 13, 1685, to December 8, 1686. A comparison between the rough and finished journals is of interest; sometimes the entries are almost identical and in the same court hand, again there is a complete change of order, and the rough journal will bear copious corrections. Blathwayt made a large number of the entries in the first volume, and it is a much finer piece of work than the second, which was Povey's handiwork, written in his cramped hand and bearing Blathwayt's frequent corrections. The first

dition to the Journal and the various colonial entry books, there was also the so-called "Journal of All that Passes in the Office," which runs from January 6, 1683, to December 24, 1688. It contains some of the minutes of the committee meetings on which the Journal was based, items of the business to be done in the office from day to day, and notations of when mails were sent and received. Entries appear of reams of paper sent to the various colonies for their official returns of proceedings and laws, and the names and business of those who called at the office are noted. Occasional references are found to mail sent to Blathwayt at Newmarket, where he had gone to attend the king. Most of the entries are curt, and in some instances, after the heading of "Business," come the words, "Mr. Blath[wayt] takes care."[49]

In addition to the "Journal of All that Passes in the Office," a "Book of Occurrences" was kept, which ran

volume is entitled "Journal," the second, "Minutes of the Committee." Both are folio volumes, bound in white vellum. They are called the second and third volumes of a set of three, the first of the set being the finished Journal of the Shaftesbury council, 1672–1674, of which Blathwayt took possession. The Board of Trade also had a rough journal, one volume of which is in the British Museum (Add. MSS. 8867); the others are in the Public Record Office, C.O. 391:90, etc., and run down to 1720.

[49] Only a few meetings of the committee were reported in the "Journal of All that Passes," and while some of the meetings were of major importance, there seems to have been no guiding rule. The following are the minutes of the important session of July 17, 1683:

New England	What Frigate goes that way
	A proclamation to be prepared
	Mr. Randolph to go with the Quo Warranto
A proclamation	The same Method to be used as in the case of Virginia charter, 1623
Quo Warranto	The Agents may go home
the method	Upon absolute Submission and Resignation the King will settle the Government with a salvo for every man's Property

The minutes of what took place at the meeting of the Privy Council, where

from 1678 to April, 1688.[50] It is a commonplace book, containing chiefly entries of events in Europe and the colonies. The items are military in their nature, and the volume more properly belongs to the war office. Finally, there were the magnificent entry books of patents, commissions, and charters relating to the colonies. It was for the entering of these that Blathwayt was originally employed by Southwell.[51]

During his lifetime, Blathwayt's ability was generally recognized. It won him the commendation of three monarchs and of the Earl of Sunderland, arch adviser of all of them. William III, who probably had a sounder judgment of office systems than he had of his kingdom's sensibilities or of human nature in general, told his confidant, Halifax, in 1689, when it seemed for a while that Blathwayt might be permanently dropped from the administrative cast, that Blathwayt was dull but had "a good method."[52] Hence, William argued, it was safe to leave him in admin-

the report of the committee was considered, appear on the next page as follows:

Council 20 [July?] New England	At the Council ordered That Mr. Randolph go to New England with the Quo Warranto against their charter That a Frigate bound for the West Indies carry him to Boston The New England Agents have leave to return home A Declaration to be issued conserving to the Bostoners the estates and propertys

The "Journal of All that Passes" was obviously Povey's memorandum and is entered in his hand. A small folio, bound in brown russia, it is now in the Library of Congress.

[50] C.O. 389:35. It was among the books handed over to Popple by Blathwayt in 1703.

[51] These volumes are now in the Library of Congress. Entries begin with the grant to John Cabot by Henry VII and close with 1706, although there are very few entries after 1689.

[52] Foxcroft, *The Life and Letters of* . . . *Halifax*, II, 226; entry in Spencer House "Journals," July 28, 1689.

istrative control of the army. After all, a man did not have to be a brilliant conversationalist in order to run an army, nor was it the secretary at war's business to amuse the king. William's laconic comment was no passing impulse of good nature, since he retained Blathwayt in his service until the end of his reign.

Fellow administrators recognized the soundness of Blathwayt's office methods. The precise Sir John Evelyn complimented him on his "dexterity" in business. Men like Harley, of course, maintained that Blathwayt was the poorest tool that ever dirtied paper with his official scribblings, but Harley was too blinded by his party bias ever to judge Blathwayt fairly.[53] Others, like Admiral Russell, sneered in their irritable moods at Blathwayt, "that never-erring minister."[54] This last was certainly unfair. As a matter of fact, Blathwayt was quite amenable to correction, even though James Vernon once said, in a moment of impatience, that Blathwayt was like all other men, quite unwilling ever to own himself in the wrong.[55]

Probably the most serious charges of inaccuracy and carelessness have been brought against Blathwayt by the celebrated historian, Hutchinson, who put the entire blame on him for the errors contained in the Massachusetts charter draft of 1691. The textual shortcomings of the charter, he states, had been variously attributed; by some to Sir John Somers, the colony's good friend, by others to John Locke. Hutchinson declares, however, that it was so full of mistakes, "as not to be accounted for if done by either of those great men. . . . It is more proba-

[53] *Hist. MSS. Com., Portland MSS., Harley Papers,* V, 202; Harley to a friend, Whitehall, July 12, 1712. Harley was trying to hold Blathwayt equally responsible with some of the German representatives for the maladministration of the army and army contracts, under the allies.

[54] Coxe, *Shrewsbury Correspondence,* p. 215.

[55] Vernon, *Letters Illustrative, etc.* I, 281.

ble that they should come from Mr. Blathwayt.''[56] His comment is merely another interesting example of the warped view which Massachusetts always took of Blathwayt.

Careful examination of the steps by which the charter of 1691 was drawn, shows the difficulty of proving that Blathwayt was in any way responsible for its errors. The first draft was unquestionably the work of the attorney-general, George Treby. On June 8, 1691, this was presented to the Lords of Trade, who thereupon ordered Blathwayt to make comparative abstracts of the old, and of the proposed, charter of the province. Blathwayt did so, arranging his summary in parallel columns, point by point.[57] Accordingly the two charters were discussed at length, by the Lords of Trade, during the summer of 1691, beginning with June 25th, the date on which Blathwayt had been ordered to have the abstract ready.[58] As those who have followed the history of the charter know, the Massachusetts agents were called in repeatedly by the Lords of Trade, to state their views, and they were given every opportunity to voice their objections.[59] On the basis of these objections, the draft was revised. Late in August, the charter was ready to be drawn finally, for its passage through the seals. William III had sent his consent to it from Flanders. On August 23, Blathwayt wrote to Treby, telling him that the royal consent had been granted, and that the charter's passage was to be hastened. Treby, who was taking the waters at Tunbridge Wells, was instructed either to hasten back to London to prepare the charter or send his clerk, Mr. Gwillym, to do so.[60] Treby replied,

[56] Hutchinson, *History of Massachusetts Bay* (2d ed.), I, 411; Channing, *History of the United States*, II, 283.

[57] *Cal. S. P. Col.*, 1689–1692, p. 470.   [58] *Ibid.*, 1689–1692, p. 477.

[59] *Ibid.*, pp. 470–471, 509, 511, 512, 513, 525.

[60] *Ibid.*, p. 526.

through Gwillym, that on account of his indisposition he could not possibly be back in London before September 1. However, Gwillym wrote, "If greater dispatch be necessary, please send the papers here and I will work at them."[61]

By September 6th, the second draft of the charter was ready. It was apparently Gwillym's work, but whether drawn at Tunbridge Wells or in London, we cannot say.[62] In the meantime, the Massachusetts agents had again solicited the attention of the Lords of Trade with further objections to the charter, and had been favorably received.[63] The result was that the second draft of the charter was already marked with corrections before it had passed the seals, though it was then presumably in its final shape.[64] As a result, it is not certain whether or not a third draft of the charter was prepared; but we do know that the agents continued to bring in their corrections as late as September 15th, and that they seemed to be torn by a desire for haste, on the one hand, and change in the original provisions, on the other. Finally, the document passed the great seal on October 7th.[65] Who was to blame if it came out in somewhat mangled form, still containing provisions which the agents wanted amended? Perhaps, if Hutchinson could have followed the proceedings of the Lords of Trade in their various dealings with the agents from day to day, he might have been as puzzled as we are now to place the blame for the shortcomings of the final draft.

The confidence which was placed in Blathwayt and his office books in his own day, comes out most strikingly in connection with the investigations of the parliamentary commissioners of accounts. In a sense these periodic ex-

61 *Ibid.*, p. 526.   62 *Ibid.*, p. 531.
63 *Ibid.*, pp. 527–528, 529.   64 *Ibid.*, pp. 531, 533, 535, 542.
65 *Ibid.*, p. 550.

aminations were gruelling experiences, in which the commissioners tried their best to shake Blathwayt's confidence and to put him in error. As the examinations proceeded, however, more than one tribute was paid to his skill and the trustworthy character of his records. In certain instances, the commissioners showed a shameless dependence on his testimony. They made exceedingly heavy demands, yet Blathwayt, who never fought shy of investigation, usually complied with alacrity and good grace. The examinations of his war-office records were as interesting as those of his plantation-office books, and the demands made were far more unreasonable.

In 1702, he was ordered to produce copies of all the contracts that had been made for food and forage for the army since 1689. It developed that the commissioners had first turned to the Treasury for this information, but had been referred to Blathwayt as the official most likely to have it in accessible form.[66] Blathwayt's clerks painstakingly went over the war-office records, extracting copies of the contracts. Occasionally they were obliged to admit that a contract was missing, presumably because, in the confusion resulting from Blathwayt's attendance in Flanders, it had never been entered.[67] In October, 1703, the commissioners demanded copies of all the agreements that had been made with the allies for annual subsidies for the pay of their troops and for forage in winter quarters, from April 1, 1692, to March 25, 1699.[68] Within a month, Le Bas, Blathwayt's clerk, was able to present copies of them all.

The commissioners, both of 1692 and 1702–1703, re-

[66] Add. MSS. 38709, f. 11.

[67] *Ibid.*, ff. 12, 41, 43, 45–47, 49; also 38696, f. 123; 38697, ff. 73, 117; 38700, ff. 50, 56–58; 38704, f. 45; 38705, ff. 108–110.

[68] *Ibid.*, 36863, ff. 71, 112, 115, 117; November 9, 12, 15, 1703. These folios are also numbered pp. 461, 544, 547, 552.

quested copies of the pay warrants which did not rest on
the establishments—those for clothing, victualling, transportation, subsidies, arrears, hospital expenses, apothe-
caries' services and supplies, and pensions. The paybooks
of the war office contain marginal notations which show
what warrants were copied and handed over to the commissioners in 1692.[69] In 1702, Blathwayt protested, saying
that the commissioners should not require a complete
copy of every warrant. He was willing, he said, to make
abstracts of them and to bring these in weekly, as fast as
he could, but they were too voluminous to be copied in full.
With this arrangement the commissioners had to be satisfied, making the condition that he omit only words of a
formal nature in making the abstracts.[70] They demanded,
however, that he produce all the debentures which he had
received for the Roman Catholic troops disbanded in 1689
or sent to the Channel Islands.[71] They also requested a
copy of the rules he had received for making out debentures for the forces in Flanders. At this point Blathwayt's system failed! Neither he nor his clerks could
produce a copy of the rules or of the orders for the Roman Catholic troops, although they declared they had
searched high and low for them.[72] For this failure Blathwayt had a fairly plausible explanation to give; despite
his great care, some of the office books had been lost when
his equipage had been seized by the French, in 1692.[73] Just
why these records should have gone to Flanders is a little
difficult to decide. He stated, also, that not all the pay warrants passed through his hands, and besides, even if they
had, they could easily have been lost in the rush and con-

---

[69] W.O. 25:3146, ff. 126, 147.
[70] Add. MSS. 36859, f. 22; May 16, 1702.
[71] *Ibid.*, 36860, f. 71; October 7, 1702.
[72] *Ibid.*, f. 108; also ff. 46, 92; 9755, f. 15.
[73] *Ibid.*, 36859, f. 123; 36860, f. 46.

fusion of camp life, when perforce the records had been somewhat neglected. "Being askt if all warrants did not pass his hands, he answered that there were hundreds of warrants which did not. That when there was a general in Holland he made orders and passed warrants which were good till the king ruled over them, and so many orders for payments, etc., are issued by the Treasury. And that the general often made out commissions which came not many times to his hands."[74]

On the whole, Blathwayt made an honest effort to answer the queries of the commissioners. He and his clerks made frequent visits to their office and carried on an extended correspondence with them. His testimony is in marked contrast to that of the shameless Ranelagh, whose clerks were also a poor lot.[75] Unfortunately his honesty and promptness did not always secure entire confidence in him. The commissioners, for instance, demanded a copy of all the establishments from the Restoration to 1703, and when they discovered a gap for the years from 1680 to 1684, they immediately demanded the reason and almost refused to credit his explanation that no establishment had ever been drawn for that period. They kept detecting the most minute errors and even found errors where there were none. For example, Blathwayt had a hard time convincing them that what seemed to be an unwarranted augmentation of the forces had actually been made on royal order and was quite valid.[76] They were outraged when some of the establishments were found to lack the signature of the Treasury, and they were inclined at first to discredit Blathwayt's statement that the omission was due to a shift in the board, the

---

[74] Add. MSS. 36860, f. 92; October 14, 1702; also *ibid.*, 36859, f. 141.
[75] *Ibid.*, 38708, ff. 1–190; also various references *ibid.*, 36859, 36860.
[76] *Ibid.*, 9755, ff. 59, 61; also *ibid.*, 36859, f. 126.

out-going members neglecting to sign and the incoming ones carefully avoiding doing so.[77] The unreasonable limits to which they went, can be seen from their request that Blathwayt furnish them with fresh copies of the establishments of 1692 and 1694, to replace those which they had mislaid.[78] Nor did they think it unwarranted for them to require Blathwayt to furnish them with facts which they rightfully should have gathered from other officials. Thus, in 1702, they asked Nottingham, the secretary of state, to furnish data regarding commissions, when and by whom issued; Nottingham sent his clerk to inform them that Blathwayt could better supply the information.[79] Blathwayt did so, although, when they came to him, he told them that it would be an exceedingly difficult task for him, since so many commissions had been issued of which he was never apprised, the generals in the field having the power to issue commissions without notifying him when they did so.[80]

The most annoying incident arose in 1702, with regard to the musters. Blathwayt did not keep a record of the muster rolls in his office; he had merely the muster books, which indicated whether musters had been taken and successfully completed. When the commissioners asked him to state the exact time when various officers and soldiers had come into pay, he answered that only Crawford, the commissary general of the musters, could supply that information;[81] however, he obligingly secured and dispatched to them the commissary's list of all the forces on the establishments from November 5, 1688, to December 24, 1699.[82] The commissioners told him flatly that the list

[77] *Ibid.*, 36859, f. 62.   [78] *Ibid.*, 9755, f. 27.

[79] *Ibid.*, 36859, ff. 120, 124, 144. The commissioners, however, did require Nottingham to produce the commission books in his office.

[80] *Ibid.*, 36860, f. 92.   [81] *Ibid.*, 36859, f. 25.

[82] *Ibid.*, f. 105.

was worse than useless to them, whereupon he took it back again, looked it over and huffily decided that if that was the case, the commissioners could consult the muster rolls for themselves.[83] The muster rolls could not be found. Crawford admitted this at once and gave two reasons; the fire at Whitehall in 1698, and the fact that the clerk who had taken home some of the rolls to abstract them had been so inconsiderate as to commit suicide. The rolls had never been returned by his family. Crawford then calmly referred the commissioners to Blathwayt's office, where the establishments and the pay warrants could be found.[84]

The commissioners accordingly informed Blathwayt that he would have to correct the defects in the list of musters he had originally handed in, by comparing them with the warrants in his pay books.[85] He protested vociferously, stating that his warrants were entered chronologically, not according to the way in which muster rolls were kept, by regiment, company, men within the company, etc. He had, he said, no warrants for subsistence money in his possession, and many payments had been made on verbal order from the king to the Treasury; nor did he have any records of the Dutch paymaster, Van der Esch. However, if the commissioners would but be patient, and would supply him with a list of the defects, he would see what could be done. The commissioners replied that the defects were so numerous that they could not begin to list them, and that Blathwayt would have to take the commissary's list, compare it as best he could with his pay books, and indicate where no orders were to be found in his records.[86] Rather obliquely, they hinted that some of the numerous errors might possibly be his own. Blath-

83 Add. MSS. 36859, ff. 126, 131–138.
84 *Ibid.*, f. 138.   85 *Ibid.*, f. 141.
86 *Ibid.*, f. 141.

wayt did not deny this; many of the orders, he said, had been signed hastily in camp. Resigned, he set to his task.

The search involved was tremendous. Blathwayt and his clerks slaved at it like ants, while the irresponsible Crawford and Ranelagh protested their helplessness to do anything. The clerks worked from seven in the morning until two in the afternoon; then, after two hours' respite, they began again and worked until nine at night. After two weeks, two clerks were sent over from the commissioners' office to help them.[87] On September 4, 1702, after working steadily since August 20, Sam Lynn, the chief clerk, reported that they had gone over thirteen or fourteen of the muster books but still had eleven or twelve to examine.[88] By September 10, he reported that the chore was done and brought in the list perfected to December 24, 1699. The next day Crawford was questioned on the results, and the matter must have ended to the satisfaction of the commissioners, for no further mention was made of it.[89] It is hard to say whether malice, overzealousness, or an honest desire for information prompted the commissioners.

The commissioners of 1711 were more interested in Blathwayt's records as auditor general, although they did not entirely neglect the war office. Their requests for information were somewhat extreme and really angered him far more than the demands of the commissioners of 1702. He was in a crotchety mood, too, smarting under the sting of political defeat complicated with rheumatism. He wrote from Bath, where he had gone to take the waters,

[87] *Ibid.*, f. 165.   [88] *Ibid.*, f. 171 *dorso.*

[89] *Ibid.*, 36860, ff. 10, 12. In 1715, Blathwayt was again interrogated by parliamentary commissioners on the question of musters; they wanted to know the force of a verbal order to muster complete. Blathwayt stated that he thought the commissary general was bound to obey it. (Porlock MSS.; letter draft of March 21, 1715.) Blathwayt also said in his letter that he had handed over all his muster books to St. John on leaving the war office.

that he was willing to undergo investigation, but that he had too few clerks to compile the voluminous financial accounts which the commission required, within the time allotted. Much of the information which they demanded of him, he pointed out, might better be solicited from the Board of Trade. "I take leave to observe that by the 3rd Article of the Precept I am required to exhibit upon Oath *a Distinct account of the Names of all Governors and Officers whatsoever of Her Majesty or any other Person employ'd in any of Her said Plantations, how they are respectively constituted, whether by Letters Patent or otherwise, what the Salaries, Fees and Perquisites of them and how paid* [*sic*], Which article is submitted as proper for other Offices as the Commissioners of Trade and Plantations where the Commissions of all Governors and all such Officers do cheifly pass and for the Commissioners of the Customs who appoint or recommend all Officers in the Revenue of the Plantations which have reference to Acts of Parliament and for the duty of the 4½ per cent in the Charribby Islands who are very numerous and under their Directions as well as Audited by the Auditors of the Imprest, that Revenue of late years being return'd into England in Specie and cheifly managed by Officers of the Customs here. And whereas the Officers mentioned in this article do not make any Entry of their Commissions with me or my Deputies or are any ways accomptable to me anywhere, except those employ'd in that Part of the Revenue under my Inspection, it is humbly left to your Consideration how farr I can comply as Surveyor and Auditor of such Revenues with what is demanded of me by this Article. Although [he added with a nice bit of conceit,] by my long Conversation with that part of the World, and having had a share in the Management thereof for near Thirty years past (until my dismission from the Council of Trade and Plantations) I shall endeavour, if desir'd, to give the best [account] I can either by writing or by personall attendance at my return, on the Honorable Board."[90] The commissioners, quite naturally, played up to his vanity and cajoled him by open flattery. "But as to the account of officers, governors, etc. [*sic*] in the Plantations, the Commissioners think they cannot help expecting it from you during your continuance at the Board of honorable Commissioners of Trade and Plantations, especially your being better qualified than any body to give them that account by your long converse with that part of the world."[91] As we might expect, Blathwayt rather fatuously succumbed, only too anxious to display his omniscience, although he demanded an extension of time on account of his illness.

He was infuriated, however, when he subsequently learned that the Board of Trade expected him to supply them with a complete set of accounts, too.[92] What, he asked, had become of the duplicate copies of accounts which the governors were required to transmit to the board? Why, if they had not been transmitted, did not the board compel obedience? Blathwayt's anger was distinctly theatrical. Finally, in a mock "sack-cloth-and-ashes" mood, he consented to furnish them with the information. He regarded the incident as a tribute to his superior knowledge and administrative skill, hence a personal triumph.

[90] Treas. 64:90, ff. 46–47; July 23, 1711. This was a copy of his letter draft.

[91] Huntington MSS., Blathwayt Papers relating to America, 1681–1741; Gregory King, the secretary to the commissioners, writing from Essex House, August 9, 1711. See also Blathwayt's letter of August 15, 1711.

[92] Treas. 64:90, ff. 87–88; March 5, 1712. As a matter of fact, the board's request was perfectly regular. (*Cal. S. P. Col.*, 1706–1708, pp. 430–431, 709.) Blathwayt asked that at least they send over a clerk or two to assist his, who already had more than enough to do.

There can be no doubt that England's administrative system—or that portion which came under Blathwayt's care—emerged strengthened by the treatment it had received at his hands. He made mistakes, but none of them to England's lasting damage. Many of his acts of carelessness were evidently deliberate and were due to his fee-gathering strategy, but these were all of a minor nature.[93] Most of his enemies' charges against him of mental confusion and incoherency were the result of basic differences in point of view. Thus Edward Dummer, in writing to Harley of the postal contract to the West Indies, for which he applied in 1702, said, "I have this day concluded with the Lords for the West India business my own way, and, I fancy, with some mortification to Mr. Blathwayt who has puzzled them and me very much."[94] In view of the ultimate outcome of Dummer's contract, which involved him in a heavy loss for which he petitioned official relief in 1705, Blathwayt's ideas on the matter may not have been as "puzzling" as Dummer implied. One of Blathwayt's mistakes, indeed, almost involved the English treasury in a serious loss. Much to Blathwayt's chagrin, the disreputable Ranelagh (of all people) once caught him in error in calculating the poundage. Instead of allowing the paymaster the customary 1d. on the pound, Blathwayt in haste for Flanders, had given him 4d. Although it wrung Ranelagh's heart to report the mistake— for, with a marriageable daughter to provide for, he could easily have used the extra money—he dared not do otherwise, on account of the "objection which either the commissioners of accounts or my brethren of the House of Commons may make against so large a donation."[95]

---

[93] As for instance the loss of Jeaffreson's petition for malefactors in 1683. (Jeaffreson, *A Young Squire of the Seventeenth Century*, II, 24–25.)

[94] *Hist. MSS. Com., Portland MSS., Harley Papers*, VIII, 108; August 20, 1702.

[95] Add. MSS. 9735, f. 89; also 9732, f. 43.

Obviously the example which Blathwayt held steadily before him through his entire administrative career was that which Sir Robert Southwell had set him. He never deserted his original model. In the methods he used, his relations with his clerks, his dealings with other branches of the government, his regard for public opinion, it was Southwell's standard that he followed.[96] He could not have found a better.

[96] For an early example of an instance where Southwell found Blathwayt guilty of some mistakes, see *Petty-Southwell Correspondence*, p. 106. It was extra-governmental business, a mistake which either Blathwayt or his clerk made in copying Petty's treatise, *Quantulumcumque*, in 1682.

CHAPTER XIII

EMOLUMENTS OF OFFICE
SALARIES AND FEES

"SELF-INTEREST is the main wheel by which the mighty machine of this world's affaires is moved; some will advise you as my friends, some as if particularly your own, tho' at the same tyme they have no real kindness for either of us, but aim at private advantage and interest."[1] Was it disillusionment over the way in which the machine of state at Whitehall functioned that led Christopher Jeaffreson, the youthful planter-agent from St. Christopher, to such a dismal philosophy? As agent for St. Kitts he had spent nearly four years trying to persuade Blathwayt's plantation office, as well as the office of the secretary of state, to pay some attention to the military and economic needs of his colony. He had watched the ceaseless grind of place-seeking and fee-getting and had found that, if he was to do anything for his island, he would have to fall in with the general practice, since he had no power to oppose it. He had learned that every one and everything had a price, and that the secretary of the plantation office was no exception to the general rule.

There can be no doubt that Blathwayt, not only as secretary of the plantation office, but in all of his roles, was eager for money and money's worth. Such eagerness might have led a less cautious man to ruin, but in Blathwayt's case, plainly, there was never any question as to the outcome. Too thrifty and calculating to be ruined, he

[1] Jeaffreson, *A Young Squire of the Seventeenth Century*, II, 246.

was headed for a comfortable old age. Money came his way naturally. He married a considerable fortune; he acquired offices, the combined salaries of which at one time approximated £3500; his incidental fees increased from year to year. At the end of his life he had a decade entirely free from financial worry. His acquisitive sense had, of course, its disadvantages. His career left him open to the charge of rapacity and brought him extreme unpopularity in some circles, where people were ready to say that even his interest in the colonies was purely selfish.

There is no point in denying that Blathwayt was mercenary. He has suffered unjustly, however, at the hands both of contemporaries who were eager to malign him and of historians who have drawn from inadequate evidence equally inadequate conclusions. One of the former, Charles Hatton, said that all Blathwayt's frantic efforts to get officers back to their posts late in August, 1688, were nothing more than "a piece of Mr. Blathwayt's policy to get fees for licenses to be absent, for the rumor of the Dutch invasion is generally ridiculed here."[2] The event declared against Hatton, not Blathwayt. After 1696, when Blathwayt had fallen foul of the Whig group headed by the Duke of Shrewsbury, much was said about Blathwayt's mercenary regard for the plantations, and Shrewsbury listened with great interest to the charges that Bellomont, governor of New York, hurled against Blathwayt and his appointee, the recalled Fletcher. But Shrewsbury, if Lord Ailesbury's account is to be trusted, had nothing to say in defense of himself when it came to fee-taking.[3]

It seems curious that so profound a student of English

2 *Hatton Correspondence* (Camden Society, n.s., Vol. XXIII), II, 90; letter of August 24, 1688.

3 *Memoirs of Thomas, Earl of Ailesbury*, I, 246.

government as Dr. Lowell should attach particular significance to Blathwayt's fondness for gratuities, as if Blathwayt in that respect were markedly different from other seventeenth-century officials. Of course Blathwayt allowed "inducements of a pecuniary nature" to persuade him in complying with colonial requests.[4] Nor were colonial officials slow to offer inducements of fifty or a hundred guineas when they had a special favor to ask! The whole system of British administration was organized on a fee basis, and only a fool or an idealist would have practiced a self-denying ordinance. Blathwayt was neither.

A military historian, with a curious misunderstanding of the facts, charges Blathwayt with corruption for accepting, in 1690, a pension of £1000, payable out of the Irish poundage.[5] It was, of course, a perfectly regular payment, authorized by the king, and was a use of the poundage money not at all uncommon. True, poundage was obtained by deducting from the already niggardly pay of the common soldier, but in accepting poundage money Blathwayt was simply following the general practice of his time. In 1690, he needed money in the administrative end of the Irish campaign, his work had increased three- and fourfold, and the £1000 was by way of a contingency fund, not a bonus to the secretary at war.

Another critic, relying on the statement of Sir John Evelyn, is amazed that Blathwayt's income reached the high figure of £2000 per annum and declares that only gross malpractice could ever have raised it to that amount.[6] More careful investigation of the salaries attached to Blathwayt's offices would have convinced him of

[4] Lowell, *The Government of England*, I, 177.

[5] Walton, *A History of the British Standing Army, 1660–1700*, pp. 641, 769; also *Cal. S. P. Dom.*, 1690–1691, p. 25; June 2, 1690.

[6] Jeaffreson, *A Young Squire of the Seventeenth Century*, I, 312–313; II, 11–12. The editor of the letters, John Cordy Jeaffreson, in estimating

his error. Similar investigation would have saved Professor Channing from a like misunderstanding. His statement that Blathwayt drew a salary of £1500 as secretary to the Lords of Trade is ludicrous. What Channing thought was Blathwayt's salary, was the entire establishment of the plantation office, of which only £250 was Blathwayt's.[7] Likewise, he neglected to take into account contemporary practice, when he seized upon the payment of £100 to Blathwayt by the provincial assembly of Massachusetts as probable evidence of bribery. Despite his statement that such inducements were common, this generosity on the part of the assembly was most unwonted and represented, in reality, no bribe but long over-due compensation to Blathwayt as auditor general.[8] The fact that Blathwayt took a fee of five guineas in 1676 and asked fifty pounds for the same type of service ten years later, is also no evidence of rapacity.[9] Graduated fees were the order of the day; and the first amount was paid to him as a minor clerk in the plantation office, the second as secretary to the Lords of Trade.

Blathwayt's venality, in fact, must be judged in its relation to the practices and the conditions of his age. Administrators who dealt with an impoverished Exchequer might expect grave difficulty in collecting their salaries; contemporary opinion judged them accordingly and was more or less deadened to the evils of the fee system.

values states that £2000 was equal to £10,000 at the time he was writing (1878).

7 Channing, *History of the United States*, II, 218. Channing had run across the establishment of the plantation office among the papers of the parliamentary commissioners of accounts, 1692. (*Hist. MSS. Com.*, XIV. Report, App., Pt. VI, House of Lords MSS., p. 166.)

8 Channing, *History of the United States*, II, 218, f.n.; also *Mass. Prov. Laws*, VII, 435. Goodell, the editor of the laws, puts the same interpretation on the payment, even though the law plainly states that it was given to Blathwayt as auditor general.

9 C. S. S. Higham, ''The Accounts of a Colonial Governor's Agent in the 17th Century,'' *Amer. Hist. Rev.*, XXVIII, 267, 271.

When Sir John Evelyn wrote, in 1687, that Blathwayt's "income by the Army, Council, and Secretary to the Committee for Foreign Plantations, brings in above £2000 per annum," he calculated Blathwayt's combined salaries to a nicety.[10] Of this sum, £250 represented his salary as secretary to the Lords of Trade, an increase of £100 over the amount he received in 1675, when he entered the office; £250, his income as clerk in ordinary of the council, with £100 in addition for waiting on the Lords of Trade, a more or less sinecure payment, made to the four clerks of the council; £500, his salary as auditor general; three pounds a day, or £1095 per annum, as secretary at war— a total of £2195. From time to time, there were supplementary sources to his income. Thus he was supposed to receive something by way of salary from the various colonies taken into the royal system of audit after 1680. As secretary of state to William III, he drew an official salary of £2200, the regular amount paid to the junior secretary of state. Since, however, his salary as secretary at war was reduced at the same time to a pound a day, the gain was less substantial than it appears, although it did amount to £1470. Through the years 1692 to 1701 he drew a salary of at least £3665 from his various offices, plus any sums the colonies might give him as auditor general in addition to the £500 stipulated by his patent. In 1696, with the dismissal of the Lords of Trade and the creation of the Board of Trade, he lost his salary as secretary; but as a member of the board he still received £1000, so that he added really £750 to his income, making it, for the years 1696–1701, more than £4415, yearly—no inconsiderable sum even for a great minister of state. After 1701, his salaries fell off with comparative rapidity; he ceased to attend abroad as secretary of state, and he lost his secretaryship at war in 1704, and his position on the Board of

10 Evelyn, *Diary*, entry for June 18, 1687.

Trade in 1707. Thus he could count only on £850 in official salaries; nor was he always successful in collecting that amount.[11]

His real rise to fortune, of course, came when he married Mary Wynter, but even on the basis of his salaries, he was rated, for one of his class, a wealthy man. With allowance made for change in the purchasing power of money, the modern equivalent of his salary would be about £14,000 a year, a sum to astound present-day Whitehall.[12] Moreover, to every one of his salaries Blathwayt added fees, so that the actual amount of his receipts cannot be determined, particularly since there is no trace of his personal account books. Fees were in the nature of casual revenue and must have fluctuated considerably.

On the other hand, his salaries were not all pure gain, for in two of his offices he was obliged to pay his deputies and his office establishment out of what he received. This was true of the auditor generalship, where no provision was ever made for clerk hire, even after 1696, when Blathwayt could no longer make use of the plantation office clerks.[13] In addition, he had to compensate his deputies in the colonies. We know little about the bargains he struck with them. In New York, apparently, two-fifths of the amount paid to Blathwayt was reserved to his deputy; and in Virginia, the deputy was permitted to reserve a varying percentage of his collections.[14] In any colony, the

---

[11] The £850 included £350 as clerk of the council and £500 as auditor general.

[12] It is impossible to calculate the relative purchasing power of money in Blathwayt's day and at present. Channing figured (1905) that Blathwayt's supposed salary of £1500 would be worth £5000 or £6000. A conservative estimate would fix the pound's worth in the late seventeenth century at three times its present (1931) value; a very liberal one, at five or seven times.

[13] Even when Blathwayt was employing the plantation office clerks, headed by John Povey, in the audit, he must have had to pay them something out of his own pocket.

[14] For reference to Blathwayt's arrangement with his New York deputy,

deputy auditor was at liberty to supplement his salary through fees, which, in New York at least, according to Randolph, were considerable.[15]

In the war office, we can find no special establishment for clerks in Blathwayt's time, although some such arrangement may have existed earlier.[16] From a statement made in 1690, we know that the clerks were drawing what were regarded as good salaries.[17] Whether the amount was five shillings a day for a clerk, and whether Blathwayt was permitted to include it in his incidental expense account, is not wholly clear.

Even the amount which Blathwayt retained after he had paid his clerks and deputies was subject to further

see Huntington MSS., Blathwayt Papers relating to New York, I, no paging; evidence found in the accounts of 1699. In Virginia, the deputy's salary came up repeatedly for consideration, but was ultimately fixed at 5% of the revenue collected, which usually meant about £250, plus an additional 2½% in case the deputy auditor made good his bills of payment. (Treas. 64:89, 34–40, 265–266; 277–281, 400–401; *Board of Trade Journal*, 1715–1718, p. 74.)

[15] Goodrick, *Edward Randolph*, VI, 273; Randolph to Blathwayt, Oct. 16, 1688.

[16] In January, 1670, Mathew Lock's salary was raised from ten shillings to a pound a day, with five shillings a day extra for the hire of two clerks (*Cal. S. P. Dom.*, 1670, p. 1). In 1673, Lock petitioned for an increase in salary, since the five shillings was not sufficient for his clerks and he was obliged to reimburse them out of his own pay. (*Ibid.*, 1673–1675, pp. 82–83.) His petition was granted, for he was allowed two pounds a day, inclusive of clerk hire. In January, 1680, however, he was again reduced to one pound a day. (W.O. 24:3, 5.)

[17] Egerton MSS. 2618, f. 156; Crawford, the commissary of musters, made this statement about the salaries of the clerks, in a letter to George Clarke, whom he wanted to have take over the war office, February, 1690. Five shillings a day, per clerk, was apparently the normal amount of remuneration. Lock's clerk received that, while Lock was secretary at war to the forces in Ireland. (*Hist. MSS. Com., Ormonde MSS.*, n.s., III, 394.) James Vernon drew that amount, as secretary to the Duke of Monmouth. (W.O. 24:5; S. P. Dom., Entry Bk., Vol. 44, f. 90.) Adam Cardonnel, however, received ten shillings as secretary to Marlborough. (W.O. 24:28; also W.O. 25:3138, f. 154; W.O. 25:3145, no paging, but the warrant is dated September 8, 1691; W.O. 24:884; these are references to clerks on the Irish establishments.)

deductions, in the form of fees payable to the officers of the Exchequer.[18] Treasury officials laid heavy toll on salaries at the time of payment. The precise amount Blathwayt had to pay in the case of his various offices is not easily ascertained, but it can be estimated from the fees due in the case of his salary as clerk in ordinary of the council. To secure the £125 due him every six months, he had to pay £8 :[19] the £100, which, as clerk of the council, he received for waiting on the Lords of Trade, was liable to exchequer fees of about £5; to modern eyes, these are high percentages.[20] In the case of the plantation office establishment, however, he was permitted to include in the establishment the fees which the Exchequer clerks demanded, a curious but not uncommon practice of the period, so that his own salary and that of his clerks were presumably received intact.[21] This may have been true of some of his other salaries, although there is no evidence to prove it. The best that can be said of this system of deductions is that to a certain extent it was regulated, since fees were more or less uniformly graduated.

There was also an initial toll on such of Blathwayt's offices as were secured by letters patent. The clerkship of the council, the auditor generalship, and the secretary-

---

[18] His salary as auditor general must not, of course, be included in this group, since it was paid in the colonies.

[19] Egerton MSS. 1627, ff. 67–68. This is the diary of Philip Madox, clerk both in the plantation office and in the council chamber. He was usually required to draw the salaries of the clerks in ordinary, and in securing the half-yearly salary of Musgrave reported the following fees:

Charge in receiving it at the Treasury	1:10:0
your certificate	0: 2:6
at Sir R. Howard	1:14:0
at the pells	0:18:6
at the Tellers	3:15:0
	8:00:0

[20] *Ibid.;* entry for February 19, 1686. [21] Add. MSS. 9767, 9768.

ship at war were all issued under the great seal, and must have put Blathwayt to considerable expense. Under ordinary circumstances, the office of secretary of state was also a patent office, but, since Blathwayt's appointment was somewhat irregular, a commission under the great seal was not required.[22] No record of the amounts Blathwayt had to pay in order to pilot his various commissions through the circuitous passage of the seals has come to light, but we know that John Povey had to pay £47:16:6, in order to secure his patent as clerk in ordinary of the council.[23] Blathwayt's patent as member of the Board of

[22] For a discussion of this aspect of the secretary of state's office, see Evans, *The Principal Secretary of State*, pp. 211–212, 362–363.

[23] Add. MSS. 35107, f. 43. Edward Southwell paid the fees for Povey and later submitted to him the following itemized bill:

```
July 1697
Fees for Mr. Povey's patent
30—Paid to Mr. Bernard . . . . . . . . . .  6:10:0
August 5—Paid Mr. Bernard for the bill . . . . .  6: 7:6
    Gave Mr. Shorter  . . . . . . . . . .  0: 2:6
    Gave Mr. Turner . . . . . . . . . . .  0: 2:6
6   Paid Mr. Atturneys Clerks for their fees . . . .  7: 5:0
11  Paid for 2 Docketts at the Treasury . . . . .  1:12:6
    Paid at the Signet and Privy Seal . . . . . .  6:00:0
    Paid for the Recipi & Guinee . . . . . . .  1: 7:0
13  Paid at the Patent office for the Seal . . . . .  2:00:6
17  Paid at the Patent office  . . . . . . . .  4:19:0
    gave Mr. Storey who asked something . . . . .  0: 5:0
    at the Haniper office . . . . . . . . . .  6:13:4
    paid there for the private seal . . . . . .  2:00:0
    the clerke desired something & had  . . . . .  0: 6:0
    2 other people (haf wax?) etc. had  . . . . .  0: 5:0


                                              45:15:10
                                    more          8

    4:8                                       45:16:6
    11                                     ──────────
 ────────                                    2: 0:0
 4.:19  Entring at the auditors          ──────────
          & Pells                           47:16:6
```

Trade must have cost him at least as much as it did George Stepney, who said that he had to pay seventy pounds for it out of his own pocket.[24] Generally the fee for an office varied according to its salary, but there was no hard-and-fast rule.

Only one of Blathwayt's offices cost him anything in the way of purchase money—the secretaryship at war. He counted on getting back the amount he had spent for it by selling it in his turn, but the rise of the party system prevented him. In fact, he was not able to dispose of any of his offices by sale. If we are to accept the statement of Edward Southwell, there was considerable public sentiment against an officeholder who attempted to sell an office which he had not himself originally bought. Southwell's comments grew out of the incident of 1697, when he attempted to secure the clerkship in ordinary of the council which went instead to John Povey.[25] Southwell was exceedingly annoyed, and he grew more so when Blathwayt attempted to console him by offering him his own clerkship—for a consideration. In some notes which he apparently intended to use as the basis of a petition to the king, Southwell wrote: "Lett his Majesty bee told, that never yett any Clerke was allowed to sell that came in gratis as B[lathwayt] did, and to desire he may not be allowed to sell; nor S[outhwell] obliged to buy after so many years service, even for his Majesty's honour, And the other's object[ion] he is not in want, he hopes his Majesty will not make that an Obstruction."[26]

The curious state of unpreparedness in which the

24 Clarke, ''The Board of Trade at Work,'' *Amer. Hist. Rev.*, XVII, 29; entry in the Board of Trade Journal, December 31, 1697.

25 See *supra*, p. 319, f.n. 42.

26 Add. MSS. 38861, ff. 74–75. We have said nothing about the compensation Blathwayt received as clerk in extraordinary of the council from 1678 to 1686. So little is known of the clerkship in extraordinary, which was really a supernumerary appointment, that it is not safe to make any positive state-

Treasury habitually found itself during this period does not call for extended comment. It was usually at its wits' end to provide for the ordinary expenses of government. Year after year, it was impossible to assure a definite supply of money to any of the regular branches of the civil government. Treasury officials were constantly looking for some available fund. Thus, prior to 1688, the salaries of the secretaries of state were paid first out of the farm of the post office, then out of the farm of the customs on unwrought wood, and finally, beginning with December, 1674, out of the customs in general.[27] The costs of the plantation office were met out of any one of a half-dozen funds; in 1676, out of the law duty; in 1680, out of what remained of the queen's dowry; later out of the customs; then out of the excise; or even out of the four and a half percent. duty, which, according to the original agreement with the colonies involved, was to be used only in the colonies.[28] In 1686, it was assigned to the additional duty on sugar and tobacco which was imposed that year.[29]

When ready money was lacking, the Treasury fell back upon tallies issued against the revenues still uncollected. Thus, in 1676, the plantation office establishment amounted to £834:15:4; of this, £300 was paid out of the law duty then in the Exchequer; the remainder by tallies on the receivers, or farmers, of that duty.[30] Prior to the Revolution of 1688, bills of exchange were also resorted to, and these were always at a heavy discount. After 1688, bills of exchequer were employed. This partly relieved the situation and satisfied the officeholders, espe-

ments, but no record appears of salary payments attached to it. It was probably entirely on a fee basis.

[27] Evans, *The Principal Secretary of State*, p. 212.

[28] *Cal. Treas. Bks.*, 1676–1679, Vol. V, Pt. I, 81; 1679–1680, VI, 767; 1681–1685, Vol. VII, Pt. II, 1286.

[29] Add. MSS. 9767, ff. 146–147.

[30] *Cal. Treas. Bks.*, 1676–1679, Vol. V, Pt. I, 299.

cially when payments were made in first bills of exchequer; but payments continued to be dilatory, and more often than not compensation took the form either of the hated lottery tickets or of tickets payable out of the salt duty or the even more thoroughly despised malt duties. Such tortuous methods of public finance did little to inspire either the respect or the optimism of the officeholder. There was something demoralizing in a system which compelled Blathwayt, for instance, to write to the secretary to the Treasury, in 1697, with regard to his salary as secretary of state, reminding him of "his kind promise, that the payment of his two warrants was [to be] in the first exchequer bills, as he was forced to borrow money at extravagant rates for his subscription and for his equipage."[31] It was both humiliating and discouraging when Lowndes replied, "That, as to his own particular, my Lords have ordered his warrant for £1000 for his equipage in Exchequer bills, which is the most they can appoint out of that fond [sic]; and as to his warrant for his allowance, their Lordships intend to satisfye the same, when they can make a distribution of the credit on the Mault Act."[32] Malt tickets were of little comfort to Blathwayt, drudging away in Flanders at great expense and annoyance, and to offer them was really to add insult to injury.

Payments even in malt tickets might, however, have been welcome had they been prompt; arrears were the order of the day. This was inevitable under so lax and overburdened a treasury system. Such good results as might have ensued from the establishment of the Bank of England were neutralized necessarily by the continuance of the war. Even the Peace of Ryswick did not give any relief to the harassed Treasury, for the cost of disbanding

[31] *Cal. Treas. Papers*, 1697–1702, p. 31; April 23, 1697.
[32] *Ibid.*, pp. 37–38; June, 1697.

the army and the reduced appropriations of parliament only added new difficulties. Blathwayt's relations with the Treasury were most troublesome from 1698 to 1701, when he complained continually of deferred payments.[33]

His difficulties with the Treasury arose out of the salary arrangements made for his work as secretary at war and secretary of state. He had entered on his work as secretary of state in 1692, with no preliminary agreement on the salary to be paid him, but with the promise, of course, that he would ultimately be well compensated. Nothing had been done in the matter by 1693, so in July of that year he petitioned for payment. Encouraged by his friendly counsellor, Lord Nottingham, he summoned up his courage and decided on a bold stroke. He requested that he be paid the full annual salary of a junior secretary of state, £2242, even though he served for only a portion of the year.[34] By an arrangement of 1692, he had been allowed a contingency fund of £1000 a year, to provide

[33] In the plantation office, for instance, payments were usually from three months to two years in arrears. The deficit in the establishment at the time of Charles II's death was not finally cleared until 1690–1691, and then only after the staff had taken the oath of supremacy and allegiance. (Add. MSS. 9768, ff. 1–2, 28.) Payments in this instance were made in installments and not all of the incidentals were allowed. (See also Add. MSS. 9767, ff. 131– 135, 139–145, 148–149, 166–167.)

While Blathwayt was in Temple's service at The Hague, he was paid by Temple out of the latter's official allowance. No provision was made for a salary for Blathwayt, when Temple left Holland in 1670. On Blathwayt's return to England in 1672, he promptly petitioned the Treasury for payment of his bill of £693, which apparently covered all the expenses to which he had been put. After a lapse of a few months, the Treasury complied. Blathwayt's undated petition is to be found among the Porlock MSS. The Treasury allowed it on April 20, 1672; the sign manual to the clerk of the signet was dated in May; the privy seal in June; and the actual money warrant in July, 1672. (*Cal. Treas. Bks.*, 1669–1672, Vol. III, Pt. II, 1063, 1246.)

[34] The sum of £2242 included the ancient fee of £100, a pension of £1850, and board wages of £292. (Evans, *The Principal Secretary of State*, p. 221.) For Blathwayt's petition, etc., see S. P. Dom., Entry Bk. of Petitions, 1688–

himself with an equipage; this sum corresponded in a sense to the £2000 paid the junior secretary for intelligence.[35] Although, by the second summer of Blathwayt's attendance as secretary of state, nothing had been done to provide him with a competent salary, a reduction had meanwhile been made in his salary as secretary at war, from three pounds to one pound a day, beginning with January, 1693.[36] Such a curtailment was obviously grossly unfair unless some steps were taken to offset it. Since the Treasury did nothing, Blathwayt had to petition for an adjustment. The Treasury was aware of the justice of his plea and made an arrangement to have him paid the salary he had requested, even going so far as to make it retroactive, to begin with 1692.[37]

Unfortunately, having given him the promise of payment, the Treasury discovered that there was no ready money with which to do so. Blathwayt remained patient until February, 1694, when his arrears stood at £3300. Then, rather than wait longer, he agreed to accept payment in the form of a reversion to the manor of Egham, which was held in trust by the crown, and had an annual value which presumably approximated the sum owing him. Such a complicated system of payment was not un-

1693, Vol. 235, ff. 511–512; Cal. S. P. Dom., 1693, p. 215; also Add. MSS. 37992, f. 15; Blathwayt's letter to Nottingham, July 6, 1693.

35 King's Warrants, T. 52:16, f. 163. The £1000 was to go ''towards providing horses, carriages, and other necessaries for himself and his office and defraying other extraordinary expenses, etc.'' Since, as we have said, Blathwayt's first equipage fell into the hands of the French, the king graciously allowed him first another £1000 and, when that proved insufficient, still another. (Porlock MSS.; also W.O. 25:3138, f. 256.) For a resentful reference to the king's generosity, see Hist. MSS. Com., Portland Papers, IV, 641.

36 King's Warrants, T. 52:17, f. 165; W.O. 24:20. In 1701, Blathwayt stated that the pound a day went entirely for clerk hire. (Cal. Treas. Papers, 1697–1702, p. 498.)

37 Treas. Ref. Bk., Index 4621, ff. 320–328; Cal. S. P. Dom., 1694–1695, p. 31. Blathwayt handed in his petition in July, 1693, but it took until February, 1694, for the Treasury to take final action.

usual; but, after having secured his lease, Blathwayt discovered that there were prior claims or liens upon it to the extent of £2000, and he was obliged to petition the Treasury again for still other reversions, in the futile hope of making up the amount of his deficit.[38] It was an annoying and ignoble business, to say the least.

The arrangement by which Blathwayt was to receive a salary of £2242 and an annual contingency fund of £1000 continued until 1696; then, since peace was in sight, the latter fund was cut off, and he was told to hand in a bill of extraordinary expenses at the end of his attendance, in the fall.[39] Although he found this arrangement very unsatisfactory and complained bitterly about it, he was obliged to accept it until the very end of the expeditions.[40] Moreover, after the Peace of Ryswick, the Treasury decided to reduce his salary as secretary of state to £1000, although this reduction did not begin until 1699. To this arrangement Blathwayt was irreconcilable; so at the end of the campaign in 1699, with both his regular salary and his charge of incidentals unpaid, he submitted a bill of £2632:18:0, of which £390:18:0 was for extraordinary expenses. The Treasury was obdurate. They granted his bill of incidentals without protest, but to his other request

[38] S. P. Dom., Entry Bk. of Petitions, 1688–1693, Vol. 235, ff. 511–512; Treas. Ref. Bk., Index 4621, ff. 35, 320–328; Signet Office Docquets 20, February, 1694; Cal. S. P. Dom., 1693, p. 215; 1694–1695, p. 31.

[39] There is some confusion with regard to the year this reduction began. A reference in Cal. Treas. Papers, 1557–1696, p. 535, puts it in 1696, but makes a mistake in speaking of the fund as £1000 per week instead of per year. A reference is to be found in T. 52:19, f. 219 to a royal warrant for £1000, for contingencies, in 1696. I find no such record for 1697. In 1698, Blathwayt handed in a bill for £548:10:6; in 1699, £390:18:0; in 1700, £429:18:9; in 1701, £263:18:4. (T. 52:18, ff. 134, 346; T. 60:5, ff. 277, 397; T. 29:13, ff. 211, 238: also Hist. MSS. Com., House of Lords MSS., n.s., III, 160, 168.) For a reference to £100 paid Cardonnel in 1698, for extraordinary services, see W.O. 25:3140, ff. 118–119.

[40] Cal. Treas. Papers, 1697–1702, p. 498.

they instructed Lowndes to reply, "Their Lordships, pursuant to the King's resolution of the 26 May, 1699, can pay you £1000 only for that service, which they intend to do in some short time."[41]

Blathwayt had to accept the arrangement with the best grace he could summon and trust that time would soften the heart of the king and the Treasury Lords. He expressed his vexation to his friend, Hill, who, by 1700, was a member of the Treasury. "'Twas enough though you said but little to your board about my business. The dispatch of my secret service money was very favorable and in a letter to Mr. Lowndes I accept the £1000 with a small reservation of rights and privileges which may serve my successor if it do me no good. Methinks your lordships should judge I have the same right now at least as Mr. Vernon had before my Lord Jersey's resignation. You don't desire, sure, to save money by my service. 'Twould be a severe retrenchment indeed and yet no excuse to the house of commons if I should be called to account as others for my doings. But since I am at present retrenched not to half pay but less than a third pay (and not disbanded neither) I hope the money intended for me will be ordered as soon as possible wherein I doubt not your favor."[42]

The Treasury was evidently impressed with the injustice of the situation; for, while they made no increase in his salary as secretary of state, in 1700 they did raise his salary as secretary at war to £1000, in addition to the £365 which was a part of the regular army establishment. The fact that it was to be payable out of the poundage

41 Add. MSS. 38705, ff. 115, 121; July, 1700.

42 Porlock MSS.; Loo, August 3, 1700. By the reference to James Vernon, Blathwayt must have meant the arrangement for an equal division between Jersey and Vernon of the fees which came into the secretarial offices; they would otherwise all have gone to Jersey as the more important political personage. (See Evans, *The Principal Secretary of State*, p. 216.)

proved that it was an extraordinary item, and this was brought home to Blathwayt in 1701. His salary as secretary at war was then overdue eighteen months. He applied to Ranelagh for payment, but met with the answer "that the poundage fell so short that there was nothing left of it." Blathwayt then memorialized the Treasury, "trusting" that they would do something to make good the deficit, "humbly conceiving that the execution of so painful an office as that of Secretary at Warr may deserve so favourable a consideration that he may not want the payment of the said salary, whereof eighteen months are due."[43] The Treasury instructed Lowndes to "speak with Lord Ranelagh about the poundage. But Mr. Blathwayt must be paid somewhere."[44] The distraught refrain, "But Mr. Blathwayt must be paid somewhere," amply reveals the sorry state of the Exchequer.

Worried over the fact that there was no fund out of which his arrears as secretary at war could be paid, Blathwayt returned to his plea that he at least be restored to his earlier allowance as secretary of state. Again the Treasury would make no concessions. "The King says he [Blathwayt] ought not to make such an equipage as in time of warr, and there is no room now out of contingencys. At present the King doth not see occasion for Mr. Blathwayt to encrease his equipage, or for the King to encrease his allowance, but if there be a warr, the King will consider what occasion it will give for either."[45] Blathwayt refused to be satisfied even with so final an answer and in 1701 he submitted a bill for £2963:18:4; £1000 as secretary of state, another £1000 as secretary at war,

---

[43] *Cal. Treas. Papers,* 1697–1702, p. 498; June, 1701.

[44] *Ibid.;* Blathwayt's petition had been handed in on June 18; the Treasury minute states that it was read on June 23, which was certainly expeditious.

[45] *Ibid.;* see also Add. MSS. 38706, f. 60; Blathwayt to Lowndes, July 29, 1701.

£263:18:4 for his incidental disbursements, and £700 "for a further allowance for maintaining his clerks, making up his own salary and allowance to £2000 per annum."[46] His tender failed, the Treasury disallowing the item for £700 without further comment.[47]

All of Blathwayt's salaries were borne directly or indirectly by the English Exchequer, save one, that of the auditor generalship.[48] In his patent, provision was made for the payment of £500; £150 each to be paid by Jamaica and Barbados, and £100 by Virginia and the Leeward Islands. He was far more successful in collecting his salary than might have been anticipated. His report of 1711 to the parliamentary commissioners of accounts revealed arrearages of about £2300, on first glance a large amount, but less impressive when we learn that it covered a period

[46] Treas. Min. Bk., T. 29:13, ff. 211, 238; Treas. Order Bk., T. 60:5, f. 397.

[47] When William III died, Treasury accounts disclosed an extensive list of arrears in salaries, but Blathwayt's arrears as secretary of state and secretary at war were not among them, so apparently some substitute for the poundage had been found. £2000, however, was owing him as clerk of the council and member of the Board of Trade; this was still unpaid, apparently, twelve years later. (Hardy, *Syllabus of Rymer's Foedera,* I, cxliv–cxlv; *Cal. Treas. Papers,* 1714–1719, p. 11; September 17, 1714.)

[48] Blathwayt's salary as clerk to Temple and later as clerk to the Earl of Conway, was borne indirectly by the Exchequer. We can find no evidence of the exact amounts paid him. A secretary, or first clerk, in a foreign embassy was usually paid £150 plus his living expenses. (Add. MSS. 28901, f. 133; John Ellis, first clerk in the northern office, to Sir Paul Rycaut, British resident at Hamburg, May 17, 1698.) He was recommending one of Blathwayt's former clerks, Mr. Orth. He thought Orth would consider 200 crowns and living expenses, provided he were also given his traveling expenses to Hamburg.

For material on the salaries paid to clerks in the secretarial office, and the fact that public payment was making a feeble beginning, see Evans, *The Principal Secretary of State,* pp. 164–165, 192–193; *Cal. Treas. Bks.,* 1672–1675, IV, 100, 295, 633, 755, 818; 1676–1679, Vol. V, Pt. II, 1082. Like Owen Wynne, Sir Leoline Jenkins' clerk, Blathwayt probably received £140 from Conway, besides "diet" and lodging: or, the latter might have been omitted, and £200 paid him instead, as was true of Wynne under Sunderland, Jenkins' successor.

of ten years. Jamaica was paid up; Virginia apparently owed him £200; the Leeward Islands were £800 in arrears; while Barbados, as might be expected, the worst offender, was in arrears for the entire period and owed him £1300.[49] His salary was always sent from Jamaica with fair regularity. It was first sent in bills of exchange or in pieces of eight, but beginning with 1683, bills of exchange alone were permitted, the difference in the rate of exchange to go to the Treasury.[50] The records of Virginia reveal no particular difficulty in connection with salary payments, thanks, no doubt, to the good offices of the elder and the younger Byrd. It is hard to tell what arrangements were made in the Leeward Islands for the division of the burden among the four islands. Blathwayt received his salary from them quite regularly until 1703. After the death of Colonel Codrington, the auditing system seems to have become completely demoralized, and in 1711 Blathwayt reported that the islands owed him eight years' salary. Even Barbados paid him quite promptly until 1692, when it reported that there were no funds.[51] From that time on, there was the greatest irregularity. For the decade from 1693 to 1703, bills of exchange amounting to £1745 were transmitted. Some of these proved worthless, and their payment was protested; others were sold at a tremendous discount.[52] After 1703,

[49] Treas. 64:90, ff. 52–53; also Huntington MSS., Blathwayt Papers relating to Jamaica, 1656–1711, no paging; a draft of the report of 1711.

[50] Cal. S. P. Col., 1681–1685, p. 496; order of the council of Jamaica, September 20, 1683.

[51] Ibid., 1689–1692, p. 598; Stede to Blathwayt, February 12, 1692.

[52] Blathwayt's Account Book, 1711, f. 673; Add. MSS. 38714, ff. 102–105; also Huntington MSS., Blathwayt Papers relating to Barbados, letters from the collector, Captain Thomas, November 13, 1702, and February 2, 1703. He protested bitterly that he was required to make up the loss of £100 in bills of exchange, which had been lost at sea. Judging from Blathwayt's statement in 1711, that only £1300 was owing him (the exact amount of his salary, 1703–1711), the defects in the earlier bills of exchange had been rectified.

Blathwayt regarded the situation as more or less hopeless.[53]

Of the colonies absorbed into the system after 1680, few showed any great willingness to come to an agreement with Blathwayt on the question of salary. Cranfield reported from New Hampshire in 1682, with an optimism which proved premature, "Your office of Surveyor and Auditor is owned at Council, and the Country not being able, thro poverty to make such acknowledgment as might have been expected, have passed an order for sixpence of the pound to you, or your Deputy out of all publike monies here raised, which is hoped will Countervaile in proportion what is done in other Plantations."[54] The records do not reveal that Blathwayt was very successful in collecting many New Hampshire sixpences. In 1694, Lieutenant-Governor Usher indicated a desire to secure a payment of £400 for Blathwayt, which probably represented salary due him as auditor, but the ultimate outcome of his proposal is unknown.[55] In his reports, Blathwayt never mentioned a salary from the province. Whatever payments were made, were certainly on a casual basis.

We are equally in the dark on the arrangements Blathwayt came to with Massachusetts. Randolph exerted himself to secure some form of payment that would be satisfactory to Blathwayt, who apparently was willing to accept whatever the province was willing to give him.

[53] Blathwayt, however, acknowledged a payment of £200 in 1704. (Add. MSS. 38714, ff. 107–108; Blathwayt to Captain Thomas.) Blathwayt's letter to Colonel Parke, April 30, 1706, is interesting. (Add. MSS. 38712, f. 79.)

[54] Goodrick, *Edward Randolph*, VI, 122; December 1, 1682. Cranfield's reason for securing Blathwayt so satisfactory a settlement was somewhat naïve and quite worthy of him. Now, he said, Blathwayt would further his suit for Mason's daughter with her dowry of £3000.

[55] *Cal. S. P. Col.*, 1693–1696, p. 413; November 10, 1694.

Randolph once asked Blathwayt whether he would accept a fee of £5 on every £100 of revenue collected, and in the first accounts he sent, he allowed Blathwayt £51:4:0. The money itself apparently was not forthcoming, and Randolph subsequently reported that the council would not allow it, saying that without an assembly to sanction the payment, they had no authority to act.[56] Presumably no final settlement was ever made. Two "gifts" from Massachusetts of £100 each, in 1693 and 1694, probably represented payments to Blathwayt for his services as auditor.[57] As far as we know, Blathwayt never had anything to say on the matter in any of his reports.

New York was at first amenable and in 1688 granted Blathwayt a salary of five per cent. on collections—according to Randolph, the equivalent of £100.[58] In 1692, the latter reported that the New York revenues gave such signs of increasing that he believed Blathwayt's salary would ultimately amount to £500, an expectation which needless to say was never realized.[59] Blathwayt's salary of five per cent. was, however, fairly regular until the beginning of the eighteenth century; then, in the struggles that ensued over the question of the revenue and the relative authority of the provincial treasurer and the royal collector, New York came very near to repudiating the royal audit altogether and certainly showed a keen desire to free itself of any obligation to Blathwayt. In 1704 the question of his salary came up for debate in the assembly, and, as a result of the protest made, Blathwayt was obliged to forego his allowance of five per cent. on collections and to accept a flat rate of £150.[60] The assembly im-

56 Goodrick, *Edward Randolph*, VI, 220, 232, 257.

57 *Cal. S. P. Col.*, 1693–1696, p. 298.

58 Goodrick, *Edward Randolph*, VI, 251, 273; VII, 427.

59 *Ibid.*, VII, 403.

60 *New York Provincial Assembly Journal*, I, 452, 454, 467, 468; Osgood, *The American Colonies in the 18th Century*, II, 423 et seq.

plied, both in that year and again in 1721, when the issue broke out anew, that Blathwayt had been too fond of extralegal arrangements with the colonies on the matter of salary and should have been obliged in every instance to submit them to the English Treasury for scrutiny.[61]

Maryland refused point-blank to commit itself to any binding arrangement. In 1695, four years after the audit had been introduced into the province, Governor Nicholson, who was currying favor with Blathwayt, in an effort to gain his support in securing the governorship of Virginia, bestirred himself to obtain some salary provision. He met with no response from the assembly at first, even though he offered to advance the money himself.[62] "This house having well considered your Excellency's proposal touching the gratifying the Honorable Esquire Blathwayt, and Mr. Povey, do return your Excellency our hearty thanks for your generous offer, but find ourselves altogether incapable at this time to gratify the aforesaid gentlemen, being at present willing to satisfy all such obligations as this province now lies under."[63] Nicholson, however, continued his plea, for he knew the effect his success would have on Blathwayt. Six months later, the assembly, in niggardly fashion and with open reluctance, consented to pay Blathwayt fifty guineas, and Povey, their agent, fifty pounds, provided the governor would advance the amounts.[64]

Four years later, Blakiston, Nicholson's successor,

[61] *New York Provincial Assembly Journal*, as above. In 1721, the assembly declared that Blathwayt had been severely censured, in 1704, by the English Treasury, for his conduct and had been forced to accept the flat rate of £150. In 1723, Governor Burnet reported, however, that the original agreement for 5 per cent. on collections had been restored. (Osgood, II, 424–425.)

[62] *Md. Archives*, XIX, 165, 192; *Cal. S. P. Col.*, 1693–1696, p. 484.

[63] *Md. Archives*, XIX, 165, 192; Nicholson had offered to advance £200.

[64] *Ibid.* pp. 230, 234; *Cal. S. P. Col.*, 1693–1696, p. 603.

came with instructions from the Treasury to secure Blathwayt an annual allowance. "Gentlemen," he addressed the assembly, "herewith I send a copy of the patent of the Honorable William Blathwayt, Esquire, . . . who is a person of great worth and honor and able to do you many good offices in the station he stands and for his great trouble and care in the discharge of that employment has generally a salary from most all of the plantations except this place. I therefore recommend it to your consideration to make some yearly allowance of salary whereby you will make him your friend and I am confident thereby do yourselves a signal piece of service."[65] But good offices or no good offices, it was all the same to the Maryland house of burgesses. Its members were not to be beguiled. Though they may have again remitted Blathwayt "presents" of fifty guineas, they never altered their original determination to pay him not a penny of regular salary.

Blathwayt's salary as auditor general once involved him in an altercation with the Treasury Lords. They argued that his salary was liable to the tax levied on the salaries of all English officials. Blathwayt protested on the ground that no portion of this salary was derived in England. The Treasury, however, insisted that since he exercised his office in England, it was rateable there. To this Blathwayt answered that the work was really done in the colonies, through his deputies, and that he exercised the office in much the same way as governors did who resided in England and had their deputies serving in the plantations. The Treasury then asserted, that at any rate, the four and a half percent. duty, over which, they said, Blathwayt had some control, was managed in England. Blathwayt stoutly denied that he derived any profit from

[65] *Md. Archives*, XXII, p. 357; July 22, 1699.

it.[66] Unfortunately, the outcome of this interesting dispute is unknown. As a matter of principle, Blathwayt may have been sound in his arguments, which have the same ring as some of the *"in situ"* arguments advanced by modern income taxpayers. If he was successful, it meant that his salary as auditor escaped taxation of any sort, for it was not taxed in the colonies.

Blathwayt made two other attempts to evade taxation. In 1686, a dispute arose over the collection of hearthmoney within the verge of the palace of Whitehall. Blathwayt had refused to pay the tax on his lodgings in Scotland Yard, which he had occupied since 1675.[67] In refusing, he found himself in very "respectable" company, for the Duchess of Lauderdale, the Duchess of Portland, Colonel Kirke, and even Lord Rochester, the Lord Treasurer, and Henry Guy, the secretary to the Treasury, were included among the transgressors. It became necessary for Rochester to issue a warrant to the collectors of the hearthmoney, to compel payment from inhabitants of "several such houses and lodgings (in or near the King's Palace of Whitehall) [that] have long escaped the payment of hearthmoney under pretence that they were within the Verge of said Palace, though they are not inhabited by any of his Majesty's servants by reason of any office or employments under the King."[68]

In 1714, Blathwayt addressed a memorial to the Treasury regarding a "pretended debt due to the Crown for his

[66] Porlock MSS.; no date is given, but the issue seems to have come up early in the eighteenth century, judging from the internal evidence at hand.

[67] For a reference to this grant, see item no. 108, Sotheby sales catalogue, Blathwayt MSS., April 25, 1910.

[68] *Cal. Treas. Bks.*, 1685–1688, Vol. VII, Pt. II, 1052. The members of the board of the greencloth were ordered to assist the collectors of the hearthmoney in enforcing collections. Documentary evidence is slight, but the occasion for this sudden rigor on the part of the Treasury in 1686 was doubtless the government's extreme poverty.

assessment on his place as Clerk of the Council."[69] This was the result of a threatened suit in the Court of Exchequer to collect the tax levied on his salary as clerk—a salary which had been in arrears £2000 since 1702. The amount of the tax was £55.3.4. Blathwayt's petition met with no encouragement from the Lord Treasurer, who instructed Lowndes to reply, "My Lord thinks he cannot protect any person legally against payment of any sum assessed on him; if he is illegally assessed, he may plead it in the Exchequer. His Lordship is unwilling to make a precedent which might be prejudicial." If Blathwayt's assertions were correct, he certainly had a grievance. It is hard to say whether Blathwayt thought the matter was worth the expense and annoyance of a suit in the Court of Exchequer. The incident casts a curious light on the Treasury's reasoning. In making his request to the Treasury, he seems to have followed precedent, and the refusal of the Lord Treasurer was more irregular than Blathwayt's plea.

On Blathwayt's fees and other unofficial sources of income, we have far less light than we could desire, Presumably, like other seventeenth-century officials, he regarded his salaries merely as "pegs on which to hang a fortune." The fees which he was entitled to collect in the regular course of business must have provided him with a very handsome sum annually. By royal order, he was permitted to collect a day's pay from every officer in the army whose commission he entered in his commission books, and his profits must have been very large, since every officer was required to have his commission entered in order to have his name appear on the muster rolls.[70] In

[69] *Cal. Treas. Papers,* 1714–1719, p. 11; September 17 and 22, 1714. It is possible that in 1714 Blathwayt had finally been paid his arrears as clerk of the council, and that the Treasury was simply trying to collect back taxes on them, but Blathwayt's petition does not say so.

[70] W.O. 26:6, ff. 108, 135. A secretary of state also charged the same fee

some of the commission books appear marginal notes regarding the payment of these fees. The notation "Fees dedit" Mr. Blathwayt, Mr. Cardonnel, or Mr. Thurston, as the case might be, is far more common than the entry, "No fees."[71] Blathwayt also had the right to charge a day's pay for every permit for leave of absence which he issued to officers in the army, and this source of revenue was sufficiently profitable for Hatton to question Blathwayt's motive in ordering the men back to their posts in August, 1688.[72] At first, he was also permitted to demand fees for the issuance of pay warrants to officers, but the officers protested so vigorously that, in 1687, Blathwayt's salary as secretary at war was raised from two to three pounds a day, on condition that he cease to collect these fees.[73]

Such regulations were admissions on the part of the government that salary payments were inadequate and that only concerted action on the part of the men affected would bring official relief. They were dangerous admissions of weakness, moreover, and so also were the tables of fees which were allowed to be drawn up, and occasionally posted, in some of the public offices.[74] Secretaries and

for issuing commissions. (Add. MSS. 38861, f. 116.) What arrangements were made by Blathwayt and George Clarke for the division of fees during Blathwayt's absence on the Continent, we cannot say definitely, but from one incident we gather that Blathwayt required his share, probably the larger one, at that. We know that he insisted on having the fees for commissions to officers of the marines reserved, for him, for we find Cardonnel writing to Burchett, the secretary to the Admiralty, "When you deliver the two commissions to Captain Byng and Mr. Aylmer, I entreat you will let Mr. Faulk receive the fees from them being six pounds, seven shillings, and six pence each commission, and I will call upon him for the money when it pleases God to return." (Admiralty 1:4316; entry for September, 1698.)

71 For references see W.O. 25:4.

72 *Hatton Correspondence* (Camden Society, n.s., Vol. XXIII), II, 90.

73 W.O. 26:6, f. 108; February 18, 1687.

74 For a table of fees posted in the plantation office, in 1731, see C.O. 389: 12, f. 328. The list is printed in Dickerson, *American Colonial Government*, pp.

clerks were prone to regard these light-heartedly, and they cheerfully accepted additional voluntary offerings, while the government winked at all except the most questionable practices. Thus, in 1678, the clerks of the council were forbidden to take any fees or other profits; to compensate for their losses, they had their salaries raised from £50 to £250 a year.[75] Despite this order, Blathwayt was able to charge as high as ten guineas for the issuance of desired orders in council to anxious clients, and his clerks charged from one to three guineas for copying them.[76] Blathwayt probably never, except to his closest friends, issued a document bearing an official signature without demanding a fee—usually a very high one. As clerk to Lord Conway, he was entitled to a fee of one or two pounds on all warrants bearing Conway's signature; as secretary of state himself, he could, and did, charge five pounds for securing the royal sign manual.[77]

Blathwayt naturally never set a price for a particular service, except where there was a stipulated table of fees.

72–73. From it, it is apparent that no paper could be copied for less than ten shillings; and some, like drafts of the governor's instructions, cost £12.12.0. Considering the arduous nature of the task, it is not surprising that the instructions cost twelve guineas.

[75] *Cal. Treas. Bks.*, 1676–1679, Vol. V, Pt. II, 1286. The order had evidently been issued on September 9, 1678.

[76] C. S. S. Higham, ''Accounts of a Colonial Governor's Agent,'' *Amer. Hist. Rev.*, XXVIII, 272, 275. The ten guineas in this case were collected by Blathwayt's colleague, Sir Philip Lloyd, not by Blathwayt himself. For the scale of fees paid by a person being sworn in as an officer by the Privy Council, see Add. MSS. 38861, f. 114. A privy councillor or a secretary of state, on being sworn, had to pay the clerk in attendance £10, £4 to the under clerks, £6 to the keeper of the records, £5 to the doorkeeper—in all £25.

[77] For a discussion of the fees of the secretary of state's office, see Evans, *The Principal Secretary of State*, pp. 206–210. Blathwayt got into a heated dispute with Trumbull over the secretarial fees on commissions. (*Hist. MSS. Com., Downshire MSS., Trumbull Papers*, Vol. I, Pt. II, 470; S. P. For., *Military Expeditions*, I, 17; also *Memoirs of Thomas, Earl of Ailesbury*, I, 125, 246.)

He simply prevaricated. Delicacy and the rules of the game prevented him from saying anything openly to a parsimonious client who refused to loosen his purse strings, but there were a thousand ways of indicating that Blathwayt had no intention of acting until he had the money in his hand. He had a great deal of difficulty in conveying to the high-minded agent of St. Kitts, young Christopher Jeaffreson, that the latter need never expect any malefactors to swell the population of his island until Blathwayt got his gratuity for having the matter brought up at the Privy Council meeting. Jeaffreson finally succumbed and wrote to the lieutenant-governor of St. Kitts, ''But without a gratification of twenty or thirty guynnies [*sic*] to himself [Blathwayt], at the least, I doubt much the effect of the letters or anything else.''[78] His fellow planters agreed and thought fifty guineas not too much to bestow, considering the urgency of their need.[79]

Few colonies were unwilling to offer gratuities at Whitehall when something they had set their hearts on was at stake. If England could not be won over, then let her be bought over, was the generally accepted idea. Even the godly Massachusetts was willing to offer Lord Hyde two thousand guineas for the king's private use, if the charter could be retained.[80] Virginia, in 1692, concerned over the fate of a port bill at the hands of the Privy Council, decided that it was worth while sending Blathwayt £200 for his services in having it allowed.[81] Since the act was subsequently disallowed, the query naturally arises, what became of the £200? Was it ever sent, and if so, did Blathwayt feel free to accept it?

[78] Jeaffreson, *A Young Squire of the Seventeenth Century*, I, 141–147; II, 8–50, scattered references.

[79] *Ibid.*, II, 58–59.

[80] Kimball, *The Public Life of Joseph Dudley*, p. 15.

[81] *Cal. S. P. Col.*, 1689–1692, pp. 630–631.

Not all the colonies were as trusting as Plymouth. During the controversy over the issue of a charter for the province, Governor Hinckley wrote Blathwayt a pleading letter, closing it with the statement: "We shall not show ourselves ungrateful to either of you [Randolph and Blathwayt] for your labor of love therein. I hope the small gratuity sent to you through Mr. Jeffon will not be offensive to you or Mr. Randolph."[82] Probably Maryland was the only colony to enter any definite protest against the fees charged in the plantation office. In 1697, when Maryland was particularly out of sympathy with both Blathwayt and Povey, the provincial secretary, fresh from a trip to England, presented a letter from Povey to the following effect, "that he would give in no particular of fees due to the plantation office, for presenting several addresses and other business before the King in Council and the Right Honorable the Lords of the Committee for Trade and Plantations, for the services of this province, but left this matter wholly to the consideration of the assembly."[83] Povey had sadly misjudged the temper of the provincial assembly, and he rued the day he had resolved to do Maryland any service without first having been assured of payment, for he received the laconic reply, "The house do think they have sufficiently gratified Mr. Povey to discharge those fees if any due."[84]

Fond as Blathwayt was of all sorts of gratuities and favors—and he accepted almost any gift, from sturgeon, fresh from the North Sea, Spanish bricks of tobacco, or orange marmalade from Barbados, to ermine from New England for a cloak for Mrs. Blathwayt—his contemporaries did not regard him as abnormally covetous. His observance of the tenth commandment was probably in

[82] *Mass. Hist. Soc. Coll.*, 4th ser., I, 94.
[83] *Md. Archives*, XXII, 52.
[84] *Ibid.*, pp. 128–129; March 31, 1698.

keeping with the best seventeenth-century standards. Contemporary judgment also rated him honest. No one who had been guilty of very flagrant abuses could have withstood as searching investigation at the hands of the commissioners of accounts as Blathwayt did. Those who attacked him for his avarice were very often his would-be successors in an office and his financial success must always have been very painful to competitors. Those who charged him with bribery were men like Lord Bellomont and Sir Francis Nicholson, whose views were too biased to be accepted at their face value. Any wild dream of colonial wealth which that dubious rogue Edward Cranfield had for himself and Blathwayt could take on formidable proportions if Bellomont chose to magnify it.

From time to time, of course, Blathwayt's name was linked with various land schemes in the colonies; this, for a man in his position, was perfectly normal. There seems to have been nothing illicit in any of his alleged designs. It would not have been surprising if he had occasionally succumbed to dreams of colonial riches, but his business acumen was sufficient to keep him from being seriously interested in most of the schemes broached to him. The Million Purchase on the Merrimac River is an example of the sort of thing that frequently offered, but projects of such a minor character could scarcely have caught his fancy. Even if they did, they were not, by any standard, criminal.[85] It may or may not be significant that nearly all

[85] Richard Wharton's scheme for land development on the Merrimac River. Wharton, Joseph Dudley, and Samuel Shrimpton had purchased from the chief Indian sachem a tract of land, six by ten miles square, and had organized a company with shares at £20 each. In order "to grease the wheels" and obtain their patent of incorporation with greater ease, Dudley and Shrimpton presented Blathwayt with a share, which may, or may not, have been accepted by him; but, if it was, it did not produce the desired result. (Barnes, "Richard Wharton, a 17th Century New England Colonial," *Trans. Col. Soc. Mass.* (1924–1926), XXVI, 249.)

of the tales of this class are of a New England origin or depended on a New England setting! A West Indian venture would have had a far better chance of a successful outcome!

The story goes that Blathwayt secured the governorship of New Hampshire for Cranfield with the distinct understanding that the former was to make money out of the arrangement. Cranfield's correspondence hints at agreements of some sort or other, but if his grandiose schemes of wealth to be gleaned from impoverished New Hampshire and Maine were taken seriously by Blathwayt, the latter had less understanding of the resources of those provinces than is commonly supposed. Cranfield was, of course, either harebrained or deliberately corrupt in his management of New Hampshire. He wrote to Blathwayt in 1683, "I give you my faith that you and Mr. Randolph shall come into an equal part of everything that tends to profit. First, as to the settlement of the Province of Maine, we shall at least make £3000. The Narragansett country lies between several claimers; both parties have money, and three or four thousand pounds were not to be felt in the disposal of those lands. As for Boston, there are some persons to be exempt out of the pardon, who will buy their pardon at 8 or 10 thousand pounds' price; besides, there are several grants of town lands, which will in a year or two come to be removed, to pay above £2000 upon these new leases. The excise and Customs yearly paid come to about £1500,—and there is above £5000 money which was collected for the Evangelizing of Indians, now out at use in the country; which by commission may be inspected into and regulated: with other advantages which will arise in the settlement."[86]

Blathwayt's reply, if discovered, would throw light on

his judgment of the governor. He must have known that in backing Cranfield he was backing the wrong horse, but some mysterious personal link bound him to Cranfield.[87] At any rate, it did not take him long to discover the anemic condition of New Hampshire and the impossibility of bleeding it in any way. In the end, all that came of Cranfield's roseate prospect was the seizure of Gove's property, which yielded a paltry £200 to be divided among Blathwayt, Cooke,[88] and Cranfield.[89]

Blathwayt's motives in New Hampshire continued, however, to be suspected, and tales of his illicit designs on the province were hard to suppress. As late as 1700 Bellomont reported, "Mr. Blathwayt is intriguing to secure to himself the propriety of New Hampshire, notwithstanding the counter efforts of Allen."[90] This statement, in view of Blathwayt's well-known attitude on proprietary colonies, is somewhat surprising, but Bellomont produced what he chose to regard as irrefutable proof. "The papers I send enclosed," he wrote to Shrewsbury, ". . . will surprise, especially that which discovers Blathwait's bargain with Colonel Allen for half his pretended interest in New Hampshire and a great part of this province. I have sent the papers to my Lord Chancellor and my Lord Jersey, and I hope among you he, I mean Mr. Blathwait, will be crossbit. By this bargain of his with Allen 'tis plain who sold the lands in New York to Fletcher. If it could be lawfully done, the seizing of Colonel Allen's papers would discover this villainous bargain of Blathwait's with him, which would a thousand times more

[87] *Supra*, pp. 108, 364. Some connection with Mason and Gorges, apparently; possibly with Southwell.

[88] Presumably John Cooke, in the secretary of state's office, with whom Blathwayt was friendly.

[89] Sanborn, "Churchmen on the Pascataqua, etc.," pp. 237–238.

[90] Vernon, *Letters Illustrative, etc.*, III, 129; Vernon to Shrewsbury, August 10, 1700, basing his statement on a letter from Bellomont.

deserve an inquisition of the House of Commons than that they bestowed nine hours' debate on the 6th of last December.[91] I hope those two lords and yourself will with vigor oppose Mr. Blathwait's treacherous sale of these plantations from England. The management of them has been hitherto most ridiculous, and all by that man's means who has made a milch cow of 'em for many years together.''[92]

It seems impossible to believe that Bellomont was serious in bringing this monstrous charge, when the nature of his evidence is learned. This was a statement made by Armstrong, a naval officer, who said that Blathwayt and a lawyer named Dobbin had agreed with Colonel Allen to this transfer of New Hampshire; that Blathwayt had consented to buy out the Duke of Leeds, Lord Lonsdale, and another lord (whose name Armstrong had at first forgotten but later declared to be Leinster), who had also come to an agreement with Allen; and that the latter, owing Blathwayt the sum of £3000, had promised, before he left England for New Hampshire, to turn over one half of his claim to the province in case he could not repay the money by a given date. Even in case he did repay it, it was agreed that Blathwayt was to have a third interest as his commission for the service he had rendered Allen.[93]

The whole tale is so thin as scarcely to deserve consideration, let alone credence. Bellomont had no further

---

[91] The debate on the motion, which passed in the negative, censuring Bellomont and others for their conduct on the question of the suppression of piratical ventures, obviously those of Captain Kidd. (Cobbett, *Parl. Hist.*, 1688–1702, V, 1202.)

[92] *Cal. S. P. Col.*, 1700, pp. 372–373; June 22, 1700.

[93] *Ibid.;* also *Mass. Hist. Soc. Col.*, 6th ser., III, 526–528, for some evidence on Blathwayt's attitude toward New Hampshire at this time. He had always suspected the province's good faith, and in this instance he had a very sarcastic retort to make to agents of a province which charged its people wih a tax of £650, £300 of which they intended to use in order to send an agent to complain to the king.

proof and apparently asked for none. At the time he brought his charge, Allen's claims to New Hampshire were being hotly contested by Mason and were ultimately, although not until after Allen's death in 1706, wholly set aside. It is doubtful whether Blathwayt could have been interested in any such proposition, unless he were convinced that the claim on which it depended could be upheld in a court of law. Even if he were, the transaction was little more than a business agreement, whereby Blathwayt came to Allen's financial rescue and accepted very poor security in return. Bellomont was willing to mention the names of such great lords as Leeds, Lonsdale, and Leinster in this connection which he assumed to be dubious. Why was it so much worse for Blathwayt to have dealings with Allen than for their lordships? Or did a Whig whitewash alter the situation? Bellomont was also willing to involve the Marquis of Caermarthen, who, he said, had asked him to be particularly kind to Allen. Bellomont did not seem to regard the request as a reflection on Caermarthen's good name.

Bellomont had still another scheme of Blathwayt's reported to him. This time his informant was none other than Edward Randolph, who apparently never sensed the venom with which Bellomont regarded Blathwayt. It seems that, in 1699, Randolph heard that Blathwayt and other officials were interested in discovering gold and silver mines in South Carolina, and that James Moore, secretary of the colony, had offered to prospect for them. Randolph was alarmed by the story. Rumors of precious metals were nothing more than Indian talk, he wrote Bellomont; Moore, had better be careful, for the scheme was a dangerous encroachment on the rights of the lords proprietors, who would certainly put in a claim for a fourth part of any ore that was discovered; in the meantime they would probably regard Moore as more zealous in the royal interest than their own and would turn him out of office. Randolph went on to say that he was advising caution on the part of English officials involved (Blathwayt among them) and that he hoped Bellomont would write home in similar vein.[94] What ultimately came of the scheme is hard to say, but certainly Blathwayt never enjoyed any profits from gold or silver mined in South Carolina. As Randolph had hinted, the reports were mere Indian fabrications.

With all allowance made for gossiping exaggerations, Blathwayt undoubtedly made a very good thing out of his offices. His salaries alone would have raised him to a fair level of affluence; his numerous fees and gratuities provided a comfortable surplus. He was a man of his time, and he believed firmly in the wisdom of laying up his treasure on earth.

[94] *Cal. S. P. Col.*, 1699, pp. 112–114; Randolph to Bellomont, March 22, 1699. For Randolph's letter to the Earl of Bridgewater on the matter, see Toppan, *Edward Randolph*, II, 163–164.

CHAPTER XIV

CONCLUSION

As we pass Blathwayt's long public life in review, the facts which strike us immediately are its essential unity persisting through a diversity of duties, and Blathwayt's unfailing devotion to a rôle for which he was convinced nature had designed him. He apparently could conceive of himself in no other capacity than that of administrator, and it costs us less effort to forgive him his sense of "comfortable importance" on the matter than it did some of his contemporaries, to whom his grave omniscience on his special subjects was a constant irritant. This assurance was no passing mood or fancy. The youthful Blathwayt, who sat at his desk in Sir William Temple's office at The Hague and gravely received the news that he was to be entrusted with the mission to Amsterdam to collect data on the Genoese ship, the *Abraham's Sacrifice,* was the same Blathwayt who, many years later, resolved to go up from Dyrham with information for the parliamentary commissioners of accounts. His reaction to his task was identical in the two cases; he went stiff-necked and self-confident, with his ideas neatly docketed, ready to collect facts or to dispense them, and absolutely sure that no one else was quite so well qualified for the task as he. Nothing lastingly discomfited him; neither the humiliating—if natural—rebuffs that waited for him in Amsterdam, nor the plain determination of the commissioners to catch him tripping. It is likely that only Temple's better judgment, in the first instance, dissuaded Blathwayt and forced him to return to The Hague; in the second, not even the most pointed partisan jibes from the commissioners could prevent him from returning to his purpose—he was there to give them the benefit of his wide experience. In every office that he held, Blathwayt was always the same; self-possessed, "knowing" in the true sense of the word, for he had the solid backing of a fund of information drawn from reliable sources and intelligently digested. Although in his ideas and administrative methods Blathwayt was distinctly a man of his time, we are struck by the modernity of his style and expression. He was a purist, and even his hurriedly drafted letters and documents show unusual precision and care. His letters, in particular, are rarely marked either by the seventeenth-century floridity or the seventeenth-century colloquialisms which characterize the correspondence of many of his contemporaries. They show sparkles of wit that even the critical Matthew Prior —who had nicknamed him "the Elephant"—might have enjoyed, and their clear, vivid flow has a touch of Mr. Addison.

Since he had definitely the encyclopaedic type of mind, Blathwayt was probably incapable of brilliance; none of his offices required it, so nothing was lost. It was far more important that he be able to appear, on occasion, actually stupid. There was, for instance, more subtlety (not altogether spontaneous for he had been coached by the crown officers) than stupidity in his evidence at the Trial of the Seven Bishops. His conduct then was typical of what he could do when necessity required. As secretary of state in Flanders, this ability made him invaluable to William III, always appreciative of that particular brand of obtuseness. It often enabled Blathwayt to avoid embarrassing official complications, and he used it for his own protection in 1689–1690, when he was endeavoring to evade the simultaneous attacks of both Jacobite and Whig extremists—men like Berwick and the Earl of Monmouth. A convenient capacity for not taking offense; a smiling cheerfulness—usually quite sincere; a disconcerting, even alarming, willingness to undertake almost any task; this combination frequently enabled Blathwayt to steer clear of obstacles and to salvage offices otherwise lost. Very likely his obliging eagerness to assist young John Temple at the war office, in 1689, arose out of concern for his own security in the plantation office, where his enemies were covertly working to displace him. His finesse succeeded, and almost too well—rather to Blathwayt's discomfiture it resulted in his reinstatement as secretary at war, and ultimately entailed his going to Flanders.

A man with more independence and less firm conviction would have disdained many of Blathwayt's manoeuvres as involving a loss of self-respect; but Blathwayt was so sure that he was essential to the success of English colonial administration that he easily escapes the charge. Unless we are to believe that he loved office for its own sake, there are numerous instances where only his confidence that he was indispensable could have held him to an arduous and thankless task. Failure to secure a regular appointment as secretary of state in 1692–1693 would have driven a man of less patient spirit to resign from his *pro tem.* secretaryship. The numerous opportunities for William III to appoint him, which arose as the decade wore on, again offered ample provocation, but Blathwayt stuck meekly and stubbornly to his post. Money could not have been his motive, for he held on even after severe retrenchment had set in, merely inquiring somewhat bitterly whether the government was trying to save money on him, and reminding them that his secretaryship was after all no easy post. Possibly he kept telling himself that to give up one office was to give up all. If so, it was a reasonable fear, William III was quite capable of ruthlessly dismissing Blathwayt from all his posts—except that he found it more useful not to.

Blathwayt, although he was an administrator of high calibre and an excellent detail man, never brought out, so far as the record shows, an original idea or even a new administrative device. He came upon the administrative scene, saw that the foundations had already been laid, accepted the master plan, and proceeded to do what he could to raise a trustworthy superstructure. His vanity led him to conclude that he succeeded very well, as indeed he did. He never took credit to himself for originality he did not possess—nor did he set any great store by it. He was much fonder of a solid precedent. His importance lies in the fact that he had an accurate, though limited, perception of real issues, and that to his stubborn conviction, logical thinking, and sound judgment, he added a colossal energy. Fortunately his excessive industry was motivated by intelligent inquiry and a rational point of view, or it might have exhausted him without having done England any lasting good. Blathwayt conducted a three-ringed administrative circus with such adeptness and relatively perfect coördination that the spectacle convinced three very keen monarchs and any number of royal advisers that they had in him a rare prize in the form of a phenomenally agile drudge.

Blathwayt early displayed the qualities which go to make a good administrator; ability to take and to execute orders, capacity for working intelligently in the absence of immediate or constant direction, critical judgment in drafting correspondence and official reports, and proper regard for the care of archives. He had also the innate conservatism of the bureaucrat—love of order, respect for law, reverence for precedent—all the qualities which make for comfortable stability in administration and

which, when savored with common sense, rather expedite
than slow down its processes. It may have been Blathwayt's native shrewdness, so active in money matters and
practical affairs generally, that lent balance to many of
his official actions. Certainly he tempered most of them
with sound common sense; he knew when to strain a point,
when to meet obstinacy with obstinacy, when to admit a
compromise. Perhaps his obstinacy was developed as a result of his New England encounter; but none of the colonies saw much of Blathwayt's temporizing aspect. Indeed,
the departments at Whitehall had plenty of experience
with his stubbornness in the matter of precedent. He always had something to quote—written or unwritten law,
parliamentary statute or executive order; whatever the
time or the occasion, he never lacked an authority. The
Treasury usually respected such conduct; on occasion
they used it themselves, quite unfairly, against Blathwayt
as secretary of state *pro tem.*, in the matter of commissions of appointment and privy seals which he had countersigned; but they grew wrathful when he refused to
obey their verbal orders on the matter of foreign loans.
Blathwayt calmly told them that he had himself and his
successors in office to protect; that he respected the force
of *lex non scripta* but that he had no intention of helping
to make it—not, at least, so long as there were parliamentary commissioners of accounts in the offing. Natural
diffidence or normal caution, indeed, restrained him from
abusing the powers of any of his offices, and especially of
his *ad interim* appointment as secretary of state. As
Adam Cardonnel said, "Mr. Blathwayt always had to
have a handle or staff to go by."

In spite of the fact that Blathwayt was an active pluralist and served in comparatively new offices or ones undergoing rapid change, he actually organized the routine of
only one—the auditor general's. Even for this he cannot

be given the sole credit, since the procedure he installed was merely an adaptation of the auditing system in the English Exchequer to the royal revenues arising in the colonies. Outside the clerkship of the council, all the offices which he held were of greater administrative importance at the end of his service, but in many instances he had nothing to do with this, except so far as he gave them orderly direction and sustained virility, so making them actually more efficient. The secretaryship of state, for instance, was rapidly rising in the official scale, and nothing Blathwayt could have done or neglected would have affected this. He did, however, enable it to be adapted to a very interesting, if inevitable, war exigency, and he probably met a trying situation with far more level-headedness and *sang-froid* than the situation deserved. It is tempting to imagine that Blathwayt could have developed the secretaryship at war into a more important office, had he possessed political tact and aggressive originality. It must be borne in mind, however, that he had to cope with two very serious obstacles—a jealous secretary of state, who would have resented any invasion of authority, and a hostile house of commons which was yet to be convinced that a standing army really had a place in England's constitutional scheme. Even had he eluded parliament and Whitehall, he would still have had William III to encounter. As it was, he seems to have done a neat job in avoiding dangerous pitfalls. The development of parties lifted the office to sudden but temporary prominence, and while Blathwayt's efficiency had something to do with this, admittedly the war was the more important factor. Finally, when the emergency was over, the same political tactics allowed the office to lapse into its former place.

The expansion and development of English trade and colonial possessions were clearly the central *motif* in

Blathwayt's life and he did his best work in the plantation office and its adjunct, the auditor generalship. In his
unfailing loyalty to what we now regard as a fallacious
economic theory and in his almost painful devotion to a
Utopian concept of colonial domain, he did not stand
alone, and his contemporaries, whether they liked his
ideal or not, regarded it as a practicable one. A great part
of Blathwayt's official life was absorbed in that administrative conflict with the proprietary and charter colonies,
which, had it not been for England's dynastic and constitutional ailments, might earlier have had a bitter and
fateful outcome. The attempt was already being made to
carry this struggle beyond its original bounds and develop it into a parliamentary combat. Protest as Blathwayt often did against the whimsical and partisan caprices of parliament, he had no objection to transferring
the colonial conflict from administrative headquarters in
Whitehall to the more spectacular stage of St. Stephen's.
After all, Blathwayt's favorite economic creed had already taken on statutory form, and with Blathwayt's help
was undergoing parliamentary revision. Like most practical people, Blathwayt was an opportunist and on this
question of colonial relations, he jumped at the remotest
possibility of advancing his ideal.

The political struggles and ambitions of the various
colonies were more than distasteful to Blathwayt; they
were incomprehensible. Religious liberty and freedom of
conscience, he was willing, as he often said, to cede to all
of them except Maryland; but beyond that he neither
could nor would go. To him, the plantations were economic adjuncts, not political units, and to waste their
energy in internal strife was to weaken their military and
economic strength. Blathwayt deplored such dissipation
as he deplored the administrative strife among colonial

agencies in Whitehall. What the colonies had in the way of representative government, they had as a matter of royal grace. He saw no reason why England and the colonies should not present a united front to France—for France was, to Blathwayt's dazzled eyes, an amazing example of what perfect administrative coöperation could accomplish. He did not even care to see Englishmen spend time and effort on further exploration or settlement "in the New World where (as he dryly said) his Majesty wants more subjects than land." It was his business to build up connections with the colonies; to break down the effect of those disconcerting distances, so great that, as Governor Lovelace of New York said, the conveyance of letters was "like the production of elephants, once almost in two years." By dinning into colonial ears his reiterated orders for regular correspondence, and by strenuous efforts to make possible a satisfactory packet-post system, Blathwayt accomplished as much as the times permitted. Only by his failure to take a determined stand to prevent the further extension to the colonies of the vicious system of patent offices and thus to strengthen the position of the governor, did he show himself lacking in a realization of what threatened England's security in the colonial domain.

Blathwayt's honest concern for the welfare—according to his ideas—of all the colonies—even of New England—is plain in the record of his works. Even in the 1680's, all earnest endeavor was not on the side of the colonies, nor all prevarication on the side of Whitehall. Blathwayt probably lived through as many wakeful nights wrestling with the problems of New England and the "proprieties" as did Increase Mather—and probably many more arduous days. Rushing through the various orders speeding Edward Randolph on his way, chafing under delays

caused by careless crown officers, attempting to countermine what he regarded as the negligence of the commissioners of the customs, or imploring the Admiralty's and
navy board's assistance in furnishing packets and convoy, he presents a picture of diligence in business which
might have edified even the New Englanders. Unfortunately this great expenditure of energy was mainly lost
motion.

The charge that he was a shameless mercenary can,
plainly, be discounted. If self-interest alone had been
driving him, he would have directed his ceaseless activity
along lines more quickly and obviously profitable than
those which he followed. Undoubtedly he regarded his
work not only as a profession but also as a business and
he had a merchant's—or a secretary of the Treasury's—
zealous interest in producing a balance sheet that showed
a neat surplus. We can afford to be as charitable as a
modern New Englander, who, in a brief evaluation of
Blathwayt's services to Massachusetts Bay, declared: "It
is certainly but justice to an officer who filled so many
important positions to the entire satisfaction of employ-
ers as different as James II and William of Orange, to
scrutinize with deliberation charges against his character
and to insist upon undoubted evidence of his personal
iniquities."[1] In the absence of absolute evidence either for
or against, we can conclude with Blathwayt's high-
minded contemporary, Sir Charles D'Avenant, that
"there hardly ever was a man who did long manage the
affairs of a large empire, whose whole actions have been
intirely [sic] blameless. . . . Either multiplicity of business makes him err, or those about him are corrupt, or he
himself is surprised in his soft hours, or love, pity, or

---

[1] "Remarks" by Abner Goodell, *Mass. Hist. Soc. Proc.* (1899, 1900), 2nd
ser., XIII, 297.

some other passion works upon him, but still something happens that cannot bear the test of severe inquiry."[2]

Blathwayt entered public life in 1668, the year following the Earl of Clarendon's disgrace and final downfall. He died in 1717, just as another great leader, Sir Robert Walpole, was beginning his long career of dominance over English politics. During this period Blathwayt was continuously in office, except for the few months from 1673 to the fall of 1675, when he was without an official berth. After 1707, and especially after 1710, when he lost his seat in the house of commons, his official rating was low, although he continued to act as clerk of the council and auditor general. While Blathwayt was plodding through his routine duties, England's constitutional system was undergoing some of the basic changes which were to transform it from arbitrary to constitutional monarchy. During this time there was no one leader whose position was preëminent, yet despite the lack of individual leadership, constitutional theories and tendencies were clarified, and various modern governmental practices were ushered in. Men still spoke ponderously of the *King in Council,* but the phrases, *His Majesty's Government* and *His Majesty's Opposition,* were already on their lips with more lively and pungent relish. The royal prerogative was still potent, but its exercise had been curbed; for the future it was to be a more effective lever in colonial than in domestic operations of government.

Administrative changes which reflected these new political practices had naturally been effected. The rise of the party system and the decline of the Privy Council was thrusting new officers into prominence. The extension of trade, the growth of the colonies, the development of the standing army, all had called for an expansion in the ad-

---

[2] *Works of Sir Charles D'Avenant* (Whitworth ed., 1771), IV, 349; "Essays upon Peace at Home and War Abroad."

ministrative branches of government. The modern departmental system was slowly though steadily emerging as a practical necessity. It was apparent that the departments of the future were to be the Admiralty, the Treasury, and the Secretariat, and that these were to have a political and administrative significance, quite apart from any centralizing body, such as the Privy Council or the Cabinet. The discerning eye might even have envisaged the division of the Secretariat into its present branches; James II listed what he regarded as a model division when he noted four major secretaryships—home affairs, foreign affairs, war, and the navy.[3] This constitutional process of administrative differentiation and elaboration went steadily forward, even while the attention of the nation was absorbed in the excitement of religious, partisan, and factional controversy.

Blathwayt played what in the modern constitutional system would be the double rôle of permanent and parliamentary undersecretary, under circumstances that were kaleidoscopic and trying in the extreme—and obviously with considerable success. He did not remain entirely blind to the changes that were going on in the relationship between sovereign and parliament, nor to the effect that the development of party machinery was to have on administrative offices as well as on political ones. He was such a poor politician, and he had so little understanding of the gradually emerging party system, that he mistook the early party turnovers for sudden reversals in personal politics, but the subsequent fashion in which he himself was turned out of office convinced him that the matter must rest on a basis other than personal. Even then, however, he never seems to have had any clear idea of what the party system really implied.

As a true bureaucrat and a staunch admirer of French

3 Clarke, *Life of James II* (London, 1816), II, 640.

administrative technique, Blathwayt's attitude toward any weakening in royal prerogative was naturally hostile. He defined prerogative, however, to mean not arbitrary governmental practices, which after all he never condoned, but the equal validity of administrative or executive order and of parliamentary statute. Undoubtedly Blathwayt would have preferred a government which rested more completely on administrative rule. He was sure that government was a profession for the expert. He accepted parliamentary control as inevitable, but he made no effort to conceal his scorn for the activities of the house of commons on a variety of subjects. On the whole he regarded parliament as likely to be more capricious than the king. His correspondence with his friend Richard Hill, during the anxious days of disbanding in 1698, reveals this. He first chose to regard parliamentary onslaughts with whimsical facetiousness and made quips about its bloodthirsty fondness for victims and its addiction to political hangings; but by 1698 he could see little that was humorous in what he regarded as the wanton disbanding of the forces—with peace still on a most uncertain foundation. As a leader in the efforts to revoke the colonial charters after 1700 he found out for himself that parliamentary opposition was indeed a factor to be considered. Sensing the situation somewhat belatedly, he made the best of it as an inescapable fact, but he never ceased to decry it when he dared. He was, in a sense, a man born out of his time. He had the theories and the temperament to have been at ease under the direction of Laud or Strafford. To the end of his days he still liked to drop sounding hints to colonial assemblies and agents of what the king might order in the "fulness of his regal authority."

Blathwayt's party affiliations were so indefinite as to mislead two historians. Primarily an administrator, his party views and sympathies were really very mildly developed. Macaulay suspected him of servile Toryism, on account of his conduct in the Trial of the Seven Bishops; and apparently that sound Whig never troubled himself to discover that Blathwayt became as faithful a servant of William III as he had been of James. Informed, he would doubtless have dismissed him from consideration as a hopeless timeserver. Mr. Courtney, Blathwayt's biographer in *The Dictionary of National Biography*, on the other hand, assumed that Blathwayt was a Whig because of the vitriolic—if rare—comments upon him by Harley and St. John. He overlooked the surpassing bitterness of hatreds within a party; Harley and his group of moderate Tories hated Blathwayt not for his political views or acts but for his loyalty to a monarch like William and to a general like Marlborough. To them, he was as contemptible as one of the Dutch favorites.

Blathwayt actually belonged to that group of Protestant Tories who were willing to go almost, but not quite, the entire length with James II on points other than religion. He was congenial with Clarendon and Rochester, and after the Revolution of 1688, he followed the standards of three able, if unpopular, Tories—Lord Nottingham, Charles Montagu, and the Earl of Godolphin. Here again, however, his administrative preoccupation rather than the blind loyalty of the partisan governed his attachment. He admired and cultivated administrative ability, financial genius, and orderly governmental housekeeping. Any hard-working Tory with sound administrative ability impressed him, and he detested a Tory who wasted time in parliamentary gyrations or partisan fulminations far more cordially than he disapproved of any Whig. Witness his suspected coolness toward the oratorical Dr. Sacheverell.

It took Blathwayt some time to realize the extent to

which partisan tactics had come to control parliamentary policies and to influence the royal will. In 1696 he accepted with a fair amount of grace the rumors that a parliamentary board of trade was to be set up, but he expressed his belief that parliament would certainly never assume administrative control of the army. Royal finesse saved William III from having to accept a board of trade set up at the wish of the house of commons, and Blathwayt apparently assumed that the king could with equal ease manage to control the new board's administrative staff. William might have done so for the time being, but he preferred to compromise and to accept the idea of Whig domination over the board. This, of course, facilitated a change to the new system which took for granted a turnover of membership with every shift in party strength. Such a system was beyond Blathwayt's comprehension.

At the very time that Blathwayt was declaring that parliament would never set up an administrative board to control the army, it actually did control the secretary at war and the paymaster general on the question of estimates, and it determined, through parliamentary commissioners of accounts, to assert as complete a control on the matter of audit. Moreover, parliament and party soon meant to turn the secretaryship at war to account, by subjecting it to the spoils system. The laugh of St. Taffy's Day, when Blathwayt was first reported dismissed from the war office, was certainly on, not with, Blathwayt, as he discovered to his sorrow.

The secure Blathwayt, who could laugh, in 1704, over dismissal from the war office, found it difficult to smile, even wryly, in 1707, over his dismissal from the Board of Trade. Time had taken the edge off his sense of humor. Moreover, England's colonial and commercial interests and the detail of army administration were not, to his way of thinking, comparable in importance. He regarded the colonies far too seriously to see anything even faintly humorous in sudden and therefore dangerous shifts in administrative control over them. His feelings in 1707 were akin to those he had had in 1696, but they were intensified, since he was older and could not so easily regain lost ground. Time, too, had dulled his perceptions as well as slackened his pace, for he actually believed that his reinstatement in office was possible; patiently, almost piteously, he awaited it. Hence his petulance and pique, in 1710, over the scurvy trick which politics played him by losing him the support of his patron, the Duke of Beaufort, and consequently his seat in the house of commons— that seat which the voters of Bath, so Blathwayt had written smugly in 1694, had given him for life. He lost it now because the Duke chose to believe a shameless political broadside, which was juggling with parliamentary votes on the question of Sacheverell. From 1710 to the end of his days, Blathwayt watched the advance of party standards with far more dismay and apprehension than he felt at the physical ailments of advancing age.

Blathwayt, always a little in the rearguard of his time, far outlived his generation, even though he was only sixty-eight years old when he died. Death had claimed all his warmest friends and co-workers—Southwell, Randolph, Williamson, and Pepys—more than a decade earlier. The crest of a great wave had borne England's administrators forward in their zealous efforts to exalt obedience to law and to compel colonial compliance. The wave was now breaking. Blathwayt's energy was still unspent, but it no longer had a satisfactory outlet. His world began to close in on him, as his hopes gradually faded. He retired to Dyrham Park—where he saw a complete fulfilment of his personal ambitions at least—and only occasionally ventured forth to London and his old haunts. When he came, however, he usually came triumphant—

with testimony for the Treasury or the parliamentary commissioners on points relating to the army or the colonies which, he observed with malice, none of his successors in office could supply. Happily for Blathwayt's self-esteem he failed to observe that, in the new orientation which party politics had assumed, he had been relegated to the unapplauded rôle of animated "entry book."

APPENDIX I

WILLIAM III'S EXPEDITIONS INTO IRELAND AND INTO THE LOW COUNTRIES[1]

June 4—September 10, 1690. Campaign into Ireland, Sir Robert Southwell in attendance.

January 17—April 13, 1691. Expedition into Holland; conference with the allies; Earl of Nottingham in attendance.

May 2—October 19, 1691. Second expedition into Holland and Flanders; Lord Sydney in attendance.

March 6—October 20, 1692. Third expedition into Holland and Flanders; Blathwayt in attendance.

April 4—October 29, 1693. Fourth expedition.

May 7—November 18, 1694. Fifth expedition.

May 12—October 16, 1695. Sixth expedition.

May 6—October 6, 1696. Seventh expedition.

April 26—November 10, 1697. Eighth expedition.

July 19—December 5, 1698. Ninth expedition.

June 4—October 17, 1699. Tenth expedition.

July 5—October 18, 1700. Eleventh expedition.

July 4—November 4, 1701. Twelfth expedition.

[1] See Luttrell, *Brief Relation*, from which account these dates have been taken.

APPENDIX II

SECRETARIES OF STATE
1689–1702

Southern Department	*Northern Department*
Shrewsbury	**Nottingham**
February, 1689—May, 1690	February, 1689—June, 1690
Nottingham	**Sydney**
June, 1690—November, 1693	December, 1690—February, 1692
	Trenchard
	March, 1693—November, 1693
Trenchard	**Shrewsbury**
November, 1693—April, 1695	March, 1694—April, 1695
Shrewsbury	**Trumbull**
April, 1695—December, 1698	May, 1695—December, 1697
Jersey	**Vernon**
May, 1699—June, 1700	December, 1697—November, 1700
Vernon	**Hedges**
November, 1700—January, 1702	November, 1700—December, 1701
Manchester	**Vernon**
January, 1702—March, 1702	January, 1702—March, 1702

BIBLIOGRAPHICAL NOTE

THREE brief articles have been found which bear directly on William Blathwayt, that by W. P. Courtney in *The Dictionary of National Biography* (V, 206), another by John Hutchinson in *Notable Middle Templars*, and a third by Miss M. Lane, entitled, "William Blathwayt, Private Secretary to William III," *Contemporary Review* (May, 1924), CXXV, 639–644, the title of which is misleading, but which is otherwise a very colorful treatment of Blathwayt's services under William from a more or less popular angle. The majority of military historians who have dealt with the growth of the war office and the secretaryship at war have mentioned him in passing. The same may be said of those who have dealt intensively with American colonial history or have made a special study of the Lords of Trade or the Board of Trade. Professor Andrews and Mr. Beer were the first to realize the importance of Blathwayt's services as auditor general of plantation revenues, and the former is the only scholar to have made a thorough summary of the activities of Blathwayt and his two successors, Horatio Walpole and Robert Cholmondeley (*Guide to the Materials for American History to 1783, in the Public Record Office of Great Britain*, II, 142–148). Throughout this study, primary dependence has been placed on source materials, though a great deal of secondary material has been found helpful.

BIBLIOGRAPHICAL AIDS

The best bibliographical aids for the unprinted sources have been: C. M. Andrews, *Guide to the Manuscript Materials for the History of the United States to 1783, in the British Museum, in Minor London Archives and in the Libraries of Oxford and Cambridge*, Washington, 1908 (prepared in collaboration with Miss

F. G. Davenport); C. M. Andrews, *Guide to the Materials for American History to 1783, in the Public Record Office of Great Britain,* two volumes, Washington, 1912–1914, which contains not only valuable descriptions of the records themselves, but equally valuable accounts of the offices to which they belonged. *Lists and Indexes,* Public Record Office, 1914, proved valuable in the examination of the manuscript materials there. C. S. S. Higham, *The Colonial Entry-Books* (S.P.C.K.), London, 1921, is a very useful account of the colonial records to be found in the Public Record Office.

Secondary Materials

General. The most useful general account is Macaulay, *History of England from the Accession of James II.* From an administrative point of view, even though it deals with an earlier period, T. F. Tout, *Chapters in the Administrative History of Mediaeval England,* five volumes, London, 1920–1930, is very valuable.

Special. For the office of secretary of state, L. B. Dibben, "Secretaries in the 13th and 14th Centuries," *Eng. Hist. Rev.,* XXV, 430 (1910); Florence G. Evans (Mrs. C. S. S. Higham), *The Principal Secretary of State,* Manchester, 1923.

For the war office, Charles M. Clode, *The Military Forces of the Crown,* two volumes, London, 1869; Sir Charles Firth, *Cromwell's Army,* London, 1910; Sir John Fortescue, *A History of the British Army,* thirteen volumes, London, 1899–1930; Sir Sibbald Scott, *The British Army,* three volumes, London, 1868–1880; Clifford Walton, *A History of the British Standing Army, 1660–1700,* London, 1894; Owen Wheeler, *The War Office, Past and Present,* London, 1914.

For the colonial aspects of Blathwayt's activities, C. M. Andrews, *British Committees, Commissions, and Councils of Trade and Plantations, 1622–1675,* Baltimore, 1908; Arthur H. Basye, *The Lords Commissioners of Trade and Plantations, 1748–1782,* New Haven, 1925; Beer, *The Old Colonial System, 1660–1754,* Part I, "The Establishment of the System," 1660–1688, two volumes, New York, 1912; Ralph P. Bieber, *The Lords of Trade and Plantations, 1675–1696,* Allentown, Pa., 1919; Beverley W.

Bond, *The Quit-Rent System in the American Colonies*, New Haven, 1919; Miss Mary P. Clarke, "The Board of Trade at Work," *Amer. Hist. Rev.*, XVII, 17–43 (October, 1911); O. M. Dickerson, *American Colonial Government, 1696–1765; a study of the British Board of Trade in its relation to the American Colonies*, Cleveland, 1912; Herbert L. Osgood, *The American Colonies in the Seventeenth Century*, three volumes, New York, 1904–1907; Herbert L. Osgood, *The American Colonies in the Eighteenth Century*, four volumes, New York, 1924; Winfred T. Root, *The Relations of Pennsylvania with the British Government, 1696–1765*, New York, 1912; Winfred T. Root, "The Lords of Trade and Plantations," *Amer. Hist. Rev.*, XXIII, 20–41 (October, 1917).

Certain biographical studies of some of Blathwayt's contemporaries furnish some valuable information on him, notably, Helen C. Foxcroft, *The Life and Letters of Sir George Savile, Bart., first Marquis of Halifax*, two volumes, London, 1898; Marion E. Grew, *William Bentinck and William III*, London, 1924; Everett Kimball, *The Public Life of Joseph Dudley*, New York, 1911; Kenneth Murdock, *Increase Mather*, Cambridge, 1925; J. R. Tanner, *Mr. Pepys, an Introduction to the Diary together with a Sketch of his Later Life*, London, 1925; Estelle Ward, *Christopher Monck*, London, 1915; Leopold Wickham-Legg, *Matthew Prior*, Cambridge, 1921.

PRINTED SOURCES

Official Documents: the standard sources, *The Calendar of State Papers Domestic, The Calendar of State Papers, Colonial, The Calendar of Treasury Books, The Calendar of Treasury Papers, The Journal of the Board of Trade, The Acts of the Privy Council, Colonial Series*, furnish invaluable, although widely scattered, information on Blathwayt's public activities. Leo F. Stock's compilation, *The Proceedings and Debates of the British Parliaments respecting North America, 1542–1727*, three volumes, Washington, 1924-1930, contains several entries on Blathwayt's participation in parliamentary debates, but the brief fashion in which the debates were reported at the time prevents us from making any accurate deduction on the influence Blathwayt wielded. *The Journal of the House of Commons, The Statutes of the Realm,* William Cobbett, *State Trials, 1687–1696,* Vol. XII, have been consulted when necessary and have proved useful.

The Royal Historical Manuscripts Commission Reports have been consulted in every instance when the dates fell within the period of Blathwayt's activities. Many are valuable, in particular, *Bath MSS.,* Vol. III (*Prior Papers*); *Ormonde MSS.,* new series; *Portland MSS.* which contain the *Harley Papers; Downshire MSS.* which contain the *Trumbull Papers.* Some material of a personal nature was found, but the majority of references are of a strictly public character.

The official colonial publications of the various states have been consulted, when there was a likelihood that they would yield information on Blathwayt. On the whole, they have proved rather barren. There are scattered references to Blathwayt to be found, however, in *Maryland Archives,* Vols. XX–XXV; *New Hampshire Provincial State, and Town Papers,* Vol. II; *Documents relative to the Colonial History of the State of New York* (ed. by E. B. O'Callaghan); *Journal of the Assembly of Provincial New York,* Vol. I; *Virginia Magazine of History and Biography.*

Year Books, Political Diaries, Tracts, Official Lists: Andros Tracts, Prince Society, Vols. V–VII, 1868–1874; E. Chamberlayne, *Angliae Notitia,* various editions, London, 1669–1708; *London Gazette;* Narcissus Luttrell, *A Brief Historical Relation of State Affairs, 1678–1714,* six volumes, Oxford, 1857. Luttrell, as a Gloucestershire man himself, probably took more interest in the official actions of Blathwayt than he might otherwise have done.

Correspondence, Diaries, Memoirs: many of the letters and journals of the period contain illuminating references to Blathwayt and his work. *The Memoirs of Thomas, Earl of Ailesbury,* two volumes, The Roxburghe Club, 1890; Duke of Berwick, *Memoirs,* Paris, 2nd ed., 1780; *Bulstrode Papers, 1667–1675,* London, 1897; *The Writings of Colonel William Byrd* (ed. John Spencer Bassett), New York, 1901; *The Correspondence of the Earl of Clarendon and the Earl of Rochester* (ed. S. F. Singer),

two volumes, London, 1828; *Clarke Papers* (ed. Sir Charles
Firth), four volumes, London, 1870–1872, valuable for back-
ground in the study of Blathwayt's activities as secretary at war;
Correspondence of the Family of Hatton, Camden Society, New
Series, Vol. XXIII, London, 1878; *Hutchinson Papers*, Prince
Society, two volumes, 1865; Christopher Jeaffreson, *A Young
Squire of the Seventeenth Century* (ed. J. C. Jeaffreson), two
volumes, London, 1878, which contains some delightful comments on Blathwayt's character and mannerisms; *The Diary of
Cotton Mather*, Massachusetts Historical Society Collections, 7th
series, Vols. V–VII, 1911–1912; *The Private Correspondence
and Miscellaneous Papers of Samuel Pepys*, 1679–1703 (ed. J. R.
Tanner), two volumes, London, 1926; *Memoirs of Edward Randolph* (ed. R. N. Toppan and A. T. S. Goodrick), Prince Society,
seven volumes, 1898–1909; *The Diary of Samuel Sewall, 1674–
1729*, Massachusetts Historical Society Collections, 5th series,
Vols. V–VII, Boston, 1878–1882; *The Official Letters of Alexan-
der Spotswood*, Virginia Historical Society, two volumes, 1882;
*The Private Correspondence of Charles Talbot, Duke of Shrews-
bury* (ed. William Coxe), London, 1821; *Letters Illustrative of
the Reign of William III* (ed. G. P. R. James), three volumes,
London, 1841, the letters which James Vernon wrote to the Duke
of Shrewsbury and which contain a great many apt references to
Blathwayt; *Letters of William III and Louis XIV and their
Ministers, 1697–1700* (ed. Paul Grimblot), two volumes, London, 1848; *The Correspondence of Fitz-John Winthrop*, Massachusetts Historical Society Collections, 5th series, Vol. VIII, 6th
series, Vol. III.

MANUSCRIPT MATERIALS

Public Record Office: The official papers of the various offices
in which Blathwayt served were consulted, State Papers Domestic, 1681–1683 (Conway period); State Papers Foreign, 1668–
1673 (Holland, Denmark, Sweden); 1681–1683 (Conway period); 1692–1701, particularly the Archives and the Military
Expeditions, the series which contains a great deal of Blathwayt's
correspondence with George Stepney, much of which is of an

intimate character; also State Papers Foreign Entry Books for the same years; State Papers Colonial, 1674–1707 and State Papers Colonial, Entry Books, 1675–1696; State Papers Military, 1660–1704.

A few Treasury books and papers were consulted, but the only one of real importance is Blathwayt's Journal, Treas. 64:88–90.

All of the War Office books and papers from 1660 to 1710 were consulted, as well as some of the Admiralty papers, especially Admiralty 1:4316, which contains the correspondence with the war office.

British Museum: A large collection of Blathwayt MSS. is to be found, the majority of them of a very formal nature. Add. MSS. 9718–9768 are manuscripts, which contain the bulk of Blathwayt's correspondence with English officials and with the envoys in the foreign service, 1692–1701, and a few scattered colonial papers, notably the account books of the Lords of Trade and Plantations (Add. MSS. 9767–9768); Add. MSS. 21486–21491, further correspondence of Blathwayt with foreign envoys; Add. MSS. 34351–34357, more manuscripts similar to the preceding; Add. MSS. 35104, Blathwayt's letter book while in the Earl of Conway's office, 1681–1683; Add. MSS. 35105–35106, letters to and from Dr. John Robinson, minister to Sweden, 1692–1705; Add. MSS. 36859–36861, the minutes of the commissioners of accounts, 1702–1703, which contain some very important material on Blathwayt; Add. MSS. 37979–37986, Blathwayt's correspondence with the various diplomatic representatives, 1681–1683; Add. MSS. 37991–37992, Blathwayt's letter books while in Flanders, 1692–1701; Add. MSS. 38694–38714, twenty volumes of Blathwayt manuscripts relating to the office of secretary at war, all very important, together with some miscellaneous papers on the colonies.

There are a few papers among the Egerton MSS. bearing on Blathwayt; Egerton MSS. 920, the letters of James Vernon to Blathwayt, 1694, 1697, 1698, 1701, are probably the most important. There are some additional Vernon letters among Additional Manuscripts, which were uncatalogued in 1925 when I examined them. All of these are very formal.

MSS. in the Possession of George Wynter Blathwayt, West Porlock House, Somersetshire: These are miscellaneous family papers, some of them personal letters, others of a very formal nature. There are, principally, some letters from the Duke of Marlborough, a diary of Edward Southwell, Blathwayt's correspondence with the deputy paymaster of the army, Richard Hill; his correspondence with Secretary of State, Sir Charles Hedges, 1701; and with John Cooke in Secretary of State's Trevor's office, 1669–1671; and some scattered letters from various colonial officials.

Library of Congress: There are some very important colonial manuscripts of an official character, notably the Rough Journal of the Lords of Trade, two volumes, 1675–1679, 1686–1688; the "Journal of All that Passes in the Plantation Office, 1683–1688"; Blathwayt's Account Book, 1711, which he presented to the commissioners of accounts; the Entry Book of Patents, Commissions, etc., relating to the Colonies, 1497–1706, three volumes; the transcript of Blathwayt's Journal, Treas. 64: 88–90; and some scattered Phillipps MSS., relating to New Hampshire, Virginia, and Maryland, but of no great importance.

Huntington Library, San Marino, California: These are Phillipps MSS. 8558, etc., and were presumably once a part of the collection of Blathwayt MSS. at Kings Weston, which were sold some time during the 18th century. There are ten volumes, neatly bound in modern bindings, and they consist of miscellaneous colonial manuscripts, letter drafts by Blathwayt, in-letters, etc. They are classified according to colonies as follows: America, 1681–1741; New York, two volumes, 1687–1713; Canada, Darien, Hudson's Bay, 1696–1699; Jamaica, 1656–1711; Virginia, 1664–1712; Maryland, 1664–1701; Antigua, Bermuda, etc., 1669–1702; Barbados, Caribbee Islands, etc., 1660–1704; New England, 1694–1695.

In addition there are some MSS. from the collection of the Earl of Bridgewater, which contain some very valuable material bearing on Blathwayt's attitude toward the Board of Trade, 1696–1697 (Ellsmere 30:C29, Vols. 137–138).

THE SALE OF BLATHWAYT MANUSCRIPTS
SOTHEBY'S, LONDON

The manuscripts which Blathwayt removed from his offices to Dyrham Park were divided after his death. A large portion of them remained at Dyrham in the custody of his eldest son, William. The rest were removed to Kings Weston, the country estate of Blathwayt's son-in-law, Edward Southwell, who probably felt that he would find them very valuable in his own public work. The manuscripts at Kings Weston ultimately passed into the hands of Sir Thomas Phillipps of Cheltenham. There have been at least five sales of Phillipps' MSS. in which Blathwayt Papers were included: one on June 15–18, 1908; another, June 6–9, 1910; a third, April 24–28, 1911; a fourth, May 19–23, 1913; a fifth, June 24–27, 1919, all at Sotheby's. The majority of the manuscripts which had been preserved at Dyrham Park were sold at Sotheby's on April 25, 1910. On November 20–21, 1912, a sale took place, also at Sotheby's, of Blathwayt's library with its impressive list of works on colonial discovery and exploration. Since in many of the catalogues the names of the buyers were indicated, attempts have been made to trace the manuscripts—without result. Dealers in manuscripts have no inclination to divulge information except to prospective buyers. Fortunately a few of the manuscripts have already found their way into public archives, notably the British Museum. These are chiefly European in their interest. The bulk of the manuscripts bearing on colonial affairs are still reposing in the hands of dealers, who in most instances are holding them for exorbitant prices.

INDEX

Abraham's Sacrifice, 73, 469-470.
Acts of Trade; effect on Ireland, 113-119; Act of 1696, 296-297.
Addington, Isaac, secretary and deputy auditor, Massachusetts and New Hampshire, 369, 375 f.n.
Admiralty Board, 12, 14, 15, 73, 127, 145-146, 222-223, 339, 345-346, 459 f.n., 479.
Admiralty, High Court of, 74, 106, 329, 334.
Ailesbury, Earl of, 16, 195, 435.
Albemarle, Duke of (George Monck), 209, 210, 242, 405.
Albemarle, Duke of, governor of Jamaica, 108-109, 113, 137.
Albemarle, Duke of, William III's favorite, 257, 259, 284.
Allen, Colonel, claims to New Hampshire, 465-467.
Andros, Sir Edmund, 108, 113, 122, 131-132, 134, 137, 180, 184, 305, 307, 308, 309, 311, 332 f.n., 344.
Anglesey, Lord Privy Seal, 105.
Angliae Notitia, 15, 408.
Archives, care of, 24-25, 26-28, 402-403, 406-407, 412-420.
Arlington, Earl of, secretary of state, 171, 190, 210, 212, 404 f.n.
Armstrong, Colonel, naval officer, 466.
Army Commissions and Commission Books, 211, 221, 269-270, 414-415, 458-459.
Army Contracts and Contractors, 287 f.n., 424-425.

Army, Increases in, 224-225.
Articles of War, 216.
Ashurst, Henry, 322, 336, 341, 343-344, 350.
Ashworth, Richard, collector in Bermuda, 182.
Atkins, Sir Jonathan, governor of Barbados, 168.
Atwood, William, chief justice of New York, 343, 349, 350.
Auditor Generalship of Plantation Revenues; creation of, 150, 157 *et seq.;* colonies under control of, 150, 160-161, 357-359; Blathwayt's patent, 158 f.n., 160; salaries of Blathwayt and his deputies, 160 f.n., 438, 441, 451-457; office staff, 403-404, 408 f.n.; archives, 417-418; policy after 1689, 355-359; relations with royal receivers, 175-178, 370-374; with provincial treasurers, 158, 159, 374-380; control over quit-rents and casual revenues, 380-387; over the four and a half per cent., 169-171, 387-391; reports to the commissioners of accounts and to the Treasury, 391-398; with the Board of Trade, 413.
Auditors of the Imprest, 390, 430.
Ayleway, Robert, 366-367 f.n.

Baber, John, 81, 345-346.
Bacon, Nathaniel, the elder, 161-162 f.n., 168 f.n., 366.
Bacon's Rebellion, 383.